M000310232

Reading and Hearing the Word

From Text to Sermon

*Essays in Honor of
John H. Stek*

Edited by Arie C. Leder

Copublished by Calvin Theological Seminary and CRC Publications
Grand Rapids, Michigan

Copublished by Calvin Theological Seminary, 3233 Burton SE, Grand Rapids, MI 49546 and CRC Publications, 2850 Kalamazoo Ave. SE, Grand Rapids, MI 49560. 1-800-333-8300

Library of Congress Cataloging-in-Publication Data
Reading and hearing the Word from text to sermon: essays in honor of John H. Stek / edited by Arie C. Leder.
    p.   cm.
    Includes bibliographical references.
    ISBN 1-56212-373-4
    1. Public worship—Sermons. 2. Stek, John H. (John Henry). I. Stek, John H. (John Henry). II. Leder, Arie C., 1946-   .
    BV15.R48   1998
    220.6—dc21   98-36775
                                                                      CIP

10 9 8 7 6 5 4 3 2 1

Contents

Preface

Dreaming about this volume began in April 1993 with Johannes Schouten, then a student at Calvin Theological Seminary. Serious planning for it started in the fall of 1995. Its completion at this time would have been impossible without the support and helpful suggestions of colleagues, students, friends, and, of course, the contributors.

The project took longer than I thought it would; about as long as friends warned me it might. And throughout the process the contributors have been patient and courteous. Not all original contributors could finish the project with us, however. Peter De Klerk, Theological Librarian, Emeritus, of Calvin Theological Seminary, looked forward to bringing Stek's bibliography up to date but passed away suddenly before he could begin. Paul W. Fields, who now serves as Theological Librarian for the seminary, willingly assumed the task. Without this bibliography the volume would have been incomplete. Thank you, Paul.

For advice on the organization of this volume I am grateful to my colleague Dr. Richard A. Muller, who, as a veteran of several multiauthor publications, helped me to think through issues related to the design of the volume. Without the funds from the Faculty Heritage Fund of Calvin Theological Seminary and personal contributions from former students and members of the Old Testament Club, colleagues, friends, and members of Fuller Avenue Christian Reformed Church in Grand Rapids, Michigan, these essays would not have been published. I thank all of these donors for their contributions. Special mention goes to Michelle Van Laren, Darren Roorda, and Johannes Schouten, members of the Old Testament Club who helped with mailing, and Jean Garehan, who faithfully kept track of the moneys received. A word of gratitude also goes to CRC Publications, especially to Gary Mulder, Executive Director, and Robert De Moor, Editor in Chief of the Education, Worship, and Evangelism Department, for being willing to accept this somewhat unusual project, and for the courtesy, patience, and professional manner of its editors, designers, and other staff. They have put a sheen to the honor this volume seeks to bring John H. Stek. Of course, any problems that remain are mine.

Tolle lege.

Arie C. Leder
Grand Rapids, Michigan
August, 1998

John Henry Stek
Professor of Old Testament
from 1963 through 1990

Arie C. Leder

I t was a typical Stek lecture, not enough time to savor the thought, just enough to hold your breath and take notes while nodding the head in agreement like an orthodox Jew at prayer. What stuck was a brief aside on the character of praise. Prof. Stek had mentioned the paper a fellow student, John Bolt, had written on the song of Hannah for TaNaK (the Old Testament Club). It was very good, he said; no, it was excellent, worthy of public praise. So we learned that praise responds to someone else's worth or deeds, and that it calls others to join in.[1] Stek did no more than what the wise have counseled: "Let another praise you, and not your own mouth; someone else, and not your own lips" (Prov. 27:2; cf. 25:27). He sought to shape us with Scripture even as Scripture had shaped him.

The essays of this volume represent but a small cross-section of the chorus that praises Stek for his contributions to the Christian Reformed Church in North America as a minister of the Word and sacraments and as a professor of Old Testament in its seminary, and to the church at large through his publications and work with the New International Version (NIV) of the Bible. We are former and present students, colleagues and friends at Calvin Theological Seminary, former and present members of the Old Testament Club at the seminary, co-workers on the NIV translation and Bible Study team, fellow members of Fuller Avenue Christian Reformed Church in Grand Rapids, Michigan, and those who bless his name when they study the Portuguese and Spanish translations of his notes on *The Writings* and *The Former Prophets*.[2] We are all beneficiaries of his devotion to theological education and scholarship. In sum, now is the time for us as "others" to praise John Henry Stek.

SERVICE IN THE CHURCH

John Henry Stek of Oskaloosa, Iowa, began his studies at Calvin College in 1942. In 1944 he was drafted into the United States Army, and he served in the infantry in the Pacific. After the war Stek returned to Calvin and received his A.B. degree (pre-

---

[1]Stek's notes on Hannah's song (*The Former Prophets. A Syllabus*, ed. Arie C. Leder [Unpublished. Grand Rapids: Calvin Theological Seminary, 1997], 40) acknowledge his indebtedness to Bolt.

[2]John H. Stek, *Los profetas anteriores*, trans. Edesio Sanchez and Kent Van Til (Unpublished. San José, Costa Rica, 1995).

seminary major) in 1949. By 1952 he had completed his Th.B. program at Calvin Theological Seminary and became the first recipient of the Diamond Jubilee Scholarship for advanced study at the Free University of Amsterdam. Illness prevented his pursuing graduate work that year. Later he continued his studies at Westminster Theological Seminary (Philadelphia), where he obtained his Th.M. degree in 1956 after defending his thesis, "The Naotic Presence of God." Subsequently he pursued doctoral studies at the University of Chicago (1965-1966) and at the Free University of Amsterdam, where he became Doctorandus (1974).[3]

Ordained a minister of the Word and sacraments in the Christian Reformed Church of Raymond, Minnesota, in 1955, Stek served the community there until 1961, when he was appointed visiting lecturer at Calvin Theological Seminary. During his ministry in Raymond, Stek served on the Board of Trustees of Calvin College and Seminary (1956-1961), as delegate to the Synods of 1957 and 1959, and as a member of the Liturgical (1957-1959) and Infallibility study committees of synod (1959-1961). He also wrote articles for church papers during that time. After his appointment to Calvin Seminary, synod appointed him to serve on various study committees: Neo-Pentecostalism (1971-1973, secretary), Revision of the Form of Subscription (1974-1976), and Inter-Church Relations (1975-1981).

In 1963 synod appointed Stek assistant professor of Old Testament at Calvin Seminary, where he served until retirement from his official duties in 1990. Besides teaching, Stek published articles in the *Calvin Theological Journal*, which he edited from 1976 to 1991 (with a hiatus from 1983 through 1985), and elsewhere (see "Bibliography of John H. Stek" at the end of this book), but he focused most of his scholarly energy and attention on the NIV. As a member of the Committee on Bible Translation (CBT) he translated, edited, revised, and approved translations submitted by others. After the publication of the NIV in 1978 Stek, as associate editor, began the arduous task of producing the NIV Study Bible. It was published in 1985.[4] At present Stek is chairman of the CBT, which oversees the review and revision of the NIV. He continues to be invited to teach courses at Calvin Seminary and is still involved with the Old Testament Club.

---

[3]He wrote his "Scriptie," a minor thesis, on Psalm 22.

[4]Stek is chief contributor to the study notes on the Psalms and the Song of Songs. He also worked on Ruth and Jonah (with Marvin R. Wilson), Isaiah and Malachi (with Herbert Wolff), and Amos (with Alan R. Millard).

TEACHING OLD TESTAMENT AT CALVIN THEOLOGICAL SEMINARY

Since its birth in 1876 the Synod of the Christian Reformed Church in North America (CRC) has made ten appointments to the chair of Old Testament at Calvin Theological Seminary.[5] An early twentieth-century controversy in the CRC about the nature of theological education indelibly placed its stamp on the seminary. The triumph of Foppe Ten Hoor's view,[6] that the seminary be understood as a church school rather than a university department, did not so much erase academic or scientific concerns as create a tension between the two approaches, as the "Janssen case"[7] demonstrated. This case and the fundamentalist-liberal controversies of the early nineteenth century shaped the teaching of the Old Testament at the seminary for decades. Martin J. Wyngaarden, appointed in the wake of Ralph Janssen's dismissal for his naturalistic views and alleged higher critical views of Scripture, opposed the naturalism of higher criticism throughout his teaching career.[8] Marten Hendrik Woudstra, trained in the Netherlands and at Westminster Theological Seminary[9] in Philadelphia, zealously maintained the Reformed hermeneutic against the challenge of the critical methodologies. His teaching, however, betrayed a methodological guardedness that reflected the orthodox-liberal conflicts that created Westminster Theological Seminary in 1933.

It was this Old Testament Department that John Henry Stek joined in 1961, at the beginning of a decade that would bring significant changes to the CRC and its seminary. In 1961 the synod of the CRC debated its study on the inspiration and infallibility of Scripture which, among other things, argued that the word "infallible" was preferable to "inerrant" for history and clarity's sake, and that the infallibility of Scripture was linked to the purpose of the author's message.[10] This debate created a

---

[5]Geerhardus Vos (1888-1893, combined with Dogmatics), Ralph Janssen (1914-1922), Martin J. Wyngaarden (1924-1961), Marten H. Woudstra (1958-1985), John H. Stek (1963-1990), David H. Engelhard (1971-1994), Raymond C. Van Leeuwen (1985-1990), Arie C. Leder (1990-present), Carl J. Bosma (1990-present), and Michael J. Williams (1997-present). Of these, the following served as Visiting Lecturer or Lecturer before their appointment to a tenure-track position: Janssen (1902-1906), Woudstra (1955-1958), Stek (1961-1963), Engelhard (1970-1971), Van Leeuwen (1981-1982), Leder (1987-1989), Williams (1995-1997).

[6]For a discussion of the debate between Foppe Ten Hoor and the views of Abraham Kuyper, see John Bolt, *Stewards of the Word: Challenges in Reformed Theological Education Today* (Calvin Theological Seminary, 1996), 88-98.

[7]For a review of the "Janssen case," see David E. Holwerda, "Hermeneutical Issues Then and Now: the Janssen Case Revisited," *Calvin Theological Journal* 24.1 (1989):7-34.

[8]See Martin J. Wyngaarden, "Concerning the biblical training for our prospective ministry," *The Banner* 60 (1925), 520; "Trends in biblical studies of Old Testament theology," *The Calvin Forum* 20 (1954-1955), 84-89; "Higher criticism of Scripture," *The Banner* 96 (April 7, 1961), 9; (April 14, 1961), 9, 29; (April 29, 1961), 9.

[9]Woudstra received his Th.D. from Westminster Theological Seminary in 1961 after defending his dissertation, "The Ark of the Covenant from Conquest to Kingship."

[10]See *Agenda, Synod of the Christian Reformed Church* (1961), 147-153.

problem for those who believed "inerrant" applied to all biblically revealed informa-tion.[11] Toward the end of the decade instruction in the biblical division curriculum would take on an explicitly canonical rather than academic character.[12] Stek was involved in both as a member of the study committee[13] and the biblical division.

If the curriculum revision in the biblical division mirrored the emphases of the Ten Hoor debate of the early part of the century, there was no return to fundamentalist-liberal debate. The synodical report on infallibility suggests, rather, that a certain rela-tionship or tie to the fundamentalist-liberal debate filtered through a Westminster con-nection and was beginning to unravel. Fred H. Klooster, for example, although in agreement with Warfield on the inspiration and authority of Scripture, disagreed with Warfield's insistence on an evidentiary basis for theology. In its place he taught Kuyper's view that faith provided such a basis. And although Ten Hoor had vigorously opposed Kuyper's views, these began to surface again during the 1950s and '60s only to become part of a general cultural upheaval within the CRC.

These cultural upheavals and the questioning of traditions would not exempt the CRC, especially during the latter half of the decade. On its college campus students challenged the Vietnam War with modest marches and confronted CRC traditions with a mock edition of its official publication, *The Banner. The Bananer* was boldly irrever-ent from beginning to end. Its cover depicted U.S. Marines on Mount Surabachi hoist-ing the flag, but the flag was replaced by a dollar bill. Conservatives in the CRC were outraged. Seminary students' reactions were somewhat milder. Noisiest in those days at seminary were the objections to studying Louis Berkhof's *Systematic Theology*, especially by some zealous members of the Groen Van Prinsterer Club and its semi-nary counterpart, *Theologia Reformanda Est*. The seminary was said to be mired in scholastic and dualistic theology for which, according to some, the only solution was

[11]There are those within the CRC, some of whom have left and now are members of the United Reformed Churches or the Orthodox Christian Reformed Churches, who argue that the 1961 report on infallibility constitutes an official turn to the left and that Report 44 of 1973 on hermeneutics nailed this direction down. The 1961 report should probably be understood as defining a traditional Reformed position and thus a turning from a "fundamentalism" that has char-acterized not a few who have left the CRC in the 1990s.

[12]About this change Stek writes: "The most significant curricular change in the Biblical Division took place in the late 1960s when we abandoned the traditional *disciplinary* division (O.T. Introduction, O.T. History, O.T. Exegesis, O.T. Theology, Ancient Near Eastern History and Archaeology) for a *canonical* division (Pentateuch, Former Prophets, Latter Prophets, Writings—and correspondingly in the New Testament). . . . The chief reason for the change was that the disciplinary division was most appropriate for the university but the canonical division was most useful in minis-terial training."—from Bolt, *Stewards of the Word*, 98. Bolt editorializes: "The ghost of Foppe Ten Hoor smiled."

[13]Wyngaarden objected to the so-called "periphery" question. See *Agenda*, 192-193.

a complete reformation of theology[14] and a revisioning of the church institute. "Reformational" students of theology were urged to reject the regular route into the ministry and to attend the Institute for Christian Studies in Toronto. Questions about candidacy for the ministry were answered with vague words about entry through the local classis. It would be a fatal attraction for some and a harbinger of things to come.

Stek became professor of Old Testament for such a time as this. He was a typical CRC product: shaped by its theological, liturgical, and ecclesiastical traditions; schooled by its educational institutions; and experienced as a minister of the Word in a small midwestern church. But he had gone beyond the community: army life in the Pacific during World War II, the intellectual challenges of Westminster in Philadelphia, Chicago, and the Free University. His teaching of the Old Testament would demonstrate connections with both worlds. It would be as different from Wyngaarden's as was Janssen's, but not for the same reasons. Stek was a churchman whose scholarship was not shaped by naturalistic concerns, but neither was he afraid to acknowledge that scientific research could occasion important questions for biblical studies. If his was considered a conservative appointment in 1961, his dedication to biblical scholarship within and for the church, especially as it touched his willingness to hear the difficult questions raised by cultural anthropology about the origin of humanity, indicate that by the 1980s this was no longer so.[15] He would not challenge the confessional foundations of teaching the Old Testament, but he did break with the intimidation that had characterized its teaching since Janssen's dismissal. This academic courage and loyalty to the church of Christ provided an intellectual and confessional continuity that embraced the challenges for and needs of students aspiring to ministry during a difficult transition in the Christian Reformed Church in North America.

READING THE OLD TESTAMENT

Stek was, and remains, a superb exegete of the biblical text. Under his tutelage, with careful attention to the text and up-to-date research by recognized scholars, the Scriptures of the old covenant spoke with freshness and relevance. He enabled his students to nurture the faithful with the treasures of these Scriptures. He did this by

---

[14]Some consider that this revision was achieved by Gordon J. Spykman, who published *A Reformational Theology: A New Paradigm for Doing Dogmatics* (Grand Rapids: Eerdmans, 1992) shortly before his death.

[15]A student's complaint about a lecture on early chapters of Genesis suggested Stek was weak on the historicity of Adam and Eve. The Board of Trustees of the Seminary appointed a committee to have conversations with Stek about this matter. Prof. Henry Zwaanstra chaired a committee composed of profs. John H. Kromminga, Carl Kromminga, Fred H. Klooster, Bastiaan Van Elderen, and Marten H. Woudstra.

example in his classroom lectures on specific texts[16] and in the Old Testament Club[17], where he moved effortlessly from text to homiletic implications with unerring insight. New students were easily frustrated by Stek's close readings of the text because his insights were so obviously true that it seemed impossible that no one had seen this before. Moreover, these biblical-theological readings were carefully executed within an obvious Reformed biblical hermeneutic. When they asked how he managed such stimulating readings, students quickly learned there were no magic buttons, that his readings were the result of a patient and arduous working with the biblical text. Of course, he was and remains uniquely gifted, but his legacy is simple: read the text with great care and attention to all it says, again and again, and let it speak; follow the contours of the narrative, no matter how long the text.

Stek's careful reading of Scripture also had consequences for a biblical-theological understanding of the Old Testament. Meredith E. Kline, one of Stek's teachers at Westminster, in his *By Oath Consigned* and *Treaty of the Great King*, argued for a reading of the biblical covenants in the context of their ancient Near Eastern backgrounds, especially the ancient suzerain-vassal treaties. Suzerain-vassal treaties were royal administrative instruments kings used to maintain their empires against internal and external disorder. Stek took this material and applied it in his close reading of the covenants as they were depicted in the biblical text. It is within the kingdom, clearly taught in the opening chapters of Genesis, according to Stek,[18] but after the rebellion of Adam and Eve and the flood, that the Lord initiates the covenantal instrument as a means of redemption, beginning with Noah and not before.[19] This reading of the bibli-

[16]See, for example, the studies on the Ehud, Deborah, and Jephthah narratives (Judg. 3:12-30; 4; 5:31; 10-12:7); notes on the Bathsheba narrative (2 Sam. 11-12); 1 Kings 22 and 2 Chronicles 20:1-30), in his syllabus for the classroom, *The Former Prophets*, 124-169.

[17]Tau Nun Kaph (TaNaK) was one of several extra-curricular clubs which students could attend during their studies at the seminary. According to the 1967-1968 Catalog, p. 24, *Tau Nun Kaph* was organized "in 1967 for the purpose of studying the Old Testament from its redemptive historical perspective in order more completely to qualify the members for preaching from the Old Testament. The club meets bi-weekly for study and discussion, based on papers submitted by members of the club. A member of the Old Testament Department serves as Faculty Sponsor." Today students present sermons as a basis for discussion. At its inception profs. Stek and Woudstra were both involved in TaNaK; they were later joined by prof. Engelhard. By the mid 70s, however, Stek had become the sole faculty sponsor, a role he continues to this day. It is also noteworthy that of the 15 clubs listed in 1967-1969 catalogs only the Seminary Choir and TaNaK remain.

[18]This view was later clearly articulated in Stek's discussion of the royal language in Genesis 1:1-2:3. See his "What Says the Scripture?" in *Portraits of Creation: Biblical and Scientific Perspectives on the World's Formation*, ed. Howard J. Van Til (Grand Rapids: Eerdmans, 1990), 232-240.

[19]The earliest written form of this position is found in his Former Prophets Syllabus, first published at Calvin Theological Seminary during the 1980s. It is found unchanged in *The Former Prophets: A Syllabus* (Calvin Seminary, 1997), 170-178. An abbreviated form may be found on p. 19 of *The NIV Study Bible*. Stek published a more extensive articulation of this position in "'Covenant' Overload in Reformed Theology," *Calvin Theological Journal* 29 (1994):12-41.

cal text, however, challenged the theological understanding that the opening chapters of Genesis teach a covenant of creation or of works.

Stek's conclusions created some differences of opinion between him and some faculty colleagues,[20] because some dogmaticians, especially those who equate covenant and kingdom,[21] held that covenant had already shaped the relationship between God and his human creatures before the fall. Stek, however, was arguing for a more careful *biblical* reading. His biblical theological reading was not new in the Reformed tradition; Stek merely brought attention to it. N. H. Ridderbos, professor of Old Testament at the Free University of Amsterdam, argued that the Reformed tradition anchored the covenant of grace (Abraham) in God himself for dogmatic reasons.[22] Fred H. Klooster, professor of systematic theology and a colleague of Stek, agreed with this position.[23] Stek's understanding of the covenants exemplifies how a close reading of the biblical text brings about clear biblical theological thinking.

And there was one other thing: Stek was not an exegetical lone wolf; he displayed and taught a willingness to learn from other students of Scripture, confessional and critical. He represented the best of the grammatical-historical-theological hermeneutic taught at Calvin Seminary.[24] Without ignoring the historical and theological, Stek amplified the grammatical by teaching students to pay attention to stylistics (poetic

---

[20]Prof. Henry Zwaanstra, colleague of Stek, remembers summer lunch hours, beside the seminary pond, when Stek shared his thoughts about such and other matters arising from his research. Profs. Klooster and Woudstra were his conversation partners. Differences between Stek and Woudstra soon emerged.

[21]For example, Craig G. Bartholomew ("Covenant and Creation: Covenant Overload or Covenantal Deconstruction," *Calvin Theological Journal* 30 [1995]:14) cites Spykman approvingly (*Reformational Theology*, 11-12) when he writes that "Covenant and kingdom are like two sides of a single coin. Accordingly, we may say that in creation God *covenanted* his kingdom into existence. After the fall, God renewed the covenant . . ." (emphasis mine).

[22]N. H. Ridderbos ("Het verbond der genade. De alomvattende conceptie van het verbond," in *Het Dogma der Kerk*, eds. G. C. Berkouwer and G. Toornvliet [Groningen: Jan Haan, 1949], 291) writes, "Rather, Scripture allows us to see [Christ's] work of redemption as the restoration of the original relationship in which human beings might live with God. However, this relationship has been placed on a new basis and received a new center in Christ. And so, Reformed dogmatics reaches back from the covenant of grace, which began after the fall, to the original relationship between God and humanity that was rooted in the image of God and labelled it, after the analogy to the Covenant of Grace, the *covenant of works*. Furthermore, by linking itself to the profound ideas which Paul developed in Rom. 5:12-21 and 1 Cor. 15:20-22 and 45-49 concerning the first human being, Adam, and the last Adam, Christ, dogmatics illuminated in various ways the difference and similarity between Creation and Re-creation, Covenant of Works and Covenant of Grace" (my translation). Ridderbos was Stek's teacher during his stay at the Free University in 1973-1974.

[23]"For such reasons I do not consider it legitimate to speak of a covenant of creation, an Edenic Covenant, an Adamic Covenant, a covenant of works, or a covenant of redemption as has been done by many in the past. Covenanting involved a unique oath-taking arrangement, and the term may not be imposed where Scripture does not do so or provide the precise elements that warrant it."—Fred H. Klooster, "The Biblical Method of Salvation: A Case for Continuity," in *Continuity and Discontinuity Perspectives on the Relationship between the Old and New Testaments. Essays in Honor of S. Lewis Johnson, Jr.*, ed. John S. Feinberg (Wheaton, Ill.: Crossway Books, 1988), 150.

[24]Louis Berkhof's *Principles of Biblical Interpretation* (Grand Rapids: Baker, 1971), first published in 1950, represents the hermeneutics associated with Calvin Theological Seminary.

and narrative) and to poetic and narrative conventions such as parallelism and meter, episodic organization, and the narrative event line. So the writings of David Noel Freedman and Meir Sternberg complemented material on redemptive-historical reading of Scripture by those of Benne Holwerda, De Graaf, and Van't Veer. To this were added the form-critical studies by Gunkel, Westermann (Psalms), Mays (Hosea and Amos), and others. None were accepted at face value; all were to be read critically. We learned to understand what we were reading.

ABOUT THE ESSAYS IN THIS VOLUME

In the light of John H. Stek's work with the biblical text in the classroom, with TaNaK, and as an NIV editor, and in view of the consequences of his teaching for preaching and theology in the church of Christ, the essays in this volume have been organized in three parts, each of which reflects an aspect of the movement from text to sermon: access to the text itself and a methodology that aids in understanding; a careful reading of the text itself, leading toward suggestions for preaching; and a theological reflection on preaching in the church.

In Part One, Kenneth L. Barker and Ronald F. Youngblood explain the importance of a good translation, how such a translation comes into existence, and the reasons for addressing a specific audience. Of course, they present their work with the NIV and the New International Reader's Version (NIrV). Bible reading begins with a text, and for most people that means one translated from the original languages. Barry L. Bandstra, using 2 Kings 5, examines the usefulness of discourse analysis for exegesis.

Part Two contains exegetical essays that move from a close reading of the text toward some suggestions for preaching. Texts were selected from sections of Scripture taught by Stek at Calvin Seminary: Pentateuch (Koopmans), Former Prophets (Leder, Vannoy), the Writings (Bosma, Seerveld, Waltke, Wolters). It is not important to explain how two essays that focus on Proverbs 10 came to be included. Call it providential serendipity. When I received the second essay on this text, I took some time to think about this unexpected complication, consulted with colleagues, and contacted the authors (Waltke and Seerveld). Each received a copy of the other's essay; neither objected to both being included. Let us take these essays, then, as an example of a fact in the history of exegesis: scholars who study the same chapter of Scripture come to conclusions that differ on the extent of the text, its structure, syntactical constructions, and so on. What better place to find two such essays than in a volume honoring a careful exegete.

Essays in Part Three reflect theologically on the life of the text in the church through preaching and application (Bolt, Plantinga, Greidanus). And Roy M. A. Berkenbosch's sermon on Samson is a fitting tribute to a teacher whose classroom work with the Samson narrative was inspiring. Paul W. Fields closes this volume with an up-to-date bibliography of the writings of John Henry Stek.

PART ONE

The Biblical Text: Translations, Versions, and Syntax

Hearing God's Word Through a Good Translation

Kenneth L. Barker

If the church is to hear God's Word with authority, with accuracy, and with clarity, it must use a good translation. But what constitutes a good translation? In my opinion, the key word is *balance*. A good translation exhibits a pleasing balance in its committee approach, in its textual basis, in its translation philosophy, in its handling of difficult passages, and in the selection of tools, reference works, commentaries, and other resources that are based on it. Those are the five areas I wish to explore, primarily from my experience as an NIV translator.[1]

A BALANCED COMMITTEE APPROACH

In 1965 a joint Bible translation committee of the Christian Reformed Church and the National Association of Evangelicals appointed a fifteen-person Committee on Bible Translation (CBT) to oversee the "preparation of a contemporary English translation of the Bible . . . as a collegiate endeavor of evangelical scholars."[2] The CBT was to have broad denominational and theological representation within evangelicalism. Yet the aim was not to produce an "evangelical" translation, but one that would accurately and clearly represent what the Bible says and means. The translators were to be fully committed to the inspiration, infallibility, and divine authority of Scripture as nothing less than the Word of God.

The working method of the NIV translators included seven steps:

1. Initial Translation Teams, composed of nearly 125 scholars from the major English-speaking countries, translated the biblical books from the Hebrew and Aramaic texts of the Old Testament and from the Greek of the New.

2. Intermediate Editorial Committees evaluated those translations and compiled suggestions for improvement.

3. General Editorial Committees evaluated the work of the two previous committees, making additional suggestions.

4. CBT evaluated all previous work and determined the final wording and content.

[1]Since I have had the privilege of working with Professor John Stek for many years on both the NIV and *The NIV Study Bible*, it is a special pleasure to contribute this chapter in his honor. In particular, I have always appreciated his excellent grasp of the whole range of biblical exegesis and biblical theology.

[2]"The Story of the New International Version" (East Brunswick, N.J. [now Colorado Springs, Colo.]: International Bible Society, 1978), 8.

5. English stylists (primarily Frank Gaebelein and Margaret Nicholson) improved the literary style of the NIV.

6. The NIV was field-tested.

7. The CBT put the NIV in final form.

What are the advantages of such a balanced and thorough committee approach to the task of Bible translation? They include these:

- No one person can spot all the problems in a translation. Since all translators have areas of strength and of weakness, a team of translators can supplement and complement each other.

- Linguistic studies are highly specialized. No one person can be an expert in all fields, such as ancient languages, textual criticism, and English style. A committee of scholars can provide specialists in each area.

- Committee work helps avoid ecclesiastical, theological, and linguistic provincialisms.

- When a translation problem arises, the committee approach is conducive to finding a solution. Vigorous discussion and cross-fertilization of ideas stimulate the mind and produce solutions that would never have been reached by a single individual.

- The multi-tiered process described above yields a finely-honed product. At the lower editorial levels, attention can be given to major problems. Once these have been solved, higher-level committees concentrate on finer points.

- The committee approach results in wider acceptance of the final product.

So a good translation will take a balanced committee approach.

A BALANCED TEXTUAL BASIS

What was the textual basis of the NIV Old Testament? The preface to the NIV answers the question in a general way:

> For the Old Testament the standard Hebrew [and Aramaic] text, the Masoretic Text as published in the latest editions of *Biblia Hebraica*, was used throughout. The Dead Sea Scrolls contain material bearing on an earlier stage of the Hebrew text. They were consulted, as were the Samaritan Pentateuch and the ancient scribal traditions relating to textual changes. Sometimes a variant Hebrew reading in the margin of the Masoretic Text was followed instead of the text itself. Such instances, being variants within the Masoretic tradition, are not

specified by footnotes. In rare cases, words in the consonantal text were divided differently from the way they appear in the Masoretic Text. Footnotes indicate this. The translators also consulted the more important early versions—the Septuagint; Symmachus and Theodotion; the Vulgate; the Syriac Peshitta; the Targums; and for the Psalms the *Juxta Hebraica* of Jerome. Readings from these versions were occasionally followed where the Masoretic Text seemed doubtful and where accepted principles of textual criticism showed that one or more of these textual witnesses appeared to provide the correct reading. Such instances are footnoted. Sometimes vowel letters and vowel signs did not, in the judgment of the translators, represent the correct vowels for the original consonantal text. Accordingly some words were read with a different set of vowels. These instances are usually not indicated by footnotes.

Let us consider three examples that show "accepted principles of textual criticism" in operation. All of them are selected from my commentary on Zechariah.[3]

One principle pertains to passages where the Hebrew manuscripts and the ancient versions all agree on a single reading that yields a good sense. In such passages we may safely assume that the original reading has been preserved.

In Zechariah 6:11, for example, the Lord instructs the prophet, "Take the silver and gold and make a crown, and set it on the head of the high priest, Joshua son of Jehozadak." Some interpreters argue that the original reading at the end of the verse was "Zerubbabel son of Shealtiel." But Eichrodt rightly considers that "the interpretation of this passage in terms of Zerubbabel, which can only be secured at the cost of hazardous conjecture, is mistaken, and that a reference to a hoped-for messianic ruler after Zerubbabel's disappearance is more in accordance with the evidence."[4] Furthermore, no Hebrew manuscripts or ancient versions have the Zerubbabel reading. Therefore, since it is a purely conjectural emendation, we reject it.

A second principle of textual criticism applies to passages where the Hebrew manuscripts and the ancient versions differ. In that situation, one should choose either the more difficult reading or the reading that most readily explains how the others arose. A more difficult reading does not mean a meaningless and corrupt reading. The end result must be a reasonable and worthy text.[5]

---

[3]K. L. Barker, "Zechariah," in *Expositor's Bible Commentary*, Vol. 7, ed. F. E. Gaebelein (Grand Rapids: Zondervan, 1985), 635 (n. on 5:6), 639, 692 (n. on 14:5).

[4]W. Eichrodt, *Theology of the Old Testament*, Vol. 2, tr. J. A. Baker (Philadelphia: Westminster, 1967), 343 n. 1.

[5]B. K. Waltke, "The Textual Criticism of the Old Testament," in *Biblical Criticism: Historical, Literary and Textual* by R. K. Harrison et al. (Grand Rapids: Zondervan, 1978), 77-78. Waltke's entire article is very helpful.

Zechariah 5:6 interprets the *ephah* or "measuring basket" (or barrel) as "the iniquity of the people throughout the land," in harmony with verse 8. But עֵינָם presents a text-critical problem. As it stands, it means "their eye" (i.e., their appearance), which does not yield a good sense (cf. the parallel in verse 8, where the woman in the basket is interpreted as wickedness personified). The NIV, probably correctly, follows one Hebrew manuscript, the Septuagint, and the Syriac in reading עֲוֹנָם ("their iniquity"). The pronominal suffix refers to the people, perhaps with specific reference to the godless rich. The only significant variation between the two readings is the Hebrew letter *waw* instead of *yodh*. In many ancient Hebrew manuscripts, the only perceptible difference between the two letters is the length of the downward stroke. A long *yodh* and a short *waw* are virtually indistinguishable, so it would be easy for a scribe to miscopy. To further support the reading, "their iniquity" (or perversity), Baldwin adds,

> The *ephah*, named by Amos in his invective on short measure given
> by the merchants (Amos 8:5), symbolized injustice *in all the land.*
> The life of the community was vitiated by iniquity that infected it in
> every part (cf. Hag. 2:14). The stinginess that prompted the making
> of false measures was a symptom of an underlying perversity that
> was at the root of perverse actions and relationships.[6]

A third principle of textual criticism relates to passages where both the Hebrew manuscripts and the ancient versions offer different readings, but a superior reading cannot be demonstrated using the above two principles. In that case, the Masoretic Text takes priority. An example of such a passage appears to be Zechariah 14:5, which reads, "You will flee by my mountain valley, for it will extend to Azel. You will flee as you fled from the earthquake in the days of Uzziah king of Judah." The NIV footnote offers this alternative translation: "My mountain valley will be blocked and will extend to Azel. It will be blocked as it was blocked because of the earthquake in the days of Uzziah king of Judah." This translation presupposes repointing the verbs to נִסְתַּם (from סתם). It is supported by the Septuagint, the Targum, and Symmachus. The Masoretic Text, on the other hand, has נַסְתֶּם (from נוס) and is supported by the Vulgate and the Peshitta.

As I perceive it, the meaning of this reading is that the newly created east-west valley (v. 4) will afford an easy means of rapid escape from the anti-Semitic onslaught detailed in verse 2 (the Mount of Olives has always constituted a serious obstacle to

[6]J. G. Baldwin, *Haggai, Zechariah, Malachi*, TOTC (Downers Grove, Ill.: InterVarsity, 1972), 128.

such an escape to the east). Since the Masoretic Text makes good sense and there is no convincing reason to change it, it is preferred.[7]

What was the textual basis of the NIV New Testament? The question is answered briefly in the preface to the NIV:

> The Greek text used in translating the New Testament was an eclectic one. No other piece of ancient literature has such an abundance of manuscript witnesses as does the New Testament. Where existing manuscripts differ, the translators made their choice of readings according to accepted principles of New Testament textual criticism. Footnotes call attention to places where there was uncertainty about what the original text was. The best current printed texts of the Greek New Testament were used.

Several sentences in this summary call for further comment. First, what is meant by an "eclectic" Greek text of the New Testament? Most textual witnesses (Greek manuscripts and papyrus fragments, the ancient versions, and Scripture quotations by the early church fathers) can be grouped into one of three major text types according to the variant readings occurring in them:

> The *Alexandrian text* was so named because it apparently emerged in and around Alexandria, Egypt. It is represented by the majority of the papyri; by several early uncial manuscripts, including ℵ (Sinaiticus), B (Vaticanus), C (Ephraemi Rescriptus); by the Coptic versions; and by significant Alexandrian church fathers, such as Clement and Origen.
>
> The *Western text* is represented by the uncial D (Bezae), the Old Latin, the Old Syriac, and the church fathers Irenaeus, Tertullian, and Jerome. Most scholars are reluctant to follow readings that have only Western support.
>
> The *Byzantine text* is represented by the vast majority of Greek manuscripts and most of the later church fathers. This text was largely preserved in the area of the old Byzantine empire, which is now Turkey, Bulgaria, Greece, Albania, and the former Yugoslavia.[8]

---

[7] For additional data on the original text of the Old Testament, see E. S. Kalland, "Establishing the Hebrew and Aramaic Text," in *The Making of the NIV*, ed. K. L. Barker (Grand Rapids: Baker, 1991), 43-50, noting the works in the "Suggested Reading" list (49-50), particularly E. R. Brotzman, *Old Testament Textual Criticism: A Practical Introduction* (Grand Rapids: Baker, 1994), B. K. Waltke (n. 5 above), and E. Wurthwein, *The Text of the Old Testament*, tr. E. F. Rhodes (Grand Rapids: Eerdmans, 1979).

[8] D. A. Black, *New Testament Textual Criticism: A Concise Guide* (Grand Rapids: Baker, 1994), 33.

The so-called *Caesarean text* (found only in the Gospels) is now sometimes referred to as "other important witnesses."[9]

There are three accepted principles that support such external manuscript evidence:

1. Generally, the earlier manuscripts are preferred.

2. Normally, the reading supported in widely separated geographical areas is preferred.

3. The reading supported by the greatest number of text types is usually preferred.

When examining internal evidence, the most important principle is this: The reading that best explains the origin of the others should be favored. This principle has several corollaries:

- The shorter reading is usually preferred.

- The more difficult reading is usually preferred.

- The reading that best accords with the writer's style and vocabulary is preferred.

- The reading that best fits the context and/or the writer's theology is usually preferred.

- In parallel passages the less harmonious reading is usually preferred.

Another principle is sometimes mentioned: Manuscripts should be weighed rather than counted. For example, preference should be given to manuscripts that have most often proved to be correct when all the other tests have been applied to them.

In conservative evangelical circles, the debate over the best Greek text of the New Testament focuses on three main options:

1. Follow the Textus Receptus ("received text"), the Greek text that lies behind the KJV.

2. Follow the readings of the majority of manuscripts.

3. Follow a reasoned eclectic approach (described above in connection with external and internal evidence).

The vast majority of specialists in Greek and New Testament (including the most conservative ones) subscribe to the latter approach. To keep things in proper perspective, however, one must remember that all Greek manuscripts and papyri agree on more than 98 percent of the New Testament Greek text. The differences, then, pertain

[9]Ibid., 63, 65.

to less than 2 percent of the total text of the New Testament and do not affect Christian doctrines. They are still intact.[10]

So a good translation will have a balanced textual basis.[11]

A BALANCED TRANSLATION PHILOSOPHY

What types of Bible translations are there? Bible translators and linguists speak of two major types of translations. The first, in which the translator pursues a word-for-word rendering, is referred to as "formal," "complete," "literal," or "gross equivalence." The New American Standard Bible (NASB) and the New King James Version (NKJV) are good examples of this approach.

It is often possible to translate literally while retaining contemporary English idiom and excellent literary style. Thousands of such renderings occur in the NIV, beginning with Genesis 1:1. "In the beginning God created the heavens and the earth" is a straightforward translation of the Hebrew text. It is also good English, so why change it?

Sometimes it is impossible to translate literally and retain natural, idiomatic, clear English. Consider the NASB rendering of Matthew 13:20: "The one on whom seed was sown on the rocky places, this is the man who hears the word and immediately receives it with joy." The NIV reads: "The one who received the seed that fell on rocky places is the man who hears the word and at once receives it with joy." Here the NASB is so woodenly literal that the result is a cumbersome, poorly constructed sentence. The NIV translation, on the other hand, is natural and smooth without sacrificing accuracy.[12]

The second major type of translation is referred to as "dynamic," "functional," or "idiomatic equivalence." Here the translator attempts a thought-for-thought rendering. The Good News Bible (GNB; also known as Today's English Version, TEV), the New Living Translation, God's Word, and the Contemporary English Version are some of the examples of this approach. These versions seek a modern cultural equivalent that will have the same effect the original message had on ancient cultures while preserving the effect of the original message. Obviously this approach is a much freer one.

---

[10]For numerous examples of a reasoned eclectic approach, see K. L. Barker, *The Accuracy of the NIV* (Grand Rapids: Baker, 1996), 52-102.

[11]For additional data on the original text of the New Testament, see R. Earle, "Establishing the Greek Text," in *The Making of the NIV* (see n. 7 above), 51-55, noting the works in the "Suggested Reading" list (55), particularly D. A. Black, *New Testament Textual Criticism* (n. 8 above); J. H. Greenlee, *Introduction to New Testament Textual Criticism*, Revised Edition (Peabody, Mass.: Hendrickson, 1995); and B. M. Metzger, *The Text of the New Testament, Third, Enlarged Edition* (New York: Oxford University Press, 1992); see also D. B. Wallace, "The Majority-Text Theory: History, Methods and Critique," *Journal of the Evangelical Theological Society* 37 (June 1994):185-215; J. R. White, *The King James Only Controversy: Can You Trust the Modern Translations?* (Minneapolis: Bethany, 1995).

[12]See H. M. Wolf, "Literal vs. Accurate," in *The Making of the NIV* (n. 7 above), 125-34.

In my opinion, the NIV fits neither of these two types of translations. After considerable personal study, comparison, and analysis, I am convinced that in order to do complete justice to translations like the NIV and the New Revised Standard Version scholars must recognize a third category: the "balanced" or "mediating" translation.

It is significant that Nida seems to open the door for a mediating position between the two main translation philosophies, theories, or methods. He writes, "Between the two poles of translating (i.e. between strict formal equivalence and complete dynamic equivalence) there are a number of intervening grades, representing various acceptable standards of literary translating."[13]

A distinction must be made between dynamic equivalence as a translation principle and dynamic equivalence as a translation philosophy. The latter exists only when a version sets out to produce a dynamic-equivalence rendering from start to finish, as the GNB did. The foreword to the *Special Edition Good News Bible*, with features by Lion (England), indicates that "word-for-word translation does not accurately convey the force of the original, so the GNB uses instead the 'dynamic equivalent,' the words which will have the same force and meaning today as the original text had for its first readers." Dynamic equivalence as a translation principle, on the other hand, is used in varying degrees by all versions of the Bible.[14] This is easily illustrated by a few selected examples.[15]

- A "literal" rendering of the opening part of the Hebrew text of Isaiah 40:2 would read: "Speak to the heart of Jerusalem." Yet all English versions (including the KJV) see the need for a dynamic-equivalence translation here.

- The KJV and the NASB read "in the ears of Jerusalem" in Jeremiah 2:2, but the NKJV and the NIV have "in the hearing of Jerusalem." Here the NKJV is just as "dynamic" as the NIV. Both wanted to communicate the meaning in a natural way to modern readers.

- In Haggai 2:16 the NASB has "grain heap," but the KJV, NKJV, and NIV all use "heap" alone. Here the formal-equivalent version, the NASB, is freer than the NIV, which is alleged by some to adhere to the dynamic-equivalence method.

- The KJV and NKJV read "no power at all" in John 19:11, whereas the NIV has only "no power." Which is following the formal-equivalence approach here and which the dynamic?

[13]E. A. Nida, *Toward a Science of Translating* (Leiden: E. J. Brill, 1964), 160.

[14]See C. Hargreaves, *A Translator's Freedom* (Sheffield: JSOT Press, 1993).

[15]Several of these examples were given to me around 1990 by Dr. Marten H. Woudstra, former professor of Old Testament at Calvin Theological Seminary.

What kind of translation, then, is the NIV? Where does it fit? While these and related questions have been addressed generally in several publications and reviews, they are addressed specifically in only one published, authoritative source by NIV translators (italics mine):

> Broadly speaking, there are several methods of translation: the concordant one, which ranges from literalism to the comparative freedom of the King James Version and even more of the Revised Standard Version, both of which follow the syntactical structure of the Hebrew and Greek texts as far as is compatible with good English; the paraphrastic one, in which the translator restates the gist of the text in his own words; and the method of equivalence, in which the translator seeks to understand as fully as possible what the biblical writers had to say (a criterion common, of course, to the careful use of any method) and then tries to find its closest equivalent in contemporary usage. In its more advanced form this is spoken of as dynamic equivalence, in which the translator seeks to express the meaning as the biblical writers would if they were writing in English today. All these methods have their values when responsibly used.
>
> As for the NIV, its method is an *eclectic* one with the emphasis for the most part on a *flexible use of concordance and equivalence*, but with a *minimum of literalism, paraphrase, or outright dynamic equivalence*. In other words, the NIV stands on *middle ground*—by no means the easiest position to occupy. It may fairly be said that the translators were convinced that, through long patience in seeking the right words, it is possible to attain a high degree of faithfulness in putting into clear and idiomatic English what the Hebrew and Greek texts say. Whatever literary distinction the NIV has is the result of the persistence with which this course was pursued.[16]

This clearly indicates that CBT attempted to make the NIV a balanced, mediating version, one that would fall halfway between the most literal and the most free. It is not, strictly speaking, a dynamic-equivalence translation. If it were, it would read in Isaiah 65:25 "snakes will no longer be dangerous" (GNB) instead of "dust will be the serpent's food." Or it would read in 1 Samuel 20:30 "You bastard!" (GNB) instead of "You son of a perverse and rebellious woman!" The NIV is an idiomatically balanced translation.

---

[16]*The Story of the New International Version* (Colorado Springs: International Bible Society, 1978), 13.

This balance was achieved by a built-in system of checks and balances that preserve the *accuracy*, *beauty*, *clarity*, and *dignity* of the original text (we called it the A-B-C-Ds of the NIV). We wanted to be *accurate*, that is, as faithful to the original text as possible. It was also important to be faithful to the target or receptor language—English, in this case. We did not want to make the mistake of creating "translation English" that would not be beautiful and natural. Accuracy, then, must be balanced by *beauty* of language. CBT attempted to make the NIV read and flow the way any great English literature should.

At the same time, we did not want to create lofty, flowery, beautiful English that would not be *clear*. A favorite illustration of lack of clarity is the KJV rendering of Job 36:33: "The noise thereof sheweth concerning it, the cattle also concerning the vapour." In the interests of *clarity* the NIV reads: "His [God's] thunder announces the coming storm; even the cattle make known its approach."

On the other hand, CBT did not want to make the mistake—in the name of clarity—of stooping to slang, vulgarisms, street vernacular, and unnecessarily undignified language. Clarity must be balanced by *dignity*, particularly since CBT's objective was to produce a general, all-church-use Bible. Some of the dynamic-equivalence versions listed above are at times unnecessarily undignified.

To sum up, we wanted accuracy, but not at the expense of beauty; we wanted beauty, but not at the expense of clarity; we wanted clarity, but not at the expense of dignity. We wanted all these in a nice *balance*. A good translation follows a balanced translation philosophy.

A BALANCED SOLUTION TO DIFFICULTIES

How should Bible translators handle difficult passages? One of the balanced ways CBT approached such problems in the NIV was to recognize viable alternative solutions. One example from the Old Testament and one from the New will illustrate the point.

In Micah 5:2 (NIV) the verse ends, ". . . whose origins are from of old, from ancient times." Footnotes provide this alternative rendering: "whose goings out are from of old, from days of eternity." Why did CBT not reverse the main text and the alternative translation found in the footnotes? It is not because of carelessness in handling Old Testament Messianic prophecies or any other doctrines, as some have charged. Many good and godly scholars differ on the contextual interpretation of certain biblical passages—Micah 5:2 happens to be one of them. Those who prefer the footnote alternative use it to argue for the eternal existence of the Messiah. Those who prefer the main text believe that the expression refers to the ancient "origins" of the Messiah in the line of David (as indicated in the Davidic covenant of 2 Samuel 7) and in the tribe of Judah (Genesis 49:10).

The majority of CBT felt that the context favored the main text: "*Bethlehem . . . of Judah*, out of *you* [emphasis mine] will come for me one who will be ruler over Israel" (note the stress on the origins of the future Davidic ruler in the Davidic town of Bethlehem). So we put that rendering in the text and the other one in the footnotes as an alternative. (Incidentally, those who favor the main text still believe in the eternal existence of the Messiah [and so in the eternal Son of God] and believe that his eternality is plainly taught in other passages, particularly in the New Testament.)

In spite of this balanced approach to alternative understandings (both of them allowed by the Hebrew lexicons), Radmacher criticizes the NIV for not putting the footnotes in the main text.[17] But White defends the NIV's decision at Micah 5:2:

> Dr. Barker's explanation of the textual choice of the NIV at Micah 5:2 makes plenty of sense, *even if you do not agree with the viewpoint held by the majority of the Translation Committee* [italics White's]. . . . the rendering is supported by solid arguments and has a firm basis in the Hebrew text itself. . . . Dr. Barker referred to his own reference note in the *NIV Study Bible* at Romans 9:5, wherein he listed a number of passages that teach the deity of Christ.[18]

The second example is taken from Hebrews 11:11, which the NIV translates "By faith Abraham, even though he was past age—and Sarah herself was barren—was enabled to become a father because he considered him faithful who had made the promise." The alternative in the footnote has "By faith even Sarah, who was past age, was enabled to bear children because she considered him faithful who had made the promise." Which is correct? As the footnote indicates, the meaning of the Greek text of this verse is uncertain and may indicate that it was Sarah who was enabled instead of Abraham. In the main text, the words "and Sarah herself was barren" are to be understood parenthetically (hence the dashes).

Bruce's fine commentary on Hebrews explains why CBT made Abraham the subject in the main text and Sarah in the footnote, though Bruce suggests still another way

---

[17]E. D. Radmacher and Z. C. Hodges, *The NIV Reconsidered: A Fresh Look at a Popular Translation* (Dallas: Redención Viva, 1990), 56-58.

[18]J. R. White, *The King James Only Controversy*, 215-16. For additional defenses of the main text of the NIV here see, e.g., R. L. Smith, *Micah-Malachi*, WBC (Waco, Tex.: Word, 1984), 42-44; L.C. Allen, *The Books of Joel, Obadiah, Jonah and Micah*, NICOT (Grand Rapids: Eerdmans, 1976), 342-47; R. B. Chisholm, Jr., *Interpreting the Minor Prophets* (Grand Rapids: Zondervan, 1990), 148-49; B. K. Waltke, "Micah," in *The Minor Prophets*, Vol. 2, ed. T. E. McComiskey (Grand Rapids: Baker, 1993), 702-05.

of working Sarah into the sentence.[19] He also points out that the major problem is that the Greek phrase for "to conceive seed" (KJV) does not mean that. Rather, it refers to the father's role in the generative process. A literal translation would be "for depositing sperm," thus more likely referring to Abraham.[20]

A good translation uses balance in handling difficult passages.[21]

A BALANCED SELECTION OF AVAILABLE RESOURCES

A truly good Bible translation will have a wide range of balanced works that are keyed to it and that support its text. Study tools, reference works, commentaries, and other resources will be based on it. The NIV, for example, has an unusual abundance of supporting resources. The following is only a partial and highly selective list of such works by category.

1. STUDY BIBLES

The NIV Study Bible
Disciples Study Bible
Life Application Bible
The New Student Bible
The Ryrie Study Bible
Thompson Chain-Reference Bible
The International Inductive Study Bible

2. CONCORDANCES, INTERLINEARS, AND TRIGLOT

NIV Exhaustive Concordance
NIV Hebrew-English Concordance
NIV Greek-English Concordance
Interlinear NIV Hebrew-English Old Testament
NIV Interlinear Greek-English New Testament
NIV Triglot Old Testament (Hebrew-Greek-NIV)

3. COMMENTARIES

New Bible Commentary 21st Century Edition (1 vol.)
International Bible Commentary (1 vol.)
Evangelical Commentary on the Bible (1 vol.)

---

[19]F. F. Bruce, *The Epistle to the Hebrews*, NICNT (Grand Rapids: Eerdmans, 1964), 299-302.

[20]Ibid., 301-02. Morris is inclined to agree with Bruce—see L. Morris, "Hebrews," in *Expositor's Bible Commentary*, Vol. 12 (see n. 3 above) , 119-20, 123 (n. on 11:11).

[21]For more illustrations of a balanced approach to solving problems, see K. L. Barker, *The Accuracy of the NIV*, particularly pp. 19-50 (containing many examples of using Hebrew grammar, syntax, semantics, exegesis, theology, textual criticism, etc., in solving translation problems).

Zondervan NIV Bible Commentary (2 vols.)
Bible Knowledge Commentary (2 vols.)

MULTI-VOLUME SETS:

Expositor's Bible Commentary
New American Commentary
New International Biblical Commentary
NIV Application Commentary

4. DICTIONARIES AND ENCYCLOPEDIAS

New International Dictionary of the Bible
Zondervan Pictorial Encyclopedia of the Bible
New International Dictionary of Old Testament Theology & Exegesis
New International Dictionary of New Testament Theology

5. TOPICAL BIBLES AND ATLASES

Zondervan NIV Nave's Topical Bible
Topical Analysis of the Bible
Zondervan NIV Atlas of the Bible

6. THE NIV ON COMPUTER

Bible Source
MacBible
Thompson Chain HyperBible
BibleMaster
CompuBible
Gramcord
Logos Bible Software
QuickVerse
WordSearch

The above works involve over a dozen different publishers. With such a wealth of supporting resources (and still more planned for the future), it is not surprising that over 30 denominations either sanction or extensively use the NIV.

So a good translation will have a wide range of balanced works available to support its text.

CONCLUSION

As indicated at the outset, if the church is to hear God's word with authority, accuracy, and clarity, it must use a good translation. Such a translation will exhibit a pleasing balance in its committee approach, in its textual basis, in its translation philosophy, in handling difficult passages, and in the selection of tools, reference works, commentaries, and other resources that are based on it. Among other things, we have attempted to demonstrate that the NIV meets these criteria.

Does all this mean that the NIV is perfect? No, it does not. In fact, no translation is perfect, for they are all made by imperfect people. Nonetheless, as I have written elsewhere, "one advantage of using the NIV is that, in spite of its imperfections, most expositors will likely experience the pleasant surprise that they are devoting less time to correcting and clarifying the text than would be the case if they were using some other English Bible."[22] I added

> Yet another advantage of using the NIV is that it is in an ongoing review process. This means that although the text is basically established, not all renderings are "engraved in rock forever," to borrow Job's words (Job 19:24). We are open to achieving an even better balance in our translations. If the reader has a problem with our rendering of a particular verse and has strong feelings about the matter, he or she may submit a suggestion or proposal to the IBS [International Bible Society] address [at the end of the Preface]. CBT will consider it.[23]

Silva puts it like this:

> When the editor of *New Horizons* asked me if I would be interested in writing a response to criticism of the NIV, I hesitated briefly. After all, I was not involved in the translating of the NIV. Morever, I think the NIV is far from perfect. During the past few years, I have been involved in the production of an "NIV-like" translation of the Bible into Spanish. This work, which involves very close comparison of the NIV with the original, has alerted me to numerous renderings that appear unsatisfying, problematic, or even plain wrong. In other words, my own list of objections is probably much longer than that of most outspoken critics of the NIV. So why would I then agree to write this article? Simply because my list of objections to *other* versions would be even longer [emphasis his]. This is not to say that all available English translations are bad. Quite the contrary! We are richly blessed by a wide variety of versions, almost all of which—when

[22]Barker, *The Accuracy of the NIV*, 103.
[23]Ibid.

compared with good translations of other literature—have to be regarded as clear and accurate, but never perfect.[24]

Whether one chooses the NIV or one of the other good translations, I believe the time has come for every denomination and every church to adopt one version as its official Bible and use it for everything—pew Bible, preaching, public reading of Scripture, Sunday school, Scripture memorization, etc. This is not to say that in the early elementary grades, and so at lower reading levels, one should not use simple, easy-reading versions like the New International Reader's Version (NIrV). Indeed, the NIrV nicely prepares the way for the transition to the NIV (on which it is based). Bastian agrees with the basic premise I have stated here:

> The time has come for each congregation to center its life on one version. . . . The plethora of Bible translations into English—approximately 70 of all or parts of the Bible in this century—may only have nourished a spirit of novelty among us, making us samplers rather than searchers.
>
> If a church is to use the Bible systematically, it must center its whole life—preaching, teaching, family, and personal devotions—upon one major version, because repetition aids learning. Moreover, a congregation working from a Bible common to both pulpit and pew receives the message by the eye gate as well as the ear gate, providing another aid to understanding. . . .
>
> You may not agree, or you may argue that the choice is much wider than I allow [he recommends the NIV over the RSV]. Either way, I hope you agree that the time has come for congregations to form their life around one major version until its great words fix themselves in the minds and hearts of worshipers of all ages.[25]

The most important thing is for a church to begin really hearing God's word through whatever good translation it selects. And may we all hear it in the frequent Hebrew and Greek sense of "hear": "listen, understand, and obey with an appropriate response."

[24]M. Silva, "Reflections on the NIV," *New Horizons* (June 1995), quoted by C. O'Brien in *Which Translation? Why We Use the New International Version of the Bible at Grace Presbyterian Church* (Jackson, Tenn.: Grace Presbyterian Church, 1997), 1.

[25]D. N. Bastian, "We Have Been Bible Samplers Long Enough," *Christianity Today* (October 8, 1982): 104.

The New International Reader's Version: What, Who, How, and Why

Ronald F. Youngblood

It is confessed that Books of Anatomy, and other Parts of necessary Science, are proper to be written; and these may be consulted by Persons who are grown up to a due Age, especially by those whose Profession requires it. There is also some Necessity of foul Narratives, where foul Crimes are committed, and ought to be publickly exposed and brought to Justice and Punishment. As the Affairs of Mankind stand, these Things cannot always be avoided: But there is no manner of Necessity that Children should read them, or rash unguarded Youth.

For some of the Reasons before mentioned there should be a wise Conduct in shewing Children what Parts of the Bible they should read: For though the Word of God expresseth all Things with due Decency, yet there are some Things which have been found necessary to be spoken of in Scripture, both in the Laws of *Moses*, and in the Representation of the Wickedness of the *Gentiles* in the New Testament, in which adult Persons have been concerned, which there is no Necessity for Children to read and hear, and they may be passed over or omitted among them. The *Jews* were wont to withhold *Solomon's Song* from their Children till they were thirty Years old: And the late pious and prudent Bishop *Tillotson* (in a Manuscript which I have seen) wishes that those Parts of the Bible wherein there are some of the Affairs of Mankind expressed *too naturally* (as he calls it) were omitted in the publick Lessons of the Church: I think they may as well be excepted also out of the common Lessons of Children, and out of the daily Course of reading in Family Worship.[1]

In his elegant eighteenth-century English prose style, Isaac Watts expresses many of the sentiments I felt nearly ten years ago when I was first asked what I thought about the feasibility and possibility of translating the entire Bible into a form that an eight-year-old child could readily understand. Is everything in the Bible suitable for children to read? Should they be exposed to the gruesome details surrounding the violent

---

[1] I. Watts, *The Improvement of the Mind: Second Part* (London: J. Buckland and T. Longman, 1782), 169-170.

deaths of an Eglon (Judg. 3:20-22), or a Goliath (1 Sam. 17:48-51), or an Asahel (2 Sam. 2:23)? Can the frank and vivid language of Genesis 38:9 or Ezekiel 23:20[2] or Amos 1:13 be softened enough so as not to scandalize needlessly the tender eyes and ears and hearts of children—or keep their parents from allowing their offspring to read those passages?[3] Indeed, might not such language produce in the impressionable minds of little ones the desire to act out in real life what they have read in Holy Scripture? Would it not be better to omit questionable sections of the text in Bibles that are intended primarily for children? In short, should not Bible translators be guided by what Watts wants?

Initially, my colleagues and associates at International Bible Society and Zondervan Publishing House found it difficult to persuade me otherwise. They wanted me to become the executive editor of a children's translation of the Bible—the *whole* Bible— aimed at a third-grade reading level. The New International Version (NIV), the world's best-selling English Bible for many years, was evaluated as having a reading level of 7.8. This meant that children in the eighth month of their seventh year of elementary school would have no particular difficulty reading it, but that children in earlier grades would only be able to read it with great effort, if at all. It would be my task to oversee the production of an edition of that Bible at a third-grade level to serve the needs of chil- dren four full grades earlier—and therefore four years younger than seventh-graders— who wanted to read the NIV but were not able to.

As I continued to weigh the pros and cons of whether young children should be pro- vided with an unexpurgated Bible prepared especially for them, I was soon forced to reckon with the fact that in the 1990s the general level of juvenile awareness con- cerning sensitive matters is quite different today than it was when I was a little boy growing up in the 1930s. That was then; this is now. The advent of television, video games, rated movies, and other forms of entertainment has inevitably exposed our children to visual and auditory experiences that I was shielded from almost com- pletely. For better or for worse, our permissive culture and our wide-open society have

---

[2]In addition to its vivid sexual allusions, the prophet Ezekiel's style and subject matter makes his book difficult to read and understand (a fact long noted in rabbinic tradition). Jerome, translator of the Latin Vulgate version, pointed out that because the book of Ezekiel is so difficult Jews under the age of thirty were forbidden to read its beginning and end- ing chapters (*Commentarium in Hiezechielem libri 14, S. Hieronymi presbyteri Opera 1/4*, Corpus Christianorum Series Latina 75 [Turnholt: Brepols, 1964], 3-4).

[3]"It is all too easy to give offence to readers by the inappropriate use of sex-related imagery. Translators therefore need not only to study the ways in which the Scriptures use such imagery, but also the ways in which the language in ques- tion does so. In this area, a special sensitivity is called for if a translation is to maintain both the meaning and the impact of the original text, and at the same time respect the readers' views of what is acceptable language for use in public" (D. J. Clark, "Sex-related Imagery in the Prophets," *The Bible Translator* 33/4 [October 1982], 413).

made the average child today much more knowledgeable and articulate about sex, violence, and the like than my rowdiest childhood peers ever were. I would be the first to insist that, for the most part, this is a situation to regret rather than to rejoice over, but to say that it does not exist would be to deny the obvious.

I agreed, however reluctantly, to direct the project that produced what came to be known as the New International Reader's Version of the Bible (NIrV). As it turned out, it was not long before my querulousness and tentativeness gave way to enthusiasm and gusto. No longer was it a matter of whether the task should be undertaken. I decided that it was high time to lay my unfounded fears to rest and to get on with the job. The remainder of this chapter will explore—in greater or lesser detail—the implied questions hinted at in its subtitle.

WHAT IS THE NIRV?

Among the first issues to be addressed was what to call the proposed version. More than twenty possibilities were suggested, including The Bible for Today's Readers, The Bible for Every Reader, Everyone's Bible, The Bible for New Readers, The User-Friendly Bible, The Bible in Simple English, God's Word for Today's Readers, Easy English Version, New Simplified International Version, Elementary English Version, Plain English Version, Basic International Version, and International Reader's Version.

We finally settled on New International Reader's Version for several reasons: (1) The name immediately connects the translation to the NIV. High reader recognition and trust, among others, are desirable qualities associated with the NIV. (2) The introduction of the word *Reader's* implies that the version is easy to read. (3) The name also suggests that the translation intends to make the Bible accessible to anyone who aspires to read it (as opposed to studying it). (4) The name allows for a target audience not restricted to children. It invites use by new readers, people who experience difficulty when they try to read, readers for whom English is a second language, and so forth. (5) As in the case of the NIV, the word *International* indicates that the version is intended for *all* English-language readers.

The final product known as the NIrV is a full-fledged, complete Bible that attempts to put into third-grade language all the words in all sixty-six books of the Bible. It is not a condensed or expurgated text—although, of course, appropriate euphemisms are employed when necessary. Building on the proved excellence and positive reputation of the NIV, the NIrV preserves the wording of that version wherever it can. No change was made merely for the sake of change. One of our goals was to produce a children's edition of the NIV that would be attractive enough to encourage its readers to "graduate" to the NIV itself when their reading ability improved.

Many qualities and characteristics of the NIV were deliberately replicated in its "kid brother." Like the NIV, the NIrV was translated and edited by people who affirm the full inspiration and infallibility of Scripture—its inerrancy, if you please. They believe the Bible to be totally trustworthy and absolutely authoritative in everything it asserts and teaches. The result is a text that is reliable in every respect.

Like the NIV, the NIrV—in one way or another—explains everything contained in the text. It leaves nothing to chance. There are no obscure passages in it. Although the NIV often employs footnotes to clarify potentially problematic or ambiguous readings, we decided early on not to include footnotes of any kind in the NIrV, feeling that to do so would distract its users and impede their reading speed. Instead, we explained everything within the text itself, making use of circumlocutions, explanatory glosses, and the like wherever necessary. To put it another way, we refused to be satisfied by mere readability. Our goal was full understandability as well. Our guiding verse, as represented in its NIrV rendering, was Nehemiah 8:8: "[The Levites] read parts of the Scroll of the Law of God to the people. They made it clear to them. They told them what it meant. So the people were able to understand what was being read." Because we were determined not to be satisfied with anything less than maximum comprehension, even educated adults have found the NIrV to be useful for a quick check on the basic meaning of a particular passage.

As in the case of the NIV, the NIrV recognizes that the literary genres in the various parts of Scripture must be given their due weight. To aid the reader in becoming somewhat familiar with several of the genres, poetry is scanned as poetry; lists are set up as lists; letters are given the format of letters; and so on.

Whatever other characteristics a Bible translation might have, accuracy is a quality of supreme importance. Keeping that in mind at all times, we wanted to make sure that the entire text of the NIrV would be not only clear but also accurate. Our watchword thus became "Get it clear and get it right," not simply "Get it done." Synoptic parallels, New Testament quotations of the Old Testament, and other similar matters were carefully checked and double-checked for accuracy and consistency. In addition, interrelationships between the two Testaments, even where only by allusion, are always made clear by placing Old Testament book name, chapter, and verse references—in small, italic type and within parentheses—in the text itself immediately after the citation or allusion.

Turning now to the "Who?" question, I will divide it into two parts: (1) What readership is the New International Reader's Version intended for? (2) What was the composition of the teams of translators and editors who produced it?

FOR WHOM IS THE NIRV INTENDED?

As I hinted above, the impetus for starting the NIrV translation project in the first place was the realization that children entering the seventh grade of elementary school often find the NIV a bit hard to read unless they consult a dictionary frequently. This means, of course, that children in earlier grades have an even harder time understanding what God is saying to them through the words of the NIV translation. The decision to produce the NIrV was prompted by a desire to provide an NIV-like translation for children as young as eight years of age. The NIrV can therefore be read for profit by all elementary-school children from the third through seventh grades, not just by third-graders.

Before our work got under way, we realized that other groups of readers could be helped by a translation like the NIrV. High on this list were people of all ages for whom English is a second language. We felt that many, if not most, of them would welcome an English-language version of the Bible that was easier to read than those currently available—including many so-called children's versions. Indeed, we deliberately avoided using the word "children" in the title of our translation to keep from offending, humiliating, or insulting the intelligence of potential adult readers.

Another group of adults who might appreciate a version that features simpler English are those with low reading skills resulting from lack of education, various learning disabilities, and/or impairments. Seventy-six percent of Americans who are unemployed cannot read well enough to hold anything but the lowest-level jobs. According to the United States Commerce Department, the country's economy suffers an estimated loss of $140 billion to $300 billion in annual productivity because an alarmingly large number of its workers are illiterate. United States Army figures reveal that more than 25 percent of its enlistees cannot read training manuals that are written at a seventh-grade level. To put it another way, a full fourth of all entry-level Army personnel cannot read the NIV with even minimum comprehension.

Other examples of such statistics abound. Two will suffice for our purposes:

> The National Adult Literacy Survey found that between 21 percent and 23 percent of American adults are functioning at Level 1 and are only able to perform tasks involving "brief, uncomplicated text." An additional 25 percent to 28 percent, representing 50 million American adults, are functioning at Level 2 and have skills that are "more varied" but "still quite limited."
>
> The typical 25-year-old male inmate functions 2-3 grade levels below the grade level actually completed; 60 percent of prison inmates are illiterate and 86 percent of all juvenile offenders have reading problems.[4]

---

[4]*Facts on Literacy in America* (Literacy Volunteers of America, 1994).

This latter statistic defines yet another subset of individuals whom, we trust, the NIrV has been destined to serve: people who are marginalized members of our society. These include prisoners, Native Americans, and other disadvantaged groups whose environment, lack of education, economic deprivation, and similar problems have inhibited their ability to become mature readers. It is not surprising that the first edition of the NIrV to be published by International Bible Society (January 1995), a New Testament entitled *The Jesus Way*, had Native Americans as its main target audience. As I write these words, a revised text of the NIrV has just been issued; its first IBS printing (1998) is called *Free on the Inside*. Its title, as well as the many helps in its introductory and concluding pages, make it clear that this particular edition was prepared especially for prisoners.

It should be obvious by now that the needs of certain groups of adults and those of children were kept in mind from the very beginning of the NIrV project. Zondervan, the commercial publisher of the NIrV, has produced adult and children's editions in tandem from the outset. Those for children include devotional and study Bibles. They sport colorful, eye-catching covers, and feature charming, captivating, many-hued paintings made especially for the NIrV by artist Joel Tanis. By way of contrast, the adult editions have a plainer cover and no artwork. All editions are set in easy-to-read type and include such helps as sectional headings and a brief dictionary that defines the relatively small number of technical words (for example, "apostle," "blessed," "circumcision," "eternal," "Passover") that all translations at every reading level can scarcely avoid.

WHO TRANSLATED AND EDITED THE NIRV?

It was not particularly difficult to assemble a number of teams composed of stellar scholars, stylists, and children's literature experts who were eager to assist in the project. Basing our *modus operandi* on the four-tiered system developed by the Committee on Bible Translation (CBT), which produced the NIV, we established four levels of activity: (1) a relatively large number of rough-draft simplifiers, (2) an Initial Simplification Committee (ISC), (3) three CBT Simplification Committees (CBTSims), and (4) a Final Review Committee (FRC).

As their title implies, the task delegated to the rough-draft simplifiers was to produce a simplified rough draft of one or more books of the Bible using the NIV as the basic text. Their mandate was threefold: to shorten the NIV sentences wherever necessary (ten words or less was the ideal), to simplify the NIV vocabulary,[5] and to leave the NIV text as it was whenever possible. The simplifiers' backgrounds were quite varied. They ranged from scholars, to pastors, to office workers, to educators, to homemakers. As might be expected, some of the best work was done by parents of young children. There were some fifteen rough-draft simplifiers in all.[6]

The ISC was made up of three children's literature experts. Their assignment was to modify the work of the rough-draft simplifiers in order to bring verbal, grammatical, and stylistic consistency to the text, and to incorporate the simplifiers' varied expressions of the biblical authors' intent. In the early stages of the project, two outside stylists made valuable contributions to the work of the simplifiers and the ISC. As all of us became better at what we were doing, our interaction made the stylists' work somewhat redundant, and their services were no longer needed.

Our work quickly taught us that the triple mandate of the simplifiers and the refining work of the ISC would not produce a finished product ready for the typesetters. We found that dividing long sentences into shorter ones could result in the loss of the overall cohesiveness and subtle connections that characterize the basic text, that exchanging a seventh-grade synonym for a third-grade word or phrase was not just a matter of verbal substitution, and that idiomatic and—more seriously—theological slippage could easily occur. In addition, most of the people who worked at the first two project levels were neither theologically trained nor expert in Hebrew, Aramaic, and Greek. That is why we needed several CBTSims.

For the most part, the members of the CBTSims were (or had been) members of the NIV CBT. The others had been coopted by the CBT to assist that body in completing work on the NIV in 1977-78. All of the CBTSim members were intimately familiar with the translation principles that guided the CBT from the very beginning of its work in the late 1960s—principles that had been developed and honed as the years passed.

---

[5]Each simplifier's constant companion for this part of their assignment was A. Mogilner, *Children's Writer's Word Book* (Cincinnati: Writer's Digest Books, 1992). Its most helpful features are an alphabetical list of all words included in the book (together with their grade levels), an introduction to the principles used in determining what constitutes an appropriate word list for each grade from kindergarten through sixth grade (for third grade helps see especially pp. 65-66), and an invaluable thesaurus that gives a children's writer different ways to say different things at different grade levels (pp. 93-346). Because of its rather garish cover it became fondly known as the "pink book."

[6]Upwards of forty people, eight of whom were CBT members, were involved in the work of translation and editing at various stages of the project. As a means of guaranteeing that the NIrV would be international in scope, Martin Selman, an Old Testament scholar who teaches in Great Britain, chaired a CBTSim Anglicization committee that modified the final text to conform its spelling, vocabulary, and turns of expression to meet the needs and expectations of the NIrV's United Kingdom readership. To ensure that the translation would be truly transdenominational, care was taken to draw the translators and editors from a wide variety of backgrounds and denominations that eventually included Assemblies of God, Baptist, Baptist General Conference, Christian Reformed, Conservative Baptist, Episcopal, Evangelical Covenant, Lutheran, Mennonite, Nazarene, Open Bible Standard, Plymouth Brethren, Presbyterian, Southern Baptist, United Presbyterian, and nondenominational.

The primary task of the CBTSims was to check the ISC draft documents to make sure that they faithfully rendered the original-language texts and that they were free of theological blunders. At the same time, they were encouraged to improve narrative flow, poetic balance, and rhetorical power, as well as to remove stylistic inconcinnities.[7]

Despite the admittedly excellent work done by the three CBTSims, it was essential to read and edit their manuscripts one final time before declaring the project concluded. We needed to make sure that literary, stylistic, and theological consistency characterized the whole. We also wanted to be certain that the finished product was readable and understandable at a third-grade level. Those tasks were assigned to the three members of the FRC. As executive editor, I chaired and gave overall leadership to the work of the committee. The other two members were Kenneth Barker, at that time the executive director of the NIV Translation Center and a long-time member of CBT, and Jean Rodwick, chair of the ISC and a children's literature expert. We labored over every verse of the Bible as submitted to us by the CBTSims until we were convinced that we had fulfilled the mandate. On February 1, 1996—four years to the day after the IBS board of directors had authorized us to begin the project—we completed the work. Although we knew that a modicum of tweaking would be required in the coming weeks[8] we celebrated the achievement by throwing a party, complete with cake and balloons.

HOW DID THE NIRV EDITORS DO THEIR WORK?

Several specific Old Testament and New Testament examples will prove useful at this point. In three parallel columns, the following chart compares the NIV rendering of the first chapter of Genesis, my earliest rough-draft attempt at simplifying it, and the final published result as it came from the hands of the FRC:

[7]In addition to producing the initial draft simplification of the book of Psalms for the NIrV, John Stek chaired one of the CBTSims throughout the duration of the project. Always the genial gadfly, he also let the rest of us know—often in no uncertain terms—when he felt we were doing a poor job or giving the task less than our best. Indeed, at one point early on he had the temerity to declare that our translation was "half-baked." But having labored with John in the general fields of Bible translation and commentary for more than a quarter of a century, I was delighted when he graciously accepted our invitation to devote large blocks of time to working on the NIrV, because I knew that he would give himself unstintingly to the task and that what he and his CBTSim team produced would be of the highest possible quality. For these and many other reasons, I am humbled and grateful for having been given the opportunity and privilege of making this modest contribution to a *Festschrift* in honor of such a choice colleague.

[8]Any Bible version worth its salt will be open to continued minor revisions: "There is a sense in which the work of translation is never wholly finished. This applies to all great literature and uniquely so to the Bible. In 1973 the New Testament in the New International Version was published. Since then, suggestions for corrections and revisions have been received from various sources. The Committee on Bible Translation carefully considered the suggestions and adopted a number of them. These were incorporated in the first printing of the entire Bible in 1978. Some additional revisions were made by the Committee on Bible Translation in 1983 and appear in printings after that date" (NIV Preface).

The Beginning (NIV)

In the beginning God created the heavens and the earth. Now the earth was formless and empty, darkness was over the surface of the deep, and the Spirit of God was hovering over the waters.

And God said, "Let there be light," and there was light. God saw that the light was good, and he separated the light from the darkness. God called the light "day," and the darkness he called "night." And there was evening, and there was morning—the first day.

And God said, "Let there be an expanse between the waters to separate water from water." So God made the expanse and separated the water under the expanse from the water above it. And it was so. God called the expanse "sky." And there was evening, and there was morning—the second day.

And God said, "Let the water under the sky be gathered to one place, and let dry ground appear." And it was so. God called the dry ground "land," and the gathered waters he called "seas." And God saw that it was good.

Then God said, "Let the land produce vegetation: seed-bearing plants and trees on the land that bear fruit with seed in it, according to their various kinds." And it was so. The land produced vegetation: plants bearing seed according to their kinds and trees bearing fruit with seed in it according to their kinds. And God saw that it was good. And there was evening, and there was morning—the third day.

The Beginning (draft)

In the beginning, God created the heavens and the earth. The earth had no form. It was also empty. Darkness was over the surface of the ocean depths. The Spirit of God was hovering over the waters.

And God said, "Let there be light." And there was light. God saw that the light was good. God separated the light from the darkness. God called the light "day," and he called the darkness "night." There was evening, and there was morning—the first day.

And God said, "Let there be a layer of air between the waters. Let it separate water from water." So God made the layer of air. He separated the water under the layer from the water above it. And it was so. God called the air "sky." There was evening, and there was morning—the second day.

And God said, "Let the water under the sky be gathered to one place. Let dry ground appear." And it was so. God called the dry ground "land." He called the gathered waters "seas." God saw that it was good.

Then God said, "Let the land grow plant life. Let there be seed-bearing plants and trees on the land. Let them bear fruit with seed in it, just like them." And it was so. The land grew plant life. It grew plants bearing seed, just like them. It also grew trees bearing fruit with seed in it, just like them. God saw that it was good. There was evening, and there was morning—the third day.

The Beginning (final result)

In the beginning, God created the heavens and the earth. The earth didn't have any shape. And it was empty. Darkness was over the surface of the ocean. At that time, the ocean covered the earth. The Spirit of God was hovering over the waters.

God said, "Let there be light." And there was light. God saw that the light was good. He separated the light from the darkness. God called the light "day." He called the darkness "night." There was evening, and there was morning. It was day one.

God said, "Let there be a huge space between the waters. Let it separate water from water." And that's exactly what happened. God made the huge space between the waters. He separated the water that was under the space from the water that was above it. God called the huge space "sky." There was evening, and there was morning. It was day two.

God said, "Let the water under the sky be gathered into one place. Let dry ground appear." And that's exactly what happened. God called the dry ground "land." He called the waters that were gathered together "oceans." And God saw that it was good.

Then God said, "Let the land produce plants. Let them bear their own seeds. And let there be trees on the land that bear fruit with seeds in it. Let each kind of plant or tree have its own kind of seeds." And that's exactly what happened.

The land produced plants. Each kind of plant had its own kind of seeds. The land produced trees that bore fruit with seeds in it. Each kind of tree had its own kind of seeds.

God saw that it was good. And there was evening, and there was morning. It was day three.

And God said, "Let there be lights in the expanse of the sky to separate the day from the night, and let them serve as signs to mark seasons and days and years, and let them be lights in the expanse of the sky to give light on the earth." And it was so. God made two great lights— the greater light to govern the day and the lesser light to govern the night. He also made the stars. God set them in the expanse of the sky to give light on the earth, to govern the day and the night, and to separate light from darkness. And God saw that it was good. And there was evening, and there was morning— the fourth day.

And God said, "Let there be lights in the sky. Let them separate the day from the night. Let them serve as signs, to mark seasons and days and years. Let them be lights in the sky to give light on the earth." And it was so. God made two great lights. He made the greater light to rule over the day. He made the lesser light to rule over the night. He also made the stars. God set the lights in the sky, to give light on the earth. He set them there to rule over the day and the night. He set them there to separate light from darkness. God saw that it was good. There was evening, and there was morning— the fourth day.

God said, "Let there be lights in the huge space of the sky. Let them separate the day from the night. Let them serve as signs to mark off the seasons and the days and the years. Let them serve as lights in the huge space of the sky to give light on the earth." And that's exactly what happened.

God made two great lights. He made the larger light to rule over the day. He made the smaller light to rule over the night. He also made the stars.

God put the lights in the huge space of the sky to give light on the earth. He put them there to rule over the day and the night. He put them there to separate light from darkness.

God saw that it was good. And there was evening, and there was morning. It was day four.

And God said, "Let the water teem with living creatures, and let birds fly above the earth across the expanse of the sky." So God created the great creatures of the sea and every living and moving thing with which the water teems, according to their kinds, and every winged bird according to its kind. And God saw that it was good. God blessed them and said, "Be fruitful and increase in number and fill the water in the seas, and let the birds increase on the earth." And there was evening, and there was morning—the fifth day.

And God said, "Let the water be filled with living creatures. Let birds fly above the earth. Let them fly across the sky." So God created the great sea creatures. He created every living and moving thing that the water is filled with. He created every winged bird. All of their young were just like them. God saw that it was good. God blessed them. He said, "Be fruitful, and multiply in number. Fill the water in the seas. Let the birds multiply on the earth." There was evening, and there was morning—the fifth day.

God said, "Let the waters be filled with living things. Let birds fly above the earth across the huge space of the sky." So God created the great creatures of the ocean. He created every living and moving thing that fills the waters. He created all kinds of them. He created every kind of bird that flies. And God saw that it was good.

God blessed them. He said, "Have little ones and increase your numbers. Fill the water in the oceans. Let there be more and more birds on the earth."

There was evening, and there was morning. It was day five.

And God said, "Let the land produce living creatures according to their kinds: livestock, creatures that move along the ground, and wild animals, each according to its kind." And it was so. God made the wild animals according to their kinds, the livestock according to their kinds, and all the creatures that move along the ground according to their kinds. And God saw that it was good.

And God said, "Let there be living creatures on the land. Let there be livestock, creatures that move along the ground, and wild animals. Let all of their young be just like them." And it was so. God made the young of the wild animals just like them. God made the young of the livestock just like them. God made the young of the creatures that move along the ground just like them. God saw that it was good.

God said, "Let the land produce all kinds of living creatures. Let there be livestock, and creatures that move along the ground, and wild animals. Let there be all kinds of them." And that's exactly what happened.

God made all kinds of wild animals. He made all kinds of livestock. He made all kinds of creatures that move along the ground. And God saw that it was good.

Then God said, "Let us make man in our image, in our likeness, and let them rule over the fish of the sea and the birds of the air, over the livestock, over all the earth, and over all the creatures that move along the ground."

So God created man in his own image, in the image of God he created him; male and female he created them.

God blessed them and said to them, "Be fruitful and increase in number; fill the earth and subdue it. Rule over the fish of the sea and the birds of the air and over every living creature that moves on the ground."

Then God said, "I give you every seed-bearing plant on the face of the whole earth and every tree that has fruit with seed in it. They will be yours for food. And to all the beasts of the earth and all the birds of the air and all the creatures that move on the ground—everything that has the breath of life in it—I give every green plant for food." And it was so.

God saw all that he had made, and it was very good. And there was evening, and there was morning—the sixth day.

Then God said, "Let us make mankind in our image. Let us make them in our likeness. Let them rule over the fish of the sea. Let them rule over the birds of the air. Let them rule over the livestock. Let them rule over all the earth. Let them rule over all the creatures that move along the ground."

So God created mankind in his own image. He created mankind in the image of God. He created them, male and female. God blessed them. He said to them, "Be fruitful, and multiply in number. Fill the earth, and master it. Rule over the fish of the sea. Rule over the birds of the air. Rule over every living creature that moves on the ground."

Then God said, "I give you every seed-bearing plant on the face of the whole earth. I give you every tree that has fruit with seed in it. They will be yours for food. I give every green plant for food to everything that has the breath of life in it." And it was so.

God saw all that he had made. And it was very good. There was evening, and there was morning—the sixth day.

Then God said, "Let us make human beings in our likeness. Let them rule over the fish in the waters and the birds of the air. Let them rule over the livestock and over the whole earth. Let them rule over all of the creatures that move along the ground."

So God created human beings in his own likeness.

He created them in the likeness of God.

He created them as male and female.

God blessed them. He said to them, "Have children and increase your numbers. Fill the earth and bring it under your control. Rule over the fish in the waters and the birds of the air. Rule over every living creature that moves on the ground."

Then God said, "I am giving you every plant on the face of the whole earth that bears its own seeds. I am giving you every tree that has fruit with seeds in it. All of them will be given to you for food.

"I am giving every green plant to all of the land animals and the birds of the air for food. I am also giving the plants to all of the creatures that move on the ground. I am giving them to every living thing that breathes." And that's exactly what happened.

God saw everything he had made. And it was very good. There was evening, and there was morning. It was day six.

In the first two verses I simplified "was formless" to "had no form." But we were told by our children's literature experts that third-graders would not understand "form" in that sense and that "had no" was stylistically awkward for them. Thus, the phrase "didn't have any shape" was our ultimate solution.

"The deep," a term that has a long history of interpretation and that is pregnant with all sorts of associations, was first changed to "the ocean depths" and then further simplified to "the ocean." But realizing that "the ocean" was hardly fraught with the significance of "the deep," we finally settled on adding the gloss "At that time, the ocean covered the earth" to bring out something of the sinister horror of the Hebrew *t^ehôm*.

The only substantive change in the paragraph describing the "first day" of creation was to call it "day one," a pattern that we followed throughout the rest of the chapter. The result was simplification and the acknowledgment of the possibility (if not the likelihood) that the order of the days of creation is more literary than chronological.[9]

With respect to day two, the KJV "firmament" had already become an "expanse" in the NIV. By the time the text reached the FRC, my initially unsatisfactory attempt ("layer of air") was changed to "huge space," a rendering that helps the reader visualize what appears to be the Genesis author's intent. "And it was so" was modernized and explained: "And that's exactly what happened."

Changes in the paragraph describing the events of day three include substituting "oceans" for "seas" (partly to eliminate the possibility of homonymic misunderstanding) and "plants" for "vegetation," and pluralizing "seed" (an abstraction that might seem odd to new readers). The only significant change in the language portraying day four was to render "greater" as "larger" and "lesser" as "smaller" for purposes of clarification and simplification.

"Be fruitful" became "Have little ones" (the divine command to animals) in the description of day five and "Have children" (the command to human beings) in that of day six. These changes nicely illustrate the importance of recognizing *usus loquendi/scribendi* among new readers.

The only other important matter that requires comment here is the change from "man" to "human beings" (twice) in the description of God's creation of human life. Since "man" means only "adult male" in the vocabulary of most eight-year-olds, we decided to clarify the term for them. In the second edition of the NIrV, however, we reverted to "man" in both cases because of the 1997 firestorm caused by the publication of an inclusive-language edition of the NIV in the United Kingdom.[10] Although the strong reaction against that edition—as well as against the NIrV and a potential NIV inclusive-language edition for North American readers—was generated more by heat than by light, it is my fervent hope that saner heads will eventually prevail, because

---

[9]For extensive treatments of arguments pro and con cf. *The Genesis Debate* (ed. Ronald F. Youngblood; Nashville: Thomas Nelson, 1986), 36-55; for a recent careful defense of the nonchronological viewpoint cf. David A. Sterchi, "Does Genesis 1 Provide a Chronological Sequence?", *Journal of the Evangelical Theological Society* 39/4 (December 1996): 529-536 (esp. p. 536).

[10]Hundreds of other noninclusive-language reversions have been made in the second edition of the NIrV as well. For lucid discussions of the whole issue of gender-neutral translation, see especially D. A. Carson, *The Inclusive-Language Debate: A Plea for Realism* (Grand Rapids: Baker, 1998); Mark L. Strauss, *Distorting Scripture? Gender-Inclusive Language and the Bible* (Downers Grove, Ill.: InterVarsity, 1998).

scholars and translators on both sides of the issue agree that a judicious use of gender-neutral or gender-inclusive language is appropriate and has had a long and distinguished history in English Bible translations that goes back for several centuries. In any case, the reversion of "human beings" to "man" in the NIrV's Genesis 1:26-27 inhibits understanding and will doubtless force many readers to seek help from a parent or teacher.

I have chosen two New Testament examples that are typical of how readability, understandability, and accuracy must interact with one another if beginning readers can reasonably be expected to comprehend what a text is saying to them. The first example is the use of the phrase "in Christ (Jesus)," which occurs 79 times in Paul's letters, most frequently in the books of Romans and Ephesians (13 times apiece). For purposes of brevity we will limit ourselves to Ephesians.[11]

NIV	NIrV
1:1: the faithful in Christ Jesus	1:1: Because you belong to Christ Jesus, you are faithful
1:3: who has blessed us in the heavenly realms with every spiritual blessing in Christ	1:3: He has blessed us with every spiritual blessing. Those blessings come from the heavenly world. They belong to us because we belong to Christ
1:10: one head, even Christ	1:10: one ruler. The ruler is Christ
1:12: the first to hope in Christ	1:12: the first to put our hope in Christ
1:20: which he exerted in Christ when he raised him from the dead	1:20: God showed when he raised Christ from the dead
2:6: God . . . seated us with him in the heavenly realms in Christ Jesus	2:6: He has seated us with him in the heavenly kingdom because we belong to Christ Jesus
2:7: expressed in his kindness to us in Christ Jesus	2:7: He has shown it by being kind to us because of what Christ Jesus has done
2:10: created in Christ Jesus to do good works	2:10: He created us to belong to Christ Jesus. Now we can do good things
2:13: in Christ Jesus you . . . have been brought near through the blood of Christ	2:13: you belong to Christ Jesus. He spilled his blood for you. That has brought you near to God
3:6: sharers together in the promise in Christ Jesus	3:6: They share in the promise. It belongs to them because they belong to Christ Jesus
3:11: which he accomplished in Christ Jesus	3:11: He has worked it out through Christ Jesus
3:21: to him be glory in the church and in Christ Jesus	3:21: Give him glory in the church and in Christ Jesus
4:32: in Christ God forgave you	4:32: God forgave you because of what Christ has done

[11] For a recent helpful (if brief) exegetical treatment of selected "in Christ (Jesus)" passages in the first three chapters of Ephesians, see B. Dale Ellenburg, "'In Christ' in Ephesians," *Mid-America Theological Journal* 20 (1996): 124-127.

In all but one of the thirteen occurrences of "in Christ (Jesus)" in Ephesians, the NIV translates the phrase literally. The exception is in 1:10, where it is rendered epexegetically ("even"), corresponding to the Hebrew *bêt essentiae*. The NIrV follows suit ("is"). In two other cases the NIrV also echoes the NIV usage. It translates "put our hope in Christ" (for idiomatic reasons) in 1:12, and in 3:21 it preserves the traditional phrase "in the church and in Christ Jesus" (even though the latter phrase remains anything but clear). In one other case the NIrV translates the preposition instrumentally ("through," 3:11), and in 1:20 it is left untranslated because it is implied in the following clause ("when [God] raised Christ from the dead"). But in the rest of the occurrences it interprets Paul's intent in one of two ways: Christians are "in Christ" in the sense that they "belong to" him (1:1, 3; 2:6, 10, 13; 3:6) or "because of what [he] has done" (2:7; 4:32).

My second New Testament example concerns a few of the typical epistolary formulae used by Paul to open each of his letters. 1 Corinthians 1:1-2a can serve as an illustration. In the NIV it reads as follows: "Paul, called to be an apostle of Christ Jesus by the will of God, and our brother Sosthenes, To the church of God in Corinth. . . . "

Because young readers could hardly be expected to understand the genre implications of that sentence, the NIrV spells out Paul's intention in this way: "I, Paul, am writing this letter. I have been chosen to be an apostle of Christ Jesus just as God planned. Our brother Sosthenes joins me in writing. We are sending this letter to you, the members of God's church in Corinth."

WHY DID WE PRODUCE THE NIRV?

"If God spare my life, ere many years I will cause a boy that driveth the plough shall know more of the Scripture than thou dost." This statement—supposedly made to a learned clergyman and widely quoted in slightly varying forms[12]—is attributed to William Tyndale, an early pioneer in the translation of Holy Scripture into the English language. It demonstrates his determination to make sure that the Bible was accessible to young readers in their mother tongue. Tyndale's concern continues to be shared by equally sensitive and perceptive believers today.

> Why do parents and teachers read Bible stories to children? We want
> our children to know and love the Bible and to know that God loves
> them. We want them to come to personal faith in Christ, and we want
> them to make right decisions about how to live their lives. Children
> need the Bible for the same reasons that adults do. Yet the Bible is
> an adult book containing complex theology along with vivid descrip-

---

[12]See, for example, F. F. Bruce, *The English Bible: A History of Translations from the Earliest English Versions to the New English Bible* (New York: Oxford University, 1961), 29; and C. Gulston, *Our English Bible: No Greater Heritage* (Grand Rapids: Eerdmans, 1961), 150.

tions of violence and sexuality. Even many adults find it confusing and difficult. Children's Bibles and Bible storybooks exist to render the Bible accessible and attractive to children, so that parents' and teachers' desires for them may be met.[13]

The *raison d'être* of Bible societies has traditionally been to provide the Scriptures to the peoples of the world in their native languages.[14] The production of Bibles tailored to readers in various age groups and at various levels of comprehension is a logical extension of that task. Indeed, Bibles written specifically for children have been available for generations.[15] For example, Annie Cressman edited a translation of the New Testament designed not only for children but also for students who were just beginning to learn English.[16] Currently there are many Bibles available at a fourth- or fifth-grade reading level that attempt to meet the needs of children and others, among them the International Children's Version, the Contemporary English Version, and the New Century Version.

What, then, is the justification for the New International Reader's Version? Why did IBS and Zondervan feel that yet another children's translation was necessary? Although we have already addressed those and related questions earlier in this paper, a few summary statements are in order.

In the United States alone, thirty million children are under eight years of age. English is a second language for thirty-two million people in America, and there are forty million Americans who read at or below the fourth-grade level. In addition, there are upwards of twenty million illiterate adults in the United States. Meeting the needs of these potential Bible readers seemed to us to be reason enough for a new, up-to-date, easy-to-read, user-friendly translation.

Furthermore, the children's Bibles now available have all been evaluated at a fourth-grade reading level or higher.[17] We sensed that large numbers of people—children and adults alike—would profit from having a copy of Scripture at the third-grade level, the one at which most children begin to read with meaningful understanding.

---

[13]Pamela J. Scalise, "Telling Old Testament Stories," *Theology, News and Notes* 44/4 (December 1997): 18. The rest of her brief essay is well worth reading, as is a companion article in the same issue by John L. Thompson and Marianne Meye Thompson ("Teaching the Bible to Children," pp. 20-21).

[14]It is not uncommon for a native recipient of a new translation to exclaim: "God speaks my language!"

[15]Children's Bibles number in the hundreds; if we include children's Bible story collections the figure would rise into the thousands. A standard work on the subject is Ruth B. Bottigheimer, *The Bible for Children: From the Age of Gutenberg to the Present* (New Haven: Yale University, 1996).

[16]*Good News for the World: The New Testament in Worldwide English* (Bombay, 1969).

[17]The International Children's Version is 3.9, which for all practical purposes is fourth grade.

Our goal was therefore 3.5 (third grade, fifth month). The final result exceeded our wildest expectations: The NIrV has been evaluated at a 2.9 reading level, a full year lower than its nearest rival.

The enthusiasm with which the NIrV has been received to this point has been gratifying to everyone who labored to produce it. Almost from the first month of its publication, it has ranked among the top ten best-selling Bible translations in the United States. More gratifying by far, of course, have been reports from people who have gained renewed understanding of the meaning of Scripture and have grown spiritually as a result of reading the NIrV. It would therefore appear to be meeting a genuine need in the lives of many readers, both young and old.

And not a moment too soon. As these words are being written, our country is still reeling from the murder of four young girls and a teacher by two boys, eleven and thirteen years old respectively, outside a middle school in Jonesboro, Arkansas. The top-rated series on cable television currently is *South Park,* a cartoon show about four profane, flatulent third-graders named Cartman, Kenny, Kyle, and Stan. Kenny, whose muffled words consist of a series of meaningless squeaks, dies violently in every episode. Kyle's all-too-predictable reaction—"O my God, they've killed Kenny!"—has become a national catchword. The show is seen by five million people each week, 5 percent of whom are under 11 years of age.[18]

It is for the spiritual benefit of such children, among countless others, that we dedicated ourselves to preparing the NIrV. Our hope and prayer is that it will play a small part in helping many young and beginning readers to reach something of the theological understanding exemplified in this brief essay by eight-year-old Danny Dutton:

> One of God's main jobs is making people. He makes these to put in place of the ones that die so there will be enough people to take care of things here on earth. He doesn't make grownups. Just babies. I think because they are smaller and easier to make. That way he doesn't have to take up His valuable time teaching them to talk and walk. He can just leave that up to the mothers and fathers. I think it works out pretty good.
>
> God's second most important job is listening to prayers. An awful lot of this goes on, as some people, like preachers and things, pray other times besides bedtime. God doesn't have time to listen to the radio or TV on account of this. As He hears everything, not only prayers, there must be a terrible lot of noise going into His ears unless He has thought of a way to turn it off.

[18]The regrettable popularity of this program is analyzed in, for example, *Time* (March 23, 1998), 75-76, and *Newsweek* (March 23, 1998), 56-62.

God sees everything and hears everything and is everywhere, which keeps Him pretty busy. So you shouldn't go wasting His time by going over your parent's head and ask for something they said you couldn't have.

Atheists are people who don't believe in God. I don't think there are any in Chula Vista. At least there aren't any who come to our church.

Jesus is God's Son. He used to do all the hard work like walking on water and doing miracles and trying to teach people about God who didn't want to learn. They finally got tired of Him preaching to them and they cursified (sic) Him but He was good and kind like His Father and He told His Father that they didn't know what they were doing and to forgive them and God said ok. His Dad (God) appreciated everything He had done and all His hard work on earth, so He told Him He didn't have to go out on the road anymore. He could stay in heaven. So He did. And now He helps His Dad out by listening to prayers and seeing which things are important for God to take care of and which ones He can take care of Himself without having to bother God with. Like a secretary only more important, of course. You can pray anytime you want and they are sure to hear you because they've got it worked out so one of them is on duty all the time.

You should always go to Sunday School because it makes God happy, and if anybody you want to make happy, it's God. Don't skip Sunday School to do something you think will be more fun like going to the beach. That is wrong, and besides the sun doesn't come out at the beach until noon, anyway.

If you don't believe in God, besides being an Atheist, you will be very lonely, because your parents can't go everywhere with you like to camp, but God can. It's good to know He's around when you're scared of the dark or when you can't swim very good and you get thrown in real deep water by big kids. But you shouldn't just always think of what God can do for you. I figured God put me here and He can take me back anytime He pleases.

And that's why I believe in God.[19]

"The kingdom of heaven belongs to such as these" (Matthew 19:14).

---

[19] A friend showed me this essay many years ago, but I have been unable to locate the young man who wrote it or to find it in any published source. I have no reason, however, to doubt its authenticity.

The Textuality of Narrative: Syntax and Reading the Hebrew Bible[1]

Barry L. Bandstra

INTRODUCTION: WHAT IS DISCOURSE ANALYSIS, AND WHY MIGHT EXEGETES USE IT?

The field of discourse analysis, though still in its adolescence, has emerged out of the intersection of sociology, linguistics, and literary criticism to become a recognized supplement to traditional grammar.[2] Recently, a number of monographs and collections of essays have appeared that display the promise of this approach when applied to biblical Hebrew (BH).[3]

Discourse analysis pays attention to the integrating features of texts at the level of the paragraph and higher. It serves as an adjunct to the more traditional practice of grammatical studies, which has focused primarily on word relationships within clauses.[4] By dealing with larger spans of text, discourse analysis can aid in identifying

[1]This essay is dedicated to my esteemed teacher, Professor John Stek, who always taught his students at Calvin Seminary to read texts—never just lines or verses. In class or in Old Testament Club we sensed that we were in the presence of a master interpreter, and that he was engaging us with the Hebrew text in unique and compelling ways. One might now say that Professor Stek was a discourse analyst. He opened our eyes to the syntactic, semantic, and stylistic structures of prose and poetry, and inspired us with the importance of reading closely the minutiae of the Hebrew text within the context of the whole.

[2]See Deborah Schiffrin, *Approaches to Discourse*. Blackwell Textbooks in Linguistics (Oxford: Blackwell, 1994) for an orientation to discourse analysis within general linguistics, and Peter J. MacDonald, "Discourse Analysis and Biblical Interpretation" in *Linguistics in Biblical Hebrew*, ed. Walter R. Bodine (Winona Lake, Ind.: 1992), 153-175 as it applies specifically to the biblical corpus. Bruce Waltke and Michael O'Connor (*An Introduction to Biblical Hebrew Syntax* [Winona Lake, Ind.: 1990], §3.3.4; hereafter Waltke and O'Connor) are cautious, perhaps overly so, about the usefulness of a discourse analytic approach to BH.

[3]See R. E. Longacre, *Joseph: A Story of Divine Providence: A Text Theoretical and Textlinguistic Analysis of Genesis 37 and 39-48* (Winona Lake, Ind.: 1989); Walter R. Bodine, *Linguistics and Biblical Hebrew*; idem., *Discourse Analysis of Biblical Literature: What It Is and What It Offers*. Semeia Studies (Atlanta: Scholars Press, 1995); Robert D. Bergen, ed., *Biblical Hebrew and Discourse Analysis* (Dallas: Summer Institute of Linguistics, 1994); Eep Talstra, ed., *Narrative and Comment: Contributions presented to Wolfgang Schneider* (Amsterdam: Societas Hebraica Amstelodamensis, 1995); and Ellen van Wolde, ed., *Narrative Syntax and the Hebrew Bible*. Papers of the Tilburg Conference 1996. Biblical Interpretation Series 29 (Leiden: E. J. Brill, 1997).

[4]By clause is meant a single well-formed predication, such as "Jacob went down to Egypt." In most cases this is equivalent to the accepted meaning of the term sentence, or complete sentence. One place the distinction between clause and sentence can be helpful is in reference to constructions that demand two clauses to be complete, as with conditional sentences, such as "If Benjamin goes down to Egypt, I will die." This is a sentence constructed of two clauses.

the subdivisions or paragraphs of a text, and it can explain the word orders and variations that map the flow of action and information.[5]

This chapter aims to do two things: first, to familiarize readers with some of the
basic contributions of discourse analylsis in key areas of syntax; second, to apply the
perspective of discourse analysis to a real text to show how interpreters of the Hebrew
Bible might make use of these perspectives in their study of Scripture.

There are two broad aspects of BH narrative textuality that discourse analysis can
illumine: the information system and the clause connection system. The information
system has to do with those components of a text that communicate information to the
reader—the knowledge content of the text. Discourse analysis assists in identifying a
text's "aboutness" by accounting for how writers intend readers to identify and track
the main participants and events narrated in the text, and to distinguish what is new
and important from what is of lesser interest.

The clause connection system addresses how the content is presented and interrelated by means of the predication system of the language, namely the verbal system,
and by the use of particles and connectives. Verbal clauses can assume different
shapes, depending on the position of the verb within the clause and the tense of the
verb itself. Different clause structures signal different relationships of clauses within
the paragraph as well as their hierarchical arrangement.

THE INFORMATION SYSTEM: HOW TO DETERMINE
WHAT A TEXT IS "ABOUT"

The information delivery and tracking system of BH concerns primarily the nominal components of the verbal clause—mainly nouns and pronouns, but also prepositional phrases and adverbs. The information system of BH mainly employs word order
within the clause and pronominal referencing across clauses to signal who and what
the text is about, and to establish what is more and what is less important.

Word Order

BH is a mix of fixed and free word order. Certain word order rules are absolute and
without exception, being set and determined by the grammar of BH. For example,
prepositions invariably come before the nouns they control; attributive adjectives

---

[5]The Masoretes who standardized the text of the Hebrew Bible included signals of text organization by the way they
punctuated the text and divided it into paragraphs and larger units. The Masoretic accent system represents their
analysis of clauses into phrases and the relationships of the phrases to each other. Paragraphs (*pisqot* or *parashiyyot*)
are marked by blocks of space (e.g. between 2 Kings 5:7 and 8). The next larger span of text, the *parasha setuma*, is
marked by a concluding **S** (e.g. after 2 Kings 5: 19 and 27). The next larger span of text, the *parasha petucha* is marked
by a concluding **P** (e.g. after 2 Kings 4:44, marking a major division between chapters 4 and 5). See Israel Yeivin
(*Introduction to the Tiberian Masorah*, ed. and trans. E. J. Revell. Masoretic Studies 5 [Missoula, Mont.: Scholars
Press, 1980]) for a full description.

come after the nouns they modify. Most of these unexceptional rules are found on the phrase level of the language.

On the other hand, the order of words and phrases on the clause level are not subject to hard-and-fast rules. In narrative, the statistically dominant order of the main components of the verbal clause is verb-subject-object, but other orders are allowable and are not statistically insignificant.

The word order of a clause can signal the topic of the clause; it can also signal if that topic is the same as that of the preceding clause or if it has changed. To understand this, a distinction between clause subject and clause topic is useful. The grammatical subject of a verbal clause is the component with which the main verb must agree in person, number, and gender. Usually, the grammatical subject is the entity performing the action represented by the verb, and can be called the actor, actant, or agent. (Of course, with passive verbs the grammatical subject is not the actant but is the receiver of the verb's action.) Grammatical subject is a morphological and syntactic category that operates on the level of the clause.

The linguistic notion called "topic" has to do with noun subjects and other nominal content, but is not defined by morphology (such as affixes or special forms) and can really only be understood when a chain of clauses is considered together. Though usually the grammatical subject of a clause is who or what the clause is "about,"[6] this is not always the case. This is where terminology can get a bit misleading. The term "subject" has a variety of meanings, including the notions of theme and topic, as in "The subject of this chapter is discourse analysis." The *grammatical* subject of a clause is not necessarily the topic of the clause, that is, who or what the clause is about.[7]

English has linguistic devices at its disposal to indicate to the reader/listener what the topic is. Sentences can have the same meaning but different topic structures:

1. Moses saw the golden calf.
2. The golden calf, Moses saw it.

In the first example, Moses is the subject and the topic. In the second example, Moses is the subject and the golden calf is the topic.

---

[6]By "aboutness" is meant roughly that about which something new is stated in a clause.

[7]Terminology has been bewilderingly diverse among linguistics who deal with the notion of topicality. Simon C. Dik (*The Theory of Functional Grammar. Part 1: The Structure of the Clause* [Dordrecht: Floris, 1989], 264) defines topicality as "the things we talk about" and distinguishes it from focality, "the most important or salient parts of what we say about the topical things." Other term pairs that have been used for the topic-focus distinction are old information-new information, given-new, theme-rheme (by the Prague School of linguistics), and topic-comment (by Halliday).

Clauses can have the same topic but different meanings and different grammatical subjects:

1. Moses, he saw Miriam dance.[8]
2. It was Moses who saw Miriam dance.[9]
3. Moses, Miriam saw him dance.
4. It was Moses whom Miriam saw dance.

In all four cases, Moses is the topic of the sentence (the sentence is "about" Moses), though only in the first two examples is he the grammatical subject.

Pronoun Referencing

A pronoun is grammatically and semantically dependent on the prior noun that it references. Without its nominal antecedent, a pronoun has no meaning. This back referencing, called "anaphora" by linguists, creates a dependency relationship as well as a semantic link between clauses. Because pronouns are anaphoric, or backward referring, they are by definition evidence of a connection. They maintain content continuity with the clause that precedes them, because the referent of the pronoun is already known by the time the pronoun is found in the narrative, and can only be recovered from the preceding context.

BH does not require a clause to have an explicit subject noun. If the main verb does not have an explicit subject noun in its clause, then the actant of the verb must be recovered from the preceding context. The person, number, and gender of the main verb narrows the range of eligible possibilities recoverable from the preceding clause. A finite verb without an independent and explicit noun subject maintains continuity with the content preceding its clause. The subject of the verb is assumed to be recoverable from the preceding context.

If a clause has an explicit subject noun, then there is a high likelihood that this clause begins a new paragraph unit. If the explicit subject noun is followed by phrases in apposition to it that further define the subject noun, as happens when such subjects are introduced for the first time, then the likelihood is even higher.

THE CLAUSE CONNECTION SYSTEM:
HOW CLAUSES FORM PARAGRAPHS

BH is syntactically paratactic but semantically hypotactic.[10] The surface level syntax of BH narrative ("and . . . and . . . and . . . ") masks a more complex underlying semantic structure of subordinations.

---

[8]In Hebrew this type of construction is called *casus pendens*. See Waltke and O'Connor §16.3.3.

[9]Linguists call this type of construction a cleft-sentence.

[10]Parataxis is the coordinate chaining of clauses, and hypotaxis is the subordinate chaining of clauses.

Verb Tense and Clause Function

Gesenius (1910), the standard reference grammar of BH, contains what has become the conventional wisdom concerning verbs in narrative:

> The *imperfect* with *waw consecutive* serves to express actions, events, or states, which are to be regarded as the temporal or logical sequence of actions, events, or states mentioned immediately before. The *imperfect consecutive* is used in this way most frequently as the *narrative tense*, corresponding to the Greek *aorist* or the Latin *historic perfect*. As a rule the narrative is introduced by a perfect, and then continued by means of imperfects with *waw consecutive*.[11]

In general, this approach to verb tenses in narrative has served readers well. Yet students of the Hebrew language have sought, especially of late, to achieve more precision concerning the differences among the various clause configurations and the verbs within them. Schneider[12] applies a discourse-based analysis of the different functions of verb tense configurations in BH. He utilizes a distinction developed by traditional Arabic grammarians, classifying clauses into two categories. Clauses are considered verb clauses if they begin with a verb; they are considered noun clauses if they begin with a noun, even if followed by a verb. These two categories are given semantic significance at the level of paragraph and whole text. Verb clauses define the action and constitute the main—or event—line of a narrative. Noun clauses provide subsidiary or "background" information.

This approach has been adopted and elaborated by Niccacci,[13] who first distinguishes two types of texts: narrative and discourse.[14] In narrative, wayyiqtol[15] presents foreground information, w-x-qatal presents backward-looking supportive information, and yiqtol presents forward-looking supportive information. In speech (Niccacci's discourse), x-yiqtol presents foreground information, x-qatal presents backward-looking supportive information, and w-qatal presents forward-looking supportive information.

---

[11]E. Kautzsch, *Gesenius' Hebrew Grammar*, ed. A. E. Cowley (2nd Edition; Oxford: Clarendon, 1910), 326, §111a.

[12]Wolfgang Schneider, *Grammatik des biblischen Hebräisch* (5th edition; München: Claudius Verlag, 1982).

[13]Alviero Niccacci, *The Syntax of the Verb in Classical Hebrew Prose* (Sheffield: JSOT Press, 1990).

[14]Better termed "speech" so as not to be confused with other senses of discourse, such as that in "discourse analysis." Some authorities use the term "discourse" to reference whole compositions.

[15]In the following schemes of clause types "w" stands for the conjunction waw, "x" for any non-verb element (such as noun, explicit pronoun, prepositional phrase, infinitive, or adverb), qatal is any perfect verb form, yiqtol is any imperfect verb form, and wayyiqtol is the waw-conversive imperfect.

Talstra[16] has developed a classification of clause types using a database approach to BH and automatic text processing, though, as he points out, in practice automatic computerized classification of clauses needs to be adjusted by human intervention. Talstra's advance over Niccacci's approach comes with his increased sensitivity to the role of nominal components in verbal clauses. Furthermore, Talstra exposes the need to account for multiple narrative levels within a text. Paragraphs are not simply linear chains of clauses, some foreground and others background. Rather, the arrangement of chains is hierarchical, with certain clauses assuming paragraph topic status, and other clause chains assuming a subsidiary information status within the text unit.

Talstra[17] proposes the following classification (with some rephrasing by this author) that additionally accounts for the presence or absence of the subject noun phrase:

w-x-qatal + explicit subject:

begins a new section with change of actants.

w-x-qatal + no explicit subject:

introduction of background information; it becomes a subsection when continued by a wayyiqtol.

wayyiqtol + explicit subject:

begins a new section with (re-)introduction of actants.

wayyiqtol + no explicit subject:

narrative continuation.

Talstra explains further that clause types defined by verb form and constituent order alone cannot effectively serve to structure a text. Additional features such as pronominal reference, conjunctions and particles, and lexical patterns are needed to accurately develop a hierarchy of clause relatedness within a text.

Representing Speech in Narrative

Direct address and dialogue are essential features of biblical narration. In fact, much of the "action" in BH narrative occurs by means of embedded speech. Alter[18] argues for the "primacy of dialogue" in BH narration, with non-speech narration serving the functions of presenting essential contextual information.

[16]Talstra, "Clause Types and Textual Structure: An Experiment in Narrative Syntax," in his *Narrative and Comment*, 166-180.

[17]Ibid., 174.

[18]Robert Alter, "Between Narration and Dialogue," in his *The Art of Biblical Narrative* (New York: Basic Books, 1981), 63-87.

The studies of Meier[19] and Miller[20] have provided a framework for understanding how speech (both direct quotations and indirect speech) are incorporated into narrative texts. One of the more intractible issues concerning speech in narrative texts has been the distribution of לֵאמֹר, translated "saying" in the KJV tradition. Miller presents a breakthrough analysis by identifying the real-life situation of לֵאמֹר-introduced speech compared to other speech. By identifying the participants' roles within speech situations, it becomes clear that non-לֵאמֹר-introduced speech typically mirrors the actual original speech situation, with speaker and addressee identifiable. לֵאמֹר-introduced speech, on the other hand, does not mirror the original situation in that the original speaker is most often not the one who actualizes the speech.[21]

Miller's precise definition of speech situations lays the groundwork for this further observation on the distribution of לֵאמֹר within BH narrative (including those few places where it is found in poetic contexts).[22] Quotation frames employing לֵאמֹר introduce direct speech situations that originally occurred elsewhere and/or at another time from the "here and now" of their enveloping narrative settings. The לֵאמֹר-introduced direct speeches are reports of speech situations that occurred "off-stage" from the main narrative's "on-stage" context. So, direct speech without לֵאמֹר represents a *record* of direct speech in the narrative's here and now. Speech introduced by לֵאמֹר contains a *report* of a prior and elsewhere speech event. While Miller does not make this generalizing discourse context observation, it correlates well with many of her research observations.

According to Miller, an analysis of verbs used with לֵאמֹר-introduced speech reports demonstrates that לֵאמֹר is used most frequently as a complement of verbs of messaging (נָגַד, "tell," and שָׁלַח, "send").[23] Since the original delivery and reception of a message occurs "off-stage" before it can be sent, this aligns with the reanimation

---

[19]Samuel A. Meier, *Speaking of Speaking: Marking Direct Discourse in the Hebrew Bible.* Vetus Testamentum Supplements 46 (Leiden: E. J. Brill, 1992).

[20]Cynthia Miller, *The Representation of Speech in Biblical Hebrew: A Linguistic Analysis.* Harvard Semitic Monograph 55 (Atlanta: Scholars Press, 1996).

[21]Regarding לֵאמֹר Cynthia Miller ("Discourse Functions of Quotative Frames in Biblical Hebrew Narrative," in *Discourse Analysis of Biblical Literature*, ed. Walter R. Bodine, 155-182) concludes: "Frames with לֵאמֹר are used to indicate that the reported speech event is less than prototypically dialogic. They are used to introduce information into the narrative without recourse to representation of the entire dialogic exchange. They are used to introduce speech acts of unknown or anonymous persons, that is, persons who are less than full characters in the narrative. Finally, they are used to relate a series of embedded quotations all of which are reported from the perspective of the principal" (178).

[22]I make this observation as what seems to be a logical extension of Miller's analysis, though she does not state her conclusion in this way. The above generalization on the discourse level situational use of לֵאמֹר stands in need of further refinement and linguistic justification, but may serve for the time being as a useful heuristic device.

[23]Miller, "Discourse Functions of Quotative Frames in Biblical Hebrew Narrative," 170.

quality of לֵאמֹר-introduced speech records. Direct speech may contain exclamatives and expressives such as אוֹי, "woe," and חָלִילָה לִי, "far be it from me," which do not occur in indirect speech or in quotations introduced by לֵאמֹר. This correlates with לֵאמֹר-introduced speech reports as referencing "off-stage" speech situations, and hence not real-time speech.

If this situational analysis of לֵאמֹר-introduced speech records is valid, then we have here an important tool for reconstructing the logistic context of speech events embedded in narrative.

DISCOURSE ANALYSIS OBSERVATIONS ON 2 KINGS 5

The account of Naaman and Elisha in 2 Kings 5 is standard BH narrative. This chapter was chosen (virtually at random) to show how some features of a discourse analytic approach apply to a real text. In particular, attention is directed to the flow of information features in the text, to clause connection and clause hierarchy indicators, and to the framing of speech within narrative.

Information System Observations

Certain clauses in the Naaman narrative illustrate some of the ways the writer maintains continuity from one clause to the next by managing the flow of information, keeping the reader interested by introducing new information into the text in a measured way. The reader should have her Biblia Hebraica open to follow the arguments, for the arguments depend on spans of text, even though only single clauses are reproduced here.

5:1b כִּי־בוֹ נָתַן־יְהוָה תְּשׁוּעָה לַאֲרָם
"For by him gave YHWH victory to Aram."
Clause Type: ky-x-qatal = backgrounding

The prepositional phrase בוֹ, an instrumental complement to the verb, would normally be expected at the end of a clause. The referent of "him" in the prepositional phrase בוֹ is Naaman. Though Naaman is not the grammatical subject of the verb, he is the topic of this clause, thus maintaining continuity with Naaman, the topic of the preceding clause.

5:2 וַאֲרָם יָצְאוּ גְדוּדִים
"And Aram, went out bands."
Clause Type: w-x-qatal = backgrounding

"Aram" stands in clause initial position syntactically unconnected within its clause. This is a marvelous example of a topic word that has no grammatical function within its clause. Aram is not the subject of the clause, nor could it be, because it is singular in number and the verb is plural. It is in the topic position, and it reestablishes the topic of Aram's military initiative, which was left off with 5:1b. This construction might be called the nominative absolute.[24]

5:17 וַיֹּאמֶר נַעֲמָן וָלֹא יֻתַּן־נָא לְעַבְדְּךָ מַשָּׂא צֶמֶד־פְּרָדִים אֲדָמָה

"And Naaman said, 'If not, may be given to your servant two mule-loads of earth.'"

Clause Type: wayyiqtol-no explicit subject = narrative continuity

The passive voice verb used here has the effect of maintaining topic continuity, because no new actant is introduced. It may also reflect power and politeness issues, whereby Naaman does not presume to ask Elisha directly but frames his request in the passive to effect deference and distance.

Clause Connection System Observations

One of the essential steps in text analysis and exegesis is delimiting the text unit and establishing its major and minor boundaries.[25] The information system and the clause connection system combine to provide a structural hierarchy to the text, delineating the unit as a whole within 2 Kings, and its subsections within chapter 5. A survey of the text structure devised by the editors of the versions reveals considerable diversity.[26]

5:1a וְנַעֲמָן שַׂר־צְבָא מֶלֶךְ־אֲרָם הָיָה אִישׁ גָּדוֹל לִפְנֵי אֲדֹנָיו

"And Naaman, commander of the army of the king of Aram, was a great man before his lord."

Clause Type: w-x-qatal = episode intial, new actant

[24]This construction does not fit the profile of casus pendens constructions, in which the fronted nominal element is resumed grammatically.

[25]See Sidney Greidanus (*The Modern Preacher and the Ancient Text* [Grand Rapids: Eerdmans, 1988], 221-222) on the exegetical importance of properly delimiting text units in Hebrew narrative.

[26]Unit breaks in the versions are marked by graphical paragraphs. New units begin with the following verses:

Biblical Hebraica Stuttgartensia: 1, 8, 15, 20
Revised Standard Version: 1, 5b, 8, 15, 19b
New Revised Standard Version: 1, 5b, 8, 15, 19b, 25
New International Version: 1, 2, 4, 7, 8, 11, 13, 15, 16, 17, 19a, 19b, 21, 22, 23, 25b, 25c, 26
New English Bible: 1, 15, 19b
New American Bible: 1, 7, 9, 13, 15, 16, 19b, 25
New Jerusalem Bible: 1, 8, 15, 19b, 25

The only unit breaks these versions have in common are at verses 1 and 15. Differences in unit delineation are due, among other things, to editorial decisions on readability. Yet the variations are enough to suggest that a discourse syntactic approach to text segmentation might be beneficial.

This is the episode initial clause; it reflects the typical structure of such clauses. New episodes typically do not begin with wayyiqtol. Note the extended introduction of Naaman, as is typical when a new major character is introduced into a new episode.

5:8a וַיְהִי כִּשְׁמֹעַ

אֱלִישָׁע אִישׁ־הָאֱלֹהִים כִּי־קָרַע מֶלֶךְ־יִשְׂרָאֵל אֶת־בְּגָדָיו וַיִּשְׁלַח אֶל־הַמֶּלֶךְ

"And when Elisha, the man of Elohim, heard that the king of Israel tore his clothes,
   he sent a message to the king (saying) . . . "

Clause type: wayyiqtol-k-infinitive = paragraph beginning

This type of temporal clause often introduces a new paragraph. וַיְהִי has been termed a "macro-syntactic sign."[27] Along with other words such as וְעַתָּה ("And now"), such markers serve to signal new units. This is confirmed by analysis of the information content of this verse. Elisha is named for the first time (he is only alluded to in 5:3 as "the prophet in Samaria"), and identified as "the man of Elohim." Likewise, "the king of Israel" is renominalized, rather than referred to by a pronoun, even though he was the subject and topic of 5:7.

5:20a וַיֹּאמֶר גֵּיחֲזִי נַעַר אֱלִישָׁע אִישׁ־הָאֱלֹהִים

"And said Gehazi, servant of Elisha the man of God"

Clause Type: wayyiqtol-explicit subject = narrative continuity

Contrary to the Masoretic text, every English version creates a paragraph break after 19a and begins a new paragraph with 19b.[28] Clearly this is in error. Whereas 19b has wayyiqtol and no explicit subject noun, indicative of continuity with the preceding clause, 20a has an explicit subject noun (Gehazi) introducing a new participant in the narrative, and no back-referencing of any kind to verse 19, indicating a new unit. Though Elisha is the subject of 19a and the pronoun referent of מֵאִתּוֹ "from him" in 19b, he is renominalized (that is, mentioned by name) in 20—a sign of discontinuity. If the clause had said "Gehazi, his servant," it would have indicated continuity.

5:25 וְהוּא־בָא

"And he entered."

Clause Type: w-x-qatal = new actant

[27]Niccacci, *The Syntax of the Verb in Classical Hebrew Prose*, 33.

[28]The MT has a setuma after verse 19, used for text division, indicating a break with the following paragraph.

This clause type effects a contrastive scenario from the end of verse 24. In that verse, Gehazi has sent away the men who helped him carry the goods. In verse 25 he goes to stand before Elisha.

Embedded Speech Observations

Dialogue and embedded speech are used extensively in 2 Kings 5. Direct quotation is found in verses 3, 5, 7, 11, 13, 15, 16, 17, 20, 25, and 26. לֵאמֹר-introduced speech is used in verses 4, 6, 8, 10, and 22. See representative and noteworthy instances below.

5:3a וַתֹּאמֶר אֶל־גְּבִרְתָּהּ אַחֲלֵי אֲדֹנִי לִפְנֵי הַנָּבִיא

"And she said to her mistress, 'If my lord was in the presence of the prophet . . . '"

Clause Type: wayyiqtol-no explicit subject = narrative continuity

This clause continues the topic (the captured Israelite handmaid) of 5:2b and contains a speech record. The setting is the "here and now" of the beginning of the narrative, in this case its Aramaean context in Naaman's household. It is typical of the direct speech records of 2 Kings 5.

5:4 וַיָּבֹא

וַיַּגֵּד לַאדֹנָיו לֵאמֹר כָּזֹאת וְכָזֹאת דִּבְּרָה הַנַּעֲרָה אֲשֶׁר מֵאֶרֶץ יִשְׂרָאֵל:

"And he (Naaman) went and told his lord, 'Such and such said the handmaid who is from the land of Israel.'"

Clause Type: wayyiqtol-wayyiqtol-no explicit subject = narrative continuity

The speech component of this sentence is clearly not a verbatim record of what was said. The phrase כָּזֹאת וְכָזֹאת "such and such" is a shorthand way of summarizing what the handmaid had earlier said.[29] It is a summarizing speech report of what was communicated to Naaman earlier and elsewhere, and employs the verb נָגַד characteristic of such speech reports.

5:6 וַיָּבֵא הַסֵּפֶר אֶל־מֶלֶךְ יִשְׂרָאֵל לֵאמֹר וְעַתָּה כְּבוֹא הַסֵּפֶר הַזֶּה אֵלֶיךָ

"'"And he brought the letter to the king of Israel, לֵאמֹר 'And now when this letter comes to you, . . .'"

Clause Type: wayyiqtol-no explicit subject = narrative continuity

In this scene Naaman takes the king of Aram's letter of introduction to the king of Israel. Again, we have a לֵאמֹר-introduced speech report, but of a kind different from 5:4. In this case the report is the record of what the letter contained. This too fits the

---

[29]Miller, *The Representation of Speech in Biblical Hebrew Narrative*, calls this semi-direct speech—speech somewhere between direct quotation (it is presented as direct quotation) and indirect speech (it is a compression of what the direct quotation must have been).

profile of לֵאמֹר-introduced speech as the secondary animation (the king of Israel reading the letter) of the primary communication, in this case the letter of recommendation.

5:8b וַיִּשְׁלַח אֶל־הַמֶּלֶךְ לֵאמֹר לָמָּה קָרַעְתָּ בְּגָדֶיךָ

"He sent (a message) to the king, לֵאמֹר 'Why did you tear your clothes . . . ' "

Clause Type: wayyiqtol-no explicit subject = narrative continuity

The לֵאמֹר-introduced speech is a report of what Elisha sent as a message to the king of Israel, presumably by the hand of a messenger. Again, the speech is a report of what was spoken "off-site" in the king's presence, and not on-stage in Elisha's neighborhood. In 5:10, also employing the verb שָׁלַח, Elisha sends a messenger to Naaman. The לֵאמֹר-introduced speech instructs him to wash in the Jordan and is the verbatim of what was delivered elsewhere from Elisha.

5:22 וַיֹּאמֶר שָׁלוֹם אֲדֹנִי שְׁלָחַנִי לֵאמֹר הִנֵּה עַתָּה זֶה בָּאוּ אֵלַי שְׁנֵי־נְעָרִים

"And he said, 'Shalom. My lord sent me (with a message), לֵאמֹר "Just now have come to me two servants . . . " ' "

Clause Type: wayyiqtol-no explicit subject = narrative continuity

Gehazi reports to Naaman the message Elisha (supposedly) had earlier and elsewhere given to him to deliver to Naaman in order to extract goods from him. Again, the לֵאמֹר-introduced clause is a message first articulated elsewhere.

In sum, close attention to the situation of speech suggests that לֵאמֹר speech is distinguished from direct quotation by time and locale. לֵאמֹר speech is a report of a speech event, whereas non-לֵאמֹר speech is a record of the original speech event. The לֵאמֹר-introduced quotations contain speech first uttered elsewhere and earlier, then revoiced in the "here and now" of the narrative. The quotations introduced without לֵאמֹר are "real-time" quotations in the context of the narrative.

The Interpretive Payoff of Discourse Analysis

When prospective students of biblical Hebrew ask me if Hebrew is more difficult to learn than Greek, I respond in a way calculated to draw them into the course. I tell them that Greek is undoubtedly more difficult to learn because it is more highly inflected than Hebrew. Greek has case endings on the nouns, Hebrew does not. Greek has a complex verbal system, with aorists and optatives and all that; Hebrew has only two verb tenses (I conveniently omit telling them about the stems and weak root verbs). Overall, there are more paradigms to memorize in Greek than in Hebrew. This really intrigues them, along with the exotic alphabet and reading "backwards."

But as all students of Hebrew know, the difficulty comes after those few paradigms are mastered. Once we get into texts, students soon learn that because Hebrew is less inflected than Greek, the interpreter must work harder to discern how the text coheres and orders itself. Morphology and clause-level syntax only take the reader so far.

Traditional BH grammar provides limited assistance for discerning text-level functions. A more comprehensive linguistic approach is needed in laying a foundation for responsible text interpretation. Discourse analysis is beginning to provide guidance on the crucial systems of topic identification and management, and the linking of clauses in their hierarchical relationships. It also has the theoretical perspective to systematically recover the situationality of BH narratives. Increasing our grasp of how a text signals its real-life context of reference can only increase our grasp of its meaning for us today. Understanding text-level features is crucial for apprehending how a writer conveys to readers the essence and the intent of the divine communication with which he has been entrusted.

PART TWO

Exegesis and Interpretation

Grave Reflections on Genesis 35:16-29: From Text to Application

William T. Koopmans

INTRODUCTION

In recent decades, it has been demonstrated repeatedly that many of the narratives in Genesis are carefully crafted. Literary artistry is skillfully employed throughout the book in order to highlight the author's intentions and to heighten the understanding of the perceptive reader.[1]

Despite significant advances in recognizing various literary techniques employed in the composition of the Genesis narratives, numerous passages still contain many questions for the exegete. A good example is Genesis 35:16-29. This pericope can be subdivided into three topical units. The first deals with Rachel and the birth of her son Benjamin (vv. 16-20), the second focuses upon Reuben and his place in the family (vv. 21-26), and the third finalizes Jacob's homecoming and the death of Isaac (vv. 27-29).

A careful scrutiny of these verses, however, including a study of their interconnections and their relationships to the broader context, has caused many scholars to question the present arrangement of Genesis 35:16-29. Employing traditional methods of source-criticism, it has become commonplace for commentators to allege that these verses contain material from J, E, and P sources.[2] While in many other parts of Genesis the final compiler or redactor is thought to have performed a masterful job of producing a pleasing narrative from a variety of sources, here the assessment of many scholars is more critical. Gerhard Von Rad, for example, calls this the "rubble of smaller or very small single traditions, often quite fragmentary in character."[3] Noting the variety of material included in these verses, he concludes that here the transition "is more awkward than almost any other place in Genesis."[4]

---

[1]See B. S. Childs, *Introduction to the Old Testament as Scripture* (Philadelphia: Fortress Press, 1979), 145-50; Robert Alter, *The Art of Biblical Narrative* (New York: Basic Books, 1981), 3-10, 41-46, 155-189; B. T. Dahlberg, "The Unity of Genesis," in *Literary Interpretations of Biblical Narratives*, Vol. 2, ed. K. R. R. Gros Louis (Nashville: Abingdon, 1982), 126-133; G. W. Coats, *Genesis: With an Introduction to Narrative Literature* (Grand Rapids: Eerdmans, 1983); H. C. White, *Narration and Discourse in the Book of Genesis* (Cambridge: Cambridge University Press, 1991); W. C. Kaiser, Jr., "Narrative," in *Cracking Old Testament Codes*, eds. D. B. Sandy and R. L. Giese, Jr. (Nashville: Broadman and Holman, 1995), 69-88.

[2]E. A. Speiser, *Genesis* (New York: Doubleday, 1964), 272-275; Claus Westermann, *Genesis 12-36: A Commentary*, trans. J. J. Scullion (Minneapolis: Augsburg, 1985), 548-549.

[3]Gerhard von Rad, *Genesis* (Philadelphia: Westminster Press, 1972), 340.

[4]Ibid., 342.

It is not difficult to understand why many commentators have concluded that the presentation of details in 35:16-29 lacks the literary depth of other narratives in the Abraham, Jacob, and Joseph cycles in Genesis.[5] The stories included in this pericope are sketched in severest brevity. The text calls the reader's attention to the events mentioned in verses 16-29, but the author does not elaborate on or develop their theological significance. The birth of Benjamin and the death of Rachel, the aggression of firstborn Reuben with Jacob's concubine Bilhah, the death of Isaac after Jacob's return to Mamre—each of these topics had the potential to be told in the pleasing and enlightening depth witnessed in other narratives. But they are undeveloped.

In light of the undeniable compositional skill employed elsewhere in the book of Genesis, however, it is worthwhile to explore the possibility that the author or redactor may have used brevity here as a deliberate literary technique.[6] The component subunits of Genesis 35:16-29 could have been skillfully stretched, the transitions smoothed and polished. But would that have promoted the overall purpose of the author?

Questions concerning the cohesion of the various details narrated in 35:16-29, as well as their connections to the broader flow and outline of the book, are not merely academic. If von Rad's opinion is correct and these verses represent a disjointed collection of literary fragments, the reader could have only minimal confidence in the author's purpose or intention. On the other hand, if it is possible to determine that the author exercised greater compositional care than is usually recognized in these verses, then one could pursue matters of purpose and message more confidently.[7]

EXEGESIS OF GENESIS 35:16-29

In order to study the present composition and intention of Genesis 35:16-29, it is first of all helpful to determine the relationship of these verses to the broader context. Clearly, 35:16-29 falls at a pivotal point in the overall arrangement of the book. It has been previously recognized that a major structuring element employed throughout Genesis is identifiable in the *toledoth* arrangements.[8] Genesis 36:1 marks the beginning of the ninth *toledoth*; chapter 36 is devoted entirely to a description of the lineage

---

[5]It is generally recognized that the patriarchal accounts that make up Genesis 12-50 divide into the three "cycles" mentioned above; see Th. C. Vriezen and A. S. van der Woude, *Literatuur van Oud-Israel* (Katwijk aan Zee: Servire, 1980), 159-160.

[6]See G. J. Wenham, *Genesis 16-50* (Dallas: Word Books, 1994), 321, 328-331.

[7]We deem this to be a more objective method by which to pursue the author's purpose than is the conversational, readers' responses approach attested in the recent collage of ideas published by B. Moyers (*Genesis: A Living Conversation* [New York: Doubleday, 1996]).

[8]D. J. Wiseman, *Ancient Records and the Structure of Genesis: A Case for Literary Unity* (Nashville: Thomas Nelson, 1985), 59-60.

of Esau and the Edomites. Jacob resurfaces in 37:1 as part of a transition to the lengthy Joseph cycle.

Accordingly, from a literary perspective, Genesis 35 occupies a strategic position as it completes the main part of the Jacob cycle. The impressions left at the end of chapter 35 linger with the reader during the subsequent discussion of Esau and Edom. These impressions also set the stage for the story line to resume with Joseph in chapter 37.

After conceding the strategic literary position occupied by Genesis 35:16-29, it is helpful to pursue the manner in which the specific motifs and details of these verses connect with the broader story line of Genesis. It is not possible within the scope of this essay to deal with all the exegetical questions that arise in these verses. Our focus here will be limited more modestly to a number of key connections that link this pericope to the flow of the broader Genesis narrative and that may, therefore, provide interpretive clues to the author's or narrator's purpose in arranging the material in its present form.

The Birth of Benjamin and the Death of Rachel

Much scholarly attention has been focused on the problem of the location of Rachel's grave. Many commentators perceive a conflict between 35:16, 19 on the one hand and 1 Samuel 10:2 and Jeremiah 31:15 on the other,[9] generally concluding that Bethlehem must be a gloss here.[10] Others minimize the conflict.[11] A main point of contention involves the meaning of the enigmatic Hebrew expression כִּבְרַת־הָאָרֶץ, literally "length of land." Found only here and in 2 Kings 5:19, the expression continues to defy convincing definition.[12]

The complexity of these topographical notations warrants caution with respect to the importance of the locations. Nevertheless, the place names cannot be ignored in the process of interpretation. In 35:1-15, names and name changes are used deliberately in the flow of the narrative. Luz becomes Bethel (35:6, 15) and Jacob becomes Israel (35:10). The etymology of Allon Bacuth ("oak of weeping") is connected with the death and burial of Deborah (35:8). The deliberate use of these names in the first half

---

[9]O. Procksch, *Die Genesis* (Leipzig: A Deichertsche Verlagsbuchhandlung, 1913), 375; von Rad, *Genesis*, 340-341; M. Tsevat, "Rachel's Tomb," in *The Interpreter's Dictionary of the Bible*, Suppl. Vol. (Nashville: Abingdon, 1976), 724-725; W. H. Gispen, *Genesis III* (Kampen: J. H. Kok, 1983), 163.

[10]Westermann, *Genesis 12-36*, 554. See also Josh. 15:59 LXX.

[11]H. C. Leupold, *Exposition of Genesis*, Vol. 2, (Grand Rapids: Baker, 1942) 925f.; D. Kidner, *Genesis* (London: The Tyndale Press, 1967) 175; G. Ch. Aalders, *Genesis*, Vol. II, trans. W. Heynen (Grand Rapids: Zondervan, 1981), 166-167.; V. P. Hamilton, *The Book of Genesis: Chapters 18-50* (Grand Rapids: Eerdmans, 1995), 382.

[12]E. Vogt, "Benjamin geboren 'eine Meile' von Ephrata," *Biblica* 56 (1975): 30-35. G. J. Wenham translates it as "about two hours distance," thereby attempting to resolve the problem (*Genesis 16-50*, 326).

of chapter 35 forces one to question whether a similar technique operates in the toponyms of the last half of the chapter.

It is evident that in 35:16, 19 the primary geographical reference is to Ephrath. Significantly, it is thought that this toponym is related to the root פָּרָה "bear fruit, be fruitful."[13] It is precisely this root פָּרָה that is used in the reaffirmation of the covenant blessing to Jacob at Bethel in 35:11. Perhaps this explains why the narrator mentions that they left Bethel but did not yet reach Ephrath. The etymology of Ephrath reminds the reader of God's blessing of Jacob in which it is stated that he will be fruitful and increase in number. But they have not yet arrived at the fullness of the blessing when Rachel goes into labor with the last of the twelve sons.

The author also emphasizes the meaning of the names given to the son born there. The etymology of both "Ben-Oni" and "Benjamin" has been widely discussed.[14] Ben-Oni is generally thought to mean "son of my sorrow," and Benjamin is understood as "son of my right hand,"[15] though others understand the latter, based on Mari references, as "Son of the South."[16] Other biblical references would seem to support the definition "son of my right hand,"[17] but Jacob may very well have been employing a name more widely known, e.g. from Mari, where it originally meant "son of the South," since the "south" and "right" were considered correlates in a world oriented to the East rather than to the North.[18] It is also of interest to note that at this point Jacob was heading southward toward his home destination.

In any event, Jacob renames his son to reflect the hope of a brighter future just as God had earlier renamed him. The motif of childbirth is prominent throughout the book, which bears the name "Genesis" or "origins," and in which the author frequently theologizes at the setting of a childbirth. In that respect, what we encounter in 35:18 is consistent with the broader pattern in Genesis. Perhaps it is precisely because the reader has already been conditioned to realize the importance attached to such births

---

[13]See W. Gesenius, *Hebräisches und Aramäisches Handwörterbuch über das Alte Testament* (Leipzig: F. C. W. Vogel, 1890), 68; L. Koehler, *Lexicon in Veteris Testamenti Libros* (Leiden: E. J. Brill, 1953), 79-80.

[14]J. Muilenburg, "The Birth of Benjamin," *Journal of Biblical Literature* 75 (1956): 194-201; J. A. Soggin, "Die Geburt Benjamins, Gen XXXV 16-20(21)," *Vetus Testamentum* 11 (1961): 432-440.

[15]E.g., G. Van Groningen, "Benjamin," in *Baker Encyclopedia of the Bible*, Vol. 1 (Grand Rapids: Baker Book House, 1988), 280.

[16]H. B. Huffmon, "Benjamin, Benjaminites," in *The Interpreter's Dictionary of the Bible*, Suppl. Vol. (Nashville: Abingdon, 1976), 95-96.

[17]Gispen, *Genesis, III*, 164.

[18]See J. G. Baldwin, *The Message of Genesis 12-50* (Leicester: InterVarsity Press, 1986), 151.

that Genesis 35:16-18 can be so brief and yet so effective in advancing the flow of the narrative.

The death of Rachel, as described in 35:16-18, evokes the memory of her earlier exclamation to Jacob, "Give me children, or I'll die!" (30:1).[19] Ironically, contrary to her lament, it *was* in childbirth that she succumbed.[20] The irony is also evident when she names her first son Joseph, saying, "May the Lord add to me another son" (30:24).[21]

At their first meeting, Jacob rolled a stone away from the mouth of the well for Rachel (Genesis 29:10); in his final act of farewell he erects a memorial stone to mark her grave (35:20).[22] Similarly, the narrator tells us that when Jacob met Rachel he was moved to tears of joy, "then Jacob kissed Rachel and began to weep aloud" (29:11); at her death there is no such expression of emotion and tenderness. Although we are told elsewhere that Jacob loved Rachel (29:30), the narrator makes no mention of tenderness, affection, or sorrow at the time of her death. Is it possible that such silence is deliberate? It leaves the reader with the realization that Jacob has received from his wife the sons she longed to give him. The writer does not allow the reader to be distracted by thoughts of the emotional bond between Jacob and his wife. In a matter-of-fact approach the narrator rivets the reader's attention to the fact of Benjamin's painful arrival to complete the list of twelve sons.

In view of the various connections between the first half of Genesis 35 (at Bethel) and the episodes narrated in the second half of the chapter, it is also noteworthy that the death of Rebekah's nurse, Deborah, in 35:8 is balanced by the death of Rachel while in the company of her midwife, in 35:19. It has often been asserted that the reference to the death and burial in 35:8 is a dislocated or fragmentary insertion. To the contrary, Rendsburg has argued that that cryptic notation serves a deliberate literary purpose.[23] Our observations here support a similar conclusion with respect to the brief but strategic notation of Rachel's death and burial.

---

[19] It is not warranted to conclude, as G. W. Coats does, that Gen. 29:31-30:24 and 36:16-20 are two traditio-historically distinct units (*Genesis*, 240). On the literary techniques employed in Gen. 30:1-4, consult Alter, *The Art of Biblical Narrative*, 186-189. Additional connections are listed below with respect to Reuben's role in the rivalry between the sisters.

[20] Ronald F. Youngblood, *The Book of Genesis*, 2nd ed. (Grand Rapids: Baker Book House, 1991), 239. On the use of irony as a literary device consult E. M. Good, *Irony in the Old Testament* (Philadelphia: Westminster Press, 1965).

[21] S. H. Dresner, *Rachel* (Minneapolis: Fortress Press, 1994), 101.

[22] In keeping with a widespread practice of the day. See Brian Peckham, "Phoenicia and the Religion of Israel: The Epigraphic Evidence," in *Ancient Israelite Religion*, eds. P. D. Miller, Jr., P. D. Hanson, and S. D. McBride (Philadelphia: Fortress Press, 1987), 90 n. 23.

[23] G. A. Rendsburg, "Notes of Genesis XXXV," *Vetus Testamentum* 34 (1984): 361-366.

The Conduct of Reuben

In the preceding section we saw how the description of Rachel's death during child-birth clearly alludes to her previously expressed desire to bear children as Jacob's wife. Therefore, it is significant that immediately after the description of Rachel's death the narrator mentions Reuben's conduct with Bilhah when the family had moved on to Migdal Eder. Does the author also use this toponym deliberately? Migdal Eder means, "(watch) tower of Eder" or "(watch) tower of the flock."[24] The name Rachel means "ewe." Ironically, it is following the death of Rachel that Reuben, within the shadow of the shepherd's watch tower, takes Bilhah,[25] and Jacob, who had so success-fully shepherded the flocks of his uncle Laban in Paddan Aram, hears of it (35:21). What else would one expect of such an event happening near Migdal Eder!

Bilhah was the handmaid Rachel had pressed upon Jacob to have children in her stead (30:3-4), hoping thereby to alleviate somewhat her own sense of failure, shame, and jealousy in her rivalry with Leah. Given that background in Genesis 30, and seen in the light of the ancient Near Eastern customs, it was not necessary for the narrator to elaborate on the implications of what Reuben had done. The significance of his action would be apparent to the reader. Reuben's action was an affront to Jacob, and may well have been understood as an attempt to usurp the place of his father.[26]

In the setting of the ancient world, Reuben's aggression may or may not have been viewed as an offense against Bilhah.[27] But it almost certainly would have been received as an affront to her recently deceased mistress, Rachel. Since Reuben was the firstborn of Rachel's rival, Leah, his affront should also be read in conjunction with the antago-nism described in chapter 30. In fact, this connection is heightened by the realization that it was Reuben who found the mandrakes (30:14), considered to have aphrodisiac powers,[28] that play a role in the struggle between Rachel and Leah. Accordingly, there is an important topical connection between the death of Rachel and the action of Reuben.

What is the point of the cryptic note in 35:22, "and Israel heard of it?" Numerous commentators have suggested that this reference, standing as it does without any fur-ther elaboration of subsequent actions by Jacob, indicates the fragmentation of what

---

[24]W. Gesenius, *A Hebrew and English Lexicon of the Old Testament* (Oxford: Clarendon Press, 1975), 154.

[25]Her name seems to indicate calamity, cf. Hebrew בַּלְהָה, "terror, dreadful event, calamity, destruction."

[26]Cf. 2 Samuel 16:20-23; 1 Kings 2:22; see also 2 Samuel 3:6-11. The implications of Reuben's action are discussed by K. Armstrong (*In the Beginning: A New Interpretation of Genesis* [New York: Alfred A. Knopf, 1996], 99) and by many previous commentators.

[27]See Baldwin, *The Message of Genesis 12-50*, 152.

[28]See J. C. de Moor, *An Anthology of Religious Texts from Ugarit* (Leiden: E. J. Brill, 1987), 9 n.44.

must at one point have been a more complete story.[29] However, it is also possible that the reference was deliberately curtailed.[30] As it now stands, Jacob's silence evokes the memory of Shechem's desire to marry Dinah and of her defilement (Gen. 34).[31] Jacob heard about that matter too but did nothing until the sons came home. Moreover, the brief note in 35:22 also sets the stage for 49:4. In the narrator's presentation, Jacob keeps quiet about the affair until the sons are gathered around him for the final blessing. At that point he essentially strips Reuben of the blessing of the firstborn.[32] In the meantime, Reuben is portrayed as a man who attempts to redeem himself with actions appropriate to the eldest son (37:21-22; 42:37).[33]

The list of twelve sons indicates that in one sense the family is complete, yet the struggle that surrounds the firstborn and the birthright will continue.[34] The enumeration of the sons at this point is an integral part of the narrative because it is included at precisely the place where the roster is complete but the script for the future is still most uncertain.

The Return of Jacob and the Death of Isaac

Jacob's arrival in Mamre (35:27) sets the stage for the departure of Isaac. Here too it is important to recognize the role of the various toponyms in the progression of the Genesis narratives. There can be little doubt that the author intends the reader to recognize that Jacob's return to Mamre from Paddan Aram approximately mirrors Abraham's arrival at this place. In particular, the narrator of Genesis 12 describes his arrival at Shechem (v. 6) and at Bethel (v. 8); at both places "he built an altar to the Lord who had appeared to him" (vv. 7-8). From there, Abraham continued toward the Negev but soon arrived in Egypt because of the famine in the land (vv. 9-10). Similarly, Jacob and his family arrived at Shechem, where he set up an altar

---

[29]von Rad, *Genesis*, 341-342.

[30]M. Sternberg, *The Poetics of Biblical Narrative: Ideological Literature and the Drama of Reading* (Bloomington: Indiana University Press, 1985), 478. The silence of Jacob (which commentators found to be puzzling) is accompanied by silence from Bilhah (which commentators ignored until a recent article raised this issue; see J. A. Glancy, "The Mistress-Slave Dialectic: Paradoxes of Slavery in Three LXX Narratives," *Journal for the Study of the Old Testament* 72 [1996]: 71-87, esp. 74-77).

[31]The silence of Jacob is viewed critically by most commentators. A dissenting, but not convincing, opinion that views Jacob's reaction as being exemplary, is proposed by L. M. Bechtel ("What if Dinah Is Not Raped [Genesis 34]," *Journal for the Study of the Old Testament* 62 [1994]: 19-36). Unfortunately, Bechtel has ignored the obvious parallel between Gen. 34 and 35:22.

[32]See also 1 Chronicles 5:1.

[33]J. S. Ackerman, "Joseph, Judah, and Jacob," *Literary Interpretations of Biblical Narratives*, Vol. 2, ed. K. R. R. Gros Louis (Nashville: Abingdon, 1982), 85-113, esp. 98-100.

[34]Note how vs. 23 highlights the fact that Reuben was the firstborn.

and called it El Elohe Israel (33:18-20). Whereas in the account of Abraham only passing mention is made of the fact that there were Canaanites living in the land at the time (12:6), in the Jacob narrative an entire chapter is devoted to this theme (chapter 34). Jacob also moves from Shechem to Bethel, where he too builds an altar (35:7). Subsequent to his arrival at Mamre, Jacob and his family also eventually descend to Egypt as part of the Joseph cycle.[35]

The topographical notes that trace the return of Jacob are, therefore, not incidental. They are used to make deliberate connections between the three major cycles (Abraham, Jacob, Joseph) in the patriarchal portion of Genesis. One could call the use of connecting parallels in the various cycles a form of literary "overlay" as a variant of the type of internal overlay identified elsewhere as a device within narrative in Genesis.[36]

In 35:29, Jacob and Esau are found together at the burial of Isaac. Whereas in 32:6-8 and 33:1-17 the author highlights the tension and fear experienced by Jacob at the time of his reunion with Esau, 35:29 does not bring any such emotions into focus. Here Esau is mentioned first, perhaps to hint at his status as the firstborn. Yet the verse seems to strike a note of sober neutrality amidst other texts more explicitly judgmental of the relationship between Jacob and Esau. Elsewhere in Genesis, Esau is clearly held accountable for his part in selling the birthright and in the ensuing enmity between the brothers (Genesis 25:34; 26:35; 27:41). Also, the relationship that existed between the nations of Israel and Edom was one of escalating enmity from the time of the exodus onward.[37]

One might wonder, therefore, why Jacob and Esau are presented in 35:29 without any hint of the conflict that spans the Genesis narratives. This is probably so because in Genesis 33:16-17 they parted company neutrally and there is no intervening encounter narrated to change that mood. And, most importantly for our understanding of 35:29 (both in terms of its brevity and its implicit narrative purpose), a clue is found

---

[35]The parallels extend beyond Genesis into other books as well, especially in the descriptions of the conquest and settlement of the land. Genesis 33:17-20 may be compared with Joshua 3:14-17; 4:9, etc. Additional parallels are noted in J. N. M. Wijngaards, *The Dramatization of Salvific History in the Deuteronomic Schools* (OTS 16; Leiden: E. J. Brill, 1969). See also J. Goldingay, "The Patriarchs in Scripture and History, in *Essays on the Patriarchal Narratives*, eds. A. R. Millard and D. J. Wiseman (Winona Lake: Eisenbrauns, 1983), 1-34, esp. 20.

[36]See R. E. Longacre, "The Discourse of the Flood Narrative," *Journal of the American Academy of Religion*, XLVII/1 Supplement (March, 1979): 90-133.

[37]See M. H. Woudstra, "Edom and Israel in Ezekiel," *Calvin Theological Journal* 3 (1968): 21-35; B. Gosse, "Detournement de la vengeance du Seigneur contre Edom et les nations en Isa 63, 1-6," *Zeitschrift für die alttestamenliche Wissenschaft* 102 (1990): 105-110; W. T. Koopmans, "Poetic Reciprocation: The Oracles against Edom and Philistia in Ezek. 25:12-17," in *Verse in Ancient Near Eastern Prose*, AOAT 42, eds. J. C. De Moor and W. G. E. Watson (Neukirchen-Vluyn: Neukirchener Verlag, 1993), 113-122.

in 25:7-11. The account of Abraham's burial, attended by both Isaac and Ishmael, is mirrored with many striking parallels in the account of Isaac's burial, attended by his two sons Jacob and Esau (35:27-29).

The literary intention of the narrator in Genesis 25 is evident. Immediately after the description of Abraham's burial, the lineage of Ishmael is summarized (25:12-18), condemned with the commentary that they lived in hostility toward all their brothers (25:18), and then disregarded. From that point on, the narrative focuses upon Isaac as the heir of the covenant promises. The writer's technique at the end of the Jacob cycle is identical to the pattern established at the end of the Abraham cycle. Following the burial attended by the two brothers, in chapter 36 the Esau genealogy begins with an implicit criticism of Esau (he took his wives from the women of Canaan, 36:2; cf. 27:46). Esau's lineage, like that of Ishmael, is summarized and then disregarded as the storyline continues through the descendants of his brother.

Throughout these events in 35:16-19, we see that the author is able to employ brevity as an effective literary device precisely because the details described either form parallels to or a completion of information or events already addressed in the preceding narratives. One might call this a retrocipatory use of information as a literary device.[38]

Clearly, the narration of these various details in 35:16-29 is indispensable to the book of Genesis. When seen in connection with the broader context, they do not leave the impression of somewhat arbitrarily compiled data. To the contrary, there is evidence that the events are carefully and strategically narrated.

Previous studies have suggested that the careful literary correlations now discernible between materials often attributed to J, E, and P calls for a reexamination of the traditional theory of source documents in Genesis.[39] Our analysis does not preclude the possibility that the events described in 35:16-29 may have been known from earlier sources. In all likelihood they would have been.[40] But more important is the inescapable conclusion that in their present form these details contribute dramatically to the Jacob cycle. These verses are not a haphazard miscellany of material. Rather, there appears to be a deliberate artistry to the manner in which the rapid-fire

[38]As such, it should be viewed as a counterpart of anticipatory information, for which see N. M. Sarna, "The Anticipatory Use of Information as a Literary Feature of the Genesis Narratives," in *The Creation of Sacred Literature*, ed. R. E. Friedman (Near Eastern Studies 22, Berkeley: University of California Press, 1981), 76-82.

[39]D. W. Baker, "Diversity and Unity in the Literary Structure of Genesis," in *Essays on the Patriarchal Narratives*, eds. A. R. Millard and D. J. Wiseman (Winona Lake: Eisenbrauns, 1983), 197-215, esp. 214-215. See also G. A. Rendsburg, "Notes on Genesis XXXV," *Vetus Testamentum* 34 (1984): 361-366.

[40]Though not likely in the J, E, P framework traditionally assumed; see G. J. Wenham, "Genesis: An Authorship Study and Current Pentateuchal Criticism," *Journal for the Study of the Old Testament* 42 (1988): 3-18. For a different opinion consult S. Portnoy and D. L. Petersen, "Statistical Differences among Documentary Sources: Comments on 'Genesis: An Authorship Study,'" *Journal for the Study of the Old Testament* 50 (1991): 3-14.

narration of these events concludes the Jacob cycle and sets the stage for the Joseph cycle to follow.

FROM TEXT TO MESSAGE

It is now helpful to ask, What does Genesis 35:16-29 contribute to the broader narrative structure of the Jacob cycle? Or, to put the matter conversely, What would be lost or absent from that storyline if these verses were not included? The answer is quite revealing. In these few verses the homecoming of Jacob is completed. That completion includes many key elements anticipated earlier in the Jacob cycle. The death of Rachel marks the end of one stage in the struggle between Rachel and Leah. The birth of Benjamin completes the roster of twelve sons, but the security of the house is immediately shattered by the firstborn's indiscretion. Finally, at the death of Isaac, when Jacob and Esau stand side by side at his grave, the journey that started with Jacob's deception of his blind father comes to an end. The brevity of the scene prompts two questions: Are the brothers actually reconciled? and, more important, Which of the two brothers will remain in focus as the recipient and conveyor of the covenant blessings?"

Genesis 35:16-29 describes Jacob and his family at an important junction in the progression of redemptive history. The journey to Paddan Aram and back is complete. God has been faithful to the covenant promises made at the time of Jacob's flight (28:16-20), promises that elicited his vow of loyalty to his God (28:20). The promises and the vows have been reaffirmed at Bethel on the way home (35:9-15). As Wenham has noted, the blessing to Jacob is now expanded to include a promise of royal descendants in a manner similar to the promise to Abraham (17:6, 16).[41]

However, neither the promised blessings from God nor the personal response and commitment from Jacob precluded the struggles and hardships that would accompany the unfolding of this history. Soon after Rachel's death, Reuben's sexual aggression shattered the tranquility of the covenant family. Isaac's death, too, was a milestone shrouded in sadness. Yet at his graveside there is the reassurance that, like his father, he was gathered to his people old and full of years. Later, in the land of promise, life would continue to be a constant struggle within Jacob's family.

The life journey of God's people is often stunningly and shockingly infused with pain and brokenness. Hostility, rivalry, selfishness, and death itself repeatedly threaten the peace of all people, including the recipients of God's covenant promises. But the children of God have the assurance that the story does not end with their bro-

---

[41]Wenham, *Genesis 16-50*, 326, 329.

kenness. The journey of Jacob's homecoming, although filled with agonizing human tension, stands as a reminder that God remains faithful to his promise to care for his children while bringing them home.

In later periods of redemptive history, it was possible to look back at these events and make connections with both the suffering and the hope. In Jeremiah 31:15, Rachel is pictured weeping and mourning over her children who were removed from the land of the promise.[42] Despite the anguish of the exile, however, God's covenant promises continued to be transmitted through the heirs of salvation; another homecoming and restoration would follow (31:16-17). Centuries later, the words of Jeremiah 31:15 would take on new meaning as weeping once again was heard in the neighborhood of Bethlehem (Matt. 2:18). That child, who descended to Egypt for refuge, would return to Israel to fulfill the promises of Genesis 35:11-12. It is in the promises of that greatest son of Jacob, the son of God's right hand, that homecoming assumes its deepest comfort. The true shepherd of Israel goes before his people to prepare a place for them in his father's house (John 14:1-4).

[42]Note that prisoners from Jerusalem were detained at Ramah prior to being transported to Babylonia (Jer. 40:1).

David and Nabal: A Paradigm of Temptation and Divine Providence[1]

J. Robert Vannoy

T
he David/Nabal narrative of 1 Samuel 25 is a charming story. It is distinguished by superb characterization and a quickly moving plot. David, the anointed but uncrowned king, is harshly insulted by an unreasonable and churlish man whom he had assisted and defended. David becomes so enraged at the unexpected and unwarranted affront of this rather dimwitted individual (his name is Nabal, which in Hebrew means "fool") that he resolves to kill Nabal and his servants. When Nabal's resourceful and beautiful wife, Abigail, learns of the provocation committed by her husband, she intervenes in the dispute, and with great *élan* convinces David that he should not bring blood guilt on himself by taking revenge on her foolish husband. Upon learning of what his wife has done, Nabal's heart fails, and within ten days he is dead. David sends for Abigail, and she becomes his wife.

This fascinating story is framed by two narratives that describe how David spared the life of the reigning king, Saul, even though Saul was seeking to kill David. The relationship among these three stories in 1 Samuel 24-26 has long intrigued interpreters. The general consensus among biblical scholars has been that the two stories about David sparing Saul's life (1 Sam. 24 and 26) are variant versions of the same incident.[2]

---

[1] It's a delight for me to contribute to this volume in honor of John H. Stek, who has done so much to enhance the understanding of the Bible for students in professional and nonprofessional settings.

[2] H. P. Smith (*The Books of Samuel*, ICC [Edinburgh: T & T Clark, 1912], 216) comments, "We have reason to think, therefore, that we have two versions of the same story. It is natural to suppose that one belongs with each of the two documents which make up the bulk of the narrative already considered. . . . The slight preponderance of probability seems to me to be on the side of the latter representation (chapter 26) as more original." H. W. Hertzberg (*I & II Samuel*, OTL [Philadelphia: Westminster, 1964], 207) commenting on chapter 26 says, "It is evident that this narrative and 22:19-24:22 make use of the same material." P. K. McCarter (*I Samuel*, AB [New York: Doubleday, 1980], 386, 387) comments: "The older source critics tended to regard one [story] as derived from the other . . . in a purely literary way. . . . More recent scholars, working under the impact of the insights of form criticism, have preferred to think of a traditional source common to both accounts which developed in different ways in two locations . . . the interpretation given here . . . stands closer to that of the older literary critics, who seem more persuasive . . ." R. W. Klein (*I Samuel*, WBC [Waco: Word, 1983], 236) says, "It needs to be noticed that the two chapters [24 and 26] are probably alternate memories of one event." K. Koch (*The Growth of the Biblical Tradition* [New York: Charles Scribner's Sons, 1969]) notes (p. 144) that "literary criticism had thought that A and B [chapters 24 and 26] were derived from two individual written sources," but Koch's own view (p. 143) is that these narratives "must be two versions of the same story, both of which developed in oral form quite independently of each other."

At the same time, it has generally been held that there is little or no connection between 1 Samuel 25 and the two stories between which it is placed.[3] This conclusion has tended to isolate 1 Samuel 25 from the flow of its larger narrative context, so that it usually has been interpreted in isolation as well. As a result, this chapter has often not been viewed as contributing significantly to the forward movement of redemptive history reflected in the descriptions of events connected with David's rise to the throne. Because of the strong characterization in the narrative, especially with respect to Abigail, the story has frequently been treated primarily as a character study of Abigail as a model for the ideal traits of the good woman.[4]

1 SAMUEL 25 IN ITS NEAR CONTEXT (1 SAMUEL 24-26)

In more recent times, the relationship of the narratives in 1 Samuel 24-26 has been because of the realization that Old Testament narrative is often characterized by "gapping" or "narrative reticence." That is, questions concerning the motives, causes, and purposes of the actions of individuals within narrative units are usually not stated by the writer. This recognition is particularly important for Hebrew narrative because of its general tendency to avoid "explicit commentary" by which the narrator provides a clear assessment of the significance or purpose of the narrative within the larger composition. It is the duty of the interpreter to fill in these "gaps" in "congruity with the text's own norms."[5]

This interpretive process has given rise to a growing recognition of the importance of the technique of "narrative analogy" for the proper understanding of Old Testament narrative. Narrative analogy is the "oblique commentary" that may be made when a story is compared to other narratives within its larger context.[6] R. P. Gordon[7] has discussed the interrelatedness of 1 Samuel 24, 25, and 26 at some length on the basis of this technique of Hebrew narrative composition. Gordon[8] concludes that the central

[3]K. Koch (Ibid., 137) says that the narrative following chapter 24 which describes Nabal's folly "has nothing to do with it" [that is, with chapter 24]. He also says (p. 138) that the links between chapter 26 and the preceding chapter "are exceedingly loose."

[4]See, e.g., A. Blackwood, *Preaching from Samuel* (Nashville: Abingdon-Cokesbury, 1946), 154-159. Blackwood sees the relationship of 1 Samuel 24, 26 to 1 Samuel 25 as one of contrast. In his view, chapters 24 and 25 display envy, wrath, and attempted murder as exhibited in the behavior of Saul. In contrast to this, he finds chapter 25 to be the depiction of a charming woman "courageously intervening to avert needless bloodshed"(p. 154). Blackwood accordingly develops this theme under the following headings: 1. The sort of man a good woman should not marry (vv. 1-17). 2. The sort of woman a good man should wed (vv. 18-22). 3. How a good woman makes the best of a sorry mess (vv. 23-31). 4. How God blesses the beautiful peacemaker (vv. 32-42).

[5]M. Sternberg, *The Poetics of Biblical Narrative* (Bloomington: Indiana University Press, 1985), 188. See further chapter 6, "Gaps, Ambiguity, and the Reading Process."

[6]R. Alter, "A Literary Approach to the Bible," *Commentary* 60 (1975): 73.

[7]R. P. Gordon, "David's Rise and Saul's Demise," *Tyndale Bulletin* 31 (1980): 37-64.

[8]Ibid., 43.

thesis that emerges from this sort of analysis is that "Saul does not vanish from view in 1 Samuel 25," as might seem to be the case,[9] because Saul "is Nabal's *alter ego*."[10] This insight provides a basis for a close connection between all three narratives. 1 Samuel 24, then, is not disconnected from or unrelated to the two stories that enclose it.

Gordon substantiates this thesis compellingly. While there is neither need nor space to repeat here all the specifics of his study, the following are a few examples of the sorts of things to which Gordon calls attention. In all three stories, a "theological consideration" restrains David from seeking personal advantage through killing an antagonist (Saul or Nabal). Abigail gives elegant expression to this idea when she says to David that he should "not have on his conscience the staggering burden of needless bloodshed or of having avenged himself" (1 Sam. 25:31). In addition, Gordon points out that "psychologically Saul and Nabal are geminate [twins]. They refuse to know, in particular to acknowledge David for what he is, and they are alienated from those about them."[11]

Word repetition, an important feature of narrative analogy, also links chapters 24 to 25 and 25 to 26. Gordon comments that the "beauty of this device is that it enables the narrator to make his point with an absolute economy of words, whether it be to highlight parallelism, contrast, or development across the contextual divide."[12] One example of this occurs in 1 Samuel 26:10 where David rejects Abishai's proposal to kill Saul, saying, "As surely as the Lord lives . . . the Lord himself *will strike him*; either his time will come and he will die, or he will go into battle and perish." When we ask why David is so convinced in chapter 26 that Saul will die as a result of divine judgment, we notice that in chapter 25 the narrator has already told us that "the Lord *smote* Nabal and he died" (v. 38). Both "smote" in 25:38 and "strike" in 26:10 translate נָגַף. The repetition of this word draws a comparison between Saul and Nabal. Gordon suggests that the "manner of Nabal's death provides the key to David's confident assertion of 26:10 and herein . . . lies also a pointer to the whole narrative thrust of 1 Samuel 24-26."[13] These sorts of observations pull chapter 24-26 together into a closely connected narrative sequence.

---

[9]W. L. Humphreys ("The Tragedy of King Saul: A Study of the Structure of 1 Samuel 9-31," *Journal for the Study of the Old Testament* 6 [1978]: 19) alleges that "Saul vanishes from view" in chapter 25.

[10]A. H. Van Zyl (*I Samuël*, Old Testament [Nijkerk: Callenbach, 1989], 97) comments: "Of men de namen geheel moet transponeren (Nabal is Saul) is de vraag, maar dat Nabal een type van Saul is, dus trekken van hem heeft gekregen, staat vast." (Whether the names should be completely transposed [Nabal is Saul] is debatable. But it is clear that Nabal is a type of Saul and as such shares his characteristics.[Translation by editor.])

[11]Gordon, "David's Rise and Saul's Demise," 44.

[12]Ibid., 47.

[13]Ibid., 49.

Another consideration also links these narratives. A prominent theological concept in the entirety of 1 and 2 Samuel is divine sovereignty over all of human history. But this divine governance of human history is often more hidden than overt. The writer sees God at work behind the scenes, as it were, rather than in spectacular interventions such as by vision and miracle. Von Rad[14] comments that the writer

> depicts a succession of occurrences in which the chain of inherent cause and effect is firmly knit up—so firmly indeed that human eye discerns no point at which God could have put in his hand. Yet secretly it is he who has brought all to pass; all the threads are in his hands; his activity embraces the great political events no less than the hidden counsels of human hearts. All human affairs are the sphere of God's providential working.

Note, for example, that when Saul's forces were closing in on David in their effort to capture him, "a messenger came to Saul saying, 'Come quickly! The Philistines are raiding the land.' Then Saul broke off his pursuit of David . . . " (1 Sam. 23:26-28). From the standpoint of the narrator, this can hardly be viewed as coincidence. God was sovereignly ordering events to protect David from Saul. Numerous incidents of this kind impress on the reader the fact that everything that happens in the lives of the individuals described in the book, as well as everything that happens in the national life of Israel, lies within the sphere of God's sovereign control. This concept is one of unifying motifs of 1 Samuel 24-26.

In chapter 24, Saul suddenly and unexpectedly falls into the hands of David while David and his men are hiding in a cave. David's men interpret Saul's appearance as the Lord's providential directive to David to put Saul to death (reading 24:4 as in the NIV text note: "Today the Lord is saying to you, 'I will give your enemy into your hands for you to deal with as you wish.'"). Under temptation to seize power prematurely and deny Saul's royal office, David rose to the challenge, and continued to recognize that he should not kill Saul because he was the "anointed of the Lord." David knew how difficult it is to infallibly interpret God's providence. But he did not let this "opportunity" lead him to sin.[15] Nevertheless, he later says to Saul, "This day you have seen with your own eyes how the Lord delivered you into my hands in the cave. Some urged me to kill you, but I spared you; I said, 'I will not lift my hand against my master,

---

[14]G. Von Rad, "The Beginnings of Historical Writing in Ancient Israel," in *The Problem of the Hexateuch and Other Essays* (London: Oliver & Boyd, 1966), 201.

[15]Hertzberg, (*I & II Samuel*, 196) comments that David "complies with the will of God where it is unmistakably clear. What appears to the others as the will of God seems to him to be a temptation from which God will 'preserve' him."

because he is the Lord's anointed'" (1 Sam. 24:10). David clearly recognized God's hand in his encounter with Saul.

The central focus of chapter 26 is somewhat difficult to specify, even though the plot parallels chapter 24 in its depiction of an opportunity for David to kill Saul. In chapter 24, we find a test of David's leadership. There, the question is whether or not David will seize the throne prematurely. In chapter 26, the focus seems to be on Saul and his followers. The question is whether they will persist in refusing to recognize David as the one whom the Lord has chosen to replace Saul as king. Many related issues surface when chapter 26 is placed in its context in the flow of narratives concerning "David's rise and Saul's demise." Although these are not easily reduced to a single overarching theme, the fact that this is Saul's last chance to repent is prominent. Just as in chapter 24, however, God is providentially at work in the unfolding of events. In chapter 24, David's encounter with Saul just "happened." It is depicted as providential and unexpected. In chapter 26, however, there is an important difference. Here, Abishai's comment ("Today God has delivered your enemy into your hands" [26:8]) is similar to what David's men said in 24:5, but in contrast to chapter 24, David sets up the encounter. David's initiative makes things happen in chapter 26. When we are told that David and Abiathar crept into Saul's camp and took Saul's spear and water jug, the narrator explains that "the Lord had put them [Saul and his three thousand men] into a deep sleep" (26:12). God is at work behind the scenes to assist David in his plan to force Abner and his men to choose between Saul and himself, as well as to challenge Saul to do what is right instead of continuing his vendetta against David.

THE THEME OF 1 SAMUEL 25

This brings us back to chapter 25. On the surface, this chapter describes a conflict between David and the wealthy sheepherder Nabal. But below the surface, it depicts a surprise attack on David by the evil one, the ancient enemy of God's kingdom, an attack that this time is thwarted by a timely admonition from an unexpected source. Not only does an unnamed servant of Nabal "providentially" inform Abigail of impending disaster (25:14), Abigail herself "providentially" intervenes in the quickly developing controversy to avert a serious mistake by David (25:18-35).[16] In fact, this narrative sets forth a paradigm of temptation and divine providence. Built into the narrative is a beautiful portrait of divine providence at work in David's life.

---

[16]Klein (*I Samuel*, 250, 251) comments, "Abigail's actions are the proximate cause for David escaping guilt, but the real protector of the future king's integrity is Yahweh himself . . . . Abigail's journey to David is understood not as a valiant attempt to save her husband, much less an opportunistic attempt to join David's side. Rather, it was part of Yahweh's plan . . . . Once again Abigail's bravery is immediately reinterpreted as flowing from the actions of Yahweh God of Israel."

On another level, this narrative is both parabolic and proleptic. It is parabolic in that the relationship of David and Saul is symbolized by the relationship of David and Nabal.[17] Because of this symbolic connection, the narrative is also proleptic. The outcome of the Nabal incident reassures David about the destiny of his opponent Saul. Through these events, God is speaking to David about his future, telling David that He will eventually take care of Saul just as He has taken care of Nabal. These incidents are set in the larger context of David's rise to the throne and the series of tests through which he must pass before his eventual inauguration as the covenantal king.

If we take a closer look at 1 Samuel 25 under the theme of "A Surprise Attack on David by the Evil One," then we can capture the natural flow of the chapter in four segments: the provocation, the response, the provision, and the resolution.

The Provocation

We will discuss three aspects of the provocation David suffered: Nabal as another Saul (similarity and differences); Nabal's inflammatory provocation; and David's vulnerability at the time of the provocation.

Nabal as Another Saul (Similarity and Differences)

1 Samuel 16-31 contains a series of narratives in which the central focus is the relationship of Saul and David. But 1 Samuel 25 is quite different in character. We may wonder why the narrator would insert this story in this particular place, since it seems to break the narrative flow. Initially, we might be inclined to think that the purpose of the Nabal narrative is to provide a diversion from the "rise of David and demise of Saul" theme of the surrounding narratives. Some reflection, however, suggests that the thread of the Saul-David drama only *appears* to be set aside, because even in this narrative David is confronted with "Saul."

The verbal echoes between the three narratives of 1 Samuel 24-26 indicate that the stories are closely connected. Chapters 24 and 26 show David at his best when he spares Saul's life on two different occasions. But here, between these two narratives, David narrowly escapes a terrible failure. As we have already indicated, the story of David's encounter with Nabal has something of the character of a parable. Nabal is for David a "disguised Saul." He is a Saul whom David does not recognize, and by whom he is almost defeated.[18]

Up to this point, the evil one has been unsuccessful in pressuring David to lose his patience in his relationship with Saul. David demonstrated enormous self control when

---

[17]See H. DeJong, *De Twee Messiassen* (Kampen: Kok, 1978), 183. This volume by DeJong contains thirty-one sermons on the book of 1 Samuel, one sermon per chapter. DeJong offers many helpful insights into the homiletic use of the narratives of 1 Samuel.

[18]Ibid., 183.

he cut just a small piece from Saul's robe in the cave in En Gedi (ch. 24). But now the evil one tries a different approach. He arranges a meeting between David and Nabal in order to defeat David by a surprise attack from an entirely different direction. Here the connection between the stories of Nabal and Saul consists in the great injustice done to David, in the one instance by Saul, and in the other by Nabal. In both incidents, David must wait for justice from the hand of the Lord.[19] In the case of Saul, David understands this (1 Sam 24:12), but in the case with Nabal, he nearly takes matters into his own hands.

Nabal's fate demonstrates that David does not need to take things into his own hands, because Yahweh will intervene and cause justice to prevail. At the end of the chapter, Nabal dies, stricken by God's own hand. David's sword, which he was so ready to use (1 Sam 25:13), was not necessary to bring this about. From this incident David could infer that the Lord would do the same thing in the case of Saul. In this respect the Nabal story mirrors the Saul stories by the correspondence between the Nabal-David relationship and the Saul-David relationship. The former fulfills the function of a parable of the latter.

But there are also differences in the two stories. For one thing, there is an enormous difference in duration.[20] The Saul-David story occupies several chapters, while the Nabal story is found in a single (though lengthy) chapter. In other words, the Nabal story develops quickly in contrast to the drawn-out relationship between Saul and David. The Nabal story depicts a surprise attack on David by the evil one. It is an attempt to catch him unawares and to place a blemish on his kingship. David has very little time to reflect on his response to Nabal's outrageous behavior because his verbal assault was unexpected and required an immediate response.

McCarter points out a closely related difference between the two stories. In this story, in contrast to those of chapters 24 and 26, David's "first impulse is a violent one that must be curbed; he does not exhibit the necessary restraint spontaneously, as in the cave at En Gedi or the encampment on the hill of Hachilah, but *learns* it in the course of events."[21] By the standard's of God's kingdom, David's initial response to Nabal's provocation was not right.

Why is all this significant? It is significant because redemptive historical issues are at stake. Christ will be born from the house of David.[22] The angel Gabriel said at the announcement of the birth of Christ, "I shall give him the throne of his father David."

---

[19]De Jong, *De Twee Messiassen*, 183.

[20]Ibid., 184.

[21]McCarter, *I Samuel*, 401.

[22]De Jong, *De Twee Messiassen*, 184.

What sort of throne would the throne of David be? How could a throne blemished with blood guilt point forward to the throne of Christ, of whom it is written that "surely the justice due to me is with the Lord, and my reward with my God" (Isa. 49:4, NASB). How could a throne blemished by blood guilt anticipate the throne of the One of whom it is also written, "When they hurled their insults at him, he did not retaliate; when he suffered, he made no threats. Instead he entrusted himself to him who judges justly" (1 Pet. 2:23, NIV).

In Christ we see the true covenantal kingship revealed in all its fullness. In 1 Samuel 25 the evil one attempts to turn David away from this covenantal ideal. The evil one wants a king who takes justice into his own hands. So what the evil one had been unable to accomplish in David's relationship with Saul, he now seeks to accomplish in David's unexpected encounter with Nabal.[23]

Nabal's Inflammatory Provocation

Saul is a complex and mysterious figure. We are often not certain just how to evaluate him. His conduct is unstable and unpredictable. But Nabal is different. His ungodliness is clearly visible and recognized by all who know him, so that he is called Nabal. 1 Samuel 25:25 tells us he is just like his name (probably a nickname), which means "fool." He likes to parade his wealth for all to see. He holds a banquet "like that of a king" (25:36; one of the verbal echoes of the Saul narratives). It is certainly significant to notice the way in which the narrator introduces him in 25:2, 3.

> A certain man in Maon, who had property there at Carmel, was very wealthy. He had a thousand goats and three thousand sheep, which he was shearing in Carmel. His name was Nabal and his wife's name was Abigail. She was an intelligent and beautiful woman, but her husband, a Calebite, was surly and mean in his dealings.

Notice that his name is not given until after the description of his wealth. If you ask who Nabal is, then his riches come even before his name. In addition to his foolishness he knows no restraint. He is described as surly and mean. His diatribe against David (25:10, 11) is the means by which the evil one attempts to provoke David to anger so that he might strike back in an inappropriate manner. So Nabal's provocation is clearly inflammatory.

David's Vulnerability at the Time of the Provocation

On earlier occasions, David had received help from Samuel in sorting out his relationship with Saul. When David fled from Saul in 1 Samuel 19 he sought refuge with

---

[23]De Jong, *De Twee Messiassen*, 185.

Samuel in Naioth at Ramah. On that occasion, David and Samuel undoubtedly discussed Saul a great deal: "When David had fled and made his escape, he went to Samuel at Ramah and told him all that Saul had done to him. Then he and Samuel went to Naioth and stayed there" (1 Sam. 19:18). But this story begins with the announcement of Samuel's death (25:1). David must now make his decisions without Samuel's counsel. The death notice at the beginning of this chapter is not just a piece of irrelevant information, loosely attached to the beginning of the narrative.[24] Instead, it tells us that David is now particularly vulnerable because he has lost his most important counselor. The evil one has coordinated his attack on David at a point when he is especially susceptible to defeat. Within God's providence, this occurs to test whether David is the sort of messianic king who takes justice into his own hands, or whether he will wait upon the Lord.

The Response

David's response is precisely what might be expected. David is enraged at the insulting behavior of this arrogant man. He does what most of us would do when severely provoked—he responds in kind. In essence he says, If you want to act like that it will be the last time you treat somebody this way. He says to his men: "'Put on your swords!' So they put on their swords, and David put on his sword. About four hundred men went up with David, while two hundred stayed with the supplies" (25:13). The threefold repetition of the word "sword" (חֶרֶב) in this verse is significant. Hebrew narrative uses such repetitions to draw our attention to a particular feature of the story. David also swears, "May God deal with David, be it ever so severely, if by morning I leave alive one male of all who belong to him!" (25:22).

In this connection we encounter another expression, also highlighted by its threefold repetition, namely "delivering oneself by one's own hand" (יָשַׁע.יָד) which is translated as "avenging yourself/himself/myself" (NIV, vv. 26, 31, 33). J. F. A. Sawyer[25] understands this idiom as "taking the law into one's own hands." The NASB also translates the expression as "avenging yourself with your own hands." The NRSV speaks of "taking vengeance" with your own hand.

David's response to Nabal's insult was revenge. His intent was to take the law into his own hands in vindictive retaliation. Notice how sharply this contrasts with David's

---

[24]De Jong, *De Twee Messiassen*, 186.

[25]J. F. A. Sawyer (יָשַׁע, *TDOT*, Vol. 6 [Grand Rapids: Eerdmans, 1990], 454) comments, "The *locus classicus* of this usage is 1 S. 25:23-35, where the point at issue is whether David will accept Abigail's offer of reparation or 'take the law into his own hands' . . . and punish her husband by the sword."

response to the opportunity given him in chapter 24 to take Saul's life. On that occasion he said (24:12), "May the Lord judge between you and me. And may the Lord avenge (נָקַם) the wrongs you have done to me, but my hand will not touch you."

The Provision

In the midst of this temptation, however, the Lord provides David with a way of escape. That way of escape comes through the counsel of Abigail, Nabal's wife.[26] Abigail acts, not because she sees herself in any danger (which may well have been true, cf. 25:34), but because she sees David endangering himself. Her action seems to be born of personal faith in the promises to David (cf. 25:28-31). Abigail speaks here with the insight and authority of a prophetess concerning David's future (an echo of Hannah's prophetic insight in chapter 2). She completely understands David's reaction to Nabal, because she is Nabal's wife; what David is experiencing she has undoubtedly experienced many times over. So she prepares a gift and goes out to meet David in order to urge him not to blemish his reputation. What she says to David amounts to this, "David, you will become king someday, and in your kingship you must act in ways appropriate to the true covenantal king. You must not blemish yourself with blood guilt." In essence she says to David, "My dear brothers, take note of this: Everyone should be quick to listen, slow to speak and slow to become angry, for man's anger does not bring about the righteous life that God desires" (James 1:19-20). In contrast to David's reaction to Nabal's provocation, the true covenantal king must wait on the Lord, because the true covenantal King must lead God's people in waiting on the Lord.

This is not to say that the true covenantal king sits around and does nothing, expecting the Lord to act on his behalf. Notice that Abigail also says that David is one who fights the "battles of the Lord" (25:28). But he should fight the Lord's battles in a way that demonstrates that even in fighting he waits on the Lord.[27] The encounter with Nabal is not a "battle of the Lord." It is a personal affront, provoking David to personal revenge. Abigail is God's providential provision of escape from a serious temptation. And it is here, in connection with this providential provision, that we encounter another of the threefold verbal repetitions in the narrative. Both Abigail (25:26) and David (25:34, 39) say that the Lord "kept" (מָנַע, three times) David from doing wrong in his encounter with Nabal. This is because it is Yahweh who has sent (שָׁלַח) Abigail (25:32).

---

[26]Hertzberg (*I & II Samuel*, 203) comments, " . . . she is an instrument of the Lord to keep the future king's escutcheon clean for David." He comments further (Ibid., 204), "Through Abigail, the Lord saves David from a danger different from that in the cave with Saul, but none the less great. It consists, as has been said, in the possibility that David may take matters into his own hands and thus make himself master of his fate, instead of letting it be guided by the Lord."

[27]De Jong, *De Twee Messiassen*, 187.

The Resolution

Perhaps the most surprising aspect of this story is that David listens to Abigail. Here is a powerful person who has been seriously provoked, and who is livid with anger, yet he listens to Abigail's voice of reason. David, in fact, thanks Abigail profusely, and praises both her and God for sending her to him (בָּרַךְ, four times, 25:32, 39). David acknowledges his sin, he accepts Abigail's counsel, and he praises God for his providential leading.

1 Samuel 25 and the Church

What does the story of David and Nabal have to do with us? I suggest that this narrative calls our attention to two things.[28]

First, in its redemptive historical context, this narrative points forward to Christ. The standards kingship in Israel recognized here foreshadow and anticipate the character of the true covenantal king to come.

---

[28]The following suggestions for finding meaning for today from this Old Testament narrative are an attempt to elucidate the redemptive historical significance of this narrative in its Old Testament setting, as well as to find in it some guidance for responsible Christian living today. This raises important methodological issues, which use David's response to God's providential provision for deliverance from temptation as a model or example for our lives today. Bryan Chapell (*Christ Centered Preaching* [Baker, 1994], 281-286) warns against what he terms the "Deadly Be's" in sermonizing. He does this because this type of preaching often makes human effort "the measure and cause of godliness." This is not to say, however, that all "be messages" are wrong. Chapell comments, "There are many 'be' messages in Scripture, but they always reside in a redemptive context. Since we cannot be anything that God would approve apart from his sanctifying power, the source of that grace must permeate any exhortation for biblical behavior. 'Be' messages are not wrong in themselves; they are wrong messages *by* themselves. People cannot do or be what God requires without the work of Christ in, for, and through them. Simply railing at error and hammering at piety may convince others of their inadequacy or callous them into self-sufficiency, but these messages also keep true godliness remote. Thus, instruction in biblical behavior barren of redemptive truth only wounds, and though it is offered as an antidote to sin such preaching either promotes pharisaism or promotes despair. Christ-centered preaching accepts neither alternative (p. 285)." In "Redemptive History and Preaching" (*Pro Rege* 19/2 [1990]: 14), Sidney Greidanus notes that one of the shortcoming of redemptive-historical preaching is that it "seems to shortchange the human characters in the preaching-text." He comments, "Granted that the Bible as a whole is theocentric, it will not do to ignore its human characters in the interest of doing justice to its theocentricity" (p. 14). He then makes some insightful comments on the function of biblical characters in redemptive history and suggests (p. 14) that in finding meaning for today, biblical characters must not be isolated "from the kingdom history of which they are an integral part." Greidanus also speaks of finding in certain biblical characters "models for self-recognition." For example, Israel saw itself portrayed in the biblical narratives about Abraham, Isaac, and Jacob. Greidanus comments: "What God did for these patriarchs, he did for his people Israel. Thus Israel learned about its identity as God's covenant people—saved by grace—and about its obligation to keep the covenant. Since there is but one covenant of grace and one kingdom history, even today God's people may use these patriarchal narratives for learning their identity and obligation—provided, of course, that we take into account that we today live at a later stage of kingdom history (p. 14). Greidanus goes on to say that "it must be admitted that these 'models for self-recognition' may open the door again to example preaching with all its attendant drawbacks. Note, however, that the biblical models for self-recognition are quite different from the models for morality in example preaching. Models for self-recognition are not isolated from their biblical context, but are meaningful precisely in that context. They are not dismembered into a few elements that may transfer to individuals today, but function holistically. Also, they are relatively few in number and are entirely dependent on the intention of the author. Finally, models for self-recognition do not undermine the theocentric nature of Scripture or of the sermon, for they are models for the church of all ages precisely in their covenant relationship with God (p. 15)."

Second, this narrative calls our attention to some important truths for our own walk before God. Let me suggest several of these.

- Satan is at work in our lives just as he was in David's to lead us astray from the will of the Lord. Paul speaks of his schemes (2 Cor. 2:11), and Peter describes him as a roaring lion seeking whom he may devour (1 Pet. 5:8).

- In this narrative and today, Satan attempts to take God's people by surprise. He attacks us at our weakest points, when we least suspect his activity. We must always be on our guard.

- When we are mistreated by those around us, our response must be governed by waiting upon the Lord rather than by taking things into our own hands. Paul says, "Do not repay anyone evil for evil. Be careful to do what is right in the eyes of everybody. If it is possible, as far as it depends on you, live at peace with everyone. Do not take revenge, my friends, but leave room for God's wrath, for it is written: 'It is mine to avenge; I will repay,' says the Lord" (Rom. 12:17-19).

- In his providential governance of everything that happens in our lives, God always provides a way of escape for his people when they are tempted by Satan: "No temptation has seized you except what is common to man. And God is faithful; he will not let you be tempted beyond what you can bear. But when you are tempted, he will also provide a way out so that you can stand up under it" (1 Cor. 10:13). This story gives us a paradigm of temptation and divine providence.

- It is our responsibility to respond to God's gracious provision of a way to escape with acceptance and thanksgiving.

These are the truths that are highlighted by the verbal repetitions noted in the chapter: sword, vengeance, providence, and praise. Praise God for his marvelous grace!

The following suggestions for application of the David/Nabal narrative are an attempt to find contemporary significance from this Old Testament historical narrative in congruity with the underlying abiding truths of kingdom history that span the temporal gap from the biblical period to the present.

2 Kings 5 in the Pulpit: One Leper or Two?

Arie C. Leder

An abiding problem for those preaching Old Testament narrative is the length of the preaching units. Seldom do only a few verses form the basis of a sermon; often the narrative at hand is one or more chapters long. Respect for a narrative's definition of its own limits is a lesson John H. Stek taught and illustrated in the classroom, in reflecting on preaching the Old Testament, and in his preaching of such narrative texts.

2 Kings 5 is a very long text. Sermons on this passage address various themes. One calls attention to the faithful testimony of the young captive girl from Israel, another focuses on the inclusion of Gentiles, still others on Naaman's pride or Gehazi's avarice. This variety raises the question of the central concern of the text, which turns on the character with whom the audience is urged to identify. Textual bases for sermons also vary: 2 Kings 5:1-19a, or a smaller portion thereof, is the favorite; 2 Kings 5:19b-27 runs a close second. Often the entire chapter is read but the sermon deals with only one aspect of it. The new common lectionary lists 2 Kings 5:1-14 and 1-15ab as accompanying readings for the gospel.[1] Commentaries divide 2 Kings 5 into three subsections: 1-14, 15-19, and 20-27.[2] This variety raises the question of the best delimitation of the preaching unit.[3] In this essay I will ask and answer the question: What is the best preaching unit? Is the text about the little girl, or is it about Elisha, Naaman, or Gehazi? With whom should the audience identify?

---

[1] The sermon catalogue at the library of Calvin Theological Seminary lists at least 138 entries. Of these, 112 are based on verses 1-19a, 15 on verses 19b-27, and 11 on the entire chapter. For lectionary treatment of 2 Kings 5:1-14 see *Preaching the New Common Lectionary. Year B. Revised and Enlarged Edition. Advent, Christmas, Epiphany*, eds. Fred B. Craddock, et. al. (Nashville: Abingdon, 1984), 152-161. For 2 Kings 5:1-15ab see *Preaching the New Common Lectionary. Year C. After Pentecost.* Commentary by Fred B. Craddock, et. al. (Nashville: Abingdon, 1986), 96-104.

[2] See for example, Walter Brueggemann, *2 Kings*, Knox Preaching Guides, ed. John H. Hayes (Atlanta: John Knox, 1982), 20-22; John Gray, *I & II Kings. A Commentary*, 2nd ed. (Philadelphia: Westminster, 1970), 502-510; T. R. Hobbs, *2 Kings*. Word Biblical Commentary (Waco: Word, 1985), 55-69; Paul R. House, *1, 2 Kings*. The New American Commentary (Nashville: Broadman, 1995), 269-274; Burke O. Long, *2 Kings*. The Forms of the Old Testament Literature. Volume X (Grand Rapids: Eerdmans, 1991), 66-79; Richard D. Nelson, *First and Second Kings. Interpretation. A Bible Commentary for Teaching and Preaching* (Atlanta: John Knox, 1987), 176-183; Howard F. Vos, *1, 2 Kings*, Bible Study Commentary (Grand Rapids: Zondervan, 1989), 150-153. See also Gerhard von Rad, *Biblical Interpretations in Preaching*, trans. John E. Steely (Nashville: Abingdon, 1977), 60-64.

[3] For a useful discussion of a preaching unit see Sidney Greidanus, *The Modern Preacher and the Ancient Text* (Grand Rapids: Eerdmans, 1988), 126-128, 221-222.

APPROACHING THE TEXT

2 Kings 5 belongs to a larger complex of prophetic narrative that begins with Israel's entry into the land under Joshua's leadership and ends with Judah's removal from the land. They are exiled from the presence of God (2 Kings 17:23; 24:3, 20; cf. Gen. 3:23) because the people and their kings have disobeyed the Lord. Within this larger narrative, Kings interprets the post-Davidic kingship in the light of the Lord's promises to David to show "how that promise was aborted through the unfaithfulness of kings and people—in spite of the Lord's long-suffering mercies, stern warnings and patient wooing."[4]

At the structural center of Kings,[5] the account of the Omride dynasty features Ahab's destructive devotion to the popular Baal religion (1 Kings 16:29-34).[6] By serving and worshiping the Lord with images from the local cults, a process begun by Jeroboam (1 Kings 13), Ahab led Israel in a vigorous baalization of the faith for which he and his descendants were cursed (1 Kings 21:20-26). Within this narrative of apostasy, rebellion, and immorality are stories about the prophet Elisha who works deeds of deliverance, blessing, and healing among the remnant of God's people.[7] Within the larger narrative about the covenant leadership of the Omride dynasty, these stories accentuate Israel's failed monarchy and point to her true leader, the prophet. This also explains a unique feature of the Elisha stories: the kings do not figure prominently in them. Their absence or impotence (2 Kings 5:7) provides a foil for Israel's true leader, Elisha. Like his master Elijah, Elisha is described with the exclamation: "My father! My father! The chariots and horsemen of Israel!" (2 Kings 2:12; 13:14). And, like his master, Elisha is "the true leader of Israel—Israel's real defender against foreign oppression—not the king."[8] Among the Elisha stories, 2 Kings 5 forms part of the larger prophetic critique of Israel's (and especially her kings') disloyalty to the God of Israel.

---

[4]John H. Stek, *The Former Prophets*, A Syllabus (Unpublished. Grand Rapids: Calvin Theological Seminary, 1997), 104.

[5]So George Savran, "1 and 2 Kings," in *The Literary Guide to the Bible*, eds. Robert Alter and Frank Kermode (Cambridge: Harvard University Press, 1987), 148. Savran argues that 1 Kings 16:23-2 Kings 12 comprises this narrative. The segmentation varies. For example, 1 Kings 16:21-2 Kings 15:12 (Stek, *The Former Prophets*, 106), 1 Kings 17:1-2 Kings 8:15 (Nelson, *First and Second Kings*, 107), 1 Kings 17:1-2 Kings 11:20 (Brueggemann, *2 Kings*, 7).

[6]For a reflective study of the conflict between Elijah and Ahab in 1 Kings 16:34-19:21 see M. B. Van't Veer, *My God Is Yahweh: Elijah and Ahab in an Age of Apostasy*, trans. Theodore Plantinga (St. Catharines: Paideia, 1980).

[7]Stek, *The Former Prophets*, 95.

[8]Ibid., 93. See also Nelson, *First and Second Kings*, 162, where he writes that "the prophet is the focus of Yahweh's word and, as the bearer of this word, is the defender of Israel, whether actually engaged in war (Elisha) or not (Elijah)."

HEARING THE TEXT: A CLOSE READING OF 2 KINGS 5

Now we will consider the important literary aspects of the text with a view to understanding its frame, development, keywords, and structure.

The Frame: From One Leper to Another

2 Kings 5 is a story about leprosy (צָרַע "to be leprous," verb: 5:1, 11, 27; noun: 5:3, 6, 7, 27). All its characters are affected by the disease. Naaman has leprosy, the Hebrew maiden's hopeful comment directs Naaman to the prophet for cleansing from it, Israel's king refuses to get involved in this cleansing, Elisha prescribes the means of cleansing, Naaman rejects the prophet's word for his cleansing, his servants urge him to follow the prescription for cleansing, Naaman responds gratefully for his cleansing, Gehazi profits from Naaman's cleansing, and Elisha judges Gehazi, who becomes a leper. Naaman and Gehazi frame the narrative as complementary opposites. Moreover, the disease from which Naaman seeks release (אָסַף, "to remove" 5:6, 7, 11) now clings (דָּבַק, 5:27) to Gehazi. 2 Kings 5 takes the reader from a suffering Gentile, who is cleansed from leprosy and made whole (שָׁלוֹם, 5:19), to an Israelite who, with his descendants, suffers defilement with leprosy in perpetuity. The narrative moves from one leper to another. This frame and the connection with leprosy throughout unify 2 Kings 5. Thus the entire chapter should be considered the correct preaching unit.[9]

The Development of the Story: Plot and Character

Complications mar the narrative journey from one leper to the other. From Naaman's point of view, the problem is resolved in the last clause[10] of v. 14: "and his flesh was restored like that of a young boy and he became clean." To reach this point he had to overcome three obstacles. Upon learning from the young Israelite girl that standing "before the prophet" (5:3) would rid him of his leprosy, Naaman travels to Israel and visits the Israelite king, as instructed by his own king. But the king of Israel loudly denies he can heal, questions Naaman's status, and suspects an Aramean plot. He doesn't send Naaman to the prophet; Israel's king is ignorant of the prophet. Elisha solves this first obstacle. When he hears about Naaman's predicament, he urges him to come visit so "that he will know that there is a prophet in Israel" (5:8).

When he arrives at Elisha's house, Naaman has to stand at the door until a mere messenger greets him with Elisha's instructions for his cleansing. This creates a

---

[9]John Gray, *I & II Kings*, Old Testament Library, 3rd edit. (London: SCM Press, 1977), 502; Brueggemann, *2 Kings*, 20; Long, *2 Kings*, 67.

[10]The NIV translation places the prepositional phrase "like a young boy" at the end. In the Hebrew the clause "and he became clean" comes last.

second obstacle: Naaman is humiliated and furious. He expected the prophet to perform magic on the spot, and washing in the lowly Jordan cannot compare with the rivers of Damascus.[11] Only his servants' pleas move him to wash in the Jordan seven times, "according to the word of the man of God" (5:14). And so he was healed.

Naaman returns to Elisha to acknowledge God's power (5:15, cf. v. 8). To show his gratitude he urges gifts upon Elisha, who refuses them. Naaman's status as a new creature causes another obstacle: the worship of the other gods.[12] He takes along some earth from the land of Israel. He also petitions Elisha about taking his master into the temple of Rimmon (5:18). He describes himself as a willing servant of Elisha four times (cf. 5:15); he is eager to maintain his status. Elisha appears to grant his request and dismisses him in peace. But on his way home a fourth obstacle interrupts Naaman's peace: Gehazi's deceitful request for gifts in Elisha's name. Why complicate the narrative with these obstacles?[13]

Whereas the first three narrative complications develop the relationship between Naaman and Elisha, the fourth begins to develop the relationship between Elisha and his servant Gehazi. The Gentile Naaman had been angry with Elisha's instructions but, having submitted to him, he leaves his presence wholly clean and in peace (5:15, 19a). The text signals this conversion with the phrase "and his flesh was restored . . . like that of a young boy." Gehazi, the Israelite servant of Elisha (5:25), refuses to submit to the prophet's judgment about the gifts and goes his own way, only to leave Elisha's presence a leper (5:27).

This contrast between Naaman's actions in 5:15-19a and Gehazi's in 5:19b-27 suggests that 5:15-19a functions as a transitional unit. It brings the Naaman story to an unexpected closure—a Gentile's gratitude and his concern for proper worship of the Lord. It also forms the basis of the subsequent action and its own surprising conclusion: an Israelite's infection with leprosy. With the Gehazi story, beginning in 5:20, the account begun with Naaman is no longer one about the conversion of a Gentile. Now it is the story of Israel's "conversion." The unclean becomes clean, and the clean unclean.

Two things occasion this terrible conversion: Gehazi's deceitful request for gifts and his attitude toward the prophet. Unlike Naaman (5:15), Gehazi does not acknowledge Elisha as the bearer of God's Word. He treats him as an incompetent businessman who

---

[11] A painful and ironic mirror which reflects Israel's seeking help from "the rivers of Damascus," i.e. treaties with foreign kings, looking to the local religions to solve their religious needs.

[12] See p. 104 for more on the phrase "other gods."

[13] Commentators suggest that the Gehazi story at one time circulated separately. This may lead one to the exegetical conclusion that the Naaman and Gehazi pericopes ought to be treated separately. Most commentators, however, argue that the entire chapter is a unit. The frame of "one leper to another" bears this out.

fails to recognize a good deal (5:20). But it is Gehazi himself who fails to recognize the good in Naaman's conversion: he calls him "this Aramean" (5:20). Like Israel's king, Gehazi does not know "that there is a God in Israel" and that Elisha is his chosen servant. The first and the last people Naaman encounters in Israel (the king and Gehazi) are blind to this reality. Ironically, the Gentile, Naaman, is favored by God (5:1) and speaks words that should freely flow from Israel's lips (5:15, 17a), but the two Israelites behave like Gentiles who do not know God. The only Israelite other than Elisha who guides Naaman to the truth is the little girl who dwells in lonely exile.

The narrator of 2 Kings 5 leads the audience from Naaman the Gentile leper, through four complications, to the terrible "conversion" of Gehazi. For the Israelite audience, the first three complications present obstacles to the Gentile's healing. They might initially enjoy Naaman's frustrations, but the obstacles' resolution inevitably draws the audience to consider his cleansing, his confession, and his petition. This narrative strategy also draws the audience to Elisha. Once they are in his narrative presence, the fourth complication introduces the real conflict of this narrative: Gehazi versus Elisha. Israel beholds herself represented in the attitudes and conduct of Gehazi.

The plot of this narrative, centering on the terrible "conversion" of the clean to the unclean, is carefully dramatized with three named and *full-fledged* characters: Naaman, Elisha, and Gehazi. They are accompanied by the captive Israelite maid, the king, Elijah's messenger, and Naaman's servants, crucial agents[14] who move Naaman towards Elisha. Of these the young captive provides a critical contrast to the king and Gehazi. She stands out for what she knew and told in exile; the king and Gehazi for their folly, ignorance, and deceit in the land where the prophet lived. However, at end of the narrative only one contrast stands out—the contrast between the converted cleansed Gentile Naaman and the "converted" unclean Israelite Gehazi.

Keywords and Phrases

Several clusters of keywords and phrases support the above description of plot and character, and can help us consider the structure of 2 Kings 5.

The keyword "leprosy" has been discussed above. A second keyword, the verb "to give" (נָתַן), introduces the theme of giving and gifts. In 5:1 it tells the audience that the Lord gave Aram victory through Naaman; later Naaman asks for a gift (יֻתַּן) of soil in order to worship the Lord who has cleansed him (5:17). When Gehazi requests a part of the gift Elisha refused, Naaman gives it to two servants who carry it for Gehazi (5:22,

---

[14]See Adele Berlin, *Poetics and Interpretation of Biblical Narrative* (Sheffield: The Almond Press, 1983), 23, 32 for a definition of *full-fledged* and *agent*.

23). But the gift is spoiled by Gehazi's leprosy. The irony of a gift that cannot be enjoyed is emphasized by the verb "to take" (לְקַח, 5:15-16, 20, 23, 24, 26).[15] What Naaman urges Elisha to take and is refused (5:15-16) Gehazi asks for and takes (5:26, cf. Elisha's speech).

The phrases "young maid/young man" are also repeated several times. We read that a young Hebrew girl (נַעֲרָה קְטַנָּה, 5:2, 4) wishes Naaman could see the prophet in Samaria. After Naaman bathes in the Jordan, "his flesh was restored to that of a young boy" (נַעַר קָטֹן, 5:14). This repetition of phrases links the captive Hebrew maiden with her Gentile master and highlights Naaman's change of status: he begins anew with the body of a young boy. He is no longer one Gentile among many. Now he belongs to those Gentiles such as Jethro and Rahab who acknowledge the true God. He is a changed man, a convert! His testimony is clear: "Now I know that there is no God in all the world except in Israel" (5:15). But the young man (נַעַר, 5:20) Gehazi does not acknowledge Naaman's change of status: he calls Naaman "this Aramean" (5:20). When Naaman asks him if everything is all right (שָׁלוֹם, 5:21) Gehazi says it is (שָׁלוֹם, 5:22), but then he disturbs the peace by claiming that Elisha's visitors, two young men (נְעָרִים, 5:22), need money and clothing. Naaman's two servants (נְעָרָיו, 5:23) carry the gifts ahead of Gehazi. The repetition of נַעֲרָה-נַעַר unifies the story, develops a contrast and tension among the characters, and takes the reader to Elisha's devastating speech in 5:26. Gehazi also becomes a changed man!

Several word clusters appear almost exclusively in 5:1-14: "to turn" (5:10, 14 [שָׁבָה, 5:2]), "to be clean" (5:10, 12, 13, 14), and "to remove" (5:6-7, 11). The noun "leprosy," as it describes Naaman's condition, occurs in 5:1, 3, 6-7, 11; it occurs in 5:27 with respect to Gehazi. The occurrence of "to return" in 5:15 ("and he returned to the man of God") forms a literary hinge with the verb in 5:14. After the introduction (5:1), the narrative moves from the capture (וַיִּשְׁבּוּ, 5:2) of the young Hebrew girl (נַעֲרָה קְטַנָּה), to her wish that her master travel to Samaria to be cured, and then to Naaman's flesh becoming (וַיָּשָׁב, 5:14) like that of a young boy (נַעַר קָטֹן). So Naaman becomes clean (וַיִּטְהָר).

The verb "to turn back, return" (שׁוּב) in 5:14 performs a double function: with "to take captive" (שָׁבָה) in 5:2 it forms a frame, and it constitutes the fulfillment of the prophetic word in 5:10 (וְיָשֹׁב). Naaman's cleansing is the climax of this scene. It will allow him into the presence of God, i.e. the prophet. Other word clusters are found in 5:15-27: "as surely as the Lord lives" (5:16, 20), "peace" (5:19, 21, 22), "your servant" (5:15, 17², 18², 25 ["his servants," 5:13]), and "to take." These repetitions form part of

---

[15]It also occurs in 5:5 where it anticipates its dynamic use in scene two, 2 Kings 5:15-27.

a narrative action framed by the verb "to stand" (עָמַד, 5:15, 16, 25 [cf. 5:9]). This verb consistently depicts Naaman and Gehazi in the presence of Elisha. In Elisha's presence Naaman declares himself to be "your servant" and the words ring true; in contrast, Gehazi's "your servant" sounds hypocritical. Similarly, the verb "to take" contrasts Naaman and Gehazi in the presence of Elisha. Finally, in contrast to Elisha, the phrases "as the Lord lives" and "all is well" sound hollow when Gehazi speaks them.

These repetitions support the contrasts and inversions detected in the development and also suggest the presence of two subunits: 5:1-14 and 5:15-27.

Structure

Further examination confirms the presence of two scenes. Scene 1 introduces and resolves the problem of Naaman's leprosy; it moves from a valiant but leprous soldier to a cleansed young man. At the climax of this scene, the phrase "according to the word of the man of God" (כִּדְבַר אִישׁ הָאֱלֹהִים, 5:14) emphasizes Naaman's submission to Elisha. The cluster of words unique to its narrative interests and an inner frame constructed by the verbs "to take captive" (שָׁבָה, 5:2) and "to return" (שׁוּב, 5:14) further support the unity of this scene.

Scene 2 opens with the cleansed Naaman returning to Elisha's presence and ends with the leprous Gehazi moving away from the prophet's presence ("He went back . . . and stood before him," וַיָּשָׁב . . . וַיַּעֲמֹד לְפָנָיו in 5:15 with "Then he left his presence a leper," וַיֵּצֵא מִלְּפָנָיו מְצֹרָע in 5:27). In this scene the dynamics turn on the contrast between Naaman's desire to give Elisha a blessing, the consequence[16] of his confession that only in Israel is God to be found, and Gehazi's greedy abuse of the blessing as expressed in Elisha's rebuke in 5:26. The tension between Naaman and Elisha, resolved with Elisha's word of peace, becomes unresolved tension between Gehazi and Elisha. The unity of the scene is also supported by the repetition of words and phrases common to the narrative interest of this scene.

I have suggested that 2 Kings 5 is composed of two scenes—verses 1-14 and verses 15-27. But what about 5:15-19? Do these verses not constitute a separate unit? Or are 5:1-19 and 5:20-27 the proper subunits, each focusing on one specific person: Naaman and Gehazi? How would such changes affect the reading of the text? The verbs "to return" (וַיָּשָׁב) and "to walk" (וַיֵּלֶךְ) in verses 15 and 19 signal Naaman's movement to and from Elisha's presence. They enclose the intervening verses so that they form a separate, transitional scene, as suggested above.[17] Such a reading would produce the following chiastic structure:

---

[16]The adverb עַתָּה introduces a conclusion.

[17]Klaus Koch, *The Growth of the Biblical Tradition*, trans. S. M. Cupitt (New York: Charles Scribner's Sons, 1969), 116. Exodus 18 is similarly enclosed by Jethro's movement to the Israelite encampment and his movement away from it.

A. Naaman's leprosy healed (1-14)

B. Naaman's confession and request and Elisha's response of peace (15-19)

A¹. Gehazi receives Naaman's leprosy (20-27)

In this configuration, 5:15-19 would represent the outcome of Naaman's healing (1-14) and the basis for Gehazi's subsequent response. However, 5:15-19 can also be read as the climax of the Naaman story, for it includes his confession, his desire to give Elisha a blessing, and his request for peculiar worship practices. Then 5:20-27 focuses exclusively on Gehazi.

Several other factors compel a reading of the narrative in the two scenes as defined above. First of all, both scenes begin with Naaman in the presence of an important person—his Syrian master (5:1) and Elisha (5:15). On his first approach to Elisha, however, Naaman does not enter his presence; he stands at his door (וַיַּעֲמֹד פֶּתַח, 5:9). He enters "in his presence" (וַיַּעֲמֹד לְפָנָיו, 5:15) only in scene 2. Why the difference? Naaman may enter Elisha's presence because he has been cleansed from his leprosy. Later in scene 2 Gehazi not only stands next to Elisha (וַיַּעֲמֹד אֶל־אֲדֹנָיו, 5:25, a contrast with Naaman's submissive standing before Elisha,[18]) but he also leaves Elisha's presence as a leper (וַיֵּצֵא מִלְּפָנָיו מְצֹרָע, 5:27). Thus, while Naaman's returning to and leaving Elisha's presence frame 5:15-19, this unit initiates action that stands in direct contrast to Gehazi's in 5:20-25. Its function as a platform for subsequent contrast with Gehazi eliminates 5:15-19 as the climax of 5:1-14.

Other contrasts also support defining 5:15-27 as a unified second scene. They link Naaman and Gehazi with Elisha for evaluation and for highlighting the contrasts between Gehazi and Elisha, or between Gehazi and Naaman. Note the following: Elisha and Gehazi's oath "as the Lord lives" (5:16, 20), their use of the word "peace" (5:19, 21, 22), and Naaman's self-description as "your servant" (5:15, 17, 18) compared with Gehazi's hollow self-description (5:25). These contrasts reveal Gehazi's character: he abuses the name of the Lord; he says "Peace!" when there is no peace (cf. Jer. 6:14; 8:11), and falsely describes himself as a servant. They also place the Gentile Naaman's character in a positive light.

Thus the text is composed of two contrasting scenes that move the audience from a Gentile leper who seeks out the prophet to his cleansing in the Jordan—and from a Gentile thankful for his cleansing to a deceitful Israelite who becomes leprous. Each of the scenes may be further subdivided. Scene 1, part one, moves from the king of Aram (5:1) to the king of Israel (5:7) who receives the royal message with fear. Part two is framed by the phrase "the man of God" (5:8, 14); it begins with a temporal clause

---

[18]Long, *2 Kings*, 76.

describing how Elisha replaced the king. Scene 2, part one, is enclosed by Naaman's returning to and leaving Elisha; part two is dominated by Gehazi's deceitful request and ends with the leaving of the servants who helped carry the gifts. Part three begins with a specific focus on Gehazi in Elisha's presence and ends with his leaving.[19] This analysis produces the following outline:

I. Naaman the Aramean general is cleansed from his leprosy by washing in the Jordan according to the word of the man of God (5:1-14).

  A. Naaman travels from the King of Aram to the King of Israel (5:1-7).

  B. Naaman's leprosy is cleansed by his obedience to the word of Elisha (5:8-14).

II. Naaman the cleansed Gentile enters Elisha's presence and the Israelite Gehazi leaves Elisha as a leper (5:15-27).

  A. Naaman's confession, blessing, and request for a gift in Elisha's presence. He leaves in peace (5:15-19).

  B. Gehazi's oath, request for and receipt of a gift. The gift bearers leave (5:20-24).

  C. In Elisha's presence Gehazi lies about Naaman's gifts. He leaves as a leper (5:25-27).

2 Kings 5 may be summarized as follows: Upon the advice of a young Hebrew girl, the Aramean general Naaman seeks out the prophet Elisha, by whose instructions he is cured from his leprosy. Naaman enters Elisha's presence and confesses his trust in the God of Israel; Elisha's servant Gehazi, who takes gifts which Elisha had refused, leaves Elisha's house as a leper. Stated simply, a Gentile leper is cured in Israel by a prophet of God; the Israelite servant of the prophet becomes leprous.

TOWARD PREACHING 2 KINGS 5

The Identity of the Audience

Greidanus argues that identification links the audience with the narrated events and their characters and opens the audience to the compelling power of the narrative to induce a particular response.[20] With whom does or should the audience of 2 Kings 5 identify as it hears the account of these two conversions? The answer depends on the

---

[19]2 Kings 5:25 opens with a disjunctive clause that interrupts the narrative flow. The narrative uses the same verbs to depict Gehazi's entrance into Elisha's presence as it uses for Naaman—"to come" and "to stand" (5:25, cf. 5:15).

[20]For a discussion of a definition of identification, its problems, and proper use, see Greidanus, *The Modern Preacher and the Ancient Text*, 175-181.

intended audience, and on the narrative's clues about the characters with whom the audience should identify.

Whatever the original socio-historical[21] context of the events narrated in 2 Kings 5, their literary context[22] must determine the intended audience. The brief account of Jehoiachin's elevation (2 Kings 25:27-30) points to the community exiled from God's presence (2 Kings 17:7-23; 24:3-4, 20) as the primary audience. For a community that had been focused on Jerusalem and the temple, their destruction meant the end of their world; for a people thoroughly shaped by God's promises to David, the imprisonment of his descendants was total humiliation. For a community whose loyal kings had trusted the Lord and kept his commandments (Hezekiah, 2 Kings 18:5-6), who had restored the temple and law to their rightful places (Josiah, 2 Kings 22, 23), the exile brought burdensome existential questions: Why has this happened to us? Why has God allowed the land of his inheritance, his temple, to be defiled by foreigners? What about God's promises concerning David and his city? Is there any hope? For this community the brief account of Jehoiachin's release at the end of a devastating prophetic critique provided the hope of God's word to David (2 Sam. 7:11b-16).

The exilic community was the primary intended audience of Kings. The account reminds them how the Lord built his temple in Israel's midst and gave her peace under Solomon; how so many of her kings broke with the Lord's ways and how many prophets warned them and the people (2 Kings 17:13, 23). It also confronts the exiles with their own easy submission to culturally relevant worship at Bethel and Dan, their building of high places "from watchtower to fortified city . . . in all their towns" and their setting up "sacred stones and Asherah poles on every high hill and under every spreading tree" (2 Kings 17:10-11) under the direction of Jeroboam, Ahab, and Manasseh. But they also hear of the covenant trust of Hezekiah, the loyalty of Josiah, and the faithful ministry of Elijah and Elisha. What do they hear in 2 Kings 5?

[21]For studies on the history of the composition, see Martin Noth, *The Deuteronomistic History*. JSOT Supplement 15 (Sheffield: Sheffield Press, 1981); Frank M. Cross, "The Themes of the Book of Kings and the Structure of the Deuteronomistic History," in *Canaanite Myth and Hebrew Epic: Essays in the History of the Religion of Israel* (Cambridge: Harvard University Press, 1973), 274-289; Richard D. Nelson, *The Double Redaction of the Deuteronomistic History* (Sheffield: JSOT Press, 1981).

[22]Greidanus, *The Modern Preacher and the Ancient Text*, 80-81, 215. In his discussion of historical interpretation, Greidanus argues for the original historical setting and audience but does not distinguish between these and the literary setting of narrative reports or prophetic speeches. For example, does the phrase "the original hearers" of the Lord's speech at Sinai (Ex. 19-24) refer to those who were present or those who heard it as it was first inscripturated?

The Audience and Identification with the Text

The exilic audience would have had little trouble identifying with Kings' account since it rehearses the community's own relatively recent past—the kings, prophets, and the people's apostasy, though distant, are no strangers. Kings reminds them how their past actions brought about the exile and it reminds them what the future may hold in the light of God's promises. This promised future is possible only if identification is based on a sharing of the narrated past and a willingness to submit to the narrative's claims about the audience. For exilic Israel, this basis was physical and confessional, for they were Abraham's descendants. Nonphysical descendants of Abraham, then and now, could base their identification with this text on the acknowledgment that it rehearses the past of a community they have joined as their own (Josh. 2:11; Ruth 1:16, 17; Gal. 3:8, 12-13, 29). Those who do not regard themselves as part of the religious community whose historical antecedents are narrated in Kings do not constitute its intended audience, then or now. Such will find themselves in the narrative only by a most general analogy of human religious experience.

Kings, then, does not directly address any or every people; it does not directly place its claims on any exiled group that yearns for a homeland, or on any community that suffers some form of oppression. Many exiled groups may identify with some of the experiences of the Israelite exiles; they may even uphold the historical character of the text and the events it depicts. But unless there is a redemptive-historical, organic relationship between the originally intended covenant audience and its post-Pentecost continuation, as depicted in the entire Scriptures, the Kings narrative is not addressed to them. Only within this organic connection is Israel's unique election intended seriously and addressed authentically by the text. Those who would claim 2 Kings 5 as part of the canonical text would also submit to it as normative for their faith and conduct.

Although this answer does not completely solve the problem of historical distance, it does link God's people today with 2 Kings 5. This chapter is authoritative divine speech about our own past for the sake of our faith and conduct in the present with a view to the future of the community. Through this text we hear God's voice as authentically and authoritatively as did our ancestors in the faith.

The Audience and Its Identification with the Characters of the Text

No less than ten characters occupy the narrative stage of 2 Kings 5. With whom will or should the audience identify, and why? Preachers often focus on the Hebrew maiden's brave testimony, on Naaman's healing, or on Gehazi's avarice. Elisha generally receives little attention. But is it the preacher's decision to determine the character with whom the congregation should identify? Does the text, its structure and development, point the audience in a particular direction? A closer look at the role of the characters is helpful.

The narrative flows from Naaman through Elisha to Gehazi, or from a Gentile leper who is cleansed to the prophet's Israelite servant who becomes leprous. So the text indicates these three as full-fledged characters. They alone are named. None of them is a "flat" figure; they all exhibit a broad range of traits and are realistically portrayed.[23] Among the other figures, Israel's king is a *type*, one who represents all Israelite kings who fail in their task. Others are *agents* who fulfill a function of the plot. Both the types and the agents contribute to and participate in the contrasts between the full-fledged characters. For example, the young Hebrew girl is an obvious contrast with the the Hebrew king, as are Naaman's servants with Elisha's. Full-fledged characterization and naming indicate that Naaman, Elisha, and Gehazi are candidates with whom the audience could identify. The frame of the text and the reversal of the status quo supports the candidacy of Naaman and Gehazi; the prophet Elisha is the crucial instrument in effecting this reversal. These three characters also play a major role in creating the fundamental tension of the narrative—the tension between the unclean and the clean, the Gentile and the Jew, the nations and the land of Israel. The text moves the audience to identify with Naaman and Gehazi in their respective relationships to the prophet Elisha.

The primary audience experienced the tension between unclean and clean as exiles among the unclean Gentiles, far from the clean land of promise. In 2 Kings 5, Israel encounters an upside-down world: the Gentile who is cleansed and the Israelite who becomes unclean. Even worse, the cleansed Gentile confesses that there is no God in the earth except in Israel (5:15; cf. Ex. 18:11), and does so by acknowledging God's prophet (cf. 5:8). The Israelite confesses no such thing. The primary audience is now in exile, because they have disregarded the prophets (2 Kings 17:13, 23). They are unclean, so close to the rivers Naaman praised so highly, and so far from the waters of the insignificant Jordan. But the streams of Babylon cannot quench their thirst (Ps. 137:1).

There is more. When Naaman returns to the Gentile world he vows no longer to worship "other gods" (אֱלֹהִים אֲחֵרִים, 5:17). Worship of other gods had been Israel's fundamental problem since entering the land. God had forbidden it from the beginning (Ex. 20:3; 23:13; 34:14; Deut. 5:7; 6:14; 7:4; 8:19, etc.), and Israel had sworn total submission to the Lord before Joshua (Josh. 24:16). But soon after his death she turned from the Lord to "other gods" (Judg. 2:12, 17, 19; 10:13; 1 Sam. 8:8; 1 Kings 9:6, 9;

---

[23]Berlin, *Poetics and Interpretation of Biblical Narrative*, 23, 32. The following definitions of *type* and *agent* are also Berlin's.

11:4, 10; 14:9). For this, she was removed from the land (2 Kings 17:7, 35, 37; 22:17). Naaman's anticipation of and solution to the problem of worshiping God at home stands in sharp contrast to Israel's easy worship of "other gods" in the land. Finally, Naaman's initial reservations about bathing in the Jordan and declaring his homeland's waters as equally efficacious reflect for Israel her rejection of the means of grace appointed by the Lord. The prophets had reminded her, but it was more important to be like the nations. And now they were scattered among them.

In these ways the text urges its original audience to consider the cleansed Naaman, his confession, and his expressed devotion, and to reflect on her own unclean condition far away from "the land." She is urged to identify with him because he speaks and acts in the tones of a righteous Israelite. There is no greater irony: the unclean, leprous, Gentile general leaves his land to become clean in Israel under the prophet Elisha's ministrations. Expelled from the land, Israel hears this narrative in unclean Gentile territory. Confronted with Naaman, will Israel be moved to jealousy and look to God and hear his appointed servant?

The narrative develops Gehazi's character in reaction to Elisha's refusal to accept Naaman's gifts. The cleansing that brings one into God's presence cannot be bought (Isa. 55:1-2; Matt. 10:8). Elisha's firm refusal of Naaman's offer is underscored by the oath "As the Lord lives" (חַי יהוה, 5:16, 20), accompanied by "before whom I stand" (אֲשֶׁר־עָמַדְתִּי לְפָנָיו). This language is typical of the true prophet and it indicates that he stands in the very presence of God (2 Kings 22:19; Jer. 23:18, 22). He refuses the proferred "blessing" (בְּרָכָה, 5:15; cf. Gen. 14:22, 23). Naaman has been healed by God's grace alone, and he responds appropriately. Gehazi reacts differently to Naaman's healing. Swearing the same oath as Elisha, but without the phrase "before whom I stand," he pursues Naaman to take what Elisha had not. The absence of this phrase suggests a critique: the presence of God does not shape Gehazi's response to Naaman's healing. In this way he abuses the name of God.

The text offers another critique of Gehazi when it describes him as standing *next* to Elisha (וַיַּעֲמֹד אֶל־אֲדֹנָיו, 5:25) and not in his presence, like Naaman (cf. לְפָנָיו וַיַּעֲמֹד, 5:16). This suggests that, although Gehazi was constantly around the prophet, his faith and conduct were not shaped by the words of the prophet. He even lies to him. In contrast, Naaman identifies himself to Elisha as "your servant" (עַבְדֶּךָ, 5:15, 17, 18) and willingly submits to him. Gehazi also uses the phrase "your servant" (עַבְדֶּךָ, 5:25), but his actions belie his words. He abuses the name of the Lord and his prophet to further his own interests. Abuse of the divine name and ignoring the prophets was Israel's traditional sin. It led to their taking what did not belong to them (1 Kings 21; Amos 5:4-12).

This brings us to the items Elisha lists in his rebuke of Gehazi. The list of plunder is problematic because it contains items that Gehazi did not request from Naaman. The silver and clothing (5:22-23) Gehazi received are mentioned first in Elisha's list, but then he adds "olive groves, vineyards, flocks, herds, or menservants and maidservants" (5:26). None of these appears earlier in 2 Kings 5. Why are they mentioned? Long thinks of the rebuke as prophetic hyperbole, rhetorical exaggeration that depicts Gehazi "like some corrupt royal tyrant,"[24] but he fails to follow up on this fruitful comment. If we compare this list with that in 1 Sam. 8:15-17, several similarities appear:

2 Kings 5:26	1 Samuel 8:15-17
silver	———
clothes	———
olive groves)	olive groves (15)
vineyards	vineyards (15)
flocks	flocks (17)
herds	———
menservants	menservants (15)
maidservants	maidservants (16)

These similarities recall Samuel's warning about the excesses of Israel's kings and so reminds Israel that she wanted a king, that she had said: "we will be like all other nations, with a king to lead us and go out before us and fight our battles" (1 Sam. 8:20). The kings' zealous pursuit to be like the nations and their failure to look only to the Lord for blessing brought Israel and Judah to ruin among the nations. Israel became an outcast, expelled from the presence of God; she became unclean like the nations.

But the list begins with a question: "Is this the time to take . . . ?" (5:26b). To what does "time" refer? Given that Gehazi abuses the "new born" Naaman, it seems that it refers to the time of God's grace shown to the Gentile Naaman through his prophet.[25] By prefacing the list of royal abuses with this question, the original audience hears Elisha asking Gehazi, "Now that you have seen God's grace to a total unworthy, an unclean Gentile, how could you practice the wickedness of the kings that brought Israel to her uncleanness?"

---

[24]Long, *2 Kings*, 76. Hobbs, *2 Kings*, 68, points to the "comprehensive catalogs of wealth and prosperity" that can be seen as a gift of God, temptation to apostasy, or a sign of greed, but he does not follow this up with respect to the kings.

[25]Time is understood variously by commentators: "a time of hardship for others," Hobbs, *2 Kings*, 68; a time "for spiritual transformation . . . ought not to have been profaned," Long, *2 Kings*, 76; "when God is working a healing and conversion, greed has no place," Nelson, *First and Second Kings*, 180.

By applying this list to Gehazi, Elisha links him with Israel's ruinous monarchy, which ignored the prophets of God and could not direct the needy to them (cf. 5:7). If Gehazi's deceitful strategy identifies Gehazi with the selfishness of the unnamed king in Samaria, then Elisha's rebuke ties him to the kingship responsible for Israel's exile.[26] The text encourages its original audience to consider Gehazi as a mirror of its own uncleanness, to see in him the leadership that failed to rule righteously and ignored God's chosen servants, to recognize in him their own sinful yearning for the rivers of Damascus and their own neglect of the means of God's grace, so that they might confess God's righteous judgment of their uncleanness and call upon him to deliver them from their distress. The uncleanness of Israel's exile is not the time (5:26b) to practice the wickedness of their ancestors. Let them contemplate Elisha's judgment that "Naaman's leprosy will cling to you and to your descendants forever" (5:27).

Elisha's question and Gehazi's leprosy encourages the exilic community to wonder if there is any hope. Can she be cleansed like Naaman? What must she do? How can this terrible reversal be undone? In faraway Babylon and in Egypt God's people hear Elisha's question to Gehazi: Is the time of your exile a time to continue to insist on being like the nations? Look what it got you! How long will you follow your kings? In the context of Jehoiachin's release, there is a glimmer of hope; the Lord has not forgotten his promise to David. In the meantime Israel waits in lonely exile for the Lord to reveal himself in power.

The Church and 2 Kings 5

The church is not in exile; nor is she Jewish. But as a Gentile church engrafted into the root (Rom. 11:16-18) she has inherited this narrative as divine normative address for her faith and conduct. For a time *she* is the peculiar object of God's affections, as were the Jews before (Romans 11:11ff.). Now she is the community cleansed by the blood of the Lamb who stands against the unclean world as did Israel against the unclean nations. She is the community in whose midst God has disclosed himself by a chosen servant, Jesus Christ. And because of his presence she is an experienced witness of God's grace and the means by which he administers it—the Word and the sacraments. This allows the church to identify herself with Israel as the audience of this text. But what about the exile? How can the church identify with Israel's historical location? Two homiletical approaches are possible: the hortatory and the penitential.

---

[26]My colleague Carl J. Bosma notes that the words of the unnamed king in 2 Kings 5:7, "Can I kill and bring back to life?" echo the words of Hannah in 1 Samuel 2:6: "The Lord brings death and makes alive." Indeed, the monarchy (and the people) has suffered the consequences of Gehazi's leprosy: they were cast out from the presence of God (2 Kings 24:3, 20). They who had received life were now dead in their trespasses and sins.

The hortatory approach assumes a dissimilarity of historical situation. Nevertheless, the church's history includes epochs of disobedience that are acknowledged and mirrored in the local experience in some way. For this situation, the text, like the letters to the seven churches, presents an opportunity to reflect upon her faith and conduct. 2 Kings 5 exhorts the church not to take God or his grace for granted, not to develop church leaders like businesses or concoct means of grace not appointed by God himself. The sermon then is instructive about the temptations in the environment and the sad results of ignoring God's ways of grace and neglecting his chosen servant Jesus Christ. Above all, the sermon will place Gehazi's condition before the church as a possible future. If God abandoned the Jews for a while in order to save the Gentiles, how much more will he reject the engrafted but fruitless olive branch for the sake of the root? As God cleansed Naaman and through Elisha made Gehazi unclean, so God could do with the Gentile church in this or that particular place and "remove your lampstand from its place" (Rev. 2:5). We might say that in this case there is only one leper, Gehazi the Israelite, who mirrors the actual results for Israel. But there is the possibility of two: the Gentile church may become leprous for her disobedience.

The penitential approach assumes a similar historical situation—where the church acknowledges she is far from what she ought to be, where she acknowledges specific acts of disobedience, and where she recognizes that she stands more with the local culture and its religious directions (cf. Neh. 9:5-37, esp. vv. 36-37) than against it. In this case, Gehazi depicts the real situation; the church is unclean because she has abandoned her first love and the servant sent to reveal him, has converted grace into a profitable enterprise. If God could be gracious to Naaman, how much more to his own children? In this case it is sermonically appropriate to let the church see herself in Gehazi, who, though close to the prophet, neglected to rejoice in the gracious cleansing of Naaman but took it as an occasion to make a profit. The sermon may confront the church with an uncleanness she believed to belong only to others. Here there are two lepers: Gehazi and the church. But there is the possibility of one. The sermon will lead the church to godly sorrow, to look to the great son of David and Jehoiachin (cf. 1 John 1:9, Lam. 3:22-24).

Job 32-37: Elihu as the Mouthpiece of God

Al M. Wolters

The book of Job, long considered one of the masterpieces of world literature, continues to exert an extraordinary fascination in the closing decades of the twentieth century. The spate of lengthy studies of this enigmatic book, including many that are not part of a commentary series, shows no signs of abating. Whatever earlier generations may have seen in the story of Job, there seems to be something about the figure of Job that strikes a deep responsive chord in the souls of many of our contemporaries.

The Promethean Job, sitting alone and defiant in the ashes of his dreams, especially appeals to the imagination of many today. Both modernist and postmodernist can identify with this heroic champion of his own integrity, who dares to challenge not only traditional orthodoxy, but God himself. For late twentieth-century humanists—and their Christian sympathizers—it is not difficult to move from the text of Job to a powerful contemporary sermon.

But there is a fly in the ointment. There is much in the book of Job that sounds exactly like traditional orthodoxy, especially in the mouths of the other characters. It is true that the orthodox sayings of the three friends can quite easily be discounted, since they are condemned by God himself at the conclusion of the book. These sayings can be explained as the mindless doctrinalism to which Job himself offers a refreshing alternative, or else (since one of them is quoted as Scripture in 1 Cor. 3:19) as theological formulations that may be true in the abstract but are misapplied to the specific case of Job.

This strategy does not work in the case of Elihu, who also says many orthodox-sounding things, but who is not condemned by God. Consequently, for many interpreters who identify with the defiant Job, there is welcome evidence that the Elihu speeches are a later addition to the book and can therefore be disregarded as a secondary interpolation inserted by a small-minded champion of traditional orthodoxy. To appreciate the true genius of the original author of the book of Job, we must excise from it the five chapters containing the discourses of Elihu.

Until recently, this was the dominant opinion among critical scholars with respect to the figure of Elihu. More recently, there has been a tendency (especially in North American scholarship) to reinstate the Elihu speeches as an integral part of the book of Job. However, Elihu has returned from his literary exile with his reputation still tarnished. He may have been part of the overall literary design of the book of Job, but only as a kind of buffoon who offers comic relief in the Joban drama. He is still seen as a narrow-minded figure of fun, whose desperate efforts to salvage some remnants of orthodoxy are laughable.

I will argue that Elihu is neither extraneous to the book of Job, nor someone who is held up to ridicule, but rather that he is the mouthpiece of God. In other words, it is possible to preach on the discourses of Elihu, not as an ironic foil to outmoded orthodoxy, but as the Word of God which ought to shape a contemporary orthodoxy. I hasten to add that I do not hold this position dogmatically—it is certainly possible, and consistent with a high view of Scripture, to espouse an ironic reading of Elihu. But it is not my reading.

Since within the broader guild of contemporary biblical studies my reading of Elihu is somewhat unusual, I shall begin with a brief historical survey of interpretations of the chapters in question (Job 32-37). This will serve both to relativize the currently popular negative readings of Elihu, and to show that my own positive reading stands in a long interpretative tradition. This survey will prepare the ground for a brief presentation of the main points of my position. I will then move to an example of preaching that is based on the view that Elihu is a mouthpiece of God. However, the preaching example will not be my own, but a freshly-translated fragment from a sermon by John Calvin. I will conclude with some reflections on Calvin's sermon and a consideration of ways in which his treatment of Elihu deserves imitation today.

HISTORICAL SURVEY

A recently published German dissertation by Harald-Martin Wahl devoted to the speeches of Elihu begins with a survey of the history of interpretation of these chapters.[1] I will rely heavily on this discussion, but will supplement it with other studies, notably L. E. Goodman's new English edition of the Job commentary of Saadiah, the great medieval Jewish exegete,[2] and the recent work by Susan E. Schreiner on Calvin's sermons on Job.[3]

[1]Harald-Martin Wahl, *Der gerechte Schöpfer: Eine redaktions- und theologiegeschichtliche Untersuchung der Elihureden—Hiob 32-37*, BZAW 207 (Berlin/New York: Walter de Gruyter, 1993), 1-35. See also the Appendix to Wahl's work, which contains a survey of twentieth-century interpretations of the Elihu speeches. A brief summary of Wahl's overall conclusions can be found in his essay "Das 'Evangelium' Elihus (Hiob 32-37)," in *The Book of Job*, BETL 114, ed. W. A. M. Beuken (Louvain: Leuven University Press/Uitgeverij Peeters, 1994), 356-361. Notably, Wahl does not mention either Saadiah or Calvin.

[2]L. E. Goodman, *The Book of Theodicy: Translation and Commentary on the Book of Job by Saadiah ben Joseph al-Fayyūmī*, Yale Judaica Series 25 (New Haven: Yale University Press, 1988).

[3]Susan E. Schreiner, *Where Shall Wisdom Be Found? Calvin's Exegesis of Job from Medieval and Modern Perspectives* (Chicago: University of Chicago Press, 1994). See also her earlier study "'Through a Mirror Dimly': Calvin's Sermons on Job," *Calvin Theological Journal* 21 (1986): 175-193.

Until the rise of modern historical criticism in the late eighteenth century, the Elihu speeches were universally considered to be an authentic and integral part of the book of Job. However, opinions were divided on the value of what Elihu had to say. The Jewish pseudepigraphical work *The Testament of Job* (first-second century A.D.) considered his words blasphemous and inspired by the devil.[4] This extremely negative assessment found only qualified support in subsequent pre-critical commentaries. Jerome (fourth-fifth century) speaks of Elihu as the type of pagan philosophers.[5] The influential work of Gregory the Great, *Moralia in Iob* (seventh century) was prepared to grant that Elihu said many things that were true, but expressed them in an arrogant and unedifying manner.[6] Thomas Aquinas had a similarly mixed opinion of Elihu.[7] Luther had little to say about Elihu, but in one place in his *Table-Talk* dismissed him as a useless *Zinglius*, "blatherer."[8]

This negative assessment, however, was definitely a minority opinion among pre-critical commentators. Some of the greatest names of Jewish and Christian exegesis looked upon Elihu as the one who offered the solution to the problem of the book of Job. Saadiah (tenth century) says, for example, of the three friends, "They are unaware, as Job is, of the proper position . . . that of Elihu,"[9] and writes of God: "He did not, however, blame Elihu, but expanded on Elihu's speech to Job, thus confirming what Elihu had said."[10] Saadiah's view is echoed by Ibn Ezra (twelfth century).[11] We find a similarly positive reading of Elihu in the *Guide of the Perplexed* of Maimonides, Ibn Ezra's younger contemporary.[12]

Among Christian exegetes, John Calvin is the great exponent of the view that Elihu speaks the truth of God. In his sermons on the book of Job, Calvin repeatedly equates the words of Elihu with the words of the Holy Spirit. Consider the following quotations from these sermons: "It is true that Elihu brings the pure word of God, and that we must consider that which comes out of his mouth as having come from the Holy Spirit."[13]

[4]Wahl, *Der gerechte Schöpfer*, 3.

[5]Ibid., 4.

[6]Ibid.

[7]Schreiner, *Where Shall Wisdom Be Found?* 131.

[8]Wahl, *Der gerechte Schöpfer*, 5.

[9]Goodman, *Book of Theodicy*, 129.

[10]Ibid., 130. See also Saadiah's discussion of Elihu in the body of his commentary (Ibid., 348-381).

[11]Wahl, *Der gerechte Schöpfer*, 4-5. Wahl fails to recognize that Ibn Ezra is dependent on Saadiah.

[12]Schreiner, *Where Shall Wisdom Be Found?* 59-70, esp. 132.

[13]*CO* 35.37. Calvin's sermons on Job are printed in volumes 33-35 of *Ioannis Calvini Opera quae Supersunt Omnia* (abbreviated *CO*) in the series *Corpus Reformatorum* (Brunsvigae: Schwetschke, 1887; repr. New York/London: Johnson Reprint Corporation and Frankfurt am Main: Minerva, 1964). The sermons on the Elihu speeches are found in *CO* 35.1-350.

"This is what the Holy Spirit has wished to teach us here through the mouth of Elihu."[14] "All the more must we remember this teaching, which is here given to us by Elihu, or rather by the Holy Spirit."[15] As a matter of fact, as Schreiner puts it, "There are few people in the Bible Calvin admires more than Elihu."[16] Because of Calvin's stature in the Protestant world, it is not surprising that his reading of the Elihu chapters had great influence among Protestant exegetes. One example is the German Pietist J. C. Dippel (eighteenth century), who defends Elihu against all his detractors.[17]

The end of the eighteenth century saw the beginning of a different era of biblical studies—an era dominated by a historical criticism that increasingly denied the literary integrity of the biblical writings. It was a sign of the times when J. G. Eichhorn, one of the founding fathers of the historical-critical approach to Scripture, tentatively suggested in 1787 that the Elihu speeches did not belong to the original book of Job.[18] In the following year, this tentative suggestion was transformed into a positive assertion by M. H. Stuhlmann, who adduced a series of arguments in favor of their secondary status.[19]

Throughout the nineteenth century, and most of the twentieth, Stuhlmann's thesis was adopted by almost all critical scholars. There were three sets of arguments that were generally accepted as leading to this conclusion:

1. The Elihu speeches seem like an erratic block within the book of Job as a whole. There is no mention of Elihu either before or after Job 32-37, and Job 38 begins with God's address to Job, not Elihu.

2. Stylistic and linguistic peculiarities distinguish Elihu's speeches from the preceding discourses. For example, Elihu, unlike the three friends, often addresses Job by name, and repeatedly quotes his words verbatim.

3. The theological content of these chapters is unoriginal: it simply repeats what the friends have already said, or anticipates the divine speeches that follow.[20]

[14]*CO* 35.283.

[15]*CO* 35.298.

[16]Schreiner, *Where Shall Wisdom Be Found?* 131. Schreiner discusses Calvin's interpretation of Elihu on pp. 131-135. See also her "'Through a Mirror Dimly,'" 185-86.

[17]Wahl, *Der gerechte Schöpfer*, 6-5.

[18]Ibid., 8-9.

[19]Ibid., 10.

[20]Ibid., 10-14.

These lines of evidence seemed to suggest that chapters 32-37 were a later inter-polation in the book of Job. Others went further, and argued that it was possible to iden-tify the hand of a number of different authors in the five chapters ascribed to Elihu.[21]

It should be noted that, in the standard critical view, Elihu is a figure who com-mands little respect. He is called "ridiculous" by H. H. Rowley,[22] "insufferable," "obnoxious," and "pretentious" by John C. L. Gibson,[23] "a fanatic and a bigot" by J. B. Curtis,[24] and "a pompous, insensitive bore" by E. M. Good.[25] Indeed, these and similar strong judgments by many contemporary exegetes have prompted the question, Why do people loathe Elihu?[26] There were, of course, always dissenters from the stan-dard critical view. A hardy sub-tradition of conservative exegetes, of various confes-sional persuasions, has continued to press the case for the overall integrity of the canonical book of Job.[27] Even Karl Budde, who in many ways is the epitome of classical German critical scholarship, tenaciously defended against all comers the view that the Elihu chapters provided the key to the entire book, highlighting the purificatory value of suffering.[28] More recently, a broad spectrum of biblical scholars, especially in North America, has returned to the view that Elihu belongs to the overall design of the book of Job. Notable names in this connection are N. H. Snaith,[29] Francis I. Andersen,[30] Robert M. Polzin,[31] J. William Whedbee,[32]

[21]Wahl, *Der gerechte Schöpfer*, 20-23.

[22]H. H. Rowley, *The Book of Job*, NCB (Grand Rapids: Eerdmans, 1970), 209.

[23]John C. L. Gibson, *Job*, Daily Study Bible (Philadelphia: Westminster Press, 1985), 281.

[24]J. B. Curtis, "Why Were the Elihu Speeches Added to the Book of Job?" *Proceedings of the Eastern Great Lakes and Midwest Biblical Societies* 8 (1988): 93.

[25]Edwin M. Good, *In Turns of Tempest: A Reading of Job, with a Translation* (Stanford: Stanford University Press, 1990), 321.

[26]Carol A. Newsom, "The Book of Job," in *The New Interpreter's Bible*, Vol. 4 (Nashville: Abingdon Press, 1996), 564.

[27]As a representative sampling of theologically conservative treatments of Job we might mention Norbert Peters, *Das Buch Job* (Münster: Aschendorff, 1928), Helmut Lamparter, *Das Buch der Anfechtung: Das Buch Hiob* (Stuttgart: Calwer, 1951), and J. H. Kroeze, *Het Boek Job*, COT (Kampen: Kok, 1961).

[28]Wahl, *Der gerechte Schöpfer*, 15-16. See also Rudolf Smend, "Karl Budde (1850-1935)," in *Language, Theology, and The Bible: Essays in Honour of James Barr*, ed. Samuel E. Balentine and John Barton (Oxford: Clarendon, 1994), 351-369, esp. 358-360.

[29]N. Snaith, *The Book of Job: Its Origin and Purpose*, SBT 2/11 (London: SCM, 1968), 72-91.

[30]Francis I. Andersen, *Job: An Introduction and Commentary*, TOTC (Downers Grove, Ill.: InterVarsity Press, 1976), 49-52.

[31]Robert M. Polzin, *Biblical Structuralism: Method and Subjectivity in the Study of Ancient Texts* (Philadelphia: Fortress Press/Missoula: Scholars Press, 1977), 57-58.

[32]J. William Whedbee, "The Comedy of Job," *Semeia* 7 (1977): 1-39.

Robert Gordis,[33] Norman C. Habel,[34] J. G. Janzen,[35] David J. A. Clines,[36] and John E. Hartley.[37]

However, as noted above, not all these newer proponents of a holistic reading of the book of Job offer a positive evaluation of Elihu's speeches. These speeches may be integral to the design of the book, but they may also represent an inferior theology. Such is the view, for example, of Whedbee, who sees Elihu as the buffoon in the "comedy" of Job, and Habel, who interprets Elihu as a brash young fool who functions as a deliberate foil and an anticlimax to Job's powerful last speech.

PERSONAL CONCLUSIONS

Against the background of this survey, I will put forward my own conclusions with respect to the Elihu discourses. I will rely on the survey to guide the reader to the bibliographical sources that contain the explicit or detailed argumentation for the positions I have adopted.

1. I take it as a basic hermeneutical starting point that a work of literature should be read as a unity, and that therefore chapters 32-37 of the book of Job should be interpreted as integral to the book as a whole. This, of course, is the historic pre-critical position, which has been quite consistently maintained by conservative biblical scholars and to which many critical exegetes have returned in recent years.

2. Affirming the authenticity of these chapters as integral to the overall literary design of the book leaves open the questions of their date and authorship. It is possible that a single author conceived the entire protean mass of the Job masterpiece at one go; it is also possible that it grew in stages, with either one or multiple authors working at it over a period of time. But the final product, the finished literary production that has been transmitted as part of the canonical Hebrew Scriptures, is most reasonably read as the creation of a single superintending intelligence (perhaps that of a final redactor). Whatever its literary pre-

---

[33]Robert Gordis, *The Book of Job: Commentary, New Translation, and Special Notes* (New York: Jewish Theological Seminary of America, 1978), 546-552.

[34]Norman C. Habel, "The Role of Elihu in the Design of the Book of Job," in *In the Shelter of Elyon: Essays on Palestinian Life and Literature in Honor of G. W. Ahlstrom*, JSOT Supp 31, eds. W. Boyd Barrick and John S. Spencer (Sheffield: JSOT Press, 1984), 81-88; and idem, *The Book of Job. A Commentary*, OTL (Philadelphia: Westminster Press, 1985), 32-33, 36-37.

[35]J. G. Janzen, *Job*, Interpretation (Atlanta: John Knox, 1985), 217-218, 221-225.

[36]David J. A. Clines, "Job" in *The International Bible Commentary*, ed. F. F. Bruce (Grand Rapids: Zondervan, 1986), 521, 541-542; and idem, *Job 1-20* WBC 17 (Dallas: Word, 1989), xli-xlii, lviii-lix.

[37]John E. Hartley, *The Book of Job*, NICOT (Grand Rapids: Eerdmans, 1988), 28-30.

history may have been (the various attempts at scholarly reconstruction are all highly speculative, and tend to cancel each other out), the book of Job should be read holistically, *as though* it had a single human author writing at one time.

3. Within the context of the book of Job as a whole, Elihu is presented in a positive light. Whereas the earlier interchanges between Job and the three friends can be characterized as a "dialogue of the deaf," Elihu takes Job seriously. He addresses Job by name, quotes his own words back to him, and presents himself as a fellow seeker after truth. Though his speeches strike the modern reader as long-winded and pompous, this impression fails to take into account the conventions of ancient (and a good deal of modern) literature. The rhetorical style of the three friends, or of Job himself, is not significantly different. It is also of great significance that Elihu is pointedly *not* condemned in chapter 42.

4. The cardinal point about Elihu, as compared to the three older friends of Job, is that he alone recognizes that Job is not being punished for his sins. He recognizes that suffering may be a *testing* of the believer—which is exactly what it was in Job's case. His criticism of Job, therefore, is not for some hypothetical past sin that explains his present suffering (as the three friends had argued), but for Job's challenge, in the midst of his suffering, of the justice of God. It is clear from the rest of the book of Job that Elihu was right, and the three friends wrong, on pivotal points: Job's previous integrity, and God's present justice.

5. Since Elihu's speeches in many ways anticipate God's own speeches in chapters 39-41, and the conclusion of chapter 38 appears to set the stage for God himself finally speaking out of the whirlwind, it is reasonable to interpret Elihu as a forerunner of God, a kind of herald who introduces God's own definitive answer to Job. In short, since he is right on the basic issues being debated between Job and the three friends, and since he introduces God within the overall literary design of the book, Elihu is presented as the mouthpiece of God.

6. Nevertheless, though he functions as God's spokesman, there is still a significant difference between Elihu's speeches and the divine speeches. From the perspective of the author of the book of Job, both speak divinely authorized truth, but Elihu does so in a pastoral way, and God in an overwhelming way. Both assert the sovereignty of God, and both call Job to task for challenging God's justice, but Elihu does so in a way that prepares Job for God. The speeches of Elihu therefore function as a kind of buffer zone between Job's defiant challenge to God's justice at the end of chapter 31 and the volcanic eruption of God's assertion of sovereignty in chapters 38-41.

Given these assumptions, it is legitimate to preach on the speeches of Elihu as the oracles of God, the inspired human prelude to the Yahweh speeches that follow. One renowned preacher who approached them in this way was John Calvin, whose sermons on the book of Job have been called "the greatest exposition of Job ever given."[38] We turn now to a selection from one of these sermons.

A PREACHING SAMPLE FROM CALVIN

Calvin's sermons on the book of Job were delivered in Geneva in the years 1554-55.[39] They were taken down in shorthand and published, and immediately became very popular. By 1574, the entire set of 159 sermons had been translated from French into English and was published in London.[40] We need to remember that Calvin was speaking extemporaneously, probably with only the Hebrew text before him. The style is therefore somewhat disjointed and colloquial. The following selection is from the beginning of Sermon 146, the last of the 28 sermons on Elihu. It is an exposition of Job 37:14-16.[41]

> "[337] *14. Hear these things Job, stand still, ponder the marvels of God. 15. Do you know how God has imposed his law on them, and how he makes the light of his cloud shine? 16. Do you understand the separations of the clouds, and the miracles of the one perfect in knowledge?* [Calvin's translation of the Hebrew]
>
> [339] If we understood what is said here about the works of God, namely that they are wondrous, there would be none of us who did not take greater care to ponder them, even given the smallness and the weakness which affect our minds. But what is the case? We deem ourselves to be so clever that with a brief glance we have soon

---

[38]Andersen, *Job*, 18.

[39]Schreiner, "'Through a Mirror Dimly'," 175.

[40]*Sermons of Maister Iohn Caluin, vpon the Booke of Job. Translated out of the French by Arthur Golding* (Londini: Impensis Georgii Bishop, 1574). This 752-page volume was recently reprinted in a facsimile edition by the Banner of Truth Trust (Edinburgh, 1993). The initial publication went through five printings in ten years; see Harold Dekker, "Introduction" to John Calvin, *Sermons from Job*, selected and translated by Leroy Nixon (Eerdmans: Grand Rapids, 1952; repr. Baker Book House: Grand Rapids, 1979), ix-xxxvii (ix). (Note that Sermon 146 is not included in Nixon's selection.)

[41]The translation is made from the French as published in *CO* 35.337-343 (in my translation, bold numbers indicate the column numbers in the printed French text). I have compared the sixteenth-century English rendering by Arthur Golding (see previous note), and the twentieth-century Dutch translation by Dirk van Dijk. For the latter, see *Stemmen uit Geneve. Preken, artikelen, brieven enz. van Johannes Calvijn* (Goudriaan [The Netherlands]: Boekhandel-Uitgeverij De Groot, 1968-1977). Sermon 146 is found in Bundel 38 (pp. 273-280) and Bundel 39 (pp. 281-287). In two places, marked in the notes, I have corrected apparent misprints in the French text.

learned everything there is to know. And yet the works of God are not appreciated by us in accordance with their worth; they are like ordinary things to us because we are used to them, and we pass them by without attention. Therefore we must pay careful attention to what is said in this verse, when Elihu on the one hand asserts that *the works of God are so many miracles,* and then says that it is necessary to *stand still* for them, given the fact that our mind is much too feeble to acquire a genuine knowledge of them so quickly. It is therefore necessary that we do our best to study them. Furthermore, we are especially commanded to *listen,* for unless God speaks concerning us, it will make no difference if we turn our full attention to pondering his works; we will never get to the main point.

Thus, there are three points that we must bear in mind. The first concerns the excellence and majesty which can be observed in all the works of God, so that they are not to be despised. And then the second point is this: since men are simple-minded and slow-witted, they must not take just a passing glance at what God presents to their view, but they must look at it closely, and make an effort to study it in a thoroughgoing manner. The third point is that they should not rely on their reason, and not think that they have sufficient ingenuity to make sound judgments, but they should realize that it is reserved for God to teach us by his word what we ought to understand, and that we must begin at that end. Until we have attended the school of God our eyes will be blinded—the works of God will pass before our eyes, but we will not have the kind of feeling for them that is required; in short, we will have no discernment until God has made us wise. Now, it's not so much that these things need to be treated at length, but they should be given careful thought by each one of us. Therefore, whenever we have occasion to gain knowledge of the works of God, let us lift up our minds on high to revere them— that is, to revere the infinite wisdom, and the power, and the justice of God which appears in them. So much for the first point.

In short, whoever reflects on the works of God without revering them—that is, without bringing them honor—and without acknowledging that they are full of wisdom, and power, and goodness, is guilty of ingratitude and sacrilege. Consequently, let us show that reverence whenever people speak to us about the works of God; let us [340] not think of them as anything but miracles which far surpass our understanding, in which God displays his majesty in such a manner that we have much to revere him for. Moreover (as we have mentioned), it is necessary on the other hand to consider what is in us, so that we will not think that we are so clever that we understand everything in an instant. Let us be content to ponder what we do not immediately understand, and let us be indefatigable in this study. If we have lived for some time in the world, and are still novices, without attaining the perfection of understanding which we might wish, let us not lose heart, but let us continue that study, for we will have accomplished a great deal if in the course of our entire lifetime we have learned to appreciate the marvels that are contained in the works of God. Now it is true that we must always go forward, and thus when it says here that we must *stand still*, it is not because we must be inactive in our observations, for our thinking about God should not prevent us from serving him and being active in the things he commands us. The very opposite is true: the more anyone ponders the works of God, the more he ought to be impelled to do his duty, he ought to be aroused and motivated even more. Even those who stand still to think about the works of God "go back" (as the proverb says[42]) "in order to take a better leap." The goal is that we should not be vagabonds. After all, we see that men run to and fro, and race about, moving hither and yon—why, they would wish to make the very world move with them, when they are so busy with their undertakings! But what is the case? They could break both their arms and their legs, and will hardly make any progress, if they do not keep to the right road. What is required then? That we have some sound pondering to guide us. Let us therefore stand still before the works of God in such a way that we are kept in check, so that we do not lose our way[43] in this manner, and are not vagabonds. But meanwhile let us also be active in what God commands us, and have our goal there.

Furthermore, let us realize that by our nature we shall not have the good sense or the wit to listen to God. After all, it is his business to show us what we must ponder in his works in order to profit by them. It is true that the pagans have had subtle discussions of the secrets of nature, and virtually nothing has been hidden from them.

[42]The French saying Calvin is referring to is *reculer pour mieux sauter*.

[43]Reading *esgarer* instead of the *esgayer* of the printed text (*CO* 35.340). This is supported by the translations of both Golding and Van Dijk.

To be sure—but it was only to waste their time in this world, and not to come to God. And what is such wisdom but abysmal confusion? For what ingratitude it is, when men scrutinize all the works of God so carefully, and do not think about the Creator, and care nothing about him! Therefore let [341] such wisdom be accursed, which wastes its time in making subtle inquiries into these lower causes,[44] and meanwhile despises the Creator. Furthermore it is also certain that God gave understanding [*l'esprit*] to those who have treated so subtly of the order of nature, but because they did not hear God speak, and did not have his word to guide them rightly, they have lost their way. For the important thing was to subject themselves to God, and to behold his glory, which appears to us in all his works. They did not do it. Therefore let us take good note that when we read these great philosophers, or hear others speak of them, and when we see that they have understood the things which to us seem to be incomprehensible—let us take note that they are so many mirrors of the blindness which is in all men until such time as God has taught them in his school. Are we more subtle than they were? Far from it—and yet we see that they have tasted nothing of God. And so when we want to understand the works of God, let us not rely on our own sharp-wittedness, or take pride in our natural power, but let us give ear to what God will say to us. And when we have been taught by his word, let us walk under his guidance, and then the works of God will be understood by us, so that we can apply them to our use and instruction. So much for the first verse.

But Elihu continues his discourse immediately. He asks *whether Job knows how God has given commands to all creatures*, how he has ordained *the clouds*, and then how he puts *light* among them—and whether he has understood the order and arrangement of the clouds, and the *marvels of him who is perfect in knowledge*. When he says, *Have you understood how God imposed his law on his creatures?* there are two things to note here. The one is that God did not only create his works once for all, but that he governs them and applies them to such use as he chooses. We have already dealt with this in the last few days, but since this statement is put here again, let us weigh it

---

[44]Reading *causes inferieures* instead of the *choses inferieures* of the printed text (*CO* 35.341). This is supported by Golding's translation (p. 685: "causes") and the repeated reference in a similar context to *causes inferieures* in the preceding sermon (*CO* 35.335).

carefully, because it teaches us a good lesson. For what would it mean if it was said only that God created the world, and that now things go on as best they can? That would be a very meagre and unprofitable teaching. That's what virtually all the pagans have made of it—I mean those who had some good seed of religion. For I leave to one side those deranged creatures who have thought that the world was eternal, as did the wisest man who ever lived, namely Aristotle. He has never had his equal, and yet he "stood still" there—and the devil led him astray, so that he had no knowledge of the Creator of the world. Although he knew that there was a God, the fact is that he did not know the creation of the world, which is like the face of God, in which God [**342**] wants us to behold him. But as for those pagans who had some seed of religion, although they recognized the fact that God had created the world, yet they had no understanding of his providence, which embraces everything, since the things that were created by his power now continue to exist by his goodness and wisdom and justice. This then was unknown to the pagans. For that reason let us take to heart the teaching which is here laid down, which is in agreement with what our Lord Jesus Christ teaches (John 5:17), that the Father is always at work, and the Son with him, who is the Wisdom of which Solomon speaks in Proverbs 8.

Well then, do we wish to have a good understanding of our confession that God is the Creator of heaven and earth? Let us immediately call this to mind, that he guides everything, and that he has not forgotten his creatures, but that he coordinates them according to his will. Consequently we can conclude that the formation of the clouds in the air does not just happen, that they do not even come into being there in accordance with the earth's wishes, but that it is God who guides everything, and who imposes his law on good weather and rain (*that* therefore comes from this sovereign dominion[45]), and that no drop of rain will ever fall, no good weather will ever come, no puff of wind will ever blow, which our Lord has not commanded, and for which these creatures (although they are without sensation) do not receive a secret impulse from the one who governs all, and who transcends all. So much for the first point. But in

---

[45]This parenthetical statement seems odd; within the context of the written text it is not clear what the pronoun "that" (*cela*) refers to. I suspect that it refers to something outside of the text, namely the rain that was falling in Geneva as Calvin was preaching.

the second place, we are taught here that we do not understand this, we do not have the intelligence to know it. It is therefore necessary that we should put ourselves under the word of God, and that faith should be our entire understanding. Thus we have on the one hand the providence of God, which is here confirmed, so that we will have no doubt that everything is governed by his will, and at the same time we need to be reminded of our limited intelligence, so that despite our inability to judge all things, because they exceed our limitations, we nevertheless do not conclude that it is all for nothing, but rather go back to what is said here: to listen. If therefore our minds are too small and too feeble, let us go back to our God, who will show us the things which are hidden and unknown to us. For it is not our place to judge of these things as our fancy takes us. After all, human understanding, when it cannot submit itself to God and his word, is a frightening spectacle of confusion. So if we cannot judge of these visible things, and matters concerning the world, unless God enlightens us by his Holy Spirit and guides us by his word, what about the eternal kingdom of God, which is incomparably higher than [**343**] anything mentioned here? We are inadequate to judge of things belonging to the world—visible things which are subject to ruin and decay. Then how will our judgment penetrate into the spiritual kingdom of God? Are we not bound to fail there? Therefore let us by all means learn to humble ourselves and to be modest. When it comes to knowing the things which properly belong to our salvation, if we wish to make good use of them, let us in the first place realize that we are incapable of knowing anything unless God teaches us. Therefore let us turn to him, and allow ourselves to be guided by his word. And when we do not see the things that we desire to understand, let us realize that our Lord wants to humble us. Let us not play the fool, and indulge in fanciful speculation, but let us be content to remember the lesson found here, which is taught us in the word of God. This, then, is the way we should put this passage into practice."

REFLECTIONS ON CALVIN'S EXPOSITION

I have chosen this selection from Calvin for a number of reasons. Not only is Calvin probably the most prominent representative of the positive interpretation of Elihu, but he is also the commanding figure in the Reformed tradition of Protestantism, to which

John Stek and I both belong. But this specific selection from Calvin's sermons on the Elihu chapter touches on another interest that I share with our honoree: the hermeneutical relations between science and Scripture. Let me single out a few of the themes in Calvin's sermon that strike me as particularly significant.

Calvin was a master of expository preaching, and his sermon follows the biblical text very closely. It is instructive to see how the first part of his sermon builds on basic points in the opening verse: "Hear these things, Job, stand still, ponder the marvels of God." It is clear from the context that the "marvels" in question (Hebrew נִפְלָאוֹת) are the works of God in nature, and Calvin unhesitatingly follows the text in equating the phenomena of nature with marvels or miracles: "the works of God are so many miracles." He makes it clear in an earlier sermon on Job that he sees no disjunction between "miracles" and "the order of nature."[46] This means that Job is commanded to "stand still" (עֲמֹד) and "ponder" (הִתְבּוֹנֵן) the phenomena of the natural world, which leads Calvin to a general discussion of the value of the investigation of nature.

But that discussion is again shaped by another important distinction in the text—that between "hearing" and "pondering." Since Elihu is the mouthpiece of God, the command to Job to hear constitutes an exhortation to listen to the word of God, as distinct from the human task to investigate nature. Again taking his cue from a feature in the text, Calvin draws the conclusion that hearing the word of God must *precede* the investigation of nature.

Having thus established a text-based framework for his discussion, he proceeds to elaborate on the general theme of what we would call "science," but which Calvin and his contemporaries considered to be part of the philosophy of nature (*philosophia naturalis*). As we follow this discussion, however, we notice a tension between two emphases with respect to scientific inquiry. The first emphasis is on the priority of hearing the word of God, and the second is on the positive command to engage in the investigation of nature.

It is clear that the first emphasis predominates in Calvin's sermon. He uses very strong language in stressing the indispensability of "attending the school of God" for those who ponder the wonders of the natural world. Unless we first listen to the Word of God, "we will never get to the main point," "our eyes will be blinded," "we will have no discernment," in fact, "we are incapable of knowing anything." The pagan philosophers who inquired into the phenomena of nature did not have access to Scripture, and therefore they only wasted their time; their wisdom is "accursed" and amounts to nothing but "abysmal confusion," or "a frightening spectacle of confusion." In a word, these thinkers are just "so many mirrors of the blindness which is in all men until such

[46]See *CO* 35.312.

time as God has taught them in his school." It is therefore necessary that we should turn to Scripture, and that "faith should be our entire understanding."

But the second emphasis is not absent from Calvin's exposition of Elihu's words. He takes seriously the fact that the text contains a divine command to "ponder" the marvels of creation. Although he uses the relatively colorless French verb *considérer* to translate the Hithpael of בִּין in the original, he may have been conscious of the fact that the Hithpael conjugation often has an intensive force. In any case, the "pondering" that he has in mind is a matter of sustained investigation. The point of the preceding command to "stand still" is that the pondering should not be a fleeting thing. Investigators "must not take just a passing glance at what God presents to their view, but they must look at it closely, and make an effort to study it in a thoroughgoing manner." Despite initial discouragements in their pondering, they must "be indefatigable in [their] study," they must "continue that study." On four different occasions, Calvin uses the French word *estude* in this connection, with its sixteenth-century connotations of assiduity and zeal. Furthermore, this kind of sustained study prevents us from becoming "vagabonds," people who are apt to lose their way and come to grief in the frenetic pace of human busyness. Such study also serves to motivate us to do our duty. Clearly, Calvin assigns a high value to the study of natural phenomena.

Moreover, despite his sweeping dismissal of pagan wisdom, Calvin also acknowledges the achievements of the pagan philosophers who engaged in the investigation of nature. He makes some extraordinary claims for their scientific insights: they "have had subtle discussions of the secrets of nature, and virtually nothing has been hidden from them," and "they have understood the things which to us seem to be incomprehensible." In fact, Aristotle is said to be "the wisest man who ever lived," a man "who has never had his equal." Most strikingly of all, Calvin also says, referring to these pagan thinkers, that "God gave *l'esprit* to those who have treated so subtly of the order of nature." I have translated the word *l'esprit* as "understanding," but it could also be rendered "the Spirit."[47] On either reading, Calvin sees the hand of God also in the achievements of pagan science.

This is not the place to discuss how these two contrasting emphases fit together in Calvin's overall theology. Such discussion would require a treatment of the familiar themes of "antithesis" and "common grace," and would need to take into account that Calvin lived before the rise of modern science, and that he was preaching to a congregation, not lecturing to theologians. We might well conclude that there are inconsistences in Calvin's extemporaneous statements on the matter, but at the same time

---

[47] We find a similar statement in Calvin's Sermon 143 on Job (*CO* 35.312): "For also who has given *l'esprit* to these secular philosophers, to know how to deal so well with the secrets of nature? God has given them this knowledge (*science*)."

acknowledge that he provides fundamental insights toward a contemporary view of Christian scholarship. All this would carry us too far afield in the present context.

Our concern at present is to observe how this selection from Calvin's preaching illustrates the movement from text to sermon in a master preacher, and to seek to learn from his example. If we grant the point that Elihu is speaking for God, to what extent is Calvin's preaching on Job 37:14-16 a model to follow, and to what extent does he illustrate mistakes that are to be avoided? Let me briefly highlight some positive and negative features.

On the positive side, Calvin sticks very close to the text. Not only is his sermon based on a direct study of the Hebrew, but the sermon follows the biblical text verse by verse. Calvin, as it were, walks his hearers through the actual words of Scripture, making them familiar with virtually every sentence. Furthermore, as we have seen, he structures the points he makes on explicit features in the biblical text. His assertion that all phenomena of nature are "miracles" is a valuable teaching, which breaks with the Scholastic notion of miracle as a suspension of the order of nature, and can be supported by Scripture. Furthermore, Calvin is insistent throughout on drawing out the practical implications for each passage of Scripture, and repeatedly states, "This is what we should remember from this text."

It is also noteworthy that Calvin, though quite capable in other contexts of producing elevated and literary French prose, adopts an unadorned and straightforward style in his preaching. He is concerned above all to communicate with his audience in language that they can understand, often using colloquial expressions and colorful everyday sayings. He puts his vast philological and theological erudition in the service of communicating the message of the text, simply and directly, to ordinary believers. In all these ways, he is a model to be emulated.

Yet the sample of Calvin's preaching we have selected also shows significant weaknesses. He gives far too much weight, for example, to the fact that the command to "hear" comes before the command to "ponder." He interprets this to mean that listening to the voice of God in Scripture should take precedence over the results of the human investigation of nature. Although this theological point is undoubtedly a valid one, it does not follow from the text. Elihu's exhortation to Job to hear does not stand in *opposition* to his exhortation to ponder, but rather *reinforces it*. In effect, Elihu is saying, "Listen carefully, Job, to the following command: ponder the wonders of God."

Furthermore, it is doubtful that the pondering that Job is exhorted to do should be interpreted as referring to the scientific investigation of nature. Job is being urged to stop and take a good look at the wonders of nature that God has created, so that he will stand in awe of the majesty of God. The point is not that he should engage in a systematic inquiry of natural phenomena, but that he should come to realize the awesome nature of the God whom he is challenging. It could perhaps be argued that awe before the marvelous works of God could also become the legitimate starting point for the development of philosophy and science, but this is not the point of Elihu's admonition to Job. At most, such an argument could be an inference or further extension of his words.

The result of these two exegetical mistakes is that the observations that Calvin here makes on the hermeneutical relations of Scripture and science lose their grounding in the text on which he is preaching. If they are to maintain their validity, they must be justified on other grounds than on the words of Elihu. Calvin falls into the ever-present temptation of the exegete and preacher: to read into the text what is not there.

A Close Reading of Psalm 13:
Daring to Ask the Hard Questions

Carl J. Bosma

I t is a privilege to dedicate this essay to Professor Emeritus John H. Stek, who introduced to me the riches of the Psalter.[1] In his classroom and writings,[2] Stek argued for a "close reading" of the biblical text that integrates the available exegetical methods. Moreover, he emphasized that the exegete must not only interpret *what* the biblical text communicates; he must especially show *how* the text communicates its messages.[3] Out of that conviction he shared the gains of form criticism and stylistics with his students.

This essay will study Psalm 13[4] from a form-critical and stylistic perspective. As a form-critical study, it will pay particular attention to the interrelationship of the form, content, and function of its basic modes of speech, highlighting stylistic elements as they illumine rhetorical functions. This study will also introduce the reader to the form, function, and theological articulation of the characteristic modes of speech in complaint psalms.

Four factors motivated my choice of Psalm 13. First, it is a complaint psalm. The disturbing fact is, as Walter Brueggemann has argued, that the contemporary church has largely purged the complaint psalms from its life and public worship in its present quest for "formless religious experience." In Brueggemann's opinion, this loss has resulted in the psychological inauthenticity of faith and in the lack of a genuine concern for social justice in the church.[5] I am convinced that effective preaching of complaint psalms will help to recover these powerful biblical texts for the faith and life of the church.

Second, Psalm 13 is a textbook example of an individual complaint psalm.[6] Although it is the shortest complaint psalm, within the compass of only six verses it

---

[1] As is evident from his notes on the psalms in the *NIV Study Bible*, Stek has studied the Psalter intensively, especially from the perspective of stylistics. In the spirit of Eccles. 12:9, he dedicated himself to the study of the prosodic, rhetorical, and architectonic forms of the psalms.

[2] See, for example, his studies "The Stylistics of Hebrew Poetry: A (Re)New(ed) Focus of Study," *Calvin Theological Journal* 9 (1974), 15-30; "When the Spirit was Poetic," *The NIV: The Making of a Contemporary Translation*, ed. Kenneth L. Barker (Grand Rapids: Zondervan, 1985), 72-87.

[3] Stek, "The Stylistics of Hebrew Poetry," 15-16.

[4] In this essay, versification of the psalms is based on BHS.

[5] Walter Brueggemann, "The Costly Loss of Lament," in *The Psalms and the Life of Faith*, ed. Patrick D. Miller (Minneapolis: Fortress, 1995), 98-111.

[6] Hermann Gunkel, *Die Psalmen* (Göttingen: Vandenhoeck & Ruprecht, 1926), 46.

exhibits superbly the essential modes of speech and movements of this literary genre: dramatic change in modes of speech from poignant protests (vv. 2-3) and passionate petitions (vv. 4-5) to (promised) praise via a persistent profession of covenant loyalty (v. 6a).

The radical transition from hurt to joy in Psalm 13 provides the third impetus for my choice. Recently, Brueggemann argued for the close yet contrastive correspondence between the movement from agony to adoration in the biblical complaint psalms to the elements of the grieving process observed by Elizabeth Kübler-Ross.[7] He then went on to say that the regular use of complaint psalms was constitutive for Israel's faith and served a rehabilitative function for those who suffered. This rehabilitative use of complaint psalms suggests that a knowledge of the modes of speech of a complaint psalm and their respective speech functions is essential for effective pastoral care.

Finally, I selected a complaint psalm because I believe that regular, effective preaching of the biblical complaint psalms enriches the congregation's understanding of prayer and has the potential for preventative pastoral care. Effective preaching of complaint psalms will once more empower believers to voice their grief in meaningful ways to the only One who is ultimately able to resolve it.

A CLOSE READING OF PSALM 13

The Complaint Proper (vv. 2-3)

Introduction

The primary function of the complaint proper is to give voice to human suffering and to identify the plaintiff's problem. Its concern, however, is not with a cathartic description of personal suffering "but with the removal of the suffering itself."[8] For this reason the complainant presents his complaint as a reproachful protest in the court of the only One who can remove suffering, the Lord who reigns as King and Judge. Because it presents the reasons for the petitions that follow (vv. 4-5), the complaint proper (vv. 2-3) is the focal point of the complaint psalm.

The complaint proper of Psalm 13 begins abruptly with a series of accusatory questions prefaced by "How long?"—questions that powerfully express the complainant's impatience and anxiety. It also contains three crucial elements:[9] the complaint about God, the complaint about personal suffering, and the complaint about the action of

---

[7] See Walter Brueggemann, "From Hurt to Joy, from Death to Life," in *The Psalms and the Life of Faith*, 89.

[8] Claus Westermann, *Praise and Lament in the Psalms* (Atlanta: John Knox, 1981), 266.

[9] These characteristics are discussed by Westerman, *Praise and Lament in the Psalms*, 169. For the theological significance see pp. 267-268.

another. The sequence in which these elements appear is important. The psalmist does not begin his prayer with a complaint against the enemy, nor with a declaration about his personal suffering, but by defiantly hurling a forceful double complaint against God. Since the complaint against God occurs in the initial position, it expresses the principal issue at stake. The sufferer's double accusatory question against God supports this. The complainant's concern about the enemy (v. 3c) comes last and, significantly, receives only a short half-line of his attention. Moreover, reading the first and third complaints together (i.e., vv. 2 and 3c) indicates that God's absence is the reason for the psalmist's unbearable personal anxiety in the face of the enemy's threatening ascendancy.

The complainant's fourfold anaphoric repetition of the accusatory question "How long?" communicates a sense of passion, urgency, turbulent impatience, extreme perplexity, and desperation. It also hammers home the petitioner's relentless insistence that something is drastically wrong, and it shows that the sting of his grief is the prolonged duration of the distress. Finally, these reproachful questions demonstrate that previous efforts to ameliorate this unbearably prolonged distress have failed (cf. Job 19:2-3). A change is long overdue!

The psalmist's bold expostulation against God consists of two disputatious questions, each of which is introduced by the interrogative "How long?" (עַד־אָנָה). Along with its initial position in the poem, the twofold repetition of this reproachful question indicates that the focus of attention falls squarely on God. The double-accusatory questions protest[10] God's unfavorable disposition toward the suppliant[11] and express the speaker's extreme perplexity and impatience with God's apparent extended disfavor. Like the repetition of "Why?" in Lamentations 5:20, the double "How long?" in this complaint allows the sufferer to voice with inordinate boldness his profound sense of abandonment by God. Unlike the accusatory question "Why?" (לָמָה, Ps. 10:1; 42:9; 44:24), the primary concern of the question "How long?" is not with the *reason* for God's apparent negative disposition toward him, or God's noninvolvement and indifference to his plight, but with the prolonged *duration* of the petitioner's suffering. Together with the verbs "to forget" and "to hide," the question "How long?" implies that God's disinterest has persisted for some time. The suppliant wants to know how long this is going to last!

---

[10] When addressed to God, this is not a polite question for information but a formal judicial protest. It amounts to a reprimand, a reproach of the Lord who has not done for his covenant partner what he may legitimately expect.

[11] Craig C. Broyles, *The Conflict of Faith and Experience in the Psalms: A Form-Critical and Theological Study*, JSOTS 52 (Sheffield: Sheffield Academic Press, 1989), 59. Broyles distinguishes two types of God-complaints: complaints that "concern Yahweh's disposition toward the psalmist" and complaints that "focus on the mode of his intervention, or non-intervention, in the affairs of the psalmist."

The First Accusation (v. 2a)

This concern is underscored in the unique, paradoxical formulation of the first question of complaint addressed against God in verse 1a. In this protest the psalmist has juxtaposed the interrogative "How long?" with the question "will [Hebrew YQTL] ... forever?"[12] The rhetorical function of this unique combination of two distinct questions is to focus God's attention on the tremendous negative impact of his inexplicable delay in coming to the psalmist's rescue. At the heart of this complaining query is *When* is this going to end? How long do I have to endure your indifference and continue to suffer?[13]

With few exceptions, the invocation of the covenantal name normally occurs at the beginning of the individual complaint psalms and may be repeated in new arrangements with other modes of speech (cf. v. 4). The invocation has four functions. First, it identifies the deity to whom the prayer is addressed and in whom the supplicant has placed his trust. Second, and in spite of the contrary evidence voiced in the complaints, the invocation lays claim to the intimate and personal (covenant) relationship between the petitioner and the Lord, demonstrating that the psalmist continues to hold on to the previously established covenant relationship.[14] In fact, even at the brink of death he stakes his whole life on it. The invocation is, in the third place, an audacious act of faith that stands in strong tension with the preceding "How long?" and the subsequent shrill cry of dereliction against God. Together with these complaints, the invocation encapsulates the living tension of despair and trust in the prayer. Fourth, in its present location the invocation of God's covenant name is a bold act of faith that functions as an overture to reestablish dialogue with the Lord[15] in a covenant context.

---

[12]Some consider this combination of "How long?" and "forever" to be a logical contradiction. At issue is the incongruent נֶצַח. However, the use of these interrogatives in the binary poetic line of Psalm 74:10 suggests to N. H. Ridderbos (*De Psalmen I* [Kampen: Kok, 1962], 156) that they were originally two distinct questions. Psalm 74:10 reads as follows: "*How long* will the enemy mock you, O God? Will the foe revile your name *forever*?" In the light of Psalm 74:10, therefore, Ridderbos suggests that in his deep anguish and frustration the psalmist has joined two originally distinct clauses into one. The resultant two-in-one solecism is an example of defective form of expression used for emphasis. It is an emotionally charged solecism that effectively communicates the troublesome (dramatic, awful) inner tension experienced by the psalmist (v. 3a). In this essay YQTL is any imperfect and QTL is any perfect form.

[13]Patrick D. Miller, Jr., *They Cried to the Lord: The Form and Theology of Biblical Prayer* (Minneapolis: Fortress, 1994), 72.

[14]Brueggemann, "From Hurt to Joy, From Death to Life," 70.

[15]Samuel E. Balentine (*Prayer in the Hebrew Bible: The Drama of Divine-Human Dialogue* [Minneapolis: Fortress Press, 1993], 149) writes: "This address or invocation establishes the prayer's intense quest for dialogue with God, the equally stubborn refusal to remain a mute partner in the divine-human enterprise. Especially in the midst of hurt and pain, one abandons monotonic passivity. These lamenters seek to engage God at all costs; they must have their say."

Since the suppliant of Psalm 13 knows the divine name, God is under a self-imposed obligation to fulfill his promise. By calling upon the divine name within the context of his daring complaint, the sufferer establishes "his right to expect some action from God."[16] Consequently, the invocation forms the ground for his complaints and the petitions that follow, reinforces the urgency of the prayer, and serves as the basis of hope for deliverance.[17]

The Accusation Proper

To fully appreciate the utter seriousness of the accusatory question "Will you forget me forever?" it is necessary to place the verb "to forget" (שָׁכַח) in its appropriate semantic field.[18] According to Samuel E. Balentine, the verb occurs mostly in the prayers of complaint with God as the subject.[19] In these prayers it occurs predominantly in the accusatory question against God and in the negative petitions that imply a complaint against God.

Two aspects of this verb's use help the reader understand the inordinate boldness of the psalmist's protest in verse 1a. First, as in Psalms 9-10, it connects the confident claim of the righteous that God does not forget their plight with the self-serving counterclaim of the wicked, who argue that, in fact, God does forget the helpless. The underlying assumption behind the vigorous affirmation of the righteous is that the Lord reigns as a just King and a righteous Judge from Zion and is a refuge for the oppressed (Ps. 9:9). Moreover, according to the motivational clause of the hymnic call to praise in Psalm 9:11-12, the Lord does not forget the cry of the afflicted (cf. Ps. 10:17-18). In this verse it is clear that the verb שָׁכַח has the cry of the afflicted as its object.

Even so, the psalmist's personal experience seems to deny the truth asserted in Psalm 9:11-12 and confirm the presumption of the arrogant wicked: "He says to himself, 'God has forgotten; he covers his face and never (לָנֶצַח) sees'" (Ps. 10:11). As far as the self-assured wicked person is concerned, God's royal "protection is not available to the helpless, and so it is an opportunity for unrequited treachery. . . ."[20] No wonder the psalmist pleads urgently with the Lord in the next verse: "Arise, Lord! Lift up your hand, O God. Do not forget the helpless" (Ps. 10:12).

---

[16]Brueggemann, "From Hurt to Joy, From Death to Life," 70.

[17]Miller, *They Cried to the Lord*, 62.

[18]According to Samuel E. Balentine (*The Hidden God: The Hiding of the Face of God in the Old Testament* [New York: Oxford, 1983], 137), the verb שָׁכַח occurs just over 100 times in the Old Testament. It occurs seventeen times with God as the subject, the majority of these in the lament psalms.

[19]Balentine, *The Hidden God*, 139.

[20]Ibid., 138.

The counterclaim of the insolent wicked in 10:11 stands in sharp contrast to the vital confession in Psalm 9:11-12, and in even sharper contrast to the psalmist's confident portrayal of the radical social reversal practiced by divine justice in Psalm 9:17-18: "The wicked return to the grave, all the nations that forget God. But the needy will not always (לָנֶצַח) be forgotten, nor the hope of the afflicted ever perish." Despite the reassuring claim that "the needy will not always (לָנֶצַח) be forgotten," the psalmist's present experience of the Lord's continued ignoring of his plight leads him to question whether the Lord is going to forget his covenant partner forever.

A second use of the verb שָׁכַח is in contexts concerned with the maintenance of the covenant relationship between Israel and the Lord. In Deuteronomy 4:23, for example, Israel is admonished "not to forget the covenant of the Lord [their] God that he made with [them]. . . ." Should Israel forget, the prescribed punishment is complete destruction (Deut. 8:19). Moreover, if Israel forgets, God will also forget! This reciprocal principle is also at work in Psalm 44, but this time from Israel's side. In their protest of innocence in verses 17 and 21, Israel complains that it has suffered unbearable shame even though it has not forgotten God, his covenant, or his name. In the light of the reciprocal principle expressed, therefore, God should come to the rescue. But God has not. On the basis of Israel's professed covenant faithfulness, it boldly raises the accusatory question in verse 24b: "Why do you hide your face and forget our misery and oppression?"

The conspicuous absence of a confession of sin in Psalm 13[21] suggests that the argument of the psalmist is the same. Consequently, his emotionally charged two-in-one accusatory question in verse 1a not only verbalizes his intense sense of alienation from God but it indicts God with breach of covenant. Out of his great consternation, the speaker places himself at risk, indignantly lodges the audacious complaint that God has forgotten his commitments with his covenant partner, and indirectly insists on Yahweh's covenant loyalty (cf. vs. 6a).

The Second Complaint Against God (v. 2b)

A second protest follows, in which the complainant accuses God of deliberately hiding his face (תַּסְתִּיר פָּנֶיךָ) from him.[22] To fully understand the significance of this idiomatic phrase, it is important to note, first of all, that with the exception of Exodus 36 and Isaiah 50:6; 53:3, this complaint always has God as the subject,[23] and it occurs

---

[21]Peter C. Craigie, *Psalms 1-50* (Waco: Word, 1983), 142; Fredrik Lindström, *Suffering and Sin: Interpretation of Illness in the Individual Complaint Psalms* (Stockhom: Almquist & Wiksell, 1994), 98; Walter Brueggemann, *The Message of the Psalms: A Theological Commentary* (Minneapolis: Augsburg, 1984), 59.

[22]The *Hiphil* indicates intentionality.

[23]Balentine, *The Hidden God*, 46.

predominantly in the Psalms.[24] Second, the idiom forms part of the language of the royal court. For example, when a human king or a member of his court turns his face towards someone seeking attention (פָּנִים; cf. 1 Kings 10:24), it is a sign of favor;[25] when the king turns his face away, it "is a sign of disfavor, refusal, or neglect."[26] Since the God of Israel is depicted as the Great King, the same meanings apply in the individual complaint psalms of the Old Testament when they report that the Lord turns his face away from or toward a suppliant who is seeking his attention (בְּקֵשׁ פָּנִים).[27] Third, this idiomatic phrase must be read in light of the common ancient Near Eastern conception that there is an intimate "connection between seeing the face of the deity and the quality of life one could expect." If the suppliant's personal god allowed the petitioner to see his face, prosperity ensued. But if the deity turned away his face, the consequences could only be negative.[28]

In this connection, two issues deserve careful attention. First, the assumption of an intimate cause-and-effect connection between sin and human suffering has led commentators to presuppose that God's hiding his face is always a direct consequence of human sin.[29] Against this popular assumption, Balentine observes the paucity of sin terminology in the lament psalms and the presence of protestations of innocence.[30] Because such protestations of innocence argue against the assumption that human suffering is necessarily caused by sin, Balentine concludes that in complaint psalms the suppliant typically protests that the Lord has intentionally abandoned him for some unspecified and inexplicable reason.[31] Such is clearly the case in Psalm 13:2b. To make matters worse, associating the hiding of God's face in verse 2b with the accusatory question "How long?" suggests that the complainant saw no imminent end to the Lord's intentional hiding. Like Job, therefore, the suppliant of Psalm 13 struggles with the problem of undeserved suffering.

Second, while the complainants do not specify the reason for God's hiddenness, they do detail its negative consequences in the complaint psalms.[32] They describe

---

[24]According to Balentine (*The Hidden God*, 45), this idiomatic phrase occurs twenty-nine times in the Old Testament. It occurs most frequently in the psalms (twelve times) and in the Prophets (eleven times). In the psalms is occurs predominantly in complaint psalms (Ps. 10:11; 13:2; 22:25; 27:9; 51:11; 69:18; 88:15; 102:3; and 143:7).

[25]Balentine, *The Hidden God*, 32.

[26]Ibid.

[27]cf., Psalms 24:6; 27:8; 105:4.

[28]Balentine, *The Hidden God*, 32. He also provides some references to the ancient Near East.

[29]For this issue I am dependent on Balentine, *The Hidden God*, 50-56. Fredrik Lindström also argues against this assumption in his *Suffering and Sin*.

[30]Balentine, *The Hidden God*, 53. The second observation is made with respect to Psalm 44:18.

[31]Ibid., 54.

[32]Balentine, *The Hidden God*, 56-65.

their estrangement and separation from God in three ways: (1) the complete breakdown of communication between God and the suppliant as it is reflected in God's refusal "to see," "to hear," or "to react;"[33] (2) the threat of the petitioner's imminent death or confinement to Sheol; and (3) God's absence from the cult center. In Psalm 13, these consequences of estrangement are elaborated in expressions of personal suffering (v. 3a) and in the complaint about the enemy's ascendancy (v. 3b). Then the complainant describes the breakdown in communication in his urgent petitions to the Lord "to look" and "to react" (v. 4ab), to restore him lest he sleep [the sleep of] death (v. 4cd).

The Complaint about Personal Suffering (v. 3a)[34]

The complaint about personal suffering is the longest independent clause in Psalm 13. Disagreements about its syntactical structure have produced different interpretations. Hans-Joachim Kraus, for example, extends the clause by ellipsis with the result that he emphasizes the petitioner's interior suffering, and then claims that verse 3a "deals with the self-examining, self-condemning, and scrupulous considerations that arise in the experience of abandonment by God. . . . " In Kraus's opinion, verse 3a centers "on the problem of the connection between grief and guilt . . . . "[35] Psalm 13, however, makes no explicit reference whatsoever to sin and guilt.

Those who prefer a more literal translation of the clause[36] understand its first part to be a graphic description of how the complainant projects one plan after another, all to no avail. In this interpretation, the verb "I am placing" (אָשִׁית) indicates an ongoing activity and suggests that the suppliant goes from one contingency plan to another as he attempts to cope with the emergency caused by the Lord's inexplicable delay. Judging from the concluding adverbial noun יוֹמָם, this is an everyday affair. The second part of the extended clause of verse 3a describes the negative result of the

---

[33]The breakdown in communication between God and the petitioner is particularly evident in the petitions in which the plea that God not hide his face is accompanied by an urgent appeal that God hear the suppliant's prayer: Ps. 69:13-17; 102:3; 143:1, 7. The triple repetition of the petition עֲנֵנִי in Ps. 69:13-17 indicates clearly that the Lord has been hiding his face. The thematic relationship between the Lord's hiddenness, prayer, and hearing is also explicit in Ps. 22:25: "He has not hidden his face from him but has heard when he cried to him."

[34]According to Westermann (*Praise and Lament in the Psalms*, 186-187) the description of the nature of the psalmist's personal suffering, an indispensable element in these psalms, varies greatly.

[35]Hans-Joachim Kraus, *The Psalms 1-59. A Commentary*, trans. Hilton C. Oswald (Minneapolis: Augsburg Publishing House, 1988), 215.

[36]J. Ridderbos, *De Psalmen I*, COT (Kampen: Kok, 1955), 109, note 2.

repeated failure of his contingency plans to meet the crisis at hand. The futile multi-plication of plans increases the "sorrow in his heart" (cf. Jer. 8:18).[37]

The Complaint about the Enemy (v. 3b)

In this complaint, the focus of attention shifts to the external forces threatening his life. The enemy's dominance marks the crowning disgrace in the speaker's personal affliction—while he is suffering, the enemy continues to ascend (יָרוּם, literally: "to be exalted").

The "enemy" is characteristically the principal subject in complaint psalms and therefore "the most elaborately developed part of the complaint proper."[38] But in Psalm 13 the complainant limits his description of the enemy's action to only one clause (v. 3b).[39] Interpretations of this striking phenomenon vary. Meir Weiss, for example, infers that the ascendancy of the enemy "is only a secondary consideration."[40] But since the speaker develops his anxiety about the enemy in the motivational clauses of verse 5, it is possible to conclude that the complaint against the enemy in verse 3b is not secondary.

Without a doubt, the psalmist is tormented more by his felt estrangement from the Lord than by the action of the enemy. In fact, the Lord's apparent abandonment of his covenant partner is ultimately the cause of the enemy's ascendancy, so much so that the speaker only devotes one half-verse to isolating and emphasizing the enemy's threat. The enemy's menace creates such a sense of urgency that the speaker cannot complete the poetic line, but moves right into the cluster of pleas of verse 4abc. He then completes this dramatic picture of the enemy's anticipated actions in the motivational clauses of verse 5.[41] This frugality of description makes the enemy difficult to identify.[42] "My enemy" (אֹיְבִי) could be read as a collective singular (cf.

---

[37]The uncommon noun יָגוֹן, "sorrow," typically occurs in descriptions of severe distress (cf., Ps. 31:11). In Psalm 13:3a it describes the complainant's inner psychological frustration and anxiety that torture his heart. It should be observed, however, that this noun is sometimes also associated with the proximity of death (cf., Ps. 116:3). This association may also be implicit here. What is implied in verse 3a is specified in verse 4d-5.

[38]Westermann, *Praise and Lament in the Psalms*, 188.

[39]A poetic line in Hebrew poetry usually consists of two half-lines, but here the petitioner employs only one half-line.

[40]Meir Weiss, *The Bible From Within: The Method of Total Interpretation* (Jerusalem: Magnes, 1984), 306.

[41]For a similar phenomenon see the half-line in Psalm 6:4b: "But you, O LORD, how long?" As Brueggemann says ("The Psalms as Prayer," *The Psalms and the Life of Faith*, 55), this accusatory question "is not a complete sentence. There is no verb."

[42]This is a common problem in the interpretation of the complaint psalms. For a discussion of the problem of the enemy of the individual see Kraus, *The Psalms*, 95-99; Helmer Ringgren, *TDOT I*, s.v. אֹיֵב, 216-218; Steven J. L. Croft, *The Identity of the Individual in the Psalms*, JSOTS 44 (Sheffield: Sheffield, 1987), 15-48. According to James L. Mays (*Psalms*, Interpretation [Louisville: John Knox, 1994], 79), the identity of the enemy is not important; the significant factor is that he "wears the mask of death."

v. 5),[43] and so may denote foreign belligerents. In this psalm, however, it probably refers to someone within the covenant community with whom the complainant is engaged in a dispute similar to the one envisioned in Psalm 127:5.[44]

For the same reason, it is difficult to specify the nature of the adversary's inimical action against the psalmist. To describe his personal enemy's anticipated hostile action, the supplicant employs the phrase "to be exalted over" (רוּם) plus the preposition (עַל). In this psalm it is only applied to the enemy of a petitioner. The precise meaning of this phrase in this particular context is disputed,[45] and translations vary.

With a human subject, the verb "to be exalted" can be used positively or negatively.[46] Negatively it refers to presumption and haughtiness (cf. 2 Sam. 22:28, Ps. 18:28). In Psalm 75:5, 6, for example, the verb depicts defiant opposition to the Lord's rule and is connected with boastful speech.[47] In view of the complainant's worry in Psalm 13:5, it seems that the nuance of Psalm 75:5, 6 also fits Psalm 13:3b. This same verb with a human subject followed by the preposition עַל plus a person is rare in the Old Testament. It is employed figuratively with "head" (רֹאשׁ) as the subject in Psalm 27:6: "Then my head will be exalted above the enemies who surround me" (סְבִיבוֹתַי וְעַתָּה יָרוּם רֹאשִׁי עַל אֹיְבַי). This figure symbolizes triumph.[48]

The question is whether the supplicant's complaint about the enemy in verse 3b is synonymous with his description of the enemy's antagonistic attitude in the motivating clause of verse 5. In my judgment, it is not because the motivating clause of verse

---

43J. Ridderbos, Psalmen 1-41, 109; A. A. Anderson, The Psalms, New Century Bible (London: Oliphants, 1972), 129. In view of the use of the plural "adversaries" in verse 5, Ridderbos also suggests that the singular may refer to the leader of the group, i.e., Saul.

44Croft, The Identity of the Individual in the Psalms, 41. Cf., 1 Kings 8.31-32. On the basis of Psalm 18:4-6, Mitchell Dahood (Psalms I 1-50, [New York: Doubleday, 1966], 77) speculates that the enemy is death. This interpretation is defended by Nicholas J. Tromp (Primitive Conceptions of Death and the Nether World in the Old Testament [Rome: Pontifical Biblical Institute, 1969], 92 and 114), is adopted by Craigie (Psalms 1-50, 142) and assumed by Lindström (Suffering and Sin, 100). The problem with this suggestion is that it conflicts with the plural synonym צָרַי, "my adversaries," in verse 5.

45Curiously, Claus Westermann (The Living Psalms [Grand Rapids: Eerdmans, 1989], 72) interprets this statement to mean that "the enemies feel able to exalt themselves over the supplicant because they view his suffering as his own fault and hence as a punishment." The problem with his interpretation is that, as we have mentioned above, in this psalm the supplicant makes no reference to sin and guilt in this psalm. For this reason, we agree with Brueggemann's (The Message of the Psalms, 59) claim: "The speaker does not for a moment entertain the thought that the trouble comes from guilt or failure. It is because of Yahweh's irresponsible absence, which is regarded as not only unfortunate, but unfaithful to covenant."

46H. P. Stähli, Theological Lexicon of the Old Testament, Vol. III, eds. Ernst Jenni and Claus Westermann, trans. Mark E. Biddle (Peabody, Mass.: Hendrikson Publishers, 1997), s.v. רוּם 1224. This work will be referred to hereafter as TLOT.

47N. A. van Uchelen, Psalmen I, POT (Nijkerk: G. F. Callenbach, 1971), 84-85.

48BDB, s.v. רוּם, 2b, p. 927; Kraus, The Psalms, 335. For this reason perhaps the NIV translates יָרוּם as "triumph."

5 is introduced by the particle "lest" (פֶּן). This syntax suggests that the anticipated victory cry "I have overcome him" (יְכָלְתִּיו) has not yet occurred. The complainant is experiencing a tension-filled "already" and "not yet" situation between his present suffering at the hand of his personal enemy (v. 3b) and the worst-case scenario that he forecasts in the motivational clauses of verse 5. On the one hand, as יָרוּם in verse 3b indicates, the enemy increasingly continues to dominate the complainant. In fact, the enemy is so powerful that the supplicant can see death crouching at his door (v. 4d). On the other hand, should the Lord continue to abandon him, he fears that his enemy's continued ascendancy will cause his death and that the enemy will exclaim, "I have overcome him!"

To appreciate the pathos of the sufferer's complaint against the enemy in verse 3b, it is necessary to understand that the verb רוּם is also employed with the Lord as subject to denote God's exalted position over the creation, and to describe the Lord's protective action as the divine Judge. In Psalm 3:4, for example, the expression "who lifts up my head" (וּמֵרִים רֹאשִׁי) denotes a juridical act "in which the judge raises up from the floor and thereby pronounces free a defendant who has prostrated himself . . . ."[49] The unique use of the syntactical construction יָרוּם עַל in Psalm 13:3b suggests that where the psalmist expected the Lord to be he now encounters the enemy. The unique use of רוּם עַל in verse 3b underscores "the abnormal situation, the reverse of what it should be."[50] Since the Lord is absent, the enemy occupies the position normally reserved for the Lord.[51]

The Petitions and Motivations (vv. 4-5)

Compelled by the ascendancy of his personal enemy and driven by the conviction that the present distress is not how the Lord intended life to be, the complainant changes his mode of speech from insistent protests to three urgent appeals bolstered by motivating "sanctions" (vv. 4-5).[52] The petition proper and its accompanying motivating clauses occupy the center position in the poem (vv. 4-5). Stylistically, the poet moves from an effective use of anaphoric repetition in the complaint proper (vv. 2-3) to a triad of bold imperatives. This lends a sense of urgency to his petitions.

[49]Kraus, *The Psalms*, 140; Stähli, *TLOT III*, 1222; Cf., Gen. 40:13; 2 Kings 25:27.

[50]C. A. Briggs, *A Critical and Exegetical Commentary on the Book of Psalms*, Vol. 1, ICC (New York: Charles Scribners' Sons, 1906), 101.

[51]J. Clinton McCann, *A Theological Introduction to the Book of Psalms: The Psalms as Torah* (Nashville: Abingdon, 1993), 91.

[52]This sudden switch in speech function confirms Westermann's claim (*Praise and Lament in the Psalms*, 266) that prayer complaint without petition is pointless. Here Westermann objects to Hermann Gunkel's claim (*Einleitung in die Psalmen: die Gattungen der religiösen Lyrik Israels* [Göttingen: Vandenhoeck & Ruprecht, 1933], 218) that the petition is the core of the complaint psalm. In Westermann's opinion, the petition issues naturally from the complaint and, consequently, the two cannot be separated.

The Petition Proper

Structurally, the central section of Psalm 13 consists of three emphatic imperatives that call for decisive divine judicial intervention—"Look . . . Answer . . . make light . . . ." These imperatives are supported by two negative final clauses. Petitions for an immediate divine intervention in individual complaint prayers normally exhibit a tripartite structure that corresponds to the three-dimensional structure of the complaint section:[53]

1. For God to be favorable (*look . . . incline yourself . . . and hear*)

2. For God to intervene (*help . . . save*)

3. For God to destroy the enemy or enemies (*destroy*).

The sequence in which these petitions occur in prayers for help varies depending on the urgency of the distress. Of the emphatic imperatives in Psalm 13:4abc, the first (הַבִּיטָה) and second (עֲנֵנִי) correspond to the first part of the three-stage petitionary structure outlined above. The third (הָאִירָה עֵינַי) matches the request for a divine salvific intervention to deliver the psalmist. Strikingly, however, there is no direct request for redress against the enemy.

Since the cluster of urgent petitions flows naturally from the complaint section (vv. 2-3), the compositional structure of the petitionary part of Psalm 13 (vv. 4-5) corresponds essentially to that of the complaint proper (vv. 2-3).[54]

Complaints (vv. 2-3)		**Petitions** (vv. 4-5)	
[2a] How long, O Lord, will you forget me? Forever?		**God**	[4a] Look!
[b] How long will you hide your face from me?			[b] Answer me, O Lord, my God!
[3a] How long must I wrestle with my thoughts with sorrow in my heart everyday?		**I**	[c] Give light to my eyes
			[d] lest I sleep in death;
[3b] How long will my enemy have the upper hand?		**Enemy**	

Comparison of the two parallel columns shows that the first imperative (הַבִּיטָה) corresponds to the second part of the complaint against the Lord (v. 2b) and emphatically demands a reversal of the Lord's hiding his face. Although the second imperative (עֲנֵנִי) fits all the questions of the complaint proper (vv. 2-3), this passionate appeal occurs typically in connection with complaints about the Lord's hiddenness. Since the final and climactic imperatival clause (הָאִירָה עֵינַי) recalls the Aaronic blessing with its understanding that the Lord's face is the source of light (Num.

---

[53]Westermann, *Praise and Lament in the Psalms*, 64.

[54]For the intimate relationship between the complaint and the petition in the individual complaint psalms see Miller, *They Cried to the Lord*, 99-102.

6:25-26; cf. Ps. 4:7; Ps. 31:17), it stands in sharp contrast with the previous complaint about the Lord's hiddenness (v. 2a). At the same time, however, it addresses the concrete need expressed in the complaint about personal suffering (v. 3a). As noted above, there is no direct demand for redress against the enemy that corresponds with the complaint about the enemy in verse 3b. This part is developed in the motivating section.

The First Petition

In the initial appeal, the petitioner pleads for the Lord's visual attention: "Look!" (הַבִּיטָה).[55] Comparison with Psalms 74:20, 80:15, 102:19, and Isaiah 63:15 indicates that the emphatic imperative "Look!" (הַבִּיטָה) in Psalm 13:4a is an abbreviation of the fuller imperative phrase that urges God to "look down from heaven"[56] at the plight of the suppliant or at the enemy.[57] This longer phrase assumes that God rules and judges from his heavenly throne, and that from his lofty position he takes note of human suffering in order to deliver the afflicted and those threatened by death. This image is clearly portrayed in Psalm 102:20: "The Lord looked down from his sanctuary on high, from heaven he viewed the earth, to hear the groans of the prisoners, to release those condemned to death." It also contrasts with the arrogant claims in Psalm 10:12 that God forgets, that he hides his face, and that he does not see (רָאָה); the righteous person is confident that God does take note (תַּבִּיט) of trouble and grief (10:14). A similar confidence probably inspired the suppliant of Psalm 13 to cry out, "Look!"

The Second Petition

The second appeal, "Answer!" (עֲנֵנִי), is joined asyndetically to the preceding supplication to express urgency. Common in individual complaint psalms,[58] this plea occurs especially in conjunction with complaints about the Lord's hiddenness.[59] Opinion differs about the nature of the response envisioned. Recent semantic analysis of the verb עָנָה argues that its primary meaning is "to react (willingly)."[60] This

---

[55] According to Anneli Aejmelaeus (*The Traditional Prayer in the Psalms*, BZAW 167 [Berlin: Walter de Gruyter, 1986], 26), this emphatic one-word urgent appeal occurs primarily in the petitions of complaint psalms. J. Clinton McCann, Jr. ("The Book of Psalms," *The New Interpreter's Bible*, Vol. IV [Nashville: Abingdon, 1996], 727) suggests that NIV's translation "Look!" is to be preferred over the NRSV's translation "Consider!"

[56] Psalms 33:10; 80:15; 102:20; 104:32; Isaiah 63:15.

[57] Suppliant: Psalm 80:15; Lamentations 1:12; 2:20; 5:1; the enemy: Lamentations 3:63 and cf. Psalms 9:13; 25:19; Lamentations 1:9.

[58] Aejmelaeus, *The Traditional Prayer in the Psalms*, 29.

[59] Cf. Psalms 27:6; 69:17; 102:2; 143:7.

[60] C. J. Labuschagne, *TLOT*, II, 927. The Lord is the subject of the verb עָנָה in seventy-eight occurrences; of these, thirty-five occur in the Psalter.

meaning for the imperative עֲנֵנִי fits the preceding emphatic command and may explain its frequent occurrence in connection with the hiddenness of God. Moreover, in the complaint psalms the command עֲנֵנִי implies that the suppliant is crying to the Lord (cf. Ps. 4:2; 27:7) and boldly demands that he respond. Finally, the expected response is not necessarily verbal.[61] In view of the declaration in Psalm 65:6 ("With awesome deeds of righteousness you respond to us . . . " נוֹרָאוֹת בְּצֶדֶק תַּעֲנֵנוּ), it may be inferred that the petition עֲנֵנִי expects a reaction in concrete deeds.

The second plea is accompanied by an invocation of the divine name "Lord" (יהוה). Expanded by the appositional phrase "*my* God" in verse 4b, this invocation buttresses in "highly relational terms" the earlier claim (v. 2a) of an intimate personal relationship between the troubled psalmist and the Lord. It also declares that the Lord is not only the God of Israel but also the God of each individual Israelite who serves him.[62] Broyles argues that the appositional phrase "my God" encapsulates the covenant relationship between the Lord and the psalmist. This covenant relationship, he writes, constitutes "the sole reason why the Lord should act on the psalmist's behalf . . . ."[63]

In the context of the pleas in verse 4abc, the petitioner's claim to intimate personal relationship with the Lord, his covenant partner, has an important double function. First, it serves as a ground of trust.[64] This grounding function is clearly articulated in the expression of confidence in Psalm 31:14 that serves as a preface to a series of plaintive pleas in verses 15-18. In this verse the speaker declares, "But I trust in you, O Lord; I say, 'You are *my God.*'" Second, as a statement of confidence that introduces a series of urgent petitions in verses 15-18, the address of intimacy also functions as a significant implicit reason for the Lord to act on the petitioner's behalf (cf. Ps. 25:2).

In the light of the above considerations, the phrase "my God" serves as an expression of confidence and as a proper basis and context for the third and climactic petition. This twofold function of the divine epithet also suggests that voicing distress before the Lord does not indicate a lack of faith. On the contrary, it is a courageous act of faith that serves as the basis for a personal address to God from the very beginning of the complaint. Without this confident faith there would be no reason to pray.

As in verse 2a, the suppliant's invocation of the divine name and the confident claim that the Lord is his personal God seems to be completely at odds with his pre-

---

[61]Labuschagne, *TLOT*, II, 928. Cf., Aejmelaeus, *The Traditional Prayer in the Psalms*, 31.

[62]Mays, *Psalms*, 79. According to N. H. Ridderbos (*De Psalmen I*, 87), this is particularly true of leaders, especially the king (cf. Ps. 22:11).

[63]Broyles, *The Conflict of Faith and Experience in the Psalms*, 121.

[64]Miller, *They Cried to the Lord*, 59.

ceding complaints that God has ignored and abandoned him. Nevertheless, in this dark hour the suppliant does not curse God to let death take over (Job 2:9). Rather, he insists on calling the Lord "my God" in an attempt to close the distance between him and the Lord.

The Third Petition

From the confidence of the second petition, the suppliant boldly moves to a third petition: "Give light to my eyes. . . . " This climactic cry for help derives its force and urgency from the following motivational clause (v. 4d) and stands in sharp contrast to the frightful experience of the Lord's hiddenness in verse 2b. This contrast implies that the Lord's turning his face toward the psalmist will lighten his eye.

The precise meaning of the suppliant's urgent entreaty in verse 4c is debated. Two lines of interpretation can be found. Some interpret the request in a figurative sense.[65] On the basis of the occurrence of the locution הָאִיר עֵינַיִם in Psalm 19:9, Proverbs 29:13, and Ezra 9:8, however, others interpret the suppliant's urgent petition in a physical sense.[66] For them it is a pressing appeal for the restoration of physical strength. Since the plaintive plea of verse 4a addresses the need articulated in the complaint of personal suffering in verse 3a, I conclude that the petitioner's eyes were dimmed by grief and, in view of the first motivational clause in verse 4d, the lack of light in the eyes implies the loss of vital powers (Ps. 38:10) and the proximity of death. For this reason, the suppliant pleads with the Lord to restore the light to his eyes. As is clear from 1 Samuel 14:27 and 29, the increase in light in the eyes means the restoration of life and vitality.[67]

Function

As judicial appeals in the Lord's court of justice, these imperatives represent the petitioner's insistence on his rights within the context of previously established precedents and promises. Because the suppliant's distress is the result of the Lord's inattentiveness, he refuses to accept this and, propelled by the urgency of the distress, appeals to the Lord to reverse the unbearable situation. The invocation of the divine name and the address of intimacy, "my God," assume a covenantal relationship that envisions the Lord's response to the distress of his covenant partner.

---

[65]Luther, for example, applies it to the removal of inner anxiety caused by the failure of the petitioner's emergency plans. See also Artur Weiser, *The Psalms* (Philadelphia: Westminster, 1962), 163.

[66]John Calvin, *Commentary on the Book of Psalms*, tr. Henry Beveridge (Grand Rapids: Baker, 1979), 184-185; J. J. Stewart Perowne, *The Book of Psalms* (Grand Rapids: Zondervan, 1976), 185; Joseph Addison Alexander, *The Psalms*, Vol. 1 (New York: Charles Scribners' Sons, 1853), 99; J. Ridderbos, *De Psalmen I*, 110-111; N. H. Ridderbos, *De Psalmen I*, 156-157; Kraus, *The Psalms*, 216; Mays, *Psalms*, 79.

[67]Sverre Aalen, *TDOT I*, s.v. אוֹר, 158.

On this basis I suggest that the suppliant's address demands immediate action in two ways. First, the voicing of distress is not merely an exercise in catharsis; it aims to secure the removal of the distress.[68] Second, the complaint does not flow from a lack of faith, but from a vital and robust faith that so addresses the Lord. Therefore, the complaint psalms are not quietistic acts of self-resignation but bold acts of faith's assertion by the Lord's covenant partner. The petitioner's imperatives are a daring act of insistent hope that stands in sharp contrast to the stage of depression in the grief process outlined by Kübler-Ross.[69]

The Motivational Clauses (vv. 4d-5)

Following typical judicial procedure, the appellant reinforces his appeals to the heavenly Judge with two negative motivational clauses (vv. 4d-5), each of which is introduced by the particle "lest" (פֶּן). These clauses have been carefully structured in a concise *chiasmus*[70] with the enemy's taunting victory cry at the center and the petitioner's fear of imminent death at the extremes.

a	[4d] ... lest I sleep (the sleep) of death(מָוֶת)		**I**
	b	[5a] lest my enemy say:	**Enemy**
		c [b] "I have overcome him!,"	
	b'	[c] [lest] my foes rejoice	**Enemy**
a'	[d] when I totter (מוֹט)		**I**

This arrangement spells out the inevitable consequences of the enemy's continuing dominance, should the Lord fail to act benevolently on behalf of his covenant partner: death (v. 4d) and the enemy's triumph (v. 5). Note also that while the petitioner dedicated only one clause to his description of the enemy's ascendancy in the complaint proper (v. 3b), he employs three motivational clauses when laying out his case in verses 4d-5. But these clauses contain no reference whatsoever to the divine name, a striking omission that underscores part of the suppliant's problem: the absence of God.

---

[68]Westermann, *Praise and Lament in the Psalms*, 266.

[69]Brueggemann, "The Formfulness of Grief," in *The Psalms and the Life of Faith*, 89.

[70]Several stylistic features support this concentric structure: The word play formed by the noun "death" (מָוֶת) and the verb "to totter" (מוֹט) indicates that verse 4d and verse 5d frame the speaker's description of the anticipated action of his personal enemy in verse 5abc. Together these two clauses constitute an instance of distant synthetic parallelism and so they must be read together, as *cause* (v. 5d) and *effect* (v. 4d). Moreover, the synonymous parallelism between the verbs "he say" (יֹאמַר) and "they rejoice" (יָגִילוּ) and the nouns "my enemy" (אֹיְבִי, sg.) and "my foes" (צָרַי, pl.), the ellipsis and double duty of the particle "lest" (פֶּן) in verse 5c, and the inversion of syntactical order of the verb and subject in verse 5a to subject and verb in verse 5c, all indicate that verse 5a parallels verse 5a, leaving the anticipated taunt at the very center in verse 5b.

Compositionally, the motivational clauses correspond to the complaint about personal suffering (v. 3a) and the complaint about the enemy (v. 3b). Verses 4d and 5d match the complaint about personal suffering in verse 3a "and understand the sufferer's grief and pains as steps on the road to death."[71] Verse 5 expands on the complaint about the enemy's dominance. Should the suppliant die, his death would certainly "mean that his foes had triumphed and this God must prevent."[72]

The First Motivational Clause (v. 4d)

The basic argument of the first motivational clause is that unless the Lord restores the suppliant (v. 4c) he will certainly die (v. 4d).[73] Thematically, this argument is closely related to the second part of the petitioner's complaint against God via the associations between the words "death" and "sorrow" in verse 3a. In Psalm 143:7, this important thematic connection is evident from the urgent plea for a response, the plaintive's petition that the Lord not hide his face, and the threat of imminent death:

[a] Answer me quickly, O Lord;	**Petition**
[b] my spirit fails.	**Motivation**
[c] Do not hide your face from me	**Petition**
[d] or I will be like those who go down to the pit.	**Motivation**

The Lord's hiding his face is tantamount to death. Similarly, the suppliant in Psalm 13 insists that the Lord stop hiding himself and react benevolently to his accusatory questions, because if he will not do so, if the present course of events remains unchanged, then death is imminent.

The Second Motivational Clause (v. 5)

The second motivational argument clarifies and develops the first. The petitioner argues that if the Lord does not act immediately on his covenant partner's requests, death is sure and the enemy will rejoice at his misfortune. To emphasize his point, the suppliant quotes what he anticipates will be the enemy's frightful taunt: "I have overcome him!"

The enemy's victory cry stands at the center of the petitioner's second motivational argument.[74] And, as in other complaint psalms,[75] this victory cry mocks the petitioner's

---

[71]Westermann, *The Living Psalms*, 73.

[72]J. Ridderbos, *De Psalmen I*, 110.

[73]Broyles, *The Conflict of Faith and Experience in the Psalms*, 90.

[74]According to Patrick D. Miller, Jr. (*Interpreting the Psalms* [Philadelphia: Fortress, 1986], 54-55), the taunt of the enemy is a central preoccupation in complaint psalms. For its negative effect on the Israelite, see N. H. Ridderbos, *De Psalmen I*, 30-31.

[75]For example, Psalms 3:2; 10:4, 6, 11, 13; 22:8; 31:2, 18; 35:21, 25; 40:15; 42:4, 11; 59:7; 71:11; 74:8; 79:10.

helplessness, suggests the Lord's indifference to the suppliant's distress, and questions his ability to provide the necessary help to reverse the petitioner's deplorable situation. In fact, quoting the enemy's anticipated victory cry clearly articulates the suppliant's awful predicament—in the present circumstances his trust in the Lord appears unfounded.[76] Indirectly, therefore, the quotation of the adversary's taunt in Psalm 13 functions as another implicit complaint against God[77] and serves as a powerful ground for an appeal to the Lord's honor[78] designed to induce God to prove his divine power.

The occasion and reason for the enemy's anticipated gloating is described in a short clause ("when I totter," כִּי אֶמּוֹט, v. 5d) which performs triple duty in the petitioner's prayer. First, it indicates the specific occasion for the suppliant's untimely death. Second, and as a result of its first function, it provides the opportunity for the enemy's derisive boasting. Finally, it also forms a striking contrast with the expression of confidence in verse 6a.

Two exegetical issues govern the interpretation of this concluding clause of the motivational section (vv. 4d-5). Is the conjunction כִּי that introduces this subordinate clause causal, temporal, or conditional? Since the anticipated victory cry "I have overcome him" in verse 5c marks the climax of the enemy's ascendancy (v. 3b), I prefer the temporal or conditional function of the conjunction כִּי (cf. בְּמוֹט, cf. Ps. 38:17), because it expresses the awful tension between the "already" of the enemy's ascendancy (v. 3b) and the "not yet" of his feared victory (v. 5). The second issue pertains to the various semantic nuances of מוֹט, a figurative verb that denotes great instability.[79] In the Old Testament this verb is employed in two antithetical, yet interrelated, overarching semantic spheres of influence that resonate in cyclically linked semantic fields (that also resonate in Ps. 13:5d). The first semantic sphere of influence employs the expression negatively (לֹא/אַבַל אֶמּוֹט) in connection with the Lord's secure establishment and preservation of creation and the city of Jerusalem (Ps. 93:1; 96:10 and 46:7; 125:1). The second sphere of semantic influence uses מוֹט to describe the chaotic convulsions of the cosmos in Psalm 46:3-4, which are intimately connected with the instability of the gods and human immorality (Ps. 82:5 and 11:3; 75:3).

These distinct usages of the verb מוֹט resonate in three thematically linked semantic fields that are important for understanding the verb's meaning and nuances in

---

[76]Miller, *They Cried to the Lord*, 73-75.

[77]Ibid., 73.

[78]J. Ridderbos, *De Psalmen I*, 110. Cf. Kraus, *The Psalms*, 216.

[79]A. Baumann, *TDOT* s.v מוֹט, 156. Significantly, of the forty times that this verb occurs in the Old Testament, twenty-six of them are found in the Psalter. According to Weiss (*The Bible From Within*, 306), it denotes the weakening of his faith. In the light of the expression of confidence in verse 6a, Weiss's opinion is not convincing.

Psalm 13:5d. First, the verb מוֹט in verse 5d is linked with death. It functions as a common metaphor that expresses fear of losing one's footing in the land of the living and falling into the netherworld.[80] The wordplay between the noun מוֹת and the verb מוֹט in verses 4d and 5d also argues for this thematic connection.[81] In the light of this thematic association, I conclude that the petitioner experiences his suffering as a manifestation of the chaotic forces of מוֹט in his life.[82]

The second semantic field describes the adversarial relationship between the righteous and the godless.[83] In their self-sufficient audacity, the ungodly claim that they will never be shaken (Ps. 10:6; cf. Ps.30:7). In sharp contrast, however, the righteous fear that the enemy will rejoice over them when they are shaken (Prov. 25:26). This dread comes to dramatic expression in Psalm 38:16: "For I said, do not let them gloat (שָׂמְחוּ), or exalt (גָּדְל) themselves over me, when my foot slips." This petition constitutes a excellent parallel to the concern of Psalm 13:5.

Third, the occurrence of מוֹט in declarations of trust and related texts (Ps. 15:5; 112:6) is important for understanding the contrast between verse 5d and verse 6a. In these declarations, the firmness that the Lord bestowed on creation serves as the basis for the stability of the righteous person who trusts the Lord (Ps. 125:1) and walks in his commandments (Ps. 15:5). Genuine stability is not a natural human resource (Ps. 30:7); only the Lord can provide it.[84] But the petitioner of Psalm 13 affirms that he is tottering and at the brink of death. Indirectly, therefore, the petitioner's preoccupation with being dislodged is intimately related to his complaint about the Lord's absence. If the Lord were present at his side, he would not be shaken.

Function

The petitioner's motivating arguments play an important rhetorical role in the judicial process. Their primary purpose is to convince the divine Judge and Warrior to comply with the stated requests and to act immediately on the petitioner's behalf. They communicate to the Lord what is at risk. In this case, it also has an indirect bearing on the Lord's own honor and character; if his covenant partner is ridiculed, then the Lord runs the risk of being ridiculed. The motivational clauses, therefore, seek to convert the suppliant's problem into God's problem and to establish an "identity of interest."[85]

---

[80]Dahood, *Psalms I*, 78. Cf. Psalms 16:8 and 10; 55:23-24; 66:9; 94:17-18.

[81]van Uchelen, *De Psalmen*, 85. A. A. Anderson (*The Book of Psalms*, I, 130) suggests it is a euphemism for death.

[82]Lindström, *Suffering and Sin*, 100.

[83]A. Baumann, *TDOT VIII*, s. v. מוֹט, 156.

[84]Ibid.

[85]The Belgic Confession § 37 identifies the cause of the believers with the "cause of the Son of God."

More specifically, they attempt to force the Lord's hand and to boldly lay claim on the Lord's response.[86]

Although the practice of presenting a convincing case to the Lord to secure a benevolent response is essential to Old Testament prayer, Miller points out that it tends to conflict with contemporary Christian conceptions of prayer. He writes,

> With our sense of the consistency of God's action, our resistance to any ideas of whimsicality in the divine intention that makes God's will dependent upon how urgently we press God, and our dependence upon the model of Christ—"Not my will but thine be done"—we properly hesitate to affirm the validity of such motivating and urging exclamations in prayer.[87]

Against this contemporary Christian (mis)conception of prayer, the petitioners in the complaint psalms trust that the Lord allows prayer to affect and move him. Their petitions are usually bolstered by motivating clauses that seek to persuade the Lord. To be sure, these motivating clauses cannot coerce the Lord, but they may persuade him.[88] For this reason, they employ rhetorically effective language. This crucial function of the motivating clauses leads Miller to conclude that "persuasion is as much the heart of the prayer as the plea."[89]

The Confession of Trust (v. 6a)

Introduction

Interpretation of the concluding section of Psalm 13 focuses on the abrupt aboutface in the mode of speech, i.e. the "abrupt change in mood"[90] from protest (vv. 2-4) and plea (vv. 4-5), to confidence (v. 6a) and praise (v. 6cd). Scholars disagree in their explanations for this sudden transition.

Those who adopt Friedrich Heiler's psychological explanation[91] and assume the compositional unity of the prayer interpret this unexpected shift in mood as a change in the

---

[86]Miller, *They Cried to the Lord*, 125-126. Brueggemann ("The Formfulness of Grief," 90) argues that such rhetorically persuasive reasons are similar to the bargaining stage in the grief process described by Kübler-Ross. However, the motivating clauses in the compaint psalms are much bolder.

[87]Miller, *Interpreting the Psalms*, 103.

[88]Miller, *They Cried to the Lord*, 125.

[89]Ibid., 126. Calvin also appears to place prayer in the context of the believer's regal office in the administration of God's cosmic rule. Commenting on verse 5, (*Commentary on the Book of Psalms*, 185-186), he writes, "We can, therefore, with confidence pray for ourselves, in the manner in which David here does for himself, only when we fight under the standard of God, and are obedient to his orders, so that our enemies cannot obtain the victory over us without wickedly triumphing over God himself."

[90]Klaus Koch, *The Growth of the Biblical Tradition* (New York: Charles Scribner's Sons, 1969), 175.

[91]Friedrich Heiler, *Prayer: A Study in the History and Psychology of Religion*, trans. S. Combe and J. E. Park (New York: Oxford, 1958), 271.

petitioner's attitude, which in turn is a psychological result of the confident affirmation of trust.[92] Others prefer a liturgical solution. They postulate that something decisive occurred in the cultic ritual between verses 2-5 and verse 6, and that this drastically altered the petitioner's situation and condition.[93] The majority of the latter adopt the hypothesis[94] that a priest uttered an unrecorded salvation oracle between verses 2-5 and verse 6.[95] In support of this, Westermann argues that the contrastive disjunctive clauses near the end of complaint psalms mark "the place at which in Psalm 12:5 the word from God stands, the place therefore at which the oracle of salvation occurs."[96]

The major problem with this popular liturgical hypothesis is that the individual complaint psalms in the Psalter contain few examples of priestly oracles of salvation.[97] Another difficulty, as Miller correctly observes, is that while some declarations of trust may have arisen from the experience of having heard a salvation oracle, this "is not necessarily the case."[98] In fact, according to Miller, it is very difficult to establish which complaint psalm is heard or "open."[99] Moreover, according to N. H. Ridderbos, in the case of Psalm 13 there is no compelling internal evidence to assume that a cultic act occurred between verse 5 and verse 6.[100] A third unresolved issue concerns the failure to provide an adequate explanation for the juxtaposition of verses 2-5 and verse 6 in the extant form of Psalm 13.[101]

---

[92]The refrain in Psalms 42:6, 12 and 43:5 serves as evidence for this connection. See, for example, Craigie (*Psalms 1-50*, 143) who writes, "it is in the nature of confidence to transform the present on the basis of past experience and thus to create hope for the future; and so the psalmist can affirm that he will "rejoice" in God's deliverance, even though it has not yet come." On this hypothesis verse 6cd functions either as anticipatory praise or a vow to praise.

[93]Brueggemann (*The Message of the Psalms*, 47) writes: "Thus, e.g. in Psalm 13, something happened between verse 4 and verse 5."

[94]F. Küchler, "Das Priestlerliche Orakel in Israel und Juda," in *Abhandlungen zur semitischen Religionsgeschichte und Sprachwissenschaft*, ed. Karl Marti [BZAW 33] 1918, 285-95; Joachim Begrich, "Das priesterliche Heilsorakel," *Zeitschrift für die alttestamentliche Wissenschaft* 52 (1934): 81-92.

[95]Cf. Lamentations 3:55 and Westermann, *Praise and Lament in the Psalms*, 69, 73.

[96]Ibid., 72

[97]Erhard S. Gerstenberger, *Psalms, Part I: With an Introduction to Cultic Poetry* (Grand Rapids: Eerdmans, 1988), n13. N. H. Ridderbos (*De Psalmen I*, 17) lists the following texts as possible examples: Psalms 12:5; 20:7; 27:14; 28:5; 32:8-9; 35:3.

[98]Miller, *They Cried to the Lord*, 127.

[99]Ibid., 133. Even Westermann (*Praise and Lament*, 73-74) has to admit that "no hard line can be drawn between petitions that have been heard and those that remain 'open.'"

[100]N. H. Ridderbos, *Die Psalmen: Stilistische Verfahren und Aufbau mit besonderer Berücksichtigung von Ps 1-41*, BZAW 117 (Berlin: Walter de Gruyter, 1972), 151-152.

[101]Tony W. Cartledge, "Conditional Vows in the Psalms of Lament: A New Approach to an Old Problem," in *The Listening Heart: Essays in Wisdom and the Psalms in honor of Roland E. Murphy*, ed. Kenneth G. Hoglund et. al. JSOTS 58 (Sheffield: JSOT, 1987), 78.

Still others reject both the psychological and the liturgical hypotheses.[102] Some of them argue for a rhetorical explanation. In their judgment, no real change in mood has occurred in the prayer. Broyles, for example, argues pointedly that verse 6cd is a vow to praise in an open petition and, as such, it does not denote or imply a change in mood.[103] The petitioner pledges to praise the Lord in response to an eagerly anticipated divine deliverance (verse 6b), but he has not dropped his complaint. For Broyles, the emphatic expression of confidence functions as a crucial, rhetorically effective, and bold move within the legal procedure that is designed to mobilize the deity to action.

In my judgment, Broyles' position is preferrable. In defense of this hypothesis I will first examine the compositional place of the expression of confidence, then probe its form and two important lexical terms, and finally examine its compositional function.

Compositional Place and Form

Confessions of trust are a common motif in the complaint psalms. Their compositional location, however, varies considerably.[104] They may occur at the beginning of a prayer (Ps. 25:1b; 31:2a; 71:1a), strategically in the body between complaint and petition (Ps. 3:4-7; 54:6), or near the conclusion of the prayer, as is the case in Psalm 13.

Broyles distinguishes three basic forms of the expression of confidence:[105]

a. An attribute is predicated of God: "God is/You are . . . "

b. An action is predicated of God: "God will/You will . . . "

c. The psalmist declares his personal trust: "But I trust . . . "

The first two forms are declarations about the Lord's attitude or action toward the petitioner. The third form is a straightforward affirmation of the suppliant's personal reliance on the Lord. The declaration of trust in Psalm 13:6a represents the third form, in which the petitioner himself is the syntactical subject. It is the simplest form of the straightforward personal affirmation of trust and it voices the petitioner's "basic trust"[106] in the Lord's reliability (חֶסֶד).

---

[102]Cf., Mays, *Psalms*, 79. Mays correctly observes that in the extant text there is no narrative setting or liturgical instruction to explain the surprising shift. In his judgment, the present form of the text leads the reader and pray-er from protest and petition to joyous praise. He claims that the text holds these three aspects together "as if to teach that they cohere in the unity of prayer." Psalm 42:8, the pivotal line of Psalms 42-43, clearly supports the coherence of petition and praise.

[103]Broyles, *The Conflict of Faith and Experience in the Psalms*, 186.

[104]Westermann, *Praise and Lament in the Psalms*, 72.

[105]Broyles, *The Conflict of Faith and Experience in the Psalms*, 41-42.

[106]For this term see Walter Brueggemann, *Theology of the Old Testament: Testimony, Dispute, Advocacy* (Minneapolis: Augsburg, 1997), 466.

Analysis of the Verb "to Trust" and the Noun חֶסֶד

In the individual complaint psalms, the verb "to trust" (בָּטַח) is one of the principal verbs for expressing personal confidence.[107] Trust is not a vague, fussy, internal feeling; it denotes a complete reliance on the Lord who intervenes in history on behalf of his covenant partner to protect him from destructive forces. Thus, in times of distress you can only survive by relying on the Lord.

In the light of the enemy's ascendance in Psalm 13:3b, it is vital to recognize the use of the verb בָּטַח in military contexts. Two aspects of its meaning stand out. The first is the sharp contrast between true and false sources of security (Ps. 40:5). This is amply illustrated by Sennacherib's attempt to undermine Hezekiah's trust in the Lord when he says, "Do not let the god you depend (בָּטַח) on deceive you when he says, 'Jerusalem will not be handed over to the king of Assyria'" (Isa. 37:10). In Sennacherib's opinion, the Lord is a deceptive source of security, and just as incapable of saving his people from the Assyrian armies as were the gods of the nations he had already defeated. For Isaiah (31:1), Egypt and military armaments are a false source of security. The only true source of security is the Lord (Isa. 26:4).

There is also the absence of fear (Isa. 12:2). Trust in the Lord is the exact opposite of fear of human beings, as Psalm 56:4-5 clearly articulates: "When I am afraid, I will trust (אֶבְטָח) in you. In God, whose word I praise, in God I trust (בָּטַחְתִּי); I will not be afraid. What can mortal man do to me?" These two aspects of meaning resonate in the expression of trust in Psalm 13:6a.

The basis for the suppliant's confident trust in Psalm 13:6a is the Lord's חֶסֶד. This noun is notoriously difficult to translate adequately.[108] More recent research[109] has underscored that this noun denotes not merely an attitude but that it refers, as the stereotypical phrase עָשָׂה חֶסֶד עִם indicates, particularly to benevolent actions in interpersonal relationships, be that in the context of human relationships or in divine and human relationships.[110] For this reason Nelson Glueck describes it as "powerful loyal aid," Katharine Doob Sakenfeld translates it as "faith in action," and Brueggemann describes it as "unearned grace in action."

---

[107]Approximately 40 percent of the occurrences of the verb בָּטַח in the Old Testament are found in the Psalter.

[108]Gordon R. Clark, *The Word Hesed in the Hebrew Bible*, JSOTS 157 (Sheffield: JSOT, 1993), 267.

[109]Nelson Glueck, *HESED in the Bible* (Cincinnati: The Hebrew Union College, 1967); Katharine Doob Sakenfeld, *The Meaning of Hesed in the Hebrew Bible: A New Inquiry* (Missoula: Scholars, 1978), 215-231.

[110]H. J. Zobel, *TDOT V*, s.v. חֶסֶד, 46.

חֶסֶד occurs predominantly in the various modes of speech of the complaint psalms.[111] Sakenfeld argues that חֶסֶד in these psalms "regularly involves rescue from dire straits as its specific action content."[112] She describes this content with the broad category of "faithful deliverance" (cf. Ps. 57:4).[113] This explains why the term חֶסֶד is primarily associated with the noun "salvation" (יְשׁוּעָה, and its synonyms) in the complaint psalms. In fact, יְשׁוּעָה (Ps. 13:6b) is a concrete expression of the Lord's חֶסֶד, in history. This is evident from the petition in Psalm 85:7: "Show us your חֶסֶד, O Lord, and grant us your salvation." In the light of the parallelism between the prepositional phrases בְּחַסְדְּךָ and בִּישׁוּעָתֶךָ in Psalm 13:6ab, I conclude that the meaning "faithful deliverance" is also present in Psalm 13. The obvious aim of the suppliant in the petitions of an individual complaint psalm is to obtain this assistance.

Sakenfeld also distinguishes five narrower semantic nuances of חֶסֶד in the Psalms, three of which resonate in Psalm 13:6a. The first and second are actually two sides of the same coin: the Lord's power and/or his ability to deliver.[114] These nuances are evident in those examples in which the noun חֶסֶד is conjoined via parallelism with the noun עֹז, "strength."[115] A variant of this nuance is the Lord's protective maintenance that prevents distress.[116] In this context, חֶסֶד refers especially to the Lord's protective presence against the powers of evil (Ps. 144:2). A third nuance is the Lord's willingness to deliver.[117] In the light of these nuances, Sakenfeld describes the action content of חֶסֶד as "the providential exercise of his power on behalf of the needy people with whom he has established a special relationship."[118]

I suggest that חֶסֶד in Psalm 13:6a denotes the Lord's benevolent readiness to provide his powerful legal assistance to the petitioner. Although the complaint in verse 2 protests against the Lord's apparent refusal to be faithful, in the expression of confidence the petitioner insists that he is securely oriented by the Lord's accessible, reliable, and powerful "faithfulness in action." In fact, indirectly he presses the Lord to activate his benevolent protective legal aid on behalf of his covenant partner.

---

[111]Sakenfeld, *The Meaning of Hesed in the Hebrew Bible*, 217.

[112]Ibid., 218.

[113]Ibid. In Psalm 57:4 חֶסֶד וְאֱמֶת are personified as a rescue squad.

[114]Sakenfeld, *The Meaning of Hesed in the Hebrew Bible*, 220-223.

[115]Exodus 15:13; Psalms 59:17; 62:12-b-13a.

[116]Sakenfeld, *The Meaning of Hesed in the Hebrew Bible*, 224-225. Cf. Psalms 21:8; 23:6; 32:10; 36:11.

[117]Ibid., 224.

[118]Ibid., 231.

Compositional Function

The assertion of personal trust in Psalm 13:6a seeks to motivate the Lord to act so that the petitioner will not be disappointed. It forms the platform from which the suppliant makes his appeal in verses 4-5 and it functions as a strong motivation for the Lord to fulfill what is requested in verse 4abc. It also functions as an indirect appeal to the Lord's powerful loyalty to induce him to right the wrongs he is experiencing.

In the light of this powerful expression of faith, it is evident that complaint prayers do not indicate a lack of faith. On the contrary, they represent an important act of faith.[119] In fact, based on the fundamental premise of the Lord's reliability and accessibility, the protest-petition-motivation sequence in these prayers are concrete evidence of a dynamic, active, genuine dialogical faith *sola gratia* within the context of the covenant.[120]

Jussive Petition

The suppliant's emphatic expression of confidence (v. 6a) should be understood as a jussive petition. A stylistic argument in favor of this interpretation is the conspicuous repetition of the noun "heart" from verse 3a. Its recurrence here envisions a dramatic transition in mood, should the Lord respond to the petitioner's plaintive pleas: a shift from "sorrow in my heart" in verse 3a to a heart filled with spontaneous joy as a result of the Lord's mighty intervention on the suppliant's behalf. Crucial to this interpretation, of course, is the assumption that the divine response has not yet occurred.

A jussive interpretation of the verbal aspect of יָגֵל allows it to be read as a self-exhortation to praise in which the petitioner, confidently assured of being heard and in joyful anticipation of God's deliverance, summons his heart to praise, "Let my heart rejoice . . . ." In this case, verse 6bcd functions as praise. It is better, however, to read the jussive as a prayer, a "request that his heart may rejoice in the experience of deliverance." As such, verse 6b functions as a polite request from a vassal to a superior—"May my heart rejoice in your victory!"—that is solidly grounded in the preceding emphatic confession of confidence in the Lord's covenant loyalty. Its basic argument is: "Since I trust in your חֶסֶד, may my heart rejoice. . . ."

For either interpretation of verse 6b, it is important to observe the striking omission of any reference to the suppliant's enemies. While reference to the enemy's dominance is made at the climax of the complaint proper (v. 3b), and the adversary's anticipated

---

[119]Cf. Miller, *They Cried to the Lord*, 130. Calvin (*Commentary on the Psalms*, I, 365) also comments on the occurrence of the verb "to cry" and the threefold repetition of "to trust" in Psalm 22:4-5.

[120]Brueggemann, "From Hurt to Joy, from Death to Life," 71.

ridicule of the suppliant occupies center stage in the motivational clauses of verse 5abc, in verse 6b the enemy is completely absent. The emphasis falls exclusively on the prepositional phrase "in your salvation" (בִּישׁוּעָתֶךָ), which constitutes the object of the petitioner's anticipated rejoicing.

As in 1 Samuel 2:1, Psalms 9:14, 20:6 and 21:1, the basis and occasion for the speaker's anticipated boisterous joy is indicated by the prepositional phrase בִּישׁוּעָתֶךָ. Two aspects of this phrase require closer attention. The first aspect concerns the meaning of the noun יְשׁוּעָה in these passages.[121] The variation in translation cited above raises the natural question: What exactly does this noun mean? Christian preachers especially must raise this question since their intended audience probably understands the term "salvation" almost exclusively as deliverance from sin. But this typical Christian understanding does not do full justice to the use of the term in Psalm 13:6b.

In the context of complaint psalms, the verb יָשַׁע and its cognate nouns are intimately related to the language of the law court and to legal protection.[122] In this forensic context, the verb יָשַׁע is employed by the oppressed in their cry for legal aid. In 2 Samuel 14:4, for example, the injured widow employs this verb in her appeal to the king: הוֹשִׁעָה הַמֶּלֶךְ, "Help, O king!" She cries out to him because it is his divinely appointed task to provide her with legal protection (Ps. 72:4, 12-14). *Mutatis mutandis*, since the Lord is the Great King, Judge, and Divine Warrior, he is also covenantally obligated to provide legal aid and protection for his covenant people when they are in distress (cf. Ps. 76:9). For this reason, persons without adequate legal protection appeal to the Lord's covenant loyalty (חֶסֶד) to help them (Ps. 6:5; 31:17). But, the verb יָשַׁע and its cognate nouns are also used to describe the positive response of the king (Ps. 72:4, 13), or God, to the cry for help.[123] In such a case they would refer to a single, concrete divine juridical intervention on behalf of an afflicted person (Ps. 76:10; 109:31). The specific nature of the Lord's legal aid depends on the nature of the distress and of the petition. For example, if the distress is of a military nature, the Lord's legal help will take the form of a military victory (Ps. 20:6, 10). In Psalm 13:6b it refers to a concrete intervention in history and may therefore be translated as "deliverance."

[121]Cf. John F. A. Sawyer, *Semantics in Biblical Research. New Methods of Defining Hebrew Words for Salvation* (Naperville, Ill.: Alec R. Allenson, 1972); John H. Stek, "Salvation, Justice and Liberation in the Old Testament," *Calvin Theological Journal* 13 (1978): 133-165.

[122]J. A. F. Sawyer, *TDOT IV*, s.v. יָשַׁע, 460.

[123]In this second sense the verb and its cognate nouns occur frequently in conjunction with expressions of confidence (Ps. 13:6; 17:7; 20:7; 25:5) and expressions of joy (1 Sam. 2:1; Ps. 9:14; 13:6).

The second aspect of the prepositional phrase בִּישׁוּעָתֶךָ that requires careful attention is the second person pronominal suffix ךָ. In Psalm 13:6b, as in Psalms 9:14, 21:1, and 106:4, it functions as a subjective genitive, thereby indicating that it is an act of God. For this reason the prepositional phrase in question is better translated as a verbal clause[124] either as "when you provide me with legal help" or "when you deliver me." The psalmist is asking the Lord to let his heart rejoice when the Lord resolves the problem of the enemy's oppressive dominance.

Vow to Praise

Introduction

The petitioner concludes his prayer with a hymnic declaration to sing to the Lord (v. 6cd), the high note of his prayer. Stimulated by the confidence in the Lord's "active grace" in verse 6a, the suppliant's wish of verse 6b becomes a reality in his public vow to praise God,[125] a vow that looks forward in complete trust to the yet-to-be-experienced divine deliverance. I will first examine the literary form of the vow proper (v. 6c), then probe the compositional function of verse 6cd, and finally discuss the concluding כִּי-clause (v. 6d).

Form of the Vow Proper (v. 6c)

Studies of the vow to praise in individual complaint psalms have focused on two forms. The first is a direct address to the Lord in the second person (Ps. 35:18), which may be expanded by a כִּי-clause (Ps. 86:12). This form of the vow to praise, however, is formally and syntactically identical to the vow to praise in a declarative psalm of an individual (cf. Ps. 56:12b-13 and 30:2), which makes it difficult to determine whether such a declaration functions as a song of thanksgiving or as a vow to praise.[126] In the second form, the speaker does not address the Lord directly in the second person but resolves to sing about him in the third person, as in Psalm 7:18. This form may also be expanded by a כִּי-clause, as in Psalm 109:31-32.

In view of the conspicuous formal differences between these two distinctive types of vows to praise in individual complaint psalms, Crüsemann raises the question whether these distinct types also have a different meaning and function. Although he

---

[124]Robert G. Bratcher and William D. Reyburn, *A Translator's Handbook on the Book of Psalms* (New York: United Bible Society, 1991), 126. Cf. Weiser, *The Psalms*, 161 ("in the help thou hast sent me"); *Revised English Bible* ("when I am brought to safety").

[125]Claus Westermann, *The Psalms: Structure, Content & Message* (Minneapolis: Augsburg, 1980), 58.

[126]With respect to voluntative declaration in Psalm 31:7-9, for example, Kraus (*Psalms 1-59*, 363) admits that it can "be understood as a vow for a future song of thanksgiving or as a song of thanksgiving itself."

does not arrive at a clear answer to this pertinent question, he postulates that the second form is a vow to praise pronounced in anticipation of a future divine deliverance.[127]

Comparison with Psalm 109:31-32 leads to the obvious conclusion that the brief vow to praise in Psalm 13:6c is an instance of the second form that has been expanded with a כִּי-clause (v. 6d). I judge, therefore, that it functions as a vow to praise in an open petition. Although the petitioner has not yet received the sure-to-be-experienced deliverance, in confident anticipation he pledges earnestly to credit the Lord for it in a public testimonial song (v. 6cd).[128]

The compositional form of Hannah's vow in 1 Samuel 1:11 illuminates the form of the vow in Psalm 13:6. Hannah's vow begins with an *invocation* of the divine name, proceeds to a *complaint* and *petition* in the protasis, and culminates in her *votive promise* in the apodosis. This sequence demonstrates, first of all, the unity of the protest-petition-votive promise sequence. No salvation oracle was inserted. In fact, Eli the priest only speaks a word of comfort after her prayer in verse 17. Consequently, it is not necessary to assume the pronouncement of a priestly oracle of salvation between verse 5 and verse 6 of Psalm 13 to account for the unexpected, radical, 180-degree turnaround in mood in verse 6. Second, the protest-petition-votive promise sequence in 1 Samuel 1:11 proves that the petitioner may address the complaint and petition directly to the Lord in the second person in the protasis and then formulate the votive promise in the third person: "Then I will give him to the Lord . . . ."[129] Together with the third person form of the vow in poetic form, it supports the third person form of the vow to praise in Psalm 13:6cd.

Note, however, that the third person address forms of the vow to praise do not identify the addressee(s). Of particular interest in this connection is the third person form of the vow of praise in Psalm 69:30-33. In this vow to praise the speaker also intercalated a jussive call to praise (v. 32) addressed to the worshipers at the cult center: "You who seek God, may your hearts live!" (v. 32b).[130] This suggests that vows to praise were occasionally made in the presence of worshipers at the cult center. Consequently, the addressees of the third-person form of the vow to praise in Psalm 13:6c could also be the worshipers at the cult center. This is important because it suggests that the practice of voicing one's complaints before the Lord was not necessarily a private matter,

[127]Frank Crüsemann, *Studien zur Formgeschichte von Hymnus und Danklied in Israel* (Neukirchen: Neukirchener Verlag, 1969), 275.

[128]Although the term "vow" is not employed in verse 6c, evidence from Psalms 22:25, 50:14-15, 56:13, 61:6, Job 22:27, Jonah 2:10 and 1 Samuel 1:11 indicates that vows were made in the complaint process.

[129]The LXX reading ἐπὶ ἐνώπιον σου has been adopted by the NRSV.

[130]In the extended second person form of the vow to praise of Psalm 22:23-31, the psalmist intercalates a summons to praise to the worshipers at the cult center in verses 23 and 24.

but could involve the community. In Hannah's case, Eli was there, even though he misdiagnosed her situation. This lends credence to Gerstenberger's claim that the aim of the individual complaint psalms was the restoration of the individual complainant to the community.[131] We read that Hannah heard the word of divine assurance from Eli, ate something, "and her face was no longer downcast" (vv. 17-18).

The communal context of (at least some) complaint psalms has, it would seem, important practical implications for the church's liturgy. It teaches us that pain cannot be voiced adequately in isolation. "In isolation," writes Brueggemann, "the power of pain grows more ominous and more hurtful."[132] Pain must be verbalized in community.[133] To that end, the biblical complaint psalms serve as model prayers for the community. This paradigmatic function is clearly indicated in the superscription above Psalm 102, which reads "A prayer of an afflicted man. When he is faint and pours out his lament before the Lord." The recital of these complaint psalms has the potential to enable the person who is suffering great pain to shape that hurt into formful grief.[134]

Compositional Place and Function

In the protest-petition-votive promise of 1 Samuel 1:11, the vow proper comes *after* the petition. This confirms Westermann's claim that the vow to praise in a complaint psalm normally occurs at the end of a supplication[135] and is integrally attached to it.[136]

Westermann's claim has important implications for its function. It indicates that there is an intimate connection between petition and praise. This agrees with Calvin's theological axiom that "the two parts of prayer are petition and thanksgiving."[137] For this reason, Calvin instructs the reader of his commentary on Psalm 13:6 as follows:

---

[131]Erhard S. Gerstenberger, *Der bittende Mensch: Bittritual und Klagelied der Einzelnen im Alten Testament* (Neukirchen: Neukirchener Verlag, 1980), 156-158.

[132]Walter Brueggemann, *Israel's Praise: Doxology against Idolatry and Ideology* (Philadelphia: Fortress, 1988), 36.

[133]See, for example, the references to the community in Psalms 3:9; 4:4-5; 28:8-9.

[134]Brueggemann, *Israel's Praise*, 136; idem., "The Formfulness of Grief," 84-97.

[135]Westermann, *Praise and Lament in the Psalms*, 75. He also claims that the vow to praise is a constant element in the individual complaint psalms. But some individual complaint psalms do not have a vow to praise. See, for example, Psalms 3, 6, and especially 88. Westermann's explanation for its omission (p. 75, note 24) is not convincing. G. Mayer (*TDOT* V, s.v. יָדָה, 431) claims that the vow to praise occurs always at the end of the complaint psalm.

[136]For the intimate connection between the petition and the vow to praise see also Cartledge, "Conditional Vows in the Psalms of Lament," 83.

[137]Cited by Heiler, *A Study in the History and Psychology of Religion*, 271. Calvin (*The Institutes of the Christian Religion, Vol. II*, ed. John T. McNeil and trans. Ford Lewis Battles [Philadelphia: Westminster, 1960], III.xx.28) claims that the two are so closely related that "they may conveniently be included under one name." In this connection he also argues that "whenever believers entreat God to do something for his name's sake . . . , they obligate themselves to give thanks. . . . "

And surely it becomes us to engage in prayer in such a frame of mind as at the same time to be ready to sing the praises of God; a thing which is impossible, unless we are fully persuaded that our prayers will not be ineffectual. We may not be wholly free from sorrow, but it is nevertheless necessary that this cheerfulness of faith rise above it, and put into our mouth a song on account of the joy which is reserved for us in the future, although not as yet experienced by us. . . .[138]

For Calvin, therefore, the vow to praise functions as thanksgiving in advance.

In addition to its anticipatory function, the vow to praise also adds argumentative weight to the petitions[139] and serves to buttress them. In Psalm 13 it adds to the argument for why the Lord should act on the suppliant's appeals in verse 4 and especially the petition in verse 6b.

To elucidate this claim it is necessary to call attention to the fact that Hannah's vow to praise is syntactically a conditional sentence. Hannah's vow, therefore, is a conditional agreement that entails a dual obligation—she is only obligated to fulfill her vow if the Lord actually remembers her (1 Sam. 1:11, 19). In view of the intregal connection between the petitions and the vow to praise the Lord through public testimony in the individual complaint psalms, the vow to praise in these psalms are also conditional agreements.[140] As such, they have a *do ut des* character. Through them, petitioners make a solemn pledge to offer praise in exchange for divine assistance in their plight.

In the vow of Psalm 13:6bc, the suppliant requests that his heart be allowed to rejoice in the Lord's victory. Then he promises, in return, to praise the Lord through public testimony. But he does not yet engage in full-fledged praise. In fact, he withholds his praise until the Lord attends to the urgent petitions voiced in verse 4 and to the jussive request in verse 6b. If the Lord really wants the speaker to praise him through public testimony, then he must first react positively to the suppliant's plaintive pleas. Naturally, should the Lord not answer these urgent demands, then the supplicant is under no obligation to fulfill the vow to praise. Consequently, the vow to

---

[138]Calvin, *Commentary upon the Book of Psalms*, 187.

[139]Westermann, *Praise and Lament in the Psalms*, 78.

[140]Cartledge ("Conditional Vows in the Psalms of Lament," 85) calls attention to the fact that the conditional nature of the vow to praise is frequently denied. Among others, he quotes, for example, Anderson's (*The Book of Psalms* I, 449) comments on Ps. 61:5: "but in the Psalter the vows may be on a higher plane: not a conditional promise of a gift, but an expression of certainty that God has already accepted the prayer."

praise contains a genuine element of bargaining power that provides the suppliant with real leverage in his attempt to mobilize God to action on his behalf.[141]

The underlying confident assumption of the vow to praise in the individual complaint psalms is that the Lord delights in public praise.[142] This conviction is clearly articulated in the vow to praise found in Psalm 69:30-31. The same claim is made in Psalm 51:16-17 in conjunction with the vow to praise in verses 14b-15. Therefore, when the suppliant of Psalm 13:6cd makes his vow to praise the Lord publicly, he is convinced that he has something the Lord really wants. Consequently, the vow to praise adds extra weight to the petitioner's argument and is specifically designed to mobilize the Lord to action on behalf of his covenant partner.

The Clause (v. 6d)

Verse 6c is accompanied by a short subordinate clause: כִּי גָמַל עָלָי (v. 6d). Scholarly interpretation of the syntactical function of this concluding climactic subordinate clause varies as a result of the diverse interpretations of verse 6c. At issue in this debate are two interrelated factors. The first factor concerns the syntactical function of the conjunction כִּי and the second pertains to the verbal aspect of the verb גָמַל.

Those who interpret verse 6cd as a song of thanksgiving in response to a heard prayer, an anticipatory song of thanksgiving, or a vow of praise in a heard petition generally interpret the conjunction כִּי causally, thus providing the reason and basis for either the song of thanksgiving or the vow to praise. As a recitative it would designate the content of the praise.[143] The NAB translation of verse 6d reflects this option: "How good our God has been to me!" Significantly, both interpretations of the syntactical function of the conjunction כִּי understand the verbal aspect of the QTL verb גָמַל as a simple past, indicating a completed event.[144]

Those who interpret verse 6cd as a vow to praise (of an open petition), however, explain the syntactical function in one of two ways. The majority ascribes a causal function to the conjunction כִּי so that verse 6d indicates the basis and reason for the vow. Others argue that the conjunction plus a QTL verb has a temporal function, so

---

[141]In his comments on the vows to praise in Psalm 35, Brueggemann (*The Message of the Psalms*, 65-67) calls this "triangling." It is the rhetorical art of lining up the Lord on the side of the suppliant, "two against one," against the personal adversary.

[142]Cartledge, "Conditional Vows in the Psalms of Lament," 85.

[143]G. Mayer, *TDOT* V, s.v. יָדָה, 434.

[144]James L. Mays (*The Lord Reigns: A Theological Handbook to the Psalms* [Louisville: Westminster/John Knox, 1994], 56) opts for this position and as a result he claims that "the hymn [v. 6cd] lays bare the foundation upon which the whole prayer is based. Somewhere, sometime, the psalmist has encountered the graciousness of God, and confidence in that grace has become the ground and support of his life."

they translate the conjunction either as "when"[145] or as "as soon as."[146] This interpretation indicates the conditional nature of the vow (v. 6cd). Both options assume the anticipatory nature of the pledged declarative praise and for this reason interpret the verbal aspect of the QTL verb גָּמַל as a "perfect of certitude" that expresses "a vivid future when the action is deemed as good as done."

Another important interpretive issue in verse 6d concerns the meaning of the QTL verb גָּמַל.[147] The problem is whether in this particular context it denotes "to deal bountifully with" (Ps. 116:7; 119:7; 142:8) or "to recompense" (Joel 4.4 [3.4]). Scholars and commentators generally agree that any idea of recompense is derived from context and not from the verb itself. Since the context of Psalm 13 does not contain any clear indication of recompense, it is inferred that in this context the verb is employed in its basic, positive sense, "to treat kindly."[148]

When the Lord is the subject of גָּמַל,[149] then this verb is frequently modified by the preposition עַל plus a noun or pronoun to designate the recipient of the divine action. This syntactical sequence (גָּמַל + עַל) connects "the divine act with the pregnant sense of 'coming upon someone from above' "[150] and, consequently, denotes a gracious beneficent act from a suzerain to a vassal. Such is especially the case when God is the subject (cf. Ps. 103:8-10 and Isa. 63:7-9). Of particular interest is the deliverance from death referred to in Psalm 103:4a and Psalm 116:7b-8: "because the Lord has dealt bountifully (גָּמַל) with you. For you have delivered my soul from death, my eyes from tears, my feet from stumbling." In view of the obvious thematic connections between Psalm 116:7b-8 and Psalm 13, I conclude that in Psalm 13:6d the verb גָּמַל refers to a future benevolent divine intervention on behalf of his covenant partner that will deliver him from the peril of death. As such, it summarizes concisely the deliverance (יְשׁוּעָה) requested in verse 6b as a beneficent divine act prompted by the Lord's חֶסֶד.

The last word of the psalm is עָלָי, "over me,"[151] which appears to be a deliberate allusion to the end of verse 3 in the complaint about the enemy. If this is the case, it marks an unmistakable contrast to the final word of the complaint in verse 3b. There the per-

[145]Cartledge ("The Conditional Vow in the Psalms of Lament," 90-91) suggests that in clauses that are subordinate to a vow to praise, the conjunction כִּי may be translated as "when" or "if" to emphasize the conditional nature of the vow. He classifies the clause in verse 6d as an "expression of confidence" (89).

[146]Craigie, *Psalms 1-50*, 141.

[147]Cf. K. Seybold, *TDOT III*, s.v. גָּמַל, 30-32.

[148]Ibid., 23. John Calvin (*Commentary on the Psalms*, 187) emphasizes this point over against those who would use this verse in support of works righteousness.

[149]As in Psalms 13:6; 103:10; 116:7, 12; 119:17; 142:.8.

[150]Seybold, *TDOT III*, s.v. גָּמַל, 30.

[151]McCann, *A Theological Introduction to the Book of Psalms*, 95.

sonal enemy "exalted *over me*" is replaced by "has dealt bountifully *over me*." A comparison of the climactic conclusion of the suppliant's prayer with its beginning reveals a sharp contrast. In the beginning, the petitioner boldly accuses the Lord of abandoning his covenant partner. At the end, he eagerly anticipates the Lord's benevolence. In an anticipatory way, that is characteristic of biblical faith, the speaker has moved from hurt to joy, from protest and petition, to (pledged) praise via a persistent profession of covenant loyalty. Clearly such prayers are courageous acts of faith.

HOMILETICAL AND PASTORAL CONSIDERATIONS

The first point that a sermon on Psalm 13 should probably make is that the petitioner's audacious questioning of God in his struggle with suffering is not an expression of doubt. Many contemporary Christians live with this fear. The sequence of parallel verbs in Psalm 22:4-5 (trusted/trusted/cried/trusted) demonstrates clearly that the cry of the complaint prayer is an act of faith.[152] In the case of Psalm 13, the petitioner's bold expostulation with God is based on his emphatic expression of confident trust in the Lord's protective "faithful love in action" (v. 6a).

Second, and intimately related to the first point, a sermon on Psalm 13 should emphasize the validity of the questions raised in verses 2-3. We live in a grief-denying culture, very likely the result of the Enlightenment. Christians have not escaped this. Indicative of this tendency are the comments of Charles H. Spurgeon in his reflection on the first complaint against God (v. 2a): "Ah, David! how like a fool thou talkest. Can God *forget?*" and "It was surely bad enough to suspect a temporary forgetfullness."[153] How different is George Herbert's affirmation in his poem "Prayer" where he calls prayer an "engine against th' Almightie, sinners towre, Reversed thunder."[154]

In an effort to correct the grief-denying tendency of our culture, therefore, the pastor could teach the validity of asking the psalmist's bold questions. As Kübler-Ross' description of the grief process has demonstrated, the psalmist's outrageous questions are the natural questions of the human grief process in the anger stage. In fact, the

---

[152]Miller, *Interpreting the Psalms*, 102. In connection with these verses, Calvin (*Commentary on the Psalms*, 365) writes, "He who pretends that he trusts in God, and yet is so listless and indifferent under his calamities that he does not implore his aid, lies shamefully." Moreover, he claims, "By prayer, then, true faith is known. . . . "

[153]C. H. Spurgeon, *The Treasury of David*, Vol. 1 (New York: Funk & Wagnalls, 1883), 168.

[154]George Herbert, *The Works of George Herbert*, ed. F. E. Hutchinson (Oxford: Clarendon, 1945), 51. See also "Artillerie," 139, l. 25: "Then we are shooters both, and thou does deigne To enter combate with us, and contest With thine own clay." Also, in the commentary on "Prayer" he observes that according to Augustine prayer has the nature of importunity: "We press, we importune God . . . Prayer hath the nature of Impudency: We threaten God in Prayer . . . And God suffers this impudency and more. Prayer hath the nature of Violence; In the public prayers of the Congregation, we besiege God, says Tertullian, and we take God prisoner, and bring God to our Conditions; and God is glad to be stratened by us in that seige" (348, Pelican edition).

Babylonian complaint psalms illustrate clearly that these are universal questions. In the lengthy prayer to Ishtar, for example, the reader can find these questions:

> How long, O my Lady, shall my adversaries be looking upon me? . . .
>
> How long, O my Lady, shall the crippled and weak seek me out? . . .
>
> How long, O my Lady, wilt thou be angered so that thy face is
> turned away?
>
> How long, O my Lady, wilt thou be infuriated so that thy spirit is
> enraged?[155]

For the Old Testament believer and for the Christian, of course, these questions are raised in a covenant context. Nevertheless, they are the questions believers ask in their suffering. Typically they ask, "If God is really with us, as he promised, then why do we suffer?"[156]

A sermon on Psalm 13 should teach the congregation, in the third place, the basic modes of speech that characterize biblical prayer. In so doing, the pastor can teach the congregation how one may articulate grief and doubt in a biblical way. It is particularly important to underscore that the recitation of a complaint psalm is not to be a gripe session to God. In the complaint psalms, protest, petition, and praise cohere in one essential unity. As is evident from Phillipians 4:6, 1 Thessalonians 5:17, 1 Timothy 2:1, and Acts 16:25, the New Testament writers were quite aware of the interrelationship between petition and prayer.[157]

Another objection to the use of the complaint psalms is that Christ has fulfilled the messages of the Psalms, including the message of the complaint psalms, and in fulfilment of the promise in Isaiah 53:6 took our infirmities upon himself and carried our sorrows (Matt. 8:17).

At least two responses are possible. First, Jesus himself used the complaint psalms on the occasion of his suffering. From the cross he cried out the words of Psalm 22:1, "My God, my God, why have you forsaken me?" Moreover, as is evident from the observation of the centurion in Luke 23:47 when Jesus cried out the words of Psalm 31:6[5], "Into your hands I commit my spirit," he recited these words as the paradig-

---

[155]James B. Pritchard ed., *Ancient Near Eastern Texts Related to the Old Testament* (Princeton: Princeton University, 1950), 384-385.

[156]In his meditation on this problem, Cornelius Plantinga (*Assurances of the Heart* [Grand Rapids: Zondervan, 1993], 38-39) calls out attention to a passage in C. S. Lewis' *A Grief Observed* in which Lewis describes the thoughts that tortured his mind: "Not that I am . . . in much danger of ceasing to believe in God. The real danger is of coming to believe such dreadful things about Him. The conclusion I dread is not 'So there's no God after all,' but 'So this is what God is really like. Deceive yourself no longer.'"

[157]Calvin (*Institutes*, III.20.28) appealed to these New Testament passages in his argument that petition and praise are two essential parts of prayer.

matic righteous sufferer. Furthermore, according to Hebrew 5:7, "he offered up prayers and petitions with loud cries and tears to the one who could save him from death. . . ." In fact, from the perspective of the complaint psalms, the resurrection was God's answer (Heb. 5:7) to Christ's complaint and petitions implied, for example, in his citation of Psalm 31:6, "Deliver me from my enemies and from those who pursue me."

Second, it is evident from Revelation 21:4, that the promise of Isaiah 25:8 ("He will swallow up death forever. The Sovereign Lord will wipe away the tears from all faces") has not yet been completely fulfilled. For this reason, the saints in Revelation 6:10 still struggle with the question of undeserved suffering and divine righteousness. In characteristic complaint language of the Old Testament they cry out, "How long, Sovereign Lord, holy and true, until you judge the inhabitants of the earth and avenge our blood?"

Finally, Walter Brueggemann's article "The Formfulness of Grief" will prove helpful in pastoral care. In this article he contrasts the five steps of the grief process outlined by Kübler-Ross to the basic outline of the complaint psalms. This comparison has proved to be particularly helpful to those who are suffering. In that connection, pastors should also invite those who are suffering to write out their own complaint prayer, following the model of those found in the Psalter.

Let us make everything known to God in prayer and praise!

Proverbs 10:1-16: A Coherent Collection?

Bruce K. Waltke

I am dedicating this article to John Stek as a token of my esteem and appreciation for him as a scholar and friend. John taught me more about translation than any other person did. He probably contributed more to the NIV than any other translator, because he combines in an incomparable way the virtues essential for the work of translation. He is a competent exegete of the Old Testament, has an ear for the English idiom, thinks very clearly, has the charismatic force of personality necessary to lead a committee, and totally dedicates himself to the task.

INTRODUCTION

Purpose

This paper investigates whether the sayings collected in Proverbs 10:1-16 exhibit a conscious arrangement into larger literary contexts, and, if so, how the larger contexts affect the interpretation of the individual sayings. The 375 proverbs of so-called Collection II (10:1-22:16), unlike Collection I (1:1-9:18) and Collection III (22:17-24:34), lack the normal syntactic links (e.g., conjunctions, particles, pronouns, and deictic references) that one expects in coherent literature. This asyndeton creates the impression that the collection is disparate, atomistic, and without coherence. However, now that we know more about the poetics of Hebrew authors, we have new access to potential connections between proverbs apart from the expected, syntactic markers. The asyndeton may be due to the literary genre.

Relevance

Because of their epigrammatic nature, interpreters can readily manipulate individual proverbs to empower their own point of view. A short section from Bertolt Brecht's *Life of Galileo* illustrates how these sayings can be twisted to suit the speaker's viewpoint. In Brecht's play, the Inquisition officially condemns Copernicus' assertion that the earth revolves around the sun. In the seventh act, Cardinal Bellarmin invites Galileo to his palace in order to discourage his further research. The following conversation ensues:

> BELLARMIN: We must move with the times. . . . If new star charts based on a new hypothesis help our mariners to navigate, then they should make use of them. We only disapprove of such doctrines as run counter to the Scriptures. . . .

GALILEO: The Scriptures . . . *"He that withholdeth corn, the people shall curse him"* [Proverbs 11:26].

BELLARMIN: *"A prudent man concealeth knowledge"* [12:23].

GALILEO: *"Where no oxen are the crib is clean: but much increase is by the strength of the ox"* [14:4].

BELLARMIN: *"He that ruleth his spirit is better than he that taketh a city"* [16:32].[1]

If the author [i.e., composer and/or editor] of Proverbs 10:1-22:16 consciously arranged the proverbs into contexts, he may have done so to protect them from performance abuse (cf. 14:21 with 14:20 and 18:10 with 18:11). However, context alone is not the panacea for protecting the vulnerable epigram from misapplication. By definition, proverbs were meant to perform in many instantiations; they depend on the wisdom and character of their audience to handle them rightly. Moreover, if the author consciously arranged Proverbs into meaningful rich contexts, then not only is the whole a helpful interpreter of its individual parts, but the sum is greater than the parts. Finally, if the author consciously arranged them into larger units, then the collection is more aesthetically pleasing, intellectually satisfying, and memorable.

Method

Scholars who deny the importance of context for interpreting sayings in Collection II are often more interested in the prehistory of the proverbs. However, this approach is speculative; the only proper analogies to illuminate the contexts of these sayings are other ancient Near Eastern literary collections. Form and tradition critics questionably look to analogies from contemporary *illiterate* peoples for insight.[2] The sayings, as we now have them, have come down to us as literature, and will be treated as such here.

To lay a foundation for the investigation, I will first sketch the history of the study of Proverbs' arrangement. I will then translate Proverbs 10:1-16 with selected exegetical notes, try to illuminate its poetics, and finally comment on the resulting sense.

By poetics, I mean several things: the author's use of key words, inclusio (i.e., marking off a literary unit by matching the end with the beginning), janus (i.e., linking sections together with a piece of literature that looks both backward and forward), catch

---

[1] B. Brecht, *Life of Galileo*, trans. J. Willett, MMP 5 (London: Reed Consumer Books, 1993), 57-58, cited by Knut Martin Heim, ("Structure and Context in Proverbs 10:1-22:16" [unpublished Ph.D. dissertation, University of Liverpool, 1996]), 1.

[2] F. W. Golka, "Die Königs—und Hofsprüche und der Ursprung der israelitischen Weisheit," *Vetus Testamentum* 36 (1986), 13-36.

words that stitch the work together, paronomasia (i.e., all sorts of sound plays often connected with sense), repetition of grammatical forms, chiasms (i.e., by reversing the structure), etc. These surface patterns that unify a work match the text's semantic units on the paradigmatic level of thought. These include structural patterns and thematic units. By matching the text's rhetorical techniques with the deep structure of its meaning, one may discern meaning-rich literary units.

HISTORY OF STUDY

In this survey of the history of the study, I leaned very heavily and with much appreciation on Knut Martin Heim (1996),[3] even as he cheerfully followed the outline of the survey by Ruth Scoralick (1995).[4]

Survey of Scholarship Denying the Existence of Structure

William McKane

McKane argued "that there is, for the most part, no context in the sentence literature" (i.e., Prov. 10:1-22:16 and 25-29).[5] This conviction is part and parcel of his program to rearrange the proverbs according to their historical development. According to McKane, the proverbs evolved from (a) those that were profane for the education of the individual, to (b) those that served the community, to (c) those that expressed "a moralism derived from Yahwistic piety."[6] For example, in his view, the word pair "righteous/wicked" belongs to category C, and the word pair "wise/fool" belongs to category A. He writes,

> Consequently, I do not propose to concern myself with the principles which are employed to group sentences in the book of Proverbs, but rather with a system of classification which is oriented towards an investigation of history of the wisdom tradition in Israel, in so far as this can be reconstructed from the sentences.[7]

R. B. Y. Scott

In his commentary on the Proverbs, Scott recognized some intentional arrangements (e.g., 16:1-7, 10, 12-15),[8] but he essentially denied their continuity: "The

---

[3]Heim, "Structure and Context in Proverbs 10:1-22:16," 5-53.

[4]R. Scoralick, *Einzelspruch und Sammlung*, BZAW 232 (Berlin, New York: Walter de Gruyter, 1995).

[5]William McKane, *Proverbs*, OTL (London: SCM Press, 1970), 10 (cf. 413-415).

[6]Ibid.

[7]Ibid., 414.

[8]R. B. Y. Scott, *Proverbs, Ecclesiastes*, AB 18 (New York: Doubleday, 1965), 17.

brevity of the proverbs [10:1-22:16] . . . , their miscellaneous subject matter and the discontinuity of their arrangement militate against the pleasure of reading them consecutively in their order."[9] In a later essay on the religious and secular contents of Proverbs, he understood Collection II as a haphazard collection of "variegated material without contextual connections."[10] He similarly thought of a reinterpretation of older traditional sayings in religious terms,[11] noting that the word-pairs "righteous/wicked" and "wise/foolish" refer to two distinct classes, "each with its appropriate destiny."[12]

Claus Westermann

Westermann reacted against efforts to find conscious arrangements.[13] His approach was governed by the form-critical conviction that the shorter sentence literature of 10:1-22:16, in contrast to the instruction literature of 1:1-9:18, was early. According to this approach, the shorter sentences originated in an oral context (the ordinary folk), while the more complex instruction literature originated at a later cultural stage at the court or in school.[14] Since he stressed that the primary *Sitz-im-Leben* of a proverb is its oral use, he denied the possibility that authors composed sayings for a written context. He could not, however, deny a relationship between some sayings in the secondary collection of the proverbs,[15] but his concern was with their alleged oral origin. This son of a professor of African studies favored using comparative materials from illiterate tribal societies to point out that a proverb given a place in a formal collection is in a second stage of development.[16]

[9]Scott, *Proverbs, Ecclesiastes*, 130.

[10]R. B. Y. Scott, "Wise and Foolish, Righteous and Wicked," in *Studies in the Religion of Ancient Israel*, ed. James L. Crenshaw, *Vetus Testamentum Supplements* 23 (Leiden: Brill, 1972), 147.

[11]Ibid., 153.

[12]Ibid.

[13]Claus Westermann, "Review of R. Van Leeuwen, *Context and Meaning in Proverbs 25-27*," *Zeitschrift für die altestamentliche Wissenschaft* 102 (1990): 165-167.

[14]Claus Westermann, *Forschungsgeschichte zur Weisheitsliteratur 1950-1990*, AzTh 71 (Stuttgart: Calwer Verlag, 1991); *Wurzeln der Weisheit* (Göttingen: Vandenhoeck & Ruprecht, 1990).

[15]Westermann, *Forschungsgeschichte*, 35-36.

[16]Ibid., 41-42; Westermann, *Wurzeln*, 122-123.

Proverb Performance Context[17]

B. Kirshenblatt-Gimblett[18]

Observing that the meaning of proverbs is often contradictory (e.g., "Haste makes waste," and "He who hesitates is lost"), Kirshenblatt-Gimblett mentioned the following factors operating in sayings according to the proverb performance school of thought.

- Proverbs express relative, not absolute truth.
- Life context determines a proverb's meaning and "truth."
- A proverb that fits semantically may not be socially appropriate for what the participants in the situation wish to accomplish.
- A person tends to select a proverb on the basis of what the life-situation requires.
- Situations can be evaluated in more than one way.[19]

Carole R. Fontaine

Fontaine also prefers to speak of "proverb performance meaning" rather than "simple proverb meaning."[20] According to her, one uses proverbs in social contexts to evaluate past actions or to affect future behavior. "The user of the saying . . . restores harmony by categorizing the situation and imposing order."[21] The collectors of proverbs, however, failed to understand the need to give full contextual data about the situation in which the saying is used. She writes,

> This, of course, is precisely what the collectors of proverbs have usually failed to do, since function in [life]-context had not been perceived as a factor which might affect meaning as a whole. For students of biblical wisdom, this means that observation of proverbs and sayings in contexts of use often must proceed outside the wisdom collections.[22]

---

[17]Fontaine defines "proverb performance" as referring to a situation in which "a certain stimulus (usually human behavior . . .) has elicited the application of the proverb to the situation" (Carole R. Fontaine, *Traditional Sayings in the Old Testament* [Sheffield: The Almond Press, 1982], 182).

[18]B. Kirshenblatt-Gimblett, "Toward a Theory of Proverb Meaning," *Proverbium* 22 (1973): 821-27.

[19]Ibid., 823, cited by Fontaine, *Traditional Sayings*, 50.

[20]Carole R. Fontaine, "Proverb Performance in the Hebrew Bible," *Journal for the Study of the Old Testament* 32 (1985): 95.

[21]Ibid., 96.

[22]Ibid., 97.

Claudia Camp

Camp developed Fontaine's treatment of "performance contexts."[23] She called for "the literary de-contextualizing of proverbs" from their "dead" collections. "Each age, each author, each work and each situation will force a new function onto the proverb. . . . It lives only when used."[24] Gathering proverbs into collections, according to her, has the following results:

- They lose their function as cultural models.
- The loss of performance context leads to the appearance of dogmatism.
- Loss of touch with the covenant context creates the appearance of a sacred-secular split.

But Camp also contends that the personification of wisdom as a female figure in the frame of the book recontextualized the individual proverbs into a new unity.[25] According to her, this personification has three interrelated functions: (1) it stresses the unity of the many facets of wisdom; (2) it has a generalizing effect to balance the "particularizing" movement of the proverbs, providing a new "performance context" for originally independent, specific, and sometimes contradictory proverbs; and (3) it transforms the abstract concept of wisdom into one attractive, inviting quality as represented in the female wisdom figure. "If the proverbs are not to die, they must be integrated into a new kind of work," she wrote.[26]

Survey of Scholarship Affirming a Context for the Individual Sayings in Proverbs 10:1-22:16

Educational Sayings

The most detailed earlier theories about "educational" sayings were developed in the commentaries of Ewald[27] and Delitzsch.[28] On this basis, Delitzsch divided Proverbs 10:1-22:16 into five parts: 10:1; 13:1; 15:20; 17:21; and 19:26. However, he could not accommodate 15:20. Some of Delitzch's suggestions were taken up by Toy[29] and

---

[23]Claudia Camp, *Wisdom and the Feminine in the Book of Proverbs* (Sheffield: Almond, 1985), 165-178.

[24]W. Mieder, "The Essence of Literary Proverb Study," *Proverbium* 23 (1974): 892, cited in Fontaine, *Traditional Sayings*, 56.

[25]Camp, *Wisdom and the Feminine*, 209-215.

[26]Ibid., 207.

[27]H. Ewald, *Die Dichter des Alten Bundes* (Göttingen, 1867²).

[28]F. Delitzsch, *Salomonisches Spruchbuch* (Leipzig: Dörffling & Franke, 1873).

[29]Crawford H. Toy, *A Critical and Exegetical Commentary on the Book of Proverbs*, ICC (Edinburgh: T. & T. Clark, 1904²).

Wildeboer,[30] the latter being used by Hermisson.[31] For the most part, however, the larger context created by such groupings were ignored in the interpretation of the isolated proverbs.

Paranomasia and Catchwords

G. Boström[32] brilliantly connected the sequential sayings in the Book of Proverbs by aural links, such as consonance, assonance, and alliteration. But the arrangement of proverbs to create meaningfully rich contexts did not interest him. St. C. Perry[33] confirmed Boström's work by a computer-based study of paronomasia in Proverbs 10:1-22:16. Nevertheless, he denied that these sound-plays between the successive proverbs provided a context that enriched the interpretation of individual sayings. Jutta Krispenz[34] identified groupings in Collections II and V (chapters 25-29) based on the repetition of phonemes as in paronomasia, catchword connections, and alliterations that in her understanding refers to the repetition. She tended to neglect other structuring devices, but she recognized groupings based on semantic content.

Theological Reinterpretation

In his earlier works, Whybray[35] accepted McKane's distinction between earlier secular materials and later theological sayings. He argued that the latter are found at strategically important places and serve to reinterpret their immediate context. "Out of a total of 53 'theological' Yahweh-sayings in Prov 10:1-22:16, only three are apparently isolated sayings, plus a further eight doubtful cases. More extensive reinterpretations occur in seven groupings: Proverbs 10:24-30; 11:17-21; 15:3-11; 16:16-20; 16:33-7:3; 20:8-12; 20:22-28." Saebo[36] independently came to the similar conclusion that Yahweh-sayings provide a context for the surrounding sayings that shape their meaning theologically.

---

[30]D. G. Wildeboer, *Die Sprüche*, KHC 15 (Freiburg, Leipzig, and Tübingen: Mohr, 1897).

[31]Hans-Jürgen Hermisson, *Studien zur israelitischen Spruchweisheit*, WMANT, 28 (Neukirchen-Vluyn: Neukirchener Verlag, 1968).

[32]G. Boström, *Paronomasi I den aeldre hebraiska Maschalliteraturen*, AUL.T 23,8 (Lund: Gleerup; Leipzig: Otto Harrassowitz, 1928).

[33]St. C. Perry, *Structural Patterns in Prov. 10:1-22:16* (Mich.: Ann Arbor, 1987).

[34]Jutta Krispenz, *Spruchkompositionen im Buch Proverbia*, EHS.T 349 (Frankfurt: Lang, 1989).

[35]R. N. Whybray, "Yahweh-sayings and Their Contexts in Proverbs 10, 1-22, 16," in *La Sagesse de l'Ancien Testament*, ed. M. Gilbert (Leuven: Leuven University Press, 1990), 153-165.

[36]M. Saebo, "From Collections to Book," in *Proceedings of the Ninth World Congress of Jewish Studies* (Jerusalem: World Union of Jewish Studies, 1986), 99-106.

Repetitions

Snell[37] provided a comprehensive study of variant repetitions in the book of Proverbs that often reach across its different collections. He was not, however, primarily interested in the contextual arrangements of sayings. In fact, he did not even entertain the notion that authors consciously employed variants to create contexts. His main interest lay in determining a relative chronology of the different collections, but the results of this approach proved inconclusive. R. Scoralick used mainly variant repetitions along with poetics—excluding semantics—as structural devices to find compositional arrangements in Proverbs 10-15.

Poetics and Sense

In 1962, Udo Skladny[38] set the stage for most subsequent discussion about the arrangement of the proverbs into semantic contexts. By using analyses of form, content, and style, and by employing statistics to quantify his findings, Skladny delineated smaller sub-collections:

A (ch. 10-15)
B (ch. 16:1-22:16)
C (ch. 25-27)
D (ch. 28-29)

This analysis conformed in part with the obvious editorial notices of the book's structure in 10:1, 22:17, 25:1, and 30. In 1968, Hermisson[39] carried both Boström's work on paronomasia and Skladny's analysis a step further by tentatively trying to discern thematic and poetic units in Collection A. In 1972, G. E. Bryce,[40] by using certain methods of French structuralism, showed that Proverbs 25:2-27 constitutes a literary unit. In 1978, B. W. Kovacs found Collection B, which he begins at 15:28, to be the embodiment of a consistent worldview.[41] In 1979, as noted, R. N. Whybray argued that an editor deliberately chose the place of the Yahweh-sayings in 10:1-22:16.[42] In 1984, R. C. Van Leeuwen,[43] by structuralism, poetics, and semantics, convincingly demonstrated that the proverbs in Collection C are arranged into larger

---

[37]Daniel C. Snell, *Twice-told Proverbs & The Composition of the Book of Proverbs* (Winona Lake: Eisenbrauns, 1993).

[38]Udo Skladny, *Die ältesten Spruchsammlungen in Israel* (Göttingen: Vandenhoeck & Ruprecht, 1962).

[39]Hermisson, *Studien zur israelitischen Spruchweisheit.*

[40]G. E. Bryce, "Another Wisdom 'Book' in Proverbs," *Journal of Biblical Literature* 91 (1972), 145-157.

[41]Brian Watson Kovacs, "Sociological-Structural Constraints Upon Wisdom: The Spatial and Temporal Matrix of Proverbs 15:28-22:16" (Ph.D. dissertation, Vanderbilt; Ann Arbor: University Microfilms International, 1978).

[42]Whybray, "Yahweh-sayings and Their Contexts in Proverbs," 153-165.

[43]Raymond C. Van Leeuwen, *Context and Meaning in Proverbs 25-27*, SBL Disseration Series 96 (Atlanta: Scholars Press, 1988; Ph.D. disseration, University of St. Michael's College, 1984).

literary compositions. In 1985, B. V. Malchow[44] proposed that Collection D is an intricately arranged collection serving as "A Manual for Future Monarchs." In 1988, Ted Hildebrandt[45] found in Proverbs 10:1-22:16 sixty-two proverbial pairs, "two proverbial sentences that are bonded together (whether by means of phonetics, semantics, syntax, rhetorical device, pragmatic situation or theme) into a higher architectonic unit." According to him, these units were "editorially intended" and reflect the "theological tendenz" and "literary sensitivity" of the collectors. In 1990, he moved beyond proverbial pairs to larger compositional units in Proverbs 10.[46] The recent commentaries by Plöger (1984),[47] Schökel (1984),[48] Meinhold (1991),[49] and Garrett (1993)[50] attempt to interpret individual proverbs within larger literary units. Meinhold succeeds best in this enterprise, though there is still much work to be done.

In his commentary, Whybray (1994)[51] tends to depreciate these earlier efforts but without critical evaluation.[52] However, he groups some proverbs into larger contexts and gives explanations of how the context of a given saying shapes its meaning and significance.[53] The recognition of groupings is even more pronounced in his monograph published in the same year, and written after his commentary.[54] Here he argued that a single proverb cannot reflect the complexity of life. The natural way to overcome this shortcoming was to combine proverbs into larger groups.[55] According to him, the combination of formal and thematic links constitutes a particularly strong case for group identification. The author constructed beginnings and endings by formalized material such as imperative instructions or by educational sayings cast in the educational lan-

[44]Bruce V. Malchow, "A Manual for Future Monarchs," *Catholic Biblical Quarterly* 47 (1985), 238-45.

[45]Theodore A. Hildebrandt, "Proverbial Pairs: Compositional Units in Proverbs 10-29," *Journal of Biblical Literature* 107 (1988): 207-224.

[46]Theodore A. Hildebrandt, "Proverbial Strings: Cohesion in Proverbs 10," *Grace Theological Journal* 11 (1990): 171-185.

[47]Otto Plöger, *Sprüche Salomos* (Proverbia), BKAT XVII/5 (Neukirchen-Vluyn: Neukirchener Verlag, 1984).

[48]L. Alonso Schökel and J. Vilchez, *Sapienciales I: Proverbios* (Madrid: Ediciones Cristiandad, 1984).

[49]Arndt Meinhold, *Die Sprüche. Teil 1: Spruche Kapitel 1-15*, Züricher Bibelkommentare, ed. Hans Heinrich Schmid, Siegfried Schulz, and Hans Weder (Zürich: Theologischer Verlag, 1991).

[50]Duane A. Garrett, *Proverbs, Ecclesiastes, Song of Songs*, The New American Commentary, ed. E. Ray Clendenen, et. al., Vol. 14 (Nashville, Tennessee: Broadman Press, 1993).

[51]R. N. Whybray, *Proverbs*, NCBC (Grand Rapids: Eerdmans, 1994).

[52]"Various attempts have been made to find other principles of arrangement [than Boström's]; but so far little progess has been made in the search for a basis for more than the formation of quite small groups of proverbs" (Ibid., 155).

[53]He divides chapter 10 into 1-5, 6-11 but then tends to treat the rest of the chapter either as individual verses or smaller units, 18-21, 23-26, 27-32.

[54]R. N. Whybray, *The Composition of the Book of Proverbs*. JSOT Supplement Series, 168 (Sheffield: JSOT Press, 1994).

[55]Ibid., 85-86.

guage of Proverbs 1-9.[56] Yahweh-sayings can complement single proverbs or comment on or sum up larger groups.[57]

Co-referentiality and Coherence

In response to scholars who denied coherence in Proverbs 10:1-22:16 and who rejected the appellations belonging to different semantic fields (e.g., "righteous/ wicked" versus "wise/fool"), Heim[58] argued that these appellations are not synonyms but co-references to the same class of persons.[59] He tried to establish their co-referentiality by demarcating the appellations and then examining the features of the persons addressed in chapter 10. Having established which appellations shared the same syntagmatic relationships, he identified which character terms can substitute for another in certain contexts within Proverbs 10. "If the commonalities are striking and they have similar features, syntagmatic relations and connotations, etc., the most plausible explanation is that they have the same referent."[60] He drew the conclusion that most positive characterizations (righteous, good, upright, blameless, wise, competent, etc.) can apply to the same referent (co-referentiality). The same is true of most negative characterizations (wicked, bad, crooked, fool, simpleton, senseless, etc.). With this tool, Heim hoped to advance the study of the poetics and sense of Proverbs 10:1-22:16.

TRANSLATION

10:1   The proverbs of Solomon:
A wise son makes his[61] father glad,[62]
but a foolish[63] son [brings][64] grief to[65] his mother.[66]

---

[56]Whybray, *The Composition of The Book of Proverbs*, 85-86.

[57]Ibid., 87.

[58]Heim, "Structure and Context in Proverbs 10:1-22:16," 57-86.

[59]See P. Cotterell and M. Turner, *Linguistics & Biblical Interpretation* (London: SPCK, 1989), 160-161.

[60]Heim, "Structure and Context in Proverbs 10:1-22:16," 60.

[61]"His" is gapped in verset A (cf. Mitchell Dahood, *Psalms III: 101-150*, AB [Garden City, N.Y.: New York, 1970], 429-430).

[62]Factitive *Piel* (Bruce K. Waltke and Michael O'Connor, *An Introduction to Biblical Hebrew Syntax* [Winona Lake, Indiana: Eisenbrauns, 1990], 24.2 [hereafter cited as *IBHS*]), and habitual non-perfective, *IBHS* 31.3b.

[63]Genitive of species (*IBHS* 9.3b; cf. genitive of genus in 15:20 [*IBHS* 9.5.3i]).

[64]Literally "is grief."

[65]A genitive of mediated object (*IBHS* 9.5.2d).

[66]The elements of the stereotype phrase "father and mother" are here broken up in the parallelism. In this binomination, "father" always occurs in verset A and "mother" in verset B.

10:2   Treasures gained by wickedness[67] do not profit,[68]
but righteousness[69] delivers from death.[70]

10:3   The LORD does not let[71] the appetite[72] of a righteous[73] person hunger,
but what the wicked[74] crave[75] he thrusts aside.

10:4   A poor person[76] is made[77] with[78] a slack[79] palm,
but the hand[80] of diligent people[81] brings[82] wealth.[83]

---

[67]Genitive of instrument (*IBHS* 9.5.1d).

[68]Unclassified *Hiphil* (*IBHS* 27.4c); root occurs mostly with לֹא and in non-perfective conjugation.

[69]Feminine צְדָקָה is a gender doublet of masculine צֶדֶק (see *IBHS* 6.4.3a); chosen there to contrast with the masculine (Adele Berlin, *The Dynamics of Biblical Parallelism* [Bloomington: Indiana University Press,1985], 41-50).

[70]"Death" refers to the grave in 2:18; 5:5; 7:27. The Tg added "evil" to death perhaps to make the proverb more creditable to human experience. The Talmud connected "life" with life after the grave (*Shabbat* 156b; *B. Bathra* 10a; *Rosh HaShana* 16b. "The proverb is still recited in some cemeteries as the mourners are encourage to make a donation" (Plaut).

[71]The *Hiphil* denotes permission (*IBHS* 27.5b).

[72]Traditional "soul," the seat of needs and desires. Dahood (*Proverbs and Northwest Semitic Philology* [Roma: Pontificium Institutum Biblicum, 1963], 18) notes that Ugaritic also collocates the *npš* 'appetite' and *hwy* in 67:I:14-15.

[73]"Righteous" refers to a person who serves the community, not the self. The "wicked" advantage themselves at the expense of the community.

[74]Hebrew parallelism typically alternates singular and plural (Berlin, *The Dynamics of Biblical Parallelism*, 41-50).

[75]A nonconventional collective singular (*IBHS* 7.2.1d). The root denotes "inordinate, unrestrained desire."

[76]A substantival participle of רֹאש. LXX (followed by Syr) facilitates the reading by πενία ἄνδρα ταπεινοῖ, "poverty brings a man low," pointing the first word as רֹאש and taking it as subject. But the vocalization of the MT is preferable (see *IBHS* 1.6.3). ταπεινοῖ is an interpretative paraphrase. A poor person lacks the means for subsistence.

[77]Vg reads *egestatem operata est manus remissa*, "a slack hand has made poverty." This facilitating reading demands revocalizing the text as עָשָׂה because the subject כַּף is feminine. MT reads literally "one makes a poor man . . . . "The indefinite subject, though usually plural with participles, is better glossed by the passive (see *IBHS* 4.4.2). The predicate participle denotes a durative, continuing situation (*IBHS* 37.6b).

[78]A non-cognate accusative denoting the organ or means by which the action is performed (see *IBHS* 10.2.1g; E. Kautzsch, *Gesenius' Hebrew Grammar*, ed. A. E. Cowley [Oxford: Clarendon Press, 1980; 1910²], 117s (hereafter *GKC*). Delitzsch questionably supplies a verb and analyzes it as direct object, "he becomes poor who bears a sluggish hand."

[79]Attributive genitive.

[80]A generic singular (*IBHS* 7.2.1d).

[81]To judge from the parallel in 13:4, יַד חָרוּצִים is a genitive of inalienable possession (*IBHS* 9.5.h).

[82]Literally "causes itself to be wealthy," a one-place *Hiphil* (*IBHS* 27.2f,g).

[83]The LXX adds the couplet between vv. 4 and 5, υἱὸς πεπαιδευμένος ἔσται, τῷ δὲ ἄνδρονι διακόνω χρήσεται, "the instructed son shall be wise and uses the fool for a servant." In some manuscripts it is added at the end of 9:12. Baumgartner (p. 101) argues that it does not fit this context well for unlike the rest of the passage it does not present a general antithesis between the wise and foolish but offers rather a more specialized contrast between the diligent man and the slack hand. On the whole the LXX renders this verse badly. Toy (*Proverbs*, 212) thinks "the whole [of this verse in the LXX] is a paraphrase which may have taken the place of an original Grk. text."

10:5   A prudent[84] son is one who gathers[85] [his food][86] in summer;
he who sleeps[87] in harvest is a shameful[88] son.[89]

10:6   Blessings[90] come to[91] the head[92] of a righteous person,
but violence[93] overwhelms[94] the mouth[95] of wicked people.[96]

10:7   The memory of a righteous person is blessed;[97]
but the name[98] of wicked people decays.[99]

10:8   The wise in heart[100] accepts commands,
but the babbling fool[101] comes to ruin.

---

[84]Lit. "who causes himself to be esteemed/declared/recognized as insightful." In this internal *Hiphil* of the *Qal* intransitive verb, "to have insight, comprehension," the subject causes itself to be or do something" (*IBHS* 27.2f).

[85]Since the topics are prudent versus wise son, the parallelism shows בַּקַּיִץ is a classifying predicate (*IBHS* 8.4.2a).

[86]The implied object is supplied from the parallel in 6:8.

[87]Unclassified *Niphal* (*IBHS*, 23, 5).

[88]Tg and Syr gloss מֵבִישׁ by "degenerate."

[89]LXX reads, "A wise son is saved from heat: but a lawless one is blighted of the winds in harvest." "The LXX rendering of the Mas. is often fairly free and may import a specific sense . . . . There is more drastic alteration of the Mas. in Prov. 10:5, where LXX speaks of destiny rather than the conduct of the prudent" (Fohrer, *TDNT*, 7. 972). See also the eschatological reconstruction of Prov. 10:25 and 11:31.

[90]LXX (so also Vg) paraphrases, εὐλογία κυρίου, "the blessing of the Lord." Syr also reads singular but Tg plural.

[91]Verb of motion elided with preposition לְ (*IBHS* 11.4.3d). Tg and Syr add "to be" with preposition "upon."

[92]According to the Hebrew idiom, blessings come to the head of the rewarded person (Delitzsch).

[93]LXX inexplicably reads πένθος ἄωρον, "untimely grief," which in Wisdom of Solomon 14:15 refers to the father's grief for the death of his child suddenly taken from him.

[94]Unclassified *Piel*.

[95]The emendation of פִּי into פְּנֵי (Graetz, Toy, Gemser, and Fichtner [BHS]) is unnecessary. "Mouth" is generic singular.

[96]Grammatically and lexically, verse 6b can also be translated "the mouth of the wicked conceals violence" (Tg. McKane, Plöger, NRSV). The following arguments support the translation (also LXX, Syr, KJV, JPS, NIV). (1) Since "head of the righteous" in verse 6a is the predicate and "mouth of the wicked" is its obvious parallel, one expects it also to function as predicate. (2) McKane, opting for the alternative, thinks verse 6b is a defective antithesis, but "violence" forms a good antithesis to "blessing" because both entail speech. (3) Since all the versets in the preceding antithetic parallels (vv. 1-5) link the comportment of the wise/righteous with their appropriate consequences, one expects the same in verse 6, but the alternative rendering of verse 6b describes only the comportment of the wicked without just recompense (Meinhold).

[97]Lit., "the memory of the righteous [is] to a blessing." "Instead of יְבֹרַךְ, לִבְרָכָה might be used; the phrase לברכה הִיה (opp. הִיה לִקְלָלָה, often used by Jeremiah) . . . paraphrases the passive, for it expresses a growing to something, and thus the entrance into a state of endurance" (Delitzsch, 213).

[98]A generic singular (*IBHS* 7.2.1d).

[99]Ehrlich, followed by Fichtner (BHS), emends to יוּקַב, "will be cursed," qal passive, non-perfective of קַבַב for a better parallel (cf. 11:26; 24:24).

[100]Genitive of species (*IBHS* 9.5.3g).

[101]Literally, "the fools of lips," a genitive of species (*IBHS* 9.5.3g).

10:9   Whoever walks in blamelessness walks securely;[102]

     but the one who makes his ways twisted[103] will suffer harm.[104]

10:10   He who maliciously[105] winks the eye[106] causes[107] trouble,

     but the babbling[108] fool comes to ruin.[109]

10:11   The mouth of the righteous is a wellspring of life,

     but the mouth of the wicked conceals[110] violence. [111]

10:12   Hatred[112] awakens[113] conflicts.[114]

     but love[115] covers up[116] all[117] transgressions.[118]

---

[102] Adverbial accusative of manner (*IBHS*, 10.2.2e) or state (10.2.2d).

[103] Factitive *Piel* of adj. עֲקֵשׁ, "twisted," "crooked" (see 2:15; 4:24). The Hebrew word pair, עֲקֵשׁ/תָּם, in its five occurrences (10:9; 11:20; 10:1; 28:6, 18) serves to define the relation between individual and community: "The person of integrity is one who accepts his own interests in terms of community. The person of perversity is one who seeks his interest apart from or in action against the community" (Walter Brueggemann, "A Neglected Sapiential Word Pair," *Zeitschrift für die alttestamentliche Wissenschaft* 89 (1977): 244.

[104] Emending MT יִוָּדֵעַ "will be known" ("found out" (NIV), to יֵרוֹעַ (cf. 11:15; 13:20) (also Graetz, Toy, Fichtner (BHS), Plöger) because MT offers no clear antithetical parallel to "walks securely." The confusion of ד and ר in both the pre-exilic and post-exilic scripts is well known. Instructively, LXX made the same error in 13:20, reading ד, not ר (MT). Delitzsch and Meinhold (p. 171), overread MT by investing it with the meaning "he will be seen through and unmasked by the wise, causing the cheat to fall." Morgenstern (p. 101) and Cohen (p. 59) invest the verb with the questionable meaning "will be instructed by discipline" (cf. Judg. 8:16; Jer. 31:18), but those contexts add the thought of discipline and a different verb is used in Jeremiah 31:18. Whybray, on the basis of Psalms 1:6; 16:2; 21:2; 24:12 adds "by the LORD," but his parallels are not cogent. In Psalm 1:6, the LORD's knowledge entails salvation, not perdition, and the other passages explicitly mention the LORD and do not use the verb "to know." D. W. Thomas (*Journal of Theological Studies* 30 [1934]: 303) connects יָרַע with Ar. *wd'*, "will be made submissive," but in addition to the questionable practice of unnecessarily reading Arabic, he also must add "will be made to submit to Yahweh's retributive discipline."

[105] In its two other occurrences (Prov. 6:13; Ps. 35:19) "wink the eye" refers to malicious facial signals (cf. Prov. 16:30). LXX also clarifies sense here by adding μετὰ δόλου, "deceitfully" but not in 6:13.

[106] The parallel proverb, 6:13, reads "with the eye."

[107] Literally, "gives" with the particular nuance of "produce" (*BDB*, p. 679, entry t (cf. 29:15; Lev. 19:28; 24:20).

[108] Literally "the fools of lips," a genitive of species (*IBHS* 9.5.3g).

[109] MT (followed essentially by Tg.) suspiciously reads the same as verse 8b, but now functions as a synthetic parallel. LXX (followed by Syr.) δὲ ἐλέγχων μετὰ παρρησίας εἰρηνοποιεῖ, "but he who rebukes openly creates peace," offers an expected antithesis. Perhaps MT suffered by dittography from verse 8b. LXX, however, represents a different recension of the book by a creative translator (see Barr, 1979, 284; Tov, 1990; Adams, 1992, 119-127).

[110] *KBL*³ 465, entry 5. Dahood (1963, 19) is not convincing that כסה can mean "uncover."

[111] In 11a the topic of the metaphor is "mouth of the righteous," making its antithesis, "mouth of the wicked," clearly the subject in verse 11b in this chiastic parallelism. "The possibility of manifold windings and turnings is a characteristic of the Mashal" (Delitzsch, 216).

[112] A substantival infinitive (*IBHS*, 36.2.1f; *KBL*³ 1249).

[113] Factititive *Polel* (*IBHS* 24.2).

[114] מְדָנִים is either a contraction of מִדְיָנִים (see 6:14) or its bi-form (see *KBL*³ 521).

[115] See n. 47. Syr may read "shame" (*bhtt'*).

[116] Same Heb.: "concealed" in verse 11b.

[117] Or "all kinds of," "of every sort" (*KBL*³ 452, entry 10).

[118] LXX reads form as a participle, "those who do not love strife" and adds the negative to obtain a parallel and a good sense. Neither James 5:20 nor 1 Peter 4:18 follow LXX.

10:13   On the lips of those with understanding[119] wisdom is found,
         but[120] a rod is for the back[121] of one who lacks sense.

10:14   The wise[122] store up knowledge,
         but the mouth of a fool is imminent terror.

10:15   The wealth of the rich person is his strong[123] city;
         the terror of the poor is their poverty.

10:16   The wage of the righteous person is surely[124] life;
         the revenue[125] of the wicked person is surely[126] sin.

10:17   Whoever keeps[127] instruction[128] is a path to[129] life,[130]
         but whoever abandons correction is one who leads astray.[131]

POETICS

To facilitate the discussion, here is a coded translation of 10:1-16 to illuminate its
poetics.

1:1a The proverbs of Solomon.

Introduction

1:1b A wise *son* makes his father glad,
1:1c but a foolish *son* [brings] grief to his mother.

[119]See 1:5, n. 11.

[120]LXX omits "but" and reads, "he that brings forth wisdom from his lips with a rod strikes the man without heart," losing the antithetical parallelism.

[121]LXX and Syr gloss "man."

[122]The emendation of adding ׳ (cf. Fichtner [BHS]) destroys the contrast between the silence of the wise with the speaking of the fool.

[123]Attributive genitive.

[124]Emphatic *lamed* in a verbless clause (see *IBHS* 11.2.10i). So also independently Dahood (1963, p. 19) and Whybray, p. 166).

[125]פְּעֻלַּת and תְּבוּאָה have the same nominal pattern that denotes the result or product of an act (*IBHS*, 5.5b).

[126]See n. 119.

[127]Independent, relative participle.

[128]LXX interpreted מוּסָר as subject and paraphrased the rest of the verse: ὁδοὺς δικαίας ζωῆς φυλάσσει παιδεία

[129]The prepositon *lamed* entails a verb of motion, "leading to."

[130]Although the translation, "the path of life guards instruction" (cf. Tg, Syr, and Vg) is grammatically possible, its sense is unclear and offers no good parallel to verset B. Furthermore, the chiastic arrangement of the versets validates the translation. As "path to life" is the antithetical parallel to "leads astray" in the outer core, so one expects the antithesis "one who keeps instruction and one who abandons reproof" in its inner core.

[131]The ancient versions, KJV, NRSV, mistook מַתְעֶה as intransitive or emended the text, but the stem in MT is clearly *Hiphil*. It is used with the object בְּנַפְשׁוֹ, "deceives himself" in Jeremiah 42:20, but it is not so restricted here and so not an exact parallel (*pace* Delitzsch, 220). The same form occurs absolutely in Isaiah 30:28 with an object other than the subject implied. Moreover, one would have to add "walks on [the way to life]" in verset A were that the restricted meaning. The participle is here construed as an independent relative participle (*IBHS* 37.5), but it could be construed as a predicate participle, "correction leads astray" (*IBHS* 37.6).

I. Wealth
A. Ethics and Theology

10:2 Treasures gained by **wickedness** do **not profit,**
but **righteousness** delivers from death.

10:3 The LORD does **not** let the appetite of a **righteous** person **hunger,**
but what the **wicked** crave he thrusts aside.

B. Practical Theology

10:4 A poor man [רָאשׁ] is made with a slack palm,
but the hand of diligent people brings wealth [תַּעֲשִׁיר].

10:5 A prudent *son* is one who gathers [his food] in summer;
he who sleeps in harvest is a shameful *son.*

II. Speech
A. Value of Wise Speech to Self

10:6 **Blessings** come to the head of a **righteous** person,
but violence overwhelms the **mouth** of wicked people.

10:7 The memory of a righteous person is **blessed**;
but the name of wicked people decays.

10:8 The wise in heart accepts commands,
but the babbling fool [**lippy** fool] comes to ruin.

10:9 Whoever walks in blamelessness walks securely;
but the one who makes his ways twisted will suffer harm.

B. Janus

10:10 He who maliciously **winks the eye** causes trouble,
but the babbling fool [**lippy** fool] comes to ruin.

C. Value of Wise Speech to Others

10:11 The **mouth** of the **righteous** is a wellspring of life,
but the **mouth** of the **wicked** conceals [יְכַסֶּה] violence.

10:12 Hatred awakens conflicts
but love covers [תְּכַסֶּה] up all transgressions.

10:13 On the **lips** of those with understanding wisdom is found,
but a rod is for the back of one who lacks sense.

10:14 The wise store up knowledge,
but the **mouth** of a fool is imminent **terror.**

10:15 The wealth of the rich [עָשִׁיר] person is his strong city;

the terror of the poor is their poverty [רֵשׁ].

10:16 The wage of the **righteous** person is surely life;

the revenue of the **wicked** person is surely sin.

Introduction

10:17 Whoever keeps instruction is a path to life,

but whoever abandons correction is one who leads astray.

Commentary on Proverbs 10:1-5

Although verse 1bc is bound to verses 1bc-5 in an inclusio, it also functions as a janus between Collections I (1:1-9:18) and II (10:1-22:16) and as an introduction to Collection II. Collection I consists primarily of admonitions from the father and mother to the son (1:8; 3:1; *passim*) to be wise, not foolish. This janus proverb also pertains to this relationship. Moreover, the juxtaposition of Woman Wisdom with the foolish woman in chapter 9 prepares the way for the antithetical parallels of chapter 10, beginning with this initial proverb.

A chiastic pattern of positive and negative appellations in the versets (or cola) of 1-5 (+- / -+ / +- / -+ / +- [i.e. wise-foolish/ill-gotten-righteousness/righteous-wicked/indolent-diligent, wise/disgraceful]) stitch the sayings together. "Son" (בֵּן), always in a bound form, constitutes an inclusio around the section (twice each in vv. 1bc and 5). The inclusio is further strengthened by their chiastic arrangement, initial in v. 1; final in v. 5. The topic of the section pertains to wealth. The co-referents "wise" (v. 1), "righteous" (vv. 2-3), "diligent" (v. 4), and "competent" (v. 5) stand in opposition to the co-referents "fool," "wicked," "slack," and "sleeper."

The proverbial pair in verses 2 and 3 is bound chiastically by the catchwords "wicked" (vv. 2a, 3b) and "righteous" (2b, 3a) and by the rare initial syntax of לֹא + *hiphil* of prefix conjugation (i.e. "do not not profit" [2a], "does not hunger" [3a]).

Hildebrandt[132] notes the assonance of the participles עֹשֶׂה, "makes," and אֹגֵר, "gathers," in 4a and 5a. Hermisson groups the pair together according to their theme (laziness and diligence) and Plöger states that verse 4 prepares for the specification of verse 5.

Commentary on Proverbs 10:6-14

In verses 6-14, the topic shifts from property/wealth to speech/communication. The two topics are connected by the first word of verse 6. "Blessing" pertains to a speech

---

[132]Theodore A. Hildebrandt, "Proverbial Poetry: its setting and syntax" (Th.D. dissertation, Grace Theological Seminary, 1985), 656.

act that mediates wealth. This subunit of the text is linked by catchwords pertaining to the organs of communication in six of its nine verses: "mouth" (vv. 6b, 11a/b, 14b), "lip" (vv. 8b, 10b, 13a), "winking eye" (v. 10a). These verses also mention other body parts: "head" (v. 6a), "heart" (v. 8a), and "back" (v. 13). Verses 6b and 11b as well as verses 8b (esp. in MT) and 10b are linked by verbatim repetitions. "Mouth of wicked/fool" forms a frame around the section (vv. 6b, 14b).

The topic is communication. We need comment only on those verses that do not specifically mention the metonymies of instruments that perform the speech act (vv. 7, 9, 12). In verse 7a, "blessed" [lit. "to blessing"] refers to verbal benedictions. In verse 9, the "walk" and "way" of the blameless and the twisted refers to their lifestyle, which presumably includes their speech. According to Heim, "vv. 13a and 12b are closely linked: a loving person covers offenses because of his wise speech."[133] Although verses 9 and 12 present truths more general than those that pertain more narrowly to communication, in light of the many clear references to communication in this unit it is reasonable to suppose that the "author" intended the truths of these proverbs to be instantiated in speech as well as in other situations.

Proverbs 10:6-14 falls into two equal halves of two proverbial pairs (vv. 6-7, 8-9; and vv. 11-12, 13-14) around a single center verse (v. 10). This janus proverb is the only single proverb in the unit; it displays a rare synonymous parallelism in Skladny's Collection A.

The first two proverbial pairs pertain to the blessings that come upon the wise communicator vis-à-vis the community's blessings (vv. 6-7), and his security (vv. 8-9), whereas fools dish out violence, social death (vv. 6-7), and ruin (vv. 8-9). I reached this evaluation independently from Hermisson, who also saw the common theme in vv. 6-9 as the ruin of the wicked/fool and the well-being of the righteous. The two proverbial pairs of the second half refer to the blessings that the wise communicator gives to the community vis-à-vis "life" (vv. 11-12),"wisdom," and "knowledge" that defuses the fool's mouth, which is implicitly likened to a time-bomb (vv. 13-14). By contrast, fools dish out violence/conflict (v. 11-12) and are an imminent terror (v. 13-14).

Verset "a" of the janus verse looks ahead to the second half of this section (i.e., "causes trouble"), and verset "b" looks back to the first half, repeating verse 8b. The final pattern of the *Niphal* prefix conjugation 3 mas. sing. weaves verses 8-10 into a seamless whole. Both halves begin with the righteous/wicked contrast (vv. 6-7 and vv. 11-12), with nominal clauses in their "a" versets, and with verbatim paronomasia in the "b" versets of verses 6b and 11b. This could be a sign of an inclusio, but the

---

[133]Heim, "Structure and Context in Proverbs 10:1-22:16," 97.

other features of the unit's poetics suggest a pattern of ABA'B' (in vv. 6-14), not of ABCB' in verses 6-11.

A brief look at the four proverbial pairs discloses the following. The first proverbial pair (vv. 6-7) is linked by the catchwords involving the lexemes בְּרָכוֹת) בְּרֹךְ, "bless-ings," and לְבְרָכָה, "to blessing"), and צַדִּיק, "righteous," in their "a" versets and רְשָׁעִים, "wicked," in their "b" versets.

Verses 8 and 9 are linked conceptually. Both deal with the security of the "wise in heart"/"blameless" and the ruin of the "lippy fool"/"perverse." Heim says, "The safety of the upright [in v. 9] is a natural outcome of the wise man's attitude in v. 8."[134] If MT is original, they are also linked by the assonance of the *Niphal 3* mas. sing. infix of the prefix conjunction in their final words (יִוָּדֵעַ, יֵלָבֵט).

The third pair (vv. 11-12) is linked lexically and phonetically by "conceal" (יְכַסֶּה, v. 11b) and "cover" (תְּכַסֶּה, v. 12b). Boström notes the phonetic similarity between "mouth of the wicked (פִּי רְשָׁעִים, v. 11b) and "transgressors" (פְּשָׁעִים, v. 12b), the latter being a collapsed form of the former. Hildebrandt (p. 664) thinks there is a con-sonance of s's between final יְכַסֶּה חָמָס ("violence covers," v. 11b) and initial שִׂנְאָה ("hatred," v. 12a).[135] Syntactically, both are chiastically structured, but in verse 11 the subject constitutes the inner core while in verse 12 it is the outer frame.

The fourth proverbial pair (vv. 13-14) is linked tightly by the lexeme חָכְמָה) חכם "wisdom"/ חֲכָמִים "wise," vv. 13a, 14a) and by the metonymy of instrument for the speech act, "lips" (v. 13a) and "mouth" (v. 14b). As in 10:2, 3 there is a linking of abstract qualities (righteousness [10:2]; wisdom [10:13]) with those who have attained those qualities (righteous [10:3]; wise men [10:14]). Verse 13a is connected with verse 11a by the synonyms "mouth of the righteous" (v. 11) and "lips of the sensible" (v. 13).

Commentary on Proverbs 10:15-16 (17)

In the last proverbial pair of the text, the topic shifts from communication/speech (vv. 6-14) back to wealth (vv. 2-5). Conceptually, the vocabulary of this pair moves from the realm of economic status, "rich" and "poor" (v. 15), to terms denoting its use, "wages" and "revenue" (v. 16). Thus there is an escalation from the possession or lack of wealth (v. 15) to its positive or negative uses (v. 16). Syntactically, all four versets are formed of nominal clauses having the same pattern of the subject [construct + noun for wealth] + predicate nominative. Three of these constructs share the assonance of the fem. sing. cstr. [ת-] (מְחִתַּת, v. 15b; פְּעֻלַּת, v. 16a; תְּבוּאַת, v. 16b), matching קִרְיַת in 15a. Finally, the verses of these two proverbs are linked asyndetically, unlike verses 6-14.

---

[134]Heim, "Structure and Context in Proverbs 10:1-22:16," 94.

[135]Hildebrandt, "Proverbial Poetry: its setting and syntax," 664.

The topics of communication/speech (vv. 6-14) and wealth (vv. 15-16) are woven together seamlessly by the catchword מְחִתָּה ("terror") of the fool's mouth (v. 15b) and of the poor's poverty (v. 16b). Boström observes the sequence of ק and ר in קְרָבָה ("imminent," v. 14b) and קִרְיַת ("city," v. 15a) (cf. initial words in vv. 10-11).

As noted, verses 2-5 and 15-16 pertain to wealth. Proverbs 10:15 is linked lexically with verse 4 by the lexeme רָאשׁ (שׁ‎אָר, "a poor person"), the first word of verse 4, and רֵאשָׁם ("their poverty"), the last word of verse 15. They are also linked by the lexeme תַּעֲשִׁיר (עשׁר, "makes rich"), the last word of verse 4, and עָשִׁיר ("a rich person") part of the initial compound of verse 15. The chiasm may help bring the pericope to closure. "The righteous" and "the wicked" of verse 16 matches the same antithesis in verse 3, which is linked by the abstract of these terms with verse 2. This inclusio closes the pericope.

Proverbs 10:17 pertains to education, using educational vocabulary drawn from Collection I. As Whybray and others noted, such educational sayings often introduce new units. The lexeme לְחַיִּים (vv. 16a, 17a) links the first pericope with this introduction.

The Sense of Proverbs 1:1-16

Without the safeguard of verse 2, one could misunderstand verse 3 to mean that the righteous never hunger and the wicked always crave. The mention of the "treasures of the wicked" in verse 2a, however, implies that, for a season, the wicked disadvantage the righteous and get away with it. By reading them together, the speech act intends that the Lord feeds the righteous and starves the wicked in the final outcome of their lifestyles. Many other proverbs, along with the initial verset of 2a, reckon with a moral world turned upside down.[136] Moreover, verse 3 shows that the Lord, not fate, guarantees the righteous will be delivered from death.

As stated in note 68, "righteousness," a key word of verses 2-3, denotes advantaging the community, whereas wickedness signifies advantaging oneself at the expense of the community. Verses 4-5 underscore that the righteous must work to produce the wealth that serves the community. Otherwise, they will join the ranks of the wicked and take from it.

Taken as a whole, this collection underscores the wisdom of prudent speech versus the folly of imprudent communication. Prudent speech enriches oneself and the community, whereas imprudent speech/communication damages both. The world of wisdom is a unified whole that serves the best interest of all. *Mutatis mutandis*, folly negatively affects all.

---

[136]Raymond C. Van Leeuwen, "Wealth and Proverty: System and Contradiction in Proverbs," *Hebrew Studies*, 33 (1992): 29.

Verse 12 probes the root—the attitudes—behind the negative and positive communications of verse 11. Out of hatred the wicked "cover over" their evil intention by their speech, while out of love the righteous "cover over" the wrong intended against them by their silence. Perhaps "mouth," explicitly mentioned twice in verse 11, is not mentioned in verse 12 to underscore the wise person's silence.

Both poor speech and material poverty entail terror and ruin: the former to the community; the latter to the individual. Verse 16 protects verse 15 against misinterpretation. Verse 15 refers to the temporal economic advantages of the rich man, verse 16 to the eternal advantages of the righteous vis-à-vis eternal life, versus sin and, by implication, death. Lest one value economic matters too highly, v. 16 is juxtaposed to bring wealth back into the realm of morality. The relationship of verses 15 and 16 is matched by the proverbial pair, 18:10, 11: "It is impossible to read 18:11 (and 10:15) without considering the telling points that are made in 18:10, 12. . . . The name of the Lord (18:11) (and not riches! 18:12) is the strong tower that provides safety, and [the rich man's] pride goes before his fall (18:12)."[137]

Read as a whole, the pericope prevents dichotomizing the righteous into two groups, those who speak wisely and those who handle their wealth prudently. A righteous person does both. A righteous person enriches his community by his speech *and* by his deeds. Indeed, one does not speak well (e.g., with honesty, charity, gentleness) unless he uses his wealth to help others.

[137]Roland E. Murphy, "Proverbs 22:1-9," *Interpretation* 41 (1987): 401.

Proverbs 10:1-22: From Poetic Paragraphs to Preaching

Calvin Seerveld

A s a Christ-believing amateur in scholarship on the book of Proverbs, I have been protected from much wrong-headed professional study in "wisdom literature" because I naively took seriously the canonic shape in which Proverbs has been accepted by the church. As a great-grandchild of the historic Reformation, my Bible reading is one that assumes "the Bible be read as sacred Scripture." This we do in the communion of the saints, living and dead, carefully trusting the text will lead the community of faith enough to find definite direction in "the manner of service which God requires of us."[1]

Such a trusting expectation is crankled by practically all Proverbs commentators—from the higher critical Crawford H. Toy (1899) to the more recent Protestant evangelical Derek Kidner (1964).[2] They treat the text like a collection of individual sayings, loose from any defined context—a kind of anthology of nuggets of wisdom arranged in apparently random fashion for our benefit and admonition. The assumed contextlessness of the sayings collected in Proverbs 10-29, however, easily makes their interpretation arbitrary, truistic, or opaque (not exactly a fertile source for a twenty-minute Sunday sermon that would bring Bible-exposed Good News).

A BRIEF HISTORY OF EXEGESIS

The background to this state of affairs is fairly well known. In 1924, Adolf Erman claimed that Proverbs 22:17-23:11 was derived from the Egyptian instruction of Amenemope. Later, Johannes Fichtner argued that biblical wisdom was derived from the ancient Near Eastern eudamonistic teachings that the Hebrews gradually nationalized with Yahwist references.[3] Subsequently, scholars sought to track these refinements, which they claimed moved from teaching mundane "folk" wisdom to the more acceptable, pious "theological wisdom."

The influential result was William McKane's decanonization of proverb sentences into three groups: advice for living a successful life, admonitions against harmful deeds to society, and Yahweh God-talk.[4]

[1]*Belgic Confession*, articles 2-7; cf. Brevard S. Childs, *Introduction to the Old Testament as Scripture* (Philadelphia: Fortress, 1979), 27-106.

[2]Crawford H. Toy, *A Critical and Exegetical Commentary on the Book of Proverbs* (Edinburgh: T. & T. Clark, 1899); Derek Kidner, *Proverbs* (Downer's Grove, Ill.: Intervarsity, 1964).

[3]J. Fichtner, *Die altorientalische Weisheit in ihrer Israelitisch-Jüdische Ausprägung* (1933).

[4]William McKane, *Proverbs* (Philadelphia: Westminster, 1970), 10-13, 415.

As late as 1979, R. N. Whybray suffered the same geneticistic approach and kept reading Proverbs as an attempt by a Yahwist editor to be "bringing 'secular' wisdom under the umbrella of Yahwism."[5] Claus Westermann still holds to the presence of unresolved opposites of "profane" and "isolated propositions about God" in Proverbs, even though he admits that this has kept biblical wisdom from playing a central role in the proclamation of the church.[6]

Udo Skladny set the record straight, as I see it. He argues that the earliest original calling of biblical proverbial wisdom is for people to respect and follow the Lord's order for everyday life, which is first of all an ordering to be trusted *("eine geglaubte Ordnung")* and obeyed truly as the Lord God's will, full of blessing.[7] Likewise, Zimmerli affirmed that "wisdom theology is Creation theology."[8] It is a false start to pit secular proverbs against sacred proverb glosses and to spend time guessing at probable stages of the compositional genealogy. Such a split orientation fosters treating Old Testament "wisdom" as a topic foreign to "salvation history."[9]

The purported derivative nature of biblical wisdom sayings, culturally dependent upon comparable Egyptian and Mesopotamian "wisdom," is no longer considered

---

[5]R. N. Whybray, "Yahweh-sayings and Their Contexts in Proverbs 10, 1-22, 16" [1979] in *La sagesse de l'ancient testament*, ed. Maurice Gilbert (Leuven: Leuven University Press, 1990), 162. Later on he writes, "it would seem we have to acknowledge three stages: a) a morally 'neutral' attitude ('old wisdom'); b) a moral attitude which expresses itself in terms of an immanent force making for just reward; c) a recognition that this just reward is not simply immanent but directly due to the personal will of Yahweh" (p. 165). In a later work (*Wealth and Poverty in the Book of Proverbs* [Sheffield: Sheffield Press, 1990], 68, n. 1) Whybray modifies his earlier formulation: "I should no longer use the term 'secular.' . . . The 'Yahweh-proverbs' may be said to represent a theological development in so far that they reflect a tendency to *clarify* Yahweh's involvement in all that happens; but—contrary to a widely held view—there is in my opinion no reason to suppose that the absence of reference to Yahweh in the majority of these proverbs necessarily implies a lack of recognition of that involvement."

[6]Claus Westermann, *Forschungsgeschichte zur Weisheitsliteratur 1950-1990* (Stuttgart:Calwer Verlag, 1991), 46-47.

[7]Udo Skladny, *Die ältesten Spruchsammlungen in Israel* (Göttingen: Vandenhoeck & Ruprecht, 1962), 89-91.

[8]Walther Zimmerli, "Ort und Grenze der Weisheit im Rahmen der alttestamentlichen Theologie," in *Gottes Offenbarung. Gesammelte Aufsätze zum Alten Testament* (München: Chr. Kaiser Verlag, 1963), 302. This essay is translated as "The Place and Limit of the Wisdom in the Framework of the Old Testament Theology," in *Studies in Ancient Israelite Wisdom*, ed. James L. Crenshaw (New York: KTAV Publishing House, 1976), 314-326.

[9]That is, as the biblical story of the exodus to the promised land. Patrick Skehan (*Studies in Israelite Poetry and Wisdom* [Washington: Catholic Biblical Association of America, 1971], 23) argues that "to ascribe a primitively 'secular' character to the origins of any phase of human life in ancient times, in or out of Israel, is to go against all that we know of ancient man . . . . The 'secular' basis for the supposition is altogether gratuitous in afflicting some unidentifiable group of ancient sages with the misfortunes of the modern agnostic." Childs (*Introduction to the Old Testament as Scripture*, 553) writes, "As sacred scripture the book (of Proverbs) was not to be read according to a history of development in the concept of wisdom, rather from a fully developed confessional standpoint."

compelling today by various specialists.[10] But McKane's wrenching apart of what is canonically given operates as a smokescreen that leaves exegetes uncertain as to what is actually given for us to read in the booked Proverbs. This is especially true in the contemporary atmosphere of wanting "living proverbs" fit for quick reading in the fast lane.

The effort to center the discussion of the proverb on its presumed oral folk wisdom origins also pushed scholarship in the wrong direction.[11] Through this approach the booked Proverbs (especially those in Proverbs 10-24) came to be considered an anthology of atomistic *logia* treating a miscellany of topics arranged at most by catch-words (Boström's paranomasia) or grouped loosely around similar themes. Perhaps Proverbs 25-29 signals a firm move from oral to "transcribed" proverbs (25:1), that is, literary deposits by educated court scribes.[12] But the presumption that the book of Proverbs is a largely unedited compilation of now contextless oral one-liners continues to dominate wisdom scholarship.[13]

Recently, however, this atomistic approach has been questioned by a qualified and tentative attempt to find unifying edited contextuality within the Proverbs text, a *Sitz im Text*.[14] Already in 1968, Hermisson carefully treated the sayings of Proverbs 10-15 with considerable cohesion, paying particular attention to how their aesthetic quality intimated a connecting order.[15] In 1988, Van Leeuwen argued: "If the text presents us with larger, unified blocks of proverbial material, the exegete possesses a much surer basis for interpretation than if only a random accretion of isolated proverbs exists."[16]

[10]The Egyptologists K. A. Kitchen, "Proverbs and Wisdom Books of the Ancient Near East: the factual history of a literary form," *Tyndale Bulletin* 28 (1977): 69-114; "Egypt and Israel during the First Millenium B.C.," *Vetus Testamentum Supplement* 40 (1986):107-23; Jutta Krispenz, *Spruchcomposition im Buch Proverbia* (Bern: Peter Lang, 1989); John Ruffle, "The Teaching of Amenenope and its Connection with the Book of Proverbs," *Tyndale Bulletin* 28 (1977): 29-68.

[11]See, for example, the work of Otto Eissfeldt, *Der Maschal im Alten Testament* (Giessen: Alfred Töpelmann, 1913).

[12]So R. B. Y. Scott, "Solomon and the Beginnings of Wisdom in Israel," *Festschrift for Harold Henry Rowley. Supplement to Vetus Testamentum III*, eds. M. Noth and D. Winton Thomas (Leiden: Brill, 1960), 272-274.

[13]McKane (*Proverbs*, 414) and Westerman (*Forschungsgeschichte*, 46) assert that didactic instruction like Proverbs 1-9, the longer and later artistically worked pieces, has a tradition separate from the original popular aphoristic tradition.

[14]Brian Watson Kovacs (*Sociological-structural Constraints upon Wisdom: the spatial and temporal matrix of Proverbs 15:28-22:16* [Dissertation Vanderbilt University, 1978], 308) writes, "the catchword and paronomastic patterns which connect various proverbs simply cannot be adventitious nor accidental. Groupings of sayings must be accounted for, along with disruptions and incursions into the text." See also Raymond C. Van Leeuwen, *Context and Meaning in Proverbs 25-27* (Atlanta: Scholars Press, 1988), 37, and Duane A. Garrett, *Proverbs, Ecclesiastes, Song of Songs.* The New American Commentary (Nashville: The Broadman Press, 1993.) In a series of articles in *Vanguard* (1972-1979), I exposited Proverbs 25-29 as an anthology of gnomic poems.

[15]Hans-Jürgen Hermisson, *Studien zur israelitischen Spruchweisheit* (Neukirchener Verlag, 1968), 180-181.

[16]Van Leeuwen, *Context and Meaning in Proverbs 25-27*, 6.

That is precisely the thesis of this article, which is dedicated in thanks to John Stek. He has always served Christ's body with his Old Testament scholarship, dedicating an incredible amount of his lifetime to carefully annotated translation (NIV study edition) of the Bible, and giving insightful lectures and valuable syllabi on Old Testament books to theological students at Calvin Seminary, in Toronto, and elsewhere over many years.

I state my thesis as follows:

> Expect poetic paragraphs within the booked Proverbs 10-29, because the artful comparisons (מְשָׁלִים) and oblique riddles (חִידֹת) are rooted historically and professionally in the office of wise leaders recounted in the Bible, and have been written down by God-breathed educated literary scribes. Finding the poetic parameters in Proverbs 10-29 so as to discern the unified paragraphs[17] will open up the book of sayings for good preaching.

CONTEXT AND TASK

Before demonstrating this thesis with Proverbs 10:1-22, I will sketch the historical and literary setting, and then present evidence that "the wise" men and women in Israel had a special task and way of presenting a word from the Lord to God's people. These matters are critical for a proper reading of the booked proverbs.

The Literary Setting

Since the superscriptions of Proverbs 1:1, 10:1, and 25:1 suggest c. 950-700 B.C.[18] to be the historical parameters for the bulk of the written material, then Proverbs should address not nomads but settled city dwellers who were becoming fairly prosperous and secularized. There was a strong farming community at the time, but the younger generation was leaving the countryside to make its fortune in Jerusalem, where the building of the temple and the royal palace were causing a construction boom. Along with the extremely high inflation rate caused by Solomon's enormous deficit financing (1 Kings 9-10, esp. 9:10-14, 10:27), the labor force's shift from herding sheep to city work upset a traditional lifestyle and the accompanying faith-commitment. Freedom from parental control and moving outside the country confines of cultic worship and rituals of sacrifice also increased the importance of education for the next generation.

---

[17]It may be useful to think of something like the various Psalms (although in Proverbs the poetic paragraphs are epigrammatic poems for speaking, not songs for singing).

[18]This dating is also supported by Kitchen on external historical-literary grounds. Cf. Kitchen, "Proverbs and Wisdom Books," 102, 108-110, and "Egypt and Israel," 119-23.

These dates for Proverbs also cover Ahab and Jezebel's appropriation of Naboth's familial homestead and Jehu's subsequent rough-and-ready retribution (1 Kings 21, 2 Kings 9). The prophets Elijah, Amos, Isaiah, and Micah proclaimed God's justice during the generations when the wise sayings and admonitions would be particularly relevant. And good kings like Hezekiah needed to train young scribes and princes to carry out godly civil administration in the outlying districts of Judah away from the courtly precincts, where judgments in civic disputes would be given orally.

It took Christa Kayatz's 1966 dissertation[19] under Gerhard von Rad to overturn earlier authorities' (e.g., Eissfeldt, Kittel, Sellin, Gressmann) post-exilic dating of Proverbs 1-9. She argued that Proverbs 1-9's familiarity with ancient Egyptian wisdom literature undermines the hypothesis that later Hellenistic sources account for biblical motifs present.[20] With Childs,[21] I hold that the Masoretic text version the church has come to live with leads it to read Proverbs 10-29 in the light of Proverbs 1-9. So the artistically nuanced Proverbs 1-9 provides a clue to the poetic compositional character of chapters 10-29, since that is the way "the wise" formulated God's word.

If Proverbs 1-9, like Proverbs 31:10-31, exemplifies the kind of poetic paragraphs booked by "the wise," then Proverbs 1-9 not only provides, as van Leeuwen writes, "a worldview and hermeneutic introduction to the short sayings and admonitions which follow,"[22] but it also suggests the poetic format normal for biblical proverbial literature. The prevalent notion that "each proverb is an independent unit that can stand alone and still have meaning," and that "textual context is not essential for interpretation," is wrong, and invites a myopic reading of Proverbs. Garrett significantly adds, "Context, however, sometimes qualifies or gives a more precise meaning to a given proverb."[23] But even Garrett's attempt to "collect" proverbs into groups needs, I think, to be driven more radically by the realization that what we have here first of all are poetic paragraphs. In poetry the chicken comes before the egg—the paragraph whole determines the sense of the separate lines. One must accept that literary critical point in order to read and exhort from the booked Proverbs in a way that "plows the word of truth rightly" (2 Tim. 2:14-19).

---

[19]Christa Kayatz, *Studien zu Proverbien 1-9. Eine form- und motivgeschichtliche Untersuchung unter Einbeziehung ägyptischen Vergleichsmaterials* (Neukirchen-Vluyn: Neukirchener Verlag, 1966).

[20]Roland E. Murphy ("Assumptions and Problems in Old Testament Wisdom Research," *Catholic Biblical Quarterly* 29 [1967]: 413) still maintained, "It is generally agreed that Prv 1-9 is a later addition and introduction to pre-exilic collections of wisdom sayings." Westermann (*Forschungsgeschichte*, 46) also still thinks Proverbs 1-9 is late. These earlier traditions of thinking about Proverbs die hard.

[21]Childs, *Introduction to the Old Testament as Scripture*, 552-555.

[22]Raymond C. Van Leeuwen, "In Praise of Proverbs," in *Pledges of Jubilee*, eds. Lambert Zuidervaart and Henry Luttikhuizen (Grand Rapids: Eerdmans, 1995), 313, n. 12.

[23]Garrett, *Proverbs, Ecclesiastes, Song of Songs*, 46.

The Historical Setting: The Place and Task of Wise Counselors in Israel

Leadership in Israel: Priests, Prophets, and Kings

After God covenanted with Israel at Mount Sinai, Moses ordained Aaron and his sons to care for the tabernacle and the ark (Lev. 8). They were in charge of sacrifices for propitiation and for thanksgiving to offset the people's sin, they gave liturgical leadership, and they were set aside for the important protocol of moving the ark (Num. 10:33-36). Levites were officially consecrated to assist in such priestly tasks in Israel (Num. 1:47-54; 3:5-13).[24] After Joshua's death, the regularly ordained priests of Aaron and Eleazer's line tended the ark at Bethel (Judg. 20:24-28), but do-it-yourself priesthoods during the days of Israel's judges (Judg. 17) showed how Israel's priesthood could deteriorate to the nadir of the abusive sons of Eli, and end shamefully with Ichabod (1 Sam. 2:12-17, 22-25; 4:1-22).

The angel of the Lord (מַלְאַךְ יהוה) had brought crucial messages from God since the olden days—to Hagar (Gen. 16:7-16), to Abraham about to sacrifice Isaac (Gen. 22:9-19), to Moses at the burning bush (Ex. 3:1-4:17), to Balaam and his ass (Num. 22:21-35), to Gideon (Judg. 6:11-24), and to Samson's prospective parents (Judg. 13). The prophet Samuel was trained by the old priest Eli during a time when the Lord God, says Scripture, was not speaking much to Israel, and when revelatory visions were infrequent (1 Sam. 3:1). The Bible tells of an unnamed seer in Gideon's day who already used the typically prophetic phrase "Thus says the Lord" (כֹּה אָמַר יהוה) (Judg. 6:7-10). Such speaking is what prophets were supposed to do, and that's what judge-prophet Samuel did when he anointed Saul to be the first king of Israel, saying, "I'll sound out to you the word of God" (1 Sam. 9:27). By the time of Elijah, Ahab, Elisha, and Jehoshaphat, there were schools for prophets in Bethel and Jericho (2 Kings 2:1-3, 15-18). When Amaziah, high priest of corrupt King Jeroboam II, labelled Amos "a visionary" (חֹזֶה), Amos was glad to tell him that he had not been to any such school, but to "Hear the Word of the Lord!" (שְׁמַע דְּבַר־יהוה) anyhow (Amos 7:10-17).

The kings of Israel were anointed to rule and protect God's people, particularly to administer justice (Deut. 17:14-20; 1 Sam. 8). There seems to be a sorting out of leadership tasks among Israel's first kings. King Saul—anointed one of the Lord (יהוה מָשִׁיחַ)—made sacrifices in Gilgal when Samuel was late, and lost his kingship because they were disobedient sacrifices (1 Sam. 13:2-15; 15:22-23). David tended burnt offerings and peace offerings before the Lord when he brought the ark to Jerusalem to centralize his tribal administration in Jerusalem, the city of God. His

---

[24]As artisans, for example, the charismatic Bezaleel from Judah, and Oholiab from Dan had crucial roles in the construction of the Tent of Meeting (Ex. 35:30-39:43).

priestly dancing pleased the Lord, if not Michal (2 Sam. 6). Young King Solomon sacrificed in Gibeon (1 Kings 3:1-15) and later offered a long priestly prayer with untold offerings at the dedication of the new temple (1 Kings 8) without punishment for mixing priestly duties with his royal tasks. King Solomon also exemplified the wisdom of God, with an encyclopedic horticultural and animal knowledge and the ability to ferret out the truth needed for making just judgments (1 Kings 3:16-28; 4:29-34).

So leaders among God's people were anointed to be priests, prophets, and kings. These posts of trust were quite differentiated, even though historical overlapping of duties existed on into the early monarchy. What needs attention, however, if we are to understand the booked Proverbs, is the fact that there emerged a loosely differentiated group of "counselors" (יֹעֵץ) of the Lord, distinct from mediating priests of the Lord in Israel, from oracular prophets of the Lord in Israel, and from the Lord's kings in Israel. They made professional in Israel the kind of guiding, teaching leadership practiced by Moses, the village elders at the gates, and the charismatic tribal judges. These "wise" persons, who served as a core of special advisers to royalty, held a definite office as normal and highly valued in the court of Israel as in the courts of surrounding countries.

Leadership in Israel: The Wise

When Pharaoh's counselors failed to interpret God-sent dreams, the wise man Joseph became Pharaoh's secretary of state. Scripture reports Pharaoh saying, "This is a man in whom is the Spirit of God; nobody sees through things as do you" (Gen. 41, esp. vv. 7-8, 38-40). Moses was also trained in Egyptian wisdom (Acts 7:17-29; Heb. 11:23-28; cf. Ex. 2:1-15). That Moses was a highly literate commander-in-chief of God's folk wandering through the desert is evident from the elaborate memorial songs he composed (Ex. 15:1-18, Deut. 32:1-47) and the poetic benedictions recorded in his name (Deut. 33). Balaam, son of Beor at Pethor on the Euphrates, was Balak's highest paid "consultant" or "wise man" (Mic. 6:5). King Balak needed advice on dealing with the horde of Israelites camped on his borders. After missing out on the honors Balak had offered him, Balaam proved his credentials as an evil "wise man" (cf. James 3:13-18) by later providing the elders of Midian with an intermarriage policy that would break the Lord's favor upon Israel (Num. 25; 31:1-20).

Such counselors of royalty—like the princesses (wise women, חַכְמוֹת) attending General Sisera's mother (Judg. 5:29)—held humble positions early on among the Lord God's people. To help him rule the unwieldy multitude of Israelites, Moses appointed "wise men, insightful, seasoned persons" selected by the various tribes to head up the civil order and to judge disputes without playing favorites (Deut. 1:9-18; cf. Ex. 18:13-27). The task of these "wise ones" was allied with ruling; they did not make laws, but they had important judicial responsibilities.

That there was still a definite place for "the wise" to give counsel in Israel during King Saul's day is clear. It was reported that the Lord was no longer answering King Saul's prayer for direction, either by the Urim (used by the priests for making important decisions—Ex. 28:30, Lev. 8:5-9, Ezra 2:59-63), or by prophetic seers, or by dreams (the peculiar interpretive task of "the wise," 1 Sam. 28:6). During King David's reign, the established practice of "wise women" in the countryside is matter-of-factly told. Joab requisitioned "a wise woman" from Tekoa—Amos' hometown—to act out a kind of morality playlet designed to give the pining David a rationale for recalling his murderer son Absalom (2 Sam. 14:1-24). It was in the office of "wise woman" that a leading woman in the city of Abel debated with General Joab and then convinced her townspeople to throw the head of Benjamite insurrectionist Sheba over the wall to save the town's inhabitants (2 Sam. 20:1-22).

The seer Nathan was King David's confidante. His story of the one little ewe lamb (2 Sam. 11:26-12:15) is a characteristic way for "the wise" to bring fools to their senses, and to give suggestive, persuasive advice to those in power. With considerable eloquence, Nathan got the dying King David to let him and Zadok the priest quickly anoint the boy Solomon to be king to foil Adonijah's bid for the throne (1 Kings 1). This consummate story-telling, roundabout, deferential, yet surprising way to bring God's specific direction to bear on life problems stamps the activity of "the wise." The crucial role Hushai and Ahithophel played at the court of David and at the headquarters of renegade Absalom is comparable to the role of the "wise women" mentioned above. Counsel was highly prized in Israel. "In those days the counsel (עֵצָה) which Ahithophel delivered was as if one consulted the very word of God" (2 Sam. 16:23).

Even King Solomon's prodigious wisdom was backed up by ranks of courtly counselors. They outlived Solomon's apostasy and death and saw their good counsel dismissed by Solomon's son Rehoboam when he formed a new cabinet of more modern "wise men," who led him to speak in a harsh spirit to the people seeking redress (1 Kings 12:1-20). This overturning of good counsel by poisoning advice (עֵצָה), with historic results of a split from David's line, was overseen by the Lord, says Scripture (1 Kings 12:15).

By the time of the God-fearing Hezekiah, the composition of a courtly council with wise counselors included figures like Shebna, a scribe or secretary, and Joah Asaphson, an historian or record-keeper. They knew Aramaic, the international language of diplomacy, and entered into high-level negotiations of royal decisions (2 Kings 18:1-19:7). So "the men of Hezekiah, King of Judah," who were given the precious task of "transcribing" the artful comparisons of Solomon (מִשְׁלֵי שְׁלֹמֹה, Prov. 25:1), were not underpaid copyists. They were educated, cultured wise men concerned with editing a canon for instructing the inexperienced and for providing "the wise" with disciplined training for setting their consciousness in awe of the Lord.[25]

Even in the run-down court of King Jehoiakim there were polyglot wise men like Daniel, Hananiah, Mishael, and Azariah. When they were taken to the palace of Babylonian Nebuchadnezzar, Daniel and his wise friends proved to be better than any of the Chaldean sorcerers, astrologers, wiseman counselors, and interpreters of dreams, because God's Spirit revealed to Daniel mysteries and made him and his God-fearing friends wise (Dan. 1:1-2:30, esp. 1:4; 2:27-28; 5:10-12).

R. N. Whybray argues for an intellectual tradition in ancient Israel that is "distinct from other traditions such as the historical, legal, cultic and prophetic." At the same time he maintains that there is no societal institution carrying this tradition, no school, "no special professional class."[26]

I find the term "intellectual" too disengaged from the determinative faith orientation that was present from the very beginnings of Israel's leadership, even in Abraham's exodus-response to the Lord (Gen. 12:1-9). It is also problematic to overdefine terms like "counselor," "teacher," "wise man," and "scribe," as if each excludes the other. Gerhard von Rad, for example, has argued that biblical words like "discipline" (מוּסָר), "discernment" (בִּין), "insightful action" (שָׂכַל), "circumspection" (עָרְמָה), and "handiness in knowing what's up" (לֶקַח) are differentiated from the other, but that these differences overlap within the family of "wisdom."[27] Moreover, "wisdom" in the Old Testament is not a matter having a "superior degree of (personal) intelligence,"[28] but of "knowing what God wants done." God can give such "understanding" to the foreign soothsayer Balaam, just as he can call the unbelieving Persian Cyrus messiah (מָשִׁיחַ) among the nations (Isa. 44:23-45:8).

I have shown how the calling to be "wise" is at home both in the tribal society Moses organized and in the precincts of Solomon's extravagant royalty. "Wise men" and "wise women" exercised a leadership among God's folk that was variegated, fluid, but constant, with certain features that identified its practice as "counsel" (עֵצָה). Differentiation of "the wise" had become commonplace by the time the prophet Jeremiah's adversaries spoke their oath to do him in, when they said, "Come, let's make plans against Jeremiah, as surely as a priest is never without law-guidance

---

[25]The word "counsel" (תַּחְבֻּלוֹת) in Prov. 1:5, reminds one of the phrase "instruction of the Lord" (νουθεσία κυρίου) in Eph. 6:4.

[26]R. N. Whybray, *The Intellectual Tradition in the Old Testament* (Berlin: Walter de Gruyter, 1974), 70, 49.

[27]Gerhard von Rad, *Wisdom in Israel*, trans. James D. Martin (London: SCM Press, 1972), 13.

[28]Whybray, *The Intellectual Tradition in the Old Testament*, 9, 117.

(תּוֹרָה), wise man without counsel (עֵצָה), and prophetic seer without the word (דָּבָר)" (Jer. 18:18).

After the exile in the day of Ezra and Nehemiah, when kings had forfeited their office among the people of God, the wise men and scribes came to the fore. Ezra was known to Artaxerxes as "priest, scribal scholar in the worded precepts of Yahweh and the ordinances for Israel" (Ezra 7:11). Indeed, that is what scribes in Israel became—Torah specialists. And it needs to be said that when the charisma of wisdom died because there was no vision among God's people, and when "the wise" began to trust their proverbs more than "standing in awe before the Lord God," when these leaders began to put stock in their Abrahamic blood rather than in obeying Yahweh's will, then we see "wise men" like Job's friends and like the scribes of Jesus' day, whether orthodox Pharisee or heterodox Sadducee.

Qoheleth[29] was one of the "wise" teachers in post-exilic Israel who was trained to lead the people in a back-and-forth, speaker-assembly, communal-probing way to determine the right direction to take. Qoheleth is a counselor and folk leader.[30] He speaks words of wisdom, makes artful comparisons, tells riddles and stories to help keep them on the Way of what is right in the eyes of God.

The Imaginative "Yes, but" Pedagogy of "the Wise," and the Literary Configuration of Proverbs 1-9

If you hear Scripture as a true story, as I do, you are startled and impressed by the way young King Solomon distributed the wisdom of God's justice when he told his courtiers to cut a child in half to determine which harlot was the mother (1 Kings 3:16-28). If such a dramatic ploy was part and parcel of "wisdom" in that day, the contests Solomon held with Egyptian and Babylonian wise men (remember Moses and Aaron's test before Pharaoh's wise men, Ex. 7:8-13)[31] were imaginative, live-wire contests to show wisdom on an international scale (1 Kings 4:29-34).

In fact, Solomon's quasi-dramatic way of bringing God's Word so vividly to bear on life's problems is the very way "the wise" we have discussed above were trained to lead the people in God's directives. I call this parry-and-thrust, parable-telling, decoy method of making a point, the "Yes, but" way of teaching God's will.

---

[29]The title of the book Ecclesiastes/Qoheleth designates the official speaker to the people assembled (קָהָל) for a special occasion.

[30]This is why in his day Luther translated the title Ecclesiates/Qoheleth as *Prediger*, that is, "preacher."

[31]" . . . wise men, hieroglyphic specialists and mumbling magicians"—the narrative pokes fun of them (Ex. 7:11) but recognizes their important official courtly task as Pharaoh's cabinet of advisors.

This "Yes, but" methodology permeates the artistic literary configuration in the canonically booked section of Proverbs 1-9. There are cohering "my child/my student" (בְּנִי) paragraphs that spin out variations on the central theme which resonates everywhere:

> to stand still, listening before the Lord God Yahweh gives you a headstart in full-bodied knowledge, in wisdom and corrective discipline—exactly what fools despise (1:7).

These בְּנִי paragraphs sport vivid quotations of tempters (1:11-14; 7:14-20) and provocative alliterative epigrams (1:17; 6:26-28). In counterpoint to these paragraphs, there are stirring appeals by Wisdom in the first person, appealing to the inexperienced to follow the ordinances of Yahweh (1:20-33; 8:1-21). Hymns about Wisdom also highlight the authority, power, and glory of living as children of Wisdom (3:13-20; 8:22-31). These poetic passages act like antiphonal recitations, heightening the one basic thrust of the whole book: live straightforwardly before the Lord, knowing what counts in all kinds of daily life matters.

And there are specially pregnant, capsule summations of the double-edged message permeating the בְּנִי paragraphs (3:11-12; 8:32-36), which festively recapitulate the theme of 1:7. Chapter 5 balances a warning about "the strange woman" and an encouragement to take joy in your wife's erotic love with an interspersed commentary. The structure of chapter 9 is similar. It climaxes the whole proem of chapters 1-9, spelling out the God-breathed point: to live with (Holy Spirited) Wisdom and to know what God wills shall bring shalom, but to set up housekeeping with godlessness and to use good gifts illicitly leads to utter ruin.[32]

---

[32]One could schematize the antiphonal artistic structure of chapters Proverbs 1-9 as follows:

introduction 1:2-6
theme of the whole 1:7

paragraphs on decisive living & temptation by what is "strange" to the Lord	WISDOM passages	
1:8-9, 10-19 (with vignette vv. 11-14) 2:1-22	1:20-21; 22-31, 32-33	appeal of Wisdom
3:1-10, 11-12 3:21-35	3:13-18, 19-20	hymn to Wisdom

4:1-9 on Wisdom as pearl of great price
4:10-19 godly Way and godless way contrasted
4:20-27 obedient heart and bodily acts
5:1-6, 7-14, 15-23 strophic caesura
6:1-5 on surety
6:6-11 on lazy fellow
6:12-15 on deceiver
6:16-19 on seven-hated matters

The literary configuration one needs to appreciate in order to understand Proverbs 1-9 and (my proposal) the book as a whole is this: think of paragraphs of variegated gnomic poetry, artistically juxtaposed as point and counterpoint, as example and repeated refrain, as graphic vignette and extended metaphor supplementing one another or in polemic contrast. Proverbs 1-9 is like a chorus of stimulating reflections, voices orchestrated on the principle of "Yes, but." The gambit "Yes, but" is the pedagogical tactic of a wise one leading the less experienced person by saying "It seems so, but have you considered this?"

God's revelation booked here in the "wise man and wise woman" format presents arranged paragraphs that need to be studied like poetry. They give an oblique presentation of reflective truth compressed rather than in a direct indicative plus imperative direction (as is the wont of Paul in the New Testament). This "Yes, but" nuanced complexity ranges in the Bible from the chorus of voices lyrically contesting erotic human love called "The Song of Songs" (7:1-9a bespeaks lust, in my reading)[33] to the book of Job with speeches permeated by laments, to the dialogical monologue wisdom of Ecclesiastes with refrains of thankful joy, to the teachings of rabbi Christ. Although booked wisdom is not in the "Thus says the Lord" manner of the prophet, and is not an atoning sacrifice offered by the priest, the "Yes, but" Scripture of interwoven poetic paragraphs is still an authoritative kerygmatic word of the Lord that gives healing words of direction.

To show the reach of the "Yes, but" way of "the wise" into the New Testament, one need but notice that Jesus renewed the wise man way of revealing God's will to the people after the intertestamentary commentators and scribes of Jesus' day had dried up its blessing (cf. Matt. 7:28-29). And Jesus "dramatized" teaching in other ways than by using parables (e.g., Matt. 13). Christ's teaching on the hillsides epitomizes the living wise man tradition of Qoheleth-rabbi: "You have heard it said, but I say"; "If your hand causes you to sin, cut it off"—cut the living baby in two! (Matt. 5-7).

6:20-21, 22-7:27 (with parable of seduction 7:6-23)
8:1-21 appeal of Wisdom
8:22-31 hymn of Wisdom, in beginning
8:32-36 closing appeal of Wisdom
9:1-6, 7-12, 13-18 strophic culmination

[33]Cf. my *The Greatest Song, in critique of Solomon*, freshly and literally translated from the Hebrew and arranged for oratorio performance [1967] (Toronto: Tuppence Press, 1988). (I cannot help but wish Duane Garrett, who repeats G. Lloyd Carr's severe judgment [Inter-Varsity Press, 1984], "that the Song, as it now stands, is unactable" [*Song of Songs*, The New American Commentary, {1993}, 359-60] could once attend one of the many performances I have directed in the last thirty years in Canada, the United States, and Europe. Their error is to force the chorus of voices in the Old Testament text into a Greek/Shakesperian concept of "drama" in order to dismiss "the dramatic interpretation.")

Also Luke reports how Jesus carried out the wise man tradition of unrehearsed interchange with disciples, crowd, and Pharisees, right after Christ's spirited exchange with those who said he exorcised by Beelzebub. Christ had just told the story (Luke 11:24-26) of the unclean spirit that is cast out, returns to find its old hideout clean but empty, gets seven other spirits worse than itself, and returns, so that the fellow is permanently worse off—filled with self-righteous demons!

> Now it happened that while Jesus was speaking these words, some woman or other in the crowd raised her voice and hollered to him, "Blessed is the belly that carried you around and the tits that gave you suck!" But Jesus said, "That's fine, [lady,] but the point is, 'Blessed are those who hear the Word of God and are busy doing it!'"
> (Luke 11:27-28)

Luke 11:27 (like Prov. 10:15) is not a text for "Mother's Day" ("May your children be like Christ")! Luke records this incident under the Spirit's guiding to show how superficial the response of Jewish approval often was to rabbi Jesus' teaching, and how Jesus here did a wise man "Yes, but" *au point.*

The woman sensed Christ had done a great deed, and defended his ministry of healing at a very fundamental level, but she didn't have a clue that Christ's exorcism act showed that the glorious rule of God was already begun on earth, and she didn't grasp the story (which Mark 3:23 calls a parable) of an exorcised evil spirit returning with seven worse ones. So the lady says, "A son like you makes a mother glad."

Christ corrects her immediately in the next verse: thank you very much, ma'am, for the support, *but* (μενοῦν) more to the point, don't put down self-righteous people in their logical contradictions, not even to be freed from dumb-making devils. The point is that you need to be cleansed from sin in order to do what God wants done. Don't congratulate me, woman. Repent and believe, fear the Lord, love your neighbor, be a steward of God's gifts to you on earth.

POETIC PARAGRAPH OF PROVERBS 10:1-22

Aware of the historical setting and literary penchant of the indirect, polemical way "the wise" make God's will known, one can hear how chapter 10:1-22 presents Wisdom (act *coram Deo*, 1:7, hate evil, 8:13) correcting the worldly-wise street "wisdom" of the day. I contend that 10:1-22 is almost as tightly composed a piece as chapter 2, which is one single ode-like sentence holding dependent "if, then" balanced clauses together in twenty-two verses that snap shut as a poem should.[34]

Translation[35] and Commentary

1. A wise son or daughter makes a father or mother's heart merry,
   and an insolent, godless child breaks its parent's heart to pieces.

2. Treasures gotten by underhanded dealings are of no use at all:
   doing what is rightly just, however, saves you from death!

3. The Lord God Yahweh never lets a man or a woman who is actually righteous stay hungry,
   but God rams the greedy desire of those who like to cut corners right back [down their throats]!

4. "A negligent empty hand brings on poverty:
   the grip of the diligent makes one rich."

5. "A fellow who gathers in at harvest time knows what he is doing:
   a fellow who oversleeps at harvest time is simply disgraceful!"

6. Genuine blessings halo the head of whoever come through with just deeds,
   while the mouth of people who don't act straight casts up a smokescreen over deeds that violate others.

7. The person who has persevered in doing what is just will be remembered as a gift of shalom,
   while the good name of those who have been guilty of crookedness shall decompose.

8. A person who is at heart wise simply carries out [his or her] tasks:
   it's the pair of slippery lips that will be smashed to bits.

9. "Who walks in wholesome ways will walk securely unafraid:
   who chooses his paths to be twisty will be discovered [tied in knots]."

10. An eye that blinks the double-crossing wink makes bitter trouble;
    [I repeat:] it's the pair of slippery lips that will be smashed to bits!

11. The mouth of folk kept truly just is a bubbling source of life;
    while the mouthing of people who don't act straight [I repeat] casts up a smoke-screen over deeds that violate others.

12. Hate rouses bickering, blistering discontent,
    while love dresses all kinds of rebellious misdeeds with clothes.

[34]2:1 My son/my daughter, if you take hold of what I say . . .
2:5 *then* you shall catch on to standing still listening before the Lord and truly find a full-bodied knowledge of God . . .
2:9 *then* you shall get to understand doing what is right, the just thing, and doing things simply the way they are set up to be—what is creationally good . . .
2:12 snatching you away safe from the way of evil . . .
2:16 snatching you away safe from the strange woman . . .
2:20 *so that* you shall be walking on the way of creationally good things . . . .

[35]The layout of my translation hints at the counterpoint connections that make the whole intelligible. "My son" (בְּנִי) paragraphs are not just referring to teenage boys. בְּנִי has the meaning of "my son, my daughter, my child, my student, my disciple," and can include adults who are humble enough to sit at the feet of "the wise" to receive teaching in God's Way. So the translation embraces the fact that בְּנִי is not gender-restrictive. My translation of רְשָׁעִים in verse 3 as "those who like to cut corners" and in verse 6 as "those who don't act straight" may set the teeth of purists on edge. But Scriptural words are more than technical terms. The words are not jargon but poetically wrought; so putting the Hebrew into English needs a little play to allow this literary quality of the worded thought to have its force. I always check out my translations with purist Buber who wrenches German into the same refined Hebraicized term every time the word appears, lest one stray beyond aesthetic limits. "Blockhead babbling" in verse 14b is my metaphoric equivalent for פִּי אֱוִיל even though "blockhead babbling" hides the fact that the Hebrew has "mouth of a fool" sounding again the "mouth of the crooked" from verse 11b.

13 You will find wisdom on the lips of an experienced, discerning person,
    but "You need a stick for the backside of anybody who at heart lacks sense."
14 Judicious men and wise women are thrifty with hard-won knowledge,
    but blockhead babblings are pregnant with disaster:
15   "Possessions are a citadel of strength to a man of wealth.
            It's poverty that ruins the poor—"
16 [No!] the handiwork and wages of a tried-and-true man or woman is full of life,
    but the income of a crooked fellow only increases his or her sin.
17 When one faithfully follows a nurturing discipline, you are on a pathway of life;
    but to pay no attention to corrective jusgments will leave you wandering around lost!

18   Lips of deceit conceal hate,
            and whoever spreads gossip is a godless, insolent fool;
19   wherever there is too much talk, the upstart misdeed will not fail to materialize—
            whoever is more chary of his or her lip movements has more sense.
20   The tongue of a tried-and-true woman or man is as valuable as the choicest silver,
            while the heart of connivers is worth next to nothing.
21   The lips of the tried-and-true woman or man will nourish many [to new life!]
            Stupidly closed fools, however, because they lack sense at heart, drop dead!
22   It is only the Lord God Yahweh's blessing that makes one rich:
            all your troubled struggle doesn't add a bit to it.

10:1 gives the usual setting, posing the alternative of "Wisdom or foolishness" in a two-generational context so important to the covenanting Lord. This introductory verse probably doubles as a common subtitle to the paragraphs that follow in chapters 10-15 until 15:33 paraphrases the cornerstone of 1:7 to end the section.

10:2 formulates the theme of the whole paragraph: crooked success is worthless, but right-doing (צְדָקָה) keeps you from a dead end. And 10:3 proclaims the Good News that the Lord provides the one with integrity (צַדִּיק) with sustenance, but frustrates the greedy wicked. It takes a saving faith to believe this thesis (as Ps. 73 and the book of Job affirm), because such truth is not observable to the naked eye.

10:4-5 counter the theme and thesis of 10:2-3 with what "people today say." Imagine verse 4 as the quip of an entrepreneur leading one of Solomon's trade missions to Hiram's court, and verse 5 as the "wisdom" of a city foreman to a work crew building the temple or Solomon's gorgeous palace, that is, as an incentive to country boys displaced in Jerusalem trying to make big money.

But 10:6-7 counters the street-smart sense and half-truth of "industry-makes-rich" (v. 4) and "those who work hard get ahead in the world" (v. 5) with the wisdom that lasting blessings (בְּרָכוֹת) come to the one with integrity (צַדִּיק, vv. 6-7) while the wicked (רְשָׁעִים) are deceitfully violent and short-lived. That is, 10:6-7 reinforces 10:2-3[36]

---

[36]No wonder the LXX added יהוה after בְּרָכוֹת in v. 6. R. B. Y. Scott (*Proverbs*, The Anchor Bible [Garden City, NY: Doubleday, 1965, 83) repeats Toy (*The Book of Proverbs*, 203) to second-guess why v. 11b doubles v. 6b. They represent an earlier generation that read doubling as scribal error rather than as poetic emphasis.

after the false lead of 10:4-5 by positing that "just-doing versus crooked acts," not "riches versus poverty," is the framework for thinking and doing wisely.

10:8-11 is a brief commentary on the point of verses 1-3 and 6-7, to make clear that being wise (חָכָם) consists in following the Lord's ordinances (מִצְוֹת, v. 8) for life. In other words, the voice of a just person, which brings life (v. 11), is precisely the opposite of being foolish (v. 8) and wicked (v. 11).

Repeating verse 8b in verse 10b and verse 6b in verse 11b corrects the false courtier's mode of operation and teaches the audience to avoid the conflagration caused by slippery lips in a competitive workforce, and a glib tongue at the office or in the neighborhood (cf. James 3:1-12). Duplicit speech entails actual destruction (vv. 8b,10b); the death of the deceitful (v. 2) is the antithesis of life (v. 11a) for the righteous (צַדִּיק).[37]

Between 10:2-11 and 10:13-22 we find the central verse of this poetic paragraph. Proverbs 10:12 exposes the nature of crookedness (רָשָׁע) and of integrity (צַדִּיק) on which one's life or death hangs. Arousing contention (making things crooked, מְעַקֵּשׁ, v.9b) is hatred in action, while love is action that covers over the nakedness of your neighbor's wrongs and evil (פְּשָׁעִים).

In the context of 10:1-22, verse 12 is as resounding a statement as Micah 6:8, which proclaims: "What does the Lord require of you? Nothing but doing what is just, loving to keep your promises, and walking humbly with your God." James quotes Proverbs 10:12 from memory as the punch line that sums up his whole letter (James 5:19-20). Peter also quotes verse 12 as the crux for life in the end times (1 Peter 4:7-11). He argues that Proverbs 10:12 teaches how the body of Christ should be "economical" (house-holding) and hospitable with its charismata. This is the clue to withstanding great troubles, says Scripture.

Verses 13 and 14 pick up the "wisdom versus foolishness" theme from verses 1 and 8. Verse 15 exemplifies this theme, but not as a plank in a biblical economic policy. Rather, 10:15 is the slogan of God's people on the make in 1 Kings 5-7: "Capital is the stronghold of the wealthy: poverty is the weak spot of the poor." Proverbs 10:15 is the proverbial recapitulation of 10:4-5 run amuck in a policy of Mammon. This policy is immediately corrected by verses. 16-17.

10:16-17 pulls the runaway concern for success and trust in money back to the orientation of Wisdom: integrity versus wickedness. These verses explicitly condemn the acquired gain, possessions, and profit of those who are devious as an increase in sin (חַטָּאת, v. 16). They declare that only the word of the righteous (צַדִּיק) brings life,

---

[37]The alliteration in verse 9a הוֹלֵךְ בַּתֹּם יֵלֶךְ בֶּטַח hints that it is a known aphorism; so the converse in verse 9b may be minted fresh for this occasion.

and that only those who follow the discipline (מוּסָר) of Wisdom are walking on the path of life (vv. 16a, 17a). So the creed of security-in-riches (10:15) is indeed the babble of fools (v. 14).

10:18-21 provides an almost line-by-line explication of verses 12-17, except for verse 15. Verse 18 links hate (שִׂנְאָה, v. 12) to being a fool (cf. vv. 1 and 14). Verse 19 emphasizes what verses 13 and 14 pronounce—too much talk is prone to misdeed (פֶּשַׁע), while the judicious (חֹשֵׂךְ) are chary of their words. Furthermore, verse 20 exposits verse 16 by saying that the tongue of the righteous (צַדִּיק) is most valuable while the conniver's (רָשָׁע) talk is worthless. Finally, verse 21 echoes verse 17's sentiment that disciplined lips will nourish many; it also sounds the note that fools (אֱוִילִים) who at heart lack sense (בַּחֲסַר־לֵב, cf. also vv. 13's contrast to v. 8) will wander around in circles, only to drop dead (cf. v. 2).

This poetic paragraph concluding verse, by using the name of YHWH to recall the Good News of verse 3, corrects all the "get rich and be safe" homespun palaver and street-smarts of verses 4, 5, and 15; the blessing of the Lord (cf. v. 6), not hard work, brings riches. Contrary to all the public opinion in boomtown Jerusalem, Judah, and Israel c. 950-750 B.C., pulling yourself up by your own bootstraps in the economy, in foreign trade, in the turmoil of civil administration and in royal court intrigue—scrambling—do not add to one's well-being: riches (v. 4b) are not the fruit of industrious labor; they come only from the hand of the Lord God's blessing upon those with integrity (צַדִּיק, v. 6).

The Paragraph and Its Message

Once one grasps that Proverbs 10:1-22 is a tightly knit poetic paragraph, its powerful message of comfort and rebuke becomes evident: curb the drive to reach prosperity by cutting corners, by talking crookedly to be impressive and to get ahead. Say "No!" to such a self-centered, selfish program of clever discontent and fermented strife, because that is hatred in action, and the end of hatred is ruin. Instead, believe that doing your ordained task is the way of genuine life. The compassionate Lord God will surely bless the one who comes through trials, withstands temptations, and deals trustworthily with colleagues and neighbors. Yahweh's blessing of shalom (veritable riches) is not something a hard-working man or woman can achieve. To know in your guts (לֵב) this truth of total dependence upon the Lord is to have a disciplined life and to be wise.[38]

---

[38]To put the literary structure of this poetic paragraph in a schematic way:

v. 1 (setting)

v. 2 theme: crooked success is worthless: right-doing keeps you from a dead-end.

So Proverbs 10:1-22 carries on in detail the very formidable choice with which Proverbs 1-9 faces every new generation: will you succumb to the seduction of what is "strange" to the Lord, the deeply foolish delights which lead to your death in hell (5:15-23, 7:21-23, 9:13-18), or will you hear the cry and accept the invitation of Wisdom to receive the Spirit[39] of knowing what is holy (1:22-33, 3:13-18, 8:4-36, 9:1-12)? Proverbs 10 develops Proverbs 1-9 by explicitly asserting that wisdom (חָכָם) shows up concretely in trustworthy right-doing (צְדָקָה), and foolishness (אֱוִיל) is embodied in crooked deeds (רָשָׁע). Heart and mouth are intimately linked: a wise heart (חֲסַר־לֵב) carries out God's ordinantial tasks with words of life (vv. 8, 11, 21); a vapid heart (חֲסַר־לֵב, vv. 13-15, 21) arouses and courts death.

This message, which links wisdom to just-doing, is in the forefront of the concern of prophets Amos, Isaiah, and Micah, who are contemporary with the later range of the Proverbs book. Spiritual wisdom is false unless it goes beyond pious sacrifices and regulated worship services and enters into the very bloodstream of society by giving justice to the downtrodden, the lonely, and the destitute, and ending the oppression of societal outcasts (Isa. 1:10-20; 29:13-24; 58-59; Amos 5-6; Mic. 2-3, 6).

The oppositional juxtaposition in Proverbs 9 of the woman Wisdom and the woman Foolishness reappears in Revelation 12 and 17 where the woman with child is saved from the dragon and from the whore of Babylonic culture.[40] Proverbs 10:1-22 ties this fundamental apocalyptic decision, which God already spelled out to Israel in the wise

v. 3 good news! the Lord protects the righteous and frustrates the wicked.
    vv. 4-5 People say . . .
        vv. 6-7   But the truth is:
        vv. 8-11   commentary on vv. 2-7
v. 12 response God wants: love your neighbour; never hate.
        vv. 13-14 Isn't it so . . .
        v. 15   People say . . .
        vv. 16-17 But the truth is:
        vv. 18-21 commentary on vv. 12-17
v. 22 good news (deepening the theme): only the Lord's blessing makes you rich.

[39]The NIV misses, it seems to me, a crucial place to help the reader see the "spirit" versus "flesh" horizon to the choice Proverbs is proclaiming by mistranslating רוּחִי in 1:23 as "thoughts." The Good News paraphrase is worse: "advice"! Petersen's *The Message* at least reads "spirit." Cf. note to RSV on Proverbs 1:23, "Heb spirit," which is dropped in NRSV.

[40]All the debate about whether "the strange woman" is a real flesh-and-blood woman (the Septuagint treats 2:16-17 as an allegorical personification and translates אִשָּׁה as ὁδός and אַלּוּף as διδασκαλίαν!), and whether capital "W" Wisdom woman is a rhetorical personification or a mythic hypostatization due to Hellenistic gnostic influence of Sophia, is simply evidence of how learned theologians do not know how to read poetic lines aright. With heavy-lidded eyes they either over-read the poetry into *theologoumena* or they mistake the allusive truth as mere dress-up embellishment. The "strange woman" (like the Babylonic harlot of Revelation) is poetic reference to your corner-store *Playboy* magazine or the Jaguar you covet to have under you, and the "Wisdom woman" is a poetic Older Testament reference, I believe, to the Holy Spirit (Prov. 2:6, 8:14-18; cf. Isa. 11:1-3, Mic. 3:8, Dan. 5:10-12).

speech of Moses generations earlier (Deut. 30: Choose the life of doing good or the death of doing evil.). Proverbs 10:1-22 reveals that the choice between life and the death is made when one's mouth nourishes the neighbor (10:21), or when one's "slippery lips" (10:8b,10b,14b-15) murder the neighbor with vain, conniving putdowns.

In Pauline fashion, Proverbs 10 takes the wisdom/folly horizons, depicted by Woman Wisdom (Proverbs 8:12) and Woman Foolishness (Prov. 9:13; Prov. 2:16; cf. Eph. 6:10-13), of Proverbs 1-9 into the tangible courts of gentle speech which sets things straight: a just deed (10:11a, 19, 20a, 21a) or the concealed hatred of ambitious, boastful, insolent talk (10:1b, 6b, 18). Later in James 3:13-18, the Newer Testament clearly proclaims this very difference between godly wisdom and demonic "wisdom" as the difference between what seeds the contention of careers and success and what sows the shalom of restorative justice (δικαιοσύνη, cf. Matt. 5:5-6).

AN OPEN CONCLUSION

How does one determine where Proverbs' poetic paragraphs begin and end? As Hermisson carefully said a generation ago, we are looking for an ordering principle that is not commonly practised today.[41] However, if we come to the text aware that the tradition of "the wise" in Israel assumed a creational theology of Yahweh's ordinances as fundamental to an obedient people of God, and if we approach the booked sayings as poetic writings, that is, as intentionally composed "Yes, but" wholes (varied wholes perhaps as diverse as the canonic psalms are), finding the paragraphic beginnings and endings in the Proverbs book will be less mysterious.

But exegetes and pastors will have to disabuse themselves of the traditional idea that Proverbs 10:1-22:16 is a collection of one-liner aphorisms and precepts.[42] Garrett's remark is true: "Identifying the small collections of proverbs is essential for the use of Proverbs in the church."[43] But Garrett still seems to work with the idea of Near Eastern paranomastic "collection" and didactic "random repetition" of formulaic sententiae.[44]

With the working presupposition that what we need to find are the artistically refined paragraphs that juxtapose and contrast epigrammatic sayings, we need to edit Proverbs into a format comparable to the Psalms. Proverbs 10:1-22 commends itself as such a literary paragraph for the following reasons.

---

[41]Hans-Jürgen Hermisson, *Studien zur israelitischen Spruchweisheit* (Neukirchener Verlag, 1968), 174.

[42]Scott, *Proverbs*, 83.

[43]Garrett, *Proverbs, Ecclesiastes, Song of Songs*, 47.

[44]Krispenz (*Spruchkompositionen im Buch Proverbia*, 161) argues that Egyptian paranomastic use is unlike that in the Old Testament book of Proverbs.

The name Yahweh appears in verses 3 and 22, and wherever it graces a poetic line one may expect something weighty to be stated, so that a Yahweh phrase initiates the train of thought like a leading paragraph sentence, or it brings the movement of a poetic whole to a conclusion, a kind of caesura.[45] Twenty-two verses is also a natural Hebraic pattern for closure, even if the whole is not an alphabetic acrostic like Proverbs 31:10-31 (or Ps. 9-10; cf. Prov. 2).

Verse 12, given special attention by the New Testament (James and 1 Peter), and the two flanking four-verse groupings I called "commentary" all highlight the importance of couplets verses 6-7 (double blessing) and verses 16-17 (double life) for explicating the theme of verse 2. There is a kind of sustained, ode-like structure to the whole.

The to-be-corrected nature of verses 4-5 and verse 15 is unambiguous when one sees their contextualization by the whole twenty-two-verse paragraph. That one should not accept Proverbs 10:15 as bona fide biblical wisdom is shown by the subparagraph Proverbs 18:10-12, which renders explicit the phantasmagorical delusions that attend those who are vainly rich.[46]

What the apostle Peter said about brother Paul's writings (2 Peter 3:14-16) is also true about the wisdom of Proverbs: too hard to understand. The poetic paragraphs of Proverbs are not popular verse. Every attempt to market them for reading like Benjamin Franklin's "Poor Richard's Almanac"—as quips for punctuating and motivating the sanctified life—misses their sturdy God-breathed point and their lasting proclamation. So long as our versified published Bible translations neglect to conceive Proverbs and to print them in collocated poetic paragraphs, we may be hindering the "simple" readers from hearing God's message.

It will take courage to buck the established tradition of Wisdom literature scholarship, which has served up Proverbs as Egyptian precepts made kosher by a Yahwist editor, and to go against the stream of making the Old Testament gospel simple. But such work has been begun by Stek, van Leeuwen, and Krispenz. It needs to be carried on so that the book of poetic paragraphs comes to be heard today as giving substance to the living water.

[45]I call this the "firefly" indicator, and am using it as one method to discern other paragraphs in Proverbs 10:23-24:34. You catch the trajectory of a firefly in the night by seeing where it lights up. Wherever Yahweh radiates a spot, a hint is given, I think, of where the poetic paragraphic point is headed.

[46]If one does not have the twenty-two-verse poetic context, one can take verses 4-5 as a straightforward work ethic opposed to laziness, which, of course, will be "complemented" by other admonitions not to trust wealth (11:28, 15:27, 23:4-5, 27:24; cf. Scott 84). Such restraint of Nature by the caution of Grace may scotch the snake of (North American) self-reliance but will not kill it as it biblically deserves.

PART THREE

Hearing the Word in the Church

The Necessity of Narrative
Imagination for Preaching

John Bolt

> *Before the message there must be the vision,*
> *before the sermon, the hymn, before the prose the poem.*
> —Amos N. Wilder[1]

My primary memories of John Stek are as teacher, mentor, and colleague—in the classroom, at Old Testament Club, around the Calvin Seminary faculty lunch table, as part of the *Calvin Theological Journal* editorial committee. I also remember well one sermon on Exodus 14 preached by John in the early 1970s at Fuller Avenue Christian Reformed Church in Grand Rapids, Michigan.

The sermon began with a pointed extended reference to Martin Luther King, Jr., and to the American civil rights movement, drawing the obvious Mosaic "let my people go" parallel. I was gripped, moved, and, if truth be told, a mite nervous about the courageous appropriation of the exodus and its application to contemporary American life—particularly in view of the passions and tensions about race that were then present in Grand Rapids and elsewhere. It was one thing for Dr. King to draw out the exodus analogy, but quite another for a seminary professor to do it in a respectable Christian Reformed pulpit. Of the thousands of sermons I have heard in my life, this remains one of the handful that were truly memorable.

In this essay I want to pay tribute to one of the truly influential teachers in my life and in the Christian Reformed Church. What he taught and what he exemplified in his preaching was the cultivation of a homiletic narrative imagination. This broad rubric enables us to link together the biblical-theological notions familiar to and favored by "Stekkies"[2] (such as the kingdom of God, covenant, salvation-history, the literary analysis we learned from Stek, and the homiletic payoff that was always the real *raison d'être* of the Old Testament Club).

---

[1] From the Foreword to *Grace Confounding: Poems by Amos N. Wilder* (Philadelphia: Fortress, 1972), ix.

[2] I trust that it is not disrespectful to link our revered mentor with such fan club or even "groupie" nomenclature as used by Star "Trekkies." At least I hope not, since the term "Stekky" to indicate the members of our clan is the sort of play on words that Professor Stek enjoys. If my etiquette has uncharacteristically failed me here, well, O. T. Club was historically something of a refuge for the "irreverent."

[3] The 1961 Christian Reformed Church Synodical Report on Inspiration and Infallibility, in my judgment, remains one of the clearest and most helpful statements on the topic.

Paying attention to language and imagination is also necessary for Reformed (and evangelical) hermeneutics, which has typically done better with formal questions of inspiration,[3] with general principles for interpretation,[4] and with biblical content,[5] than it has with more specific linguistic and literary issues arising from the biblical text.[6] The fascination with narrative that began a few decades ago in theological circles remains strong,[7] though it is generating cynicism among theologians self-consciously

[4]See Louis Berkhof's still helpful manual, *Principles of Biblical Interpretation* (Grand Rapids: Baker, 1988 [1950]).

[5]The observation in note 2 above applies equally well to the famous 1972 CRC Report 36/44 on the "Nature and Extent of Biblical Authority."

[6]Things are changing for the better, as can be seen by the significant work by Grant R. Osborne, *The Hermeneutical Spiral: A Comprehensive Introduction to Biblical Interpretation* (Downer's Grove, Ill.: InterVarsity, 1991) and the helpful, more popular introduction to biblical genres by Gordon D. Fee and Douglas Stuart, *How to Read the Bible for All Its Worth* (Grand Rapids: Zondervan, 1981). It is my impression that evangelical literary scholars generally have done better on this score than the theologians who have tended to be indifferent to the value of contemporary literary theory for biblical hermeneutics. See e.g. the Festschrift for Clyde S. Kilby, *Imagination and the Spirit: Essays in Literature and the Christian Faith*, Charles A. Huttar, ed. (Grand Rapids: Eerdmans, 1971) and, more recently, Roger Lundin, *The Culture of Interpretation* (Grand Rapids: Eerdmans, 1993). One of the reasons for this is likely the important role C. S. Lewis plays in the evangelical world, particularly in evangelical apologetics. Two exceptions are Grant Osborne's impressive *The Hermeneutical Spiral* (noted above) and the work of Kevin J. Vanhoozer; see his *Biblical Narrative in the Philosophy of Paul Ricoeur: A Study in Hermeneutics and Theology* (Cambridge and New York: Cambridge University Press, 1990); "A Lamp in the Labyrinth: The Hermeneutics of 'Aesthetic' Theology," *Trinity Journal* 8 (1987): 25-56.

[7]Recent titles include Kevin M. Bray S.J., *Story as a Way of Knowledge* (Kansas City, Mo.: Sheed and Ward, 1997); Paul Brockelman, *The Inside Story: A Narrative Approach to Religious Understanding and Truth* (Albany, NY: State University of New York Press, 1992); Richard L. Eslinger, *Narrative Imagination: Preaching the Worlds that Shape Us* (Minneapolis: Fortress, 1995); Michael Lodahl, *The Story of God: Wesleyan Theology and Biblical Narrative* (Kansas City, Mo.: Beacon Hill, 1994); Gerald Loughlin *Telling God's Story: Bible Church and Narrative Theology* (Cambridge and New York: Cambridge University Press, 1997); John Navonne, *Seeking God in Story* (Collegeville, Minn.: Liturgical Press, 1990); Adam Zachary Newton, *Narrative Ethics* (Cambridge, Mass.: Harvard University Press, 1995); Michael Roemer, *Telling Stories: Postmodernism and the Invalidation of Traditional Narrative* (Lanham, Md.: Rowman & Littlefield, 1995). This list does not include the avalanche of essays in academic journals and more "popular" magazines; two helpful anthologies of key essays are Garrett Green, ed., *Scriptural Authority and Narrative Interpretation* (Philadelphia: Fortress, 1987) and Stanley Hauerwas and L. Gregory Jones, eds., *Why Narrative? Readings in Narrative Theology* (Grand Rapids: Eerdmans, 1989). It is also significant that in an age of quickly rising and fading theological fads and strong pressure on publishers to clear old stock, key "classics" in the narrative theology "phenomenon" such as James Wm. McClendon's *Biography as Theology: How Life Stories can Remake Today's Theology* (Philadelphia: Trinity Press International, 1990 [1974]) and Michael Goldberg's *Theology and Narrative: A Critical Introduction* (Philadelphia: Trinity Press International, 1991 [1981]) are being republished. Gabriel Fackre's two-volume narrative systematic theology, *The Christian Story* (Grand Rapids: Eerdmans, 1978 [1984] and 1987), is also being reissued in 1997. Two other older works that also deserve mention are John Shea, *Stories of God* (Chicago: Thomas More, 1978) and George W. Stroup, *The Promise of Narrative Theology: Recovering the Gospel in the Church* (Atlanta: John Knox, 1981). For titles of works that more specifically address the subject of narrative and preaching, see note 47 below.

doing narrative *analysis* and among those who remind us how weary they are of those who are weary of the attention paid to narrative.[8]

Without overlooking the faddish character of some elements of the narrative phenomenon (and also recognizing that there is some validity to Wolfhart Pannenberg's contention that "the term 'story' obfuscates the truth question," and "allows one to slide over [it]"[9]) I believe that "narrative" as a biblical-theological category and enterprise is here to stay. Not only does the Bible make sense as a whole only when understood as narrative, but human life itself has a clear narrative character.[10] Here, as elsewhere, the maxim applies: *abusus non tollit usam.*

EVANGELICAL OBJECTIONS TO NARRATIVE THEOLOGY

Thanks to the misuse of narrative, we must address some objections, particularly those that have come from contemporary American evangelical theology.[11] Representative both of the critique of narrative theology and of broader evangelicalism is Carl F. H. Henry's "evangelical appraisal" of narrative theology primarily as represented by Yale's Hans Frei and Brevard S. Childs.[12] Henry regards narrative theology (along with

[8]Two examples are Gabriel Fackre's citation of Johann Baptist Metz's comment about "the damage done to narrative when it is 'pinned and classified like a butterfly in a collector's cage'" ("Narrative Theology: An Overview," *Interpretation* 37 [1983]: 340), and Stanley Hauerwas's comment ("The Church as God's New Language," in Garrett Green, ed., *Scriptural Authority and Narrative Interpretation* [Philadelphia: Fortress, 1987], 188) that "one can be told once too often that 'God made man because he loves stories.'" Both comments have taken on life of their own in subsequent citations including this one (!); also see Loughlin, *Telling God's Story*, xi.

[9]Wolfhart Pannenberg, *An Introduction to Systematic Theology* (Grand Rapids: Eerdmans, 1991), 5. cf. Carl F. H. Henry's critique of Yale theologian Hans Frei, one of the "fathers" of the renewed emphasis on narrative (especially his book, *The Eclipse of Biblical Narrative: A Study in Eighteenth and Nineteenth Century Hermeneutics* [New Haven and London: Yale University Press, 1974]) in his "Narrative Theology: An Evangelical Appraisal," *Trinity Journal* 8 (1987): 3-19. The same critique can be applied to the field of "narrative ethics" where an emphasis on character is often a strategy used to avoid moral "truths" or rule- and law-based ethics (see my "Rightly Applying the Word of Truth: The Bible and the Moral Life," *Reformation and Revival Journal* 5/5 [1996]: 53-66). In spite of the misuse of narrative, it remains my conviction that narrative categories must be included in theology (particularly in Scripture interpretation) and in ethics. This can be done without compromising doctrinal truth or ethical normativity and law. For a solid example of ethical reflection that combines narrative and law, see Richard J. Mouw, *The God Who Commands: A Study in Divine Command Ethics* (Notre Dame, Ind.: University of Notre Dame Press, 1990).

[10]"The formal quality of experience through time is inherently narrative." (Stephen Crites, "The Narrative Quality of Experience," *Journal of the American Academy of Religion*, 39 [September 1971]: 291).

[11]It needs to be noted, however, that objections to narrative theology arise from other quarters as well. See, for example, Ted L. Estess, "The Inenarrable Contraption: Reflections on the Metaphor of Story," *Journal of the American Academy of Religion* 42/3 (1974): 415-34; Michael Goldberg, "God, Action, and Narrative: Which Narrative? Which Action? Which God?" *The Journal of Religion* 68/1 (1988): 39-56; John C. Hoffman, "Metaphorical or Narrative Theology?" *Studies in Religion/Sciences Religieuses* 16/2 (1987): 173-85.

[12]See note 9 above; page references that follow in parentheses in the text are to this essay. Henry does not exclusively deal with the Yale theologians but includes James Barr, Gabriel Fackre, Mark Ellingsen, and others in his overview. *Trinity Journal* included a brief response by Hans Frei in the same issue (pp. 21-24).

"canonical" theology[13]) as a mediating position between traditional views of Scripture and the radical historical criticism of Enlightenment skepticism (4).

While he appreciates narrative theology's desire to let the Bible speak on its own terms and is willing to acknowledge that there is merit in using literary techniques rather than historical-critical methods to interpret the Bible, Henry also has serious reservations. His most telling critique concerns what he sees as the indifference of narrative theologians to historical facticity. To speak as Hans Frei does of the Gospels as "history-like" is not, Henry judges, sufficient as a "realistic reading" of their factual history, especially when the New Testament itself emphasizes the importance of historicity for such events as the resurrection (7).

According to Henry, "The notion that the narrative simply as narrative adequately nurtures faith independently of all objective historical concerns sponsors a split in the relationships of faith to reason and to history that would in principle encourage skepticism and cloud historical referents in obscurity" (11).

Henry is surely correct on this point. He is also correct in insisting that "not all of Scripture falls into the narrative genre" (10).[14] He confuses matters, however, when he uses this point to argue against the usefulness of a narrative framework to grasp the unity of Scripture and appeals instead to "a single divine Author and a single sense that permeates the diverse genres" as an alternative explanation for "an undergirding and overarching unity" (10). Divine inspiration, in other words, and not narrative, is what gives unity to the Bible.

This argument confounds matters by mixing two different issues and categories—one formal, the other material. The issue of a material *literary* unity in Scripture—given by the plot line of creation, fall, redemption, consummation—is not in opposition to the *formal* conviction about Scripture's final unity being a necessary consequence of divine inspiration by the triune God. To juxtapose them in the manner Henry does is to mix and confuse two separable categories. One can be an inerrantist and still insist that the *literary* unity of Scripture is essentially narrative. Alternatively, one can repudiate any unity in Scripture, including a *narrative* unity, if one holds a fundamentally propositionalist view of truth while regarding many of Scripture's propositions as contradicting each other.

---

[13]This is clearly a reference to the canonical-critical approach of Brevard S. Childs, whose work should not simply be identified with that of Hans Frei, though there are clear affinities. See his *Introduction to the Old Testament as Scripture* (Philadelphia: Fortress, 1979), *Old Testament Theology in a Canonical Context* (Philadelphia: Fortress, 1986), and *The New Testament as Canon: An Introduction* (Philadelphia: Fortress, 1986).

[14]For a discussion of this same point but specifically addressed to the issue of narrative preaching, see Bryan Chapell, "When Narrative is Not Enough," *Presbyterion* 22/1 (1996): 3-16.

It is clear, however, that Henry has his own good reasons for lumping together the emphasis on narrative with a rejection of biblical inspiration. His understanding is that biblical inspiration constitutes the basic unity of Scripture. He hints at this in his summary statement of reservation about narrative theology: "One discerns [in narrative theology] an enchantment with the affective, a flight from history to the perspectival that enjoins no universal truth-claims. A reflection of the revolt against reason, a reliance on 'symbolic truth' and imagination, an interest in earthly theater more than in revealed theology. In its representations of the Christian faith it too much ignores *intellectual* analysis to maintain an assured connection of confessional premises with objective reality and valid truth." Henry concludes: "The narrative approach therefore seems not fully befitting the historic Christian faith, nor fully serviceable to the need for an *intellectually compelling* argument with modernity."[15]

To gain a clear picture of what Henry means by "intellectually compelling," we need to look at his understanding of revelation and biblical truth, and the theological task of restating that truth. In other words, we need to consider Henry's view of revelation as doctrine or propositional truth.[16] According to Henry, God is revealed "in the whole canon of Scripture which objectively communicates in propositional-verbal form the content and meaning of *all* God's revelation."[17] Similarly, he defines revelation as "rational communication conveyed in intelligible ideas and meaningful words, that is, in conceptual-verbal form."[18] From this definition of revelation follows a rather straightforward theological method:

> Christian theology is the systematization of the truth-content explicit
> and implicit in the inspired writings. It consists essentially in the

---

[15]Henry, "Narrative Theology—An Appraisal," 19, emphasis added. It is worth noting that Abraham Kuyper, whose views of inspiration and and inerrancy are more "organic" than Henry's, has nonetheless a similar critique of the literary and "symbolic" in *religious life*; see his *The Antithesis Between Symbolism and Revelation* (Amsterdam and Pretoria: Höveker & Wormser, Edinburgh: T. & T. Clark, 1899).

[16]The third chapter ("Revelation as Doctrine") of Avery Dulles's *Models of Revelation* (Garden City, NY: Doubleday, 1985) provides a good summary of Henry's position. Dulles' cautionary conclusion is worth noting in view of the numerous attacks on "propositional truth" by advocates of a neo-orthodox bent who tend to void all cognitive content to biblical revelation: "In this chapter we have taken as the target a rather rigid form of the propositional model. In showing the shortcomings of this style of theology we should not be taken as implying that God's revelation is devoid of cognitive content or that the clear teachings of Scripture and the creeds are without grounds in revelation" (p. 52). I fully concur with Dulles' caution. The issue, with respect to Henry and the "evangelical" view of revelation that he represents, is not whether it is correct in affirming cognitive content to biblical revelation. Here Henry's position is a valid corrective to neo-orthodoxy. What must be asked of Henry is whether the reduction of biblical revelation to "rational communication of intelligible ideas" is a full and adequate view of revelation—one that does justice to the nature of biblical language and diversity of its literary genres.

[17]Carl F. H. Henry, *God, Revelation, and Authority*, Vol. 2 (Waco, Tex.: Word, 1979), 87; for this and some of the following citations from Henry, I am indebted to A. Dulles, *Models of Revelation*, ch. 3.

[18]Ibid., 12.

repetition, combination, and systematization of the truth of revelation in its propositionally given biblical form. The province of theology is to concentrate on the intelligible content and logical relationships of this scripturally given revelation and to present its teaching as a comprehensive whole.[19]

The question that must be asked here is whether Henry's valid concern about the misuse of narrative imagination to set aside historicity has not given way to another sort of error—pressing the entirety of Scripture and its diverse language into one—rationalist, intellectualist—mold. Do the parables of Jesus, particularly a consideration of *how* they open up the *truth* of their message, comfortably fit into such a systematization of biblical facts and data as described by Henry? Can the parable of the Pharisee and the Publican (Luke 18:9-14), for example, be reduced to propositions that would have the same impact on their listener/reader as our Lord's own actual narration? Or, to use an Old Testament example, would Nathan's confrontation of King David after his adultery with Bathsheba (2 Sam. 12) have been just as effective as "revelation" if he had simply read him the law "Thou shalt not commit adultery" instead of using the "little lamb" parable?[20] Is this how language of any sort serves to "reveal" or to "disclose"? Is the asking of such questions not to answer them?

---

[19]Carl F. H. Henry, *God, Revelation, and Authority*, Vol. 1 (Waco, Tex.: Word, 1976), 238-9. Henry's understanding of the task and method of theology is virtually identical to that of the nineteenth-century Calvinist theologian Charles Hodge: "The true method of theology is, therefore, the inductive, which assumes that the Bible contains all the facts or truths which form the contents of theology, just as the facts of nature are the contents of the natural sciences. It is also assumed that the relation of these biblical facts to each other, the principles involved in them, the laws which determine them, are in the facts themselves, and are to be deduced from them, just as the laws of nature are deduced from the facts of nature. In neither case are the principles derived from the mind and imposed upon the facts, but equally in both departments, the principles or laws are deduced from the facts and recognized by the mind." (*Systematic Theology* [New York: Charles Scribners, 1888 (1871)], I, 17)

[20]At the revelational heart of both these parables is the use of analogy or metaphor to draw the listener/reader in to make a judgment that then catches the "judge" by surprise as self-judgment. Typically, one identifies with the publican in Jesus' parable, leading to the spiritually troubling conclusion: "I thank you, Lord, that I am not like one of those self-righteous Pharisees who think they are so much better than everybody else, but rather I am humble and self-effacing like the poor publican." When one is able to articulate this, the revelatory light goes on; then and only then can a saving self-judgment take place: "Lord, be merciful to me, a sinner." The problem with a restrictive propositional model of revelation is not in what it positively affirms (cognitive content, historicity), but in its inadequacy to explain how language "discloses" or works its revelatory magic. ("Magic" here is to be understood as a figure rather than as a literal concession to New Age spirituality.)

IMAGINATION AND THE IMAGINARY

As with narrative, theological interest in imagination remains high,[21] and the concerns of evangelical theologians such as Carl Henry about narrative theology are more than matched by a broadly popular evangelical anxiety about imagination.[22] The fear expressed by many evangelicals is that the practice of "visualization" as part of a process leading to the "constructing of an alternative world" is essentially an occult, reality-manipulating technique of pagan "New Age" spirituality.[23] In the worldview of the latter, the world is remade through imagination, through forming images of a desirable goal. Mind power through the actual process of visualization is said to bring about the condition or situation desired.[24]

Fears that this "New Age" faith might lead us to delusionary and idolatrous self-deification—thinking ourselves to be gods with unlimited potential to create whatever we desire—are not unfounded, especially in certain quarters of the "health, wealth, and success" segment of American evangelicalism.[25] Yet from this legitimate concern

[21]Recent titles include Gerald J. Bednar, *Faith as Imagination: The Contribution of William F. Lynch* (Kansas City: Sheed and Ward, 1996); Eva T. H. Brann, *The World of Imagination: Sum and Substance* (Savage, Md.: Rowman & Littlefield, 1991); Walter Brueggemann, *Texts Under Negotiation: The Bible and Postmodern Imagination* (Minneapolis: Fortress, 1993); David J. Bryant, *Faith and the Play of Imagination: On the Role of Imagination in Religion* (Macon, Ga.: Mercer University Press, 1989); Richard L. Eslinger, *Narrative Imagination: Preaching the World that Shapes Us* (Minneapolis: Fortress, 1995); Garrett Greeen, *Imagining God: Theology and the Religious Imagination* (New York: Harper & Row, 1989); Stanley R. Hopper, *The Way of Transfiguration: Religious Imagination as Theopoiesis*, ed. R. Melvin Keiser and Tony Stoneburner (Louisville: Westminster/John Knox, 1992); ed. Sang Hyun Lee et. al., *Faithful Imagining: Essays in Honor of Richard R. Niebuhr* (Atlanta, Ga.: Scholars, Press, 1995); Edward Tivnan, *The Moral Imagination: Confronting the Ethical Issues of Our Day* (New York: Touchstone, 1995). Among important earlier works must be included Ray Hart, *Unfinished Man and the Imagination: Toward an Ontology and a Rhetoric of Revelation* (New York: Herder and Herder, 1968); Julian Hartt, *Theological Method and Imagination* (New York: Seabury, 1977); Gordon Kaufman, *The Theological Imagination: Constructing the Concept of God* (Philadelphia: Westminster, 1981); David Tracy, *The Analogical Imagination: Theology and the Culture of Pluralism* (New York: Crossroad, 1981); Amos N. Wilder, *Theopoetic: Theology and the Religious Imagination* (Philadelphia: Fortress, 1976).

[22]I addressed this issue with respect to Christian day-school education in *The Christian Story and the Christian School* (Grand Rapids: Christian Schools International, 1994), 199-210.

[23]See for example Dave Hunt and T. A. McMahon, *The Seduction of Christianity: Spiritual Discernment in the Last Days* (Eugene, Oreg.: Harvest, 1985); Constance Cumbey, *The Hidden Dangers of the Rainbow* (Shreveport, La.: Huntington House, 1983), and Tex Marrs, *Dark Secrets of the New Age* (Westchester, Ill.: Crossway, 1987).

[24]Ruth A. Tucker, *Another Gospel: Alternative Religions and the New Age Movement* (Grand Rapids: Zondervan, 1989), 330-31; for another helpful, balanced treatment of the New Age movement see Douglas R. Groothuis, *Confronting the New Age* (Downers Grove, Ill.: InterVarsity, 1988).

[25]See, e.g., Hank Hanegraaff, *Christianity in Crisis* (Eugene, Ore.: Harvest House, 1993). The best full historical and theological treatment of the health, wealth, and success movement in America is D. R. McDonnell, *A Different Gospel: A Historical and Biblical Analysis of the Modern Faith Movement* (Peabody, Mass.: Hendrickon, 1988); also see Bruce Barron, *The Health and Wealth Gospel* (Downers Grove, Ill.: InterVarsity, 1987).

some evangelical critics have launched indiscriminate attacks on imagination itself, along with all literary forms of fantasy, and sought to ban, among other things, the reading of C. S. Lewis's Narnia chronicles and the fantasy writings of J. R. R. Tolkien in Christian schools.[26]

It is virtually a convention in contemporary literature to begin discussions about imagination by acknowledging problems and discomforts with it. Some refer to a general "American mistrust of the imagination" resulting from a "value system dominated by Puritanism, a work ethic, and the profit motive," along with a "gender prejudice" that imagination is a "feminine trait, since it is concrete, intuitive and emotion-laden in contrast to traditional masculine characteristics of reason and objectivity."[27]

On a different note, Paul Ricoeur observes that "the entire problematic of imagination suffers from the bad reputation of the term *image*, after its misuse in the empiricist theory of knowledge." *Image* may denote "the arbitrary mention of things absent," or "portraits . . . that 'take the place of' things they represent," or "fictions that evoke not absent but non-existent things," or simply "the domain of illusions."[28] Conversely, the celebration of imagination is often part and parcel of a postmodern crusade against all expressions of metaphysical realism.[29]

The latter discomfort comes to the fore in theological discussions of imagination. There are some formal similarities here to the popular evangelical attack on imagination, namely an opposition to all forms of epistemological and ontological antirealism. Imagination is identified with the *imaginary* or *fictive*. Theologically, therefore, we are dealing with what might be called the "Feuerbach project," the effort to reduce all reli-

[26]See notes 22 and 23 above. Exceptions to such evangelical distrust should also be noted; see, eg., Cheryl Forbes, *Imagination: Embracing a Theology of Wonder* (Portland, Ore.: Multnomah, 1986). From a review of the literature on imagination it is clear that careful discernment is called for; neither simple dismissal nor uncritical acceptance is honest or helpful. As an example, the following passage is characteristic in its use of dubious language while at the same time pointing to important truths about the role of imagination in the revelation of God's promises to us that inspire hope: "The imagination is our inner rainbow in several ways. It is the bridge which joins God and the earth, the sacred and the secular, bringing them into unity in our life. The imagination enables us to live in multi-leveled, multi-colored truth, and to receive the truth which is pervaded by mist and mystery. It is also the human power that opens us to possibility and promise, the not-yet of the future. In all these ways the imagination is essential to Christian faith" (Kathleen R. Fischer, *The Inner Rainbow: The Imagination in Christian Life* [Ramsey, N.J.: Paulist, 1983], 7). It is worth noting here that the Dutch Reformed anti-Kuyperian, anti-common grace theologian Klaas Schilder objected not to fantasy but to the antipathy of many of his coreligionists to imagination and fantasy in literature; see Hans Werkman, "Schilder en de literatuur," in J. De Bruijn and G. Harinck, eds., *Geen Duimbreed: Facetten van Leven en Werk van Prof. Dr. K. Schilder 1890-1952* (Ten Have: Baarn, 1990), 106-130.

[27]Fischer, *The Inner Rainbow*, 6; Fischer is referring here to an essay by fantasy and science fiction writer Ursula LeGuin, "Why Are Americans Afraid of Dragons?" *Literary Cavalcade* (February 1981): 41-43.

[28]Paul Ricoeur, "Imagination in Discourse and Action," in *From Text to Action: Essays in Hermeneutics II*, trans. Kathleen Blamey and John B. Thompson (Evanston, Ill.: Northwestern University Press, 1991), 169-70.

[29]The same critique applies to some forms of narrative theology as well; see Ivor Jones, "Narrative Theology, Postmodernism and History," *Epworth Review* 23/1 (1996): 33-41; Bryan Chapell, "When Narrative Is Not Enough."

gious claims to purely human constructions or mere products of the imagination.[30] This understanding of the role of imagination as the sole creator of religious beliefs is, of course, unacceptable to any orthodox or evangelical theology that is committed to divine revelation as the foundation of all faith and knowledge. But, we must ask, why should the abuse of imagination rule out an understanding of its important role in Christian faith, even in the process of revelation itself?

Writer Mark Filiatreau provocatively claims that "God is a feast for the imagination; and since each human being has by definition an imagination, each Christian should be well-sated, inspired, and visionary—every day." Unfortunately, he adds, the "scandalous" truth is that many (if not most) Christians "have an imagination starved for God," in large measure because of "an undeserved distrust toward the imagination."[31] If imagination is simply one of the important human capacities or faculties of God's created imagebearers, why should it be more suspect than reason or the human will? The Enlightenment of the eighteenth century and the will-to-power Nietzscheism of twentieth-century fascism have not led North American evangelicals to similarly indiscriminate attacks on reason or will. Why should the imagination be singled out? At this point a few basic definitions are in order.

DEFINING NARRATIVE IMAGINATION

Narrative and imagination are inextricably joined; every story requires imagination in its telling and in its hearing. Narrative, according to theologian Gabriel Fackre, is "an account of events and participants moving over time and space, a recital with beginning and ending patterned by the narrator's principle of selection . . . an account of characters and events in a plot moving over time and space through conflict toward resolution."[32] The structure of narrative is fundamentally temporal: beginning, middle, end. The reason why imagination is essential to all narrative construals of meaning is that though the narrator may be omniscient, the listener or reader is bound to the specific place where the story's present action is occurring (i.e. at the point of telling). T. S. Eliot stated the problem elegantly:

[30]Gordon Kaufman's *The Theological Imagination* is a good example of such a constructionist interpretation of religion. For critique of Kaufman's position and its rejection of the idea of revelation, see Ronald F. Thiemann, "Revelation and Imaginative Construction," *Journal of Religion* 61 (1981): 242-63; for a fuller critique see David Bryant, *Faith and the Play of Imagination*, 9-64.

[31]Mark D. Filiatreau, "Make it Real: The Imagination's Role in Living Our Beliefs," *Regeneration Quarterly* (Spring 1996): 23.

[32]Gabriel Fackre, "Narrative Theology: An Overview," *Interpretation* 37 (1983): 341.

Time past and time future
Allow but a little consciousness.
To be conscious is not to be in time
But only in time can the moment . . .
Be remembered.[33]

Tied to the present moment, a hearer or reader can only grasp the larger narrative whole within which the present specific event or action is to be understood through *memory* of the narrative's past and *anticipation* of the story's end.[34] Memory and anticipation both require imagination, which is the human capacity to make *present* to our consciousness that which is either spatially or temporally absent.[35]

We can define narrative imagination as the human capacity to perceive ourselves as participants or characters in plots, including plots that are alternatives to the obvious, factual mundane narratives of our daily lives. Take, for example, Professor X—a Dutch native who immigrated to Canada, is now a Canadian citizen living as a resident alien in the United States, and who is the husband of one (American) wife and the father of three children who have dual Canadian/American citizenship. From this basic data, one level of imaginative reflection could conclude (in this case correctly) that Professor X's identity as a citizen might be oriented to a more universal notion of earthly pilgrimage or sojourning rather than intense allegiance to one specific nation. At another level, it would help to know that Professor's X's spirituality has been profoundly shaped by such scriptural passages as the Pentateuchal pilgrim narratives of Abraham, Isaac, and Jacob, the wilderness wandering of Israel, Hebrews 12:1-6, 1 Peter 2:11, Augustine's *City of God*, and John Calvin's "Golden Booklet of the Christian Life" (*Institutes*, III, vi-x). In short, Professor X lives in two different narrative worlds that have in common the notion of pilgrimage or sojourning.

I have chosen this illustration to make the point that narratologists who speak of "constructing alternative worlds through narrative"[36] should not necessarily be read as postmodern antirealists or pagan "New Agers." It is perfectly legitimate, even essential, for humans to "construct" narrative worlds of meaning in which they themselves are participants. The crucial question concerns the source and plot of the narrative

---

[33]T. S. Eliot, "Burnt Norton," lines 83-9, from *Four Quartets* (New York: Harcourt, Brace & Co., 1934).

[34]See Jacques Le Goff, *History and Memory*, trans. Stephen Rendall and Elizabeth Claman (New York: Columbia University Press, 1992).

[35]This is loosely borrowed from Immanuel Kant's definition: "*Imagination* is the faculty of representing in intuition an object that is *not itself present*." Imannuel Kant, *Critique of Pure Reason*, trans. Norman Kemp Smith (New York: St. Martin's Press, 1968), B 151; cited by Garrett Green, *Imagining God*, 62. The most thorough and balanced philosophical treatment of imagination is Eva Brann, *The World of Imagination*.

[36]As in the subtitle of Richard Eslinger's book *Narrative Imagination: Preaching the Worlds That Shape Us*.

being constructed. It is here that I suggest we think of preaching as the Holy Spirit-led task of creating an alternative narrative world through imagination.

SHAPING NEW WORLDS THROUGH PREACHING

Great stories, those that "deeply engage"[37] us, momentarily transport us to a different world—a "story world." "They seduce us," says Wayne Booth, "out of the time-bound world; if we are 'fully engaged,' we live 'elsewhere' for the time of the listening."[38] Booth suggests that we humans live in several worlds: the elemental physical-appetitive world, the conscious world of moral conflict where choices are made (including the important choice not to be captive to the appetites of the former), and, finally, the world of spiritual transcendence where we escape from ordinary time. We need not explore all the subtle nuances of Booth's observation except to note that one of the chief ways to enter this third world of transcendence is "immersion in a powerful [alternative] narrative."[39] In fact, this transcendence is precisely what happens in Christian conversion. One consciously changes the "story" frame of one's life ("I was lost and now am found"). It is the goal of narratively imaginative preaching to effect, nurture, and sustain communities and individuals in living by a new and different plot, the narrative of God's kingdom.

It may be helpful to approach this from a different angle.[40] According to Paul Ricoeur, all social worlds are ruled by "texts" that govern communal and individual narratives. Social reality, in other words, is "scripted."[41] What this means for preaching is that "people come to the preaching moment with texts already in hand that describe the world."[42] These scripts are often at odds with the gospel's own script, either through the various idolatries of our age (hedonism, civil religion, mammon, racial superiority, political correctness) or through the anxiety of hopelessness and despair. The biblical text and its proclamation need to help us construct an alternative narrative world by serving as "a counter-text that does not primarily describe but subversively redescribe reality."[43] In Brueggemann's words, "the biblical text . . . is an offer of an alternative script, and preaching this text is the exploration of how the world

---

[37]The phrase "deeply engaged" comes from Wayne C. Booth, "Story as Spiritual Quest," *Christianity and Literature* 45/2 (Winter 1996): 164.

[38]Ibid., 165.

[39]Ibid., 170.

[40]For what follows in the next paragraph I am indebted to Walter Brueggemann, "Preaching as Reimagination," *Theology Today* 52/3 (1995): 313-29.

[41]Paul Ricoeur, "From the Hermeneutics of Texts to the Hermeneutics of Action," in *From Text to Action* (Evanston, Ill.: Northwestern University Press, 1991), 105-22; cited by Brueggemann, "Preaching as Imagination," 316.

[42]Brueggemann, "Preaching as Reimagination," 316.

[43]Ibid., 319.

is if it is imagined through this alternative script."[44] The preacher's task is to imaginatively present the congregation with an alternative narrative, "to propose that the world and our lives be seen or taken *as* under the aegis of the gospel," or, in other words, "to exhibit this particular narrative script of the Bible and to show how and in what ways life will be reimagined, redescribed, and relived, if this narrative is embraced."[45]

IMAGINATIVE-NARRATIVE PREACHING OF JONAH

To prevent this discussion from becoming too abstract, let us apply the narrative/ imagination categories to Professor Stek's interpretation of the prophecy of Jonah,[46] (an essay well-known to several generations of Calvin Seminary students). In the essay, Stek immediately and simply addresses the historical question that is of so much concern to evangelicals: "The writer," he notes, "assumes the historicity of the events narrated" (23, n. 1). This personal affirmation is followed by a brief historical-contextual overview focusing on the situation of relative prosperity and security in the Israel of the eighth century B.C., a situation that led to a serious misconstrual of her elected covenantal status as God's people. "The horizon of Israel's vision of the divine purposes tended to become extremely confined. . . . To them it came to appear that all other nations of the earth existed under God only to serve Yahweh's purpose with Israel. Divine election came to be viewed only as election to privilege" (28).

The external narrative of Israel's life, marked by prosperity and security, was in fact a clear case of false consciousness. Instead of Israel seeing herself as God's chosen instrument and God thus speaking to the nations through the fidelity of his covenant people, showcasing the glory of his redemptive power and saving love, "speaking to the fallen race a new message in a new language," Israel inverted the narrative "even to the degree that Yahweh, as it would seem, was coming to be viewed as the mighty servant of Israel's national aspirations" (28). In the midst of this perverse narrative reversal reflecting a "narrow spirit of pride and complacency," (31) the prophets came with the message that Israel "has forfeited her position of privilege which she boasts; has made herself like one of the nations with no right to hope for the peculiar favor of the Lord of the nations to whom she still seems to look expectantly" (31).

Here the interpreter's own historical imagination is challenged. The narrative of the book of Jonah, it must "be remembered, is addressed to *Israel*" (32). The limits of a *mere* historical recounting of the Jonah narrative thus become apparent. Stek briefly

[44]Brueggemann, "Preaching as Reimagination," 320.

[45]Ibid., 321, 327.

[46]John H. Stek, "The Message of the Book of Jonah," *Calvin Theological Journal* 4 (1969): 23-50; references to this essay will be parenthetically included in the main text.

discusses and dismisses the challenges of certain historical-critical skeptics about the historical Jonah, but then reminds us that "assuming the historicity of the events narrated, and the memory of these events, it must be assumed that the writer of this little book, whoever he may have been, and whatever the time of his writing, had been made to see that in Jonah's mission Yahweh has spoken a word also to Israel. It is hardly doing him justice to suppose that he merely wished to chronicle a remarkable prophetic experience, with no other purpose than to preserve for posterity the memory of an historical curiosity" (34). The book of Jonah, in other words, "is *interpreted* history, the prophetic writer himself providing the interpretation, and so disclosing its inner meaning" (34).

Interpreting the prophecy of Jonah requires a controlled *literary* imagination that entails careful listening to the text. "There is no room for reading between the lines in order to supply, by means of an informed historical imagination, what has been passed over in silence" (35). Stek here draws a parallel with interpreting biblical parables where "skeletal [historical] accounts cannot but evoke in the reader's imagination a fully-fleshed reconstruction of the event." But, Stek cautions, "Nevertheless, for the reader to supply out of his imagination elements which become for him constitutive to the narrative, and to be taken account of in his understanding of the narrative, is to replace the original narrative with one of his own conceiving" (35). Instead, we must never forget to be controlled by the text: The inspired Bible "is still *literature*, and must be interpreted as such."

The key point here is that though the story's main human characters are the prophet Jonah and the citizens of Nineveh, the "writer of this narrative is addressing Israel" (35). Thus, we must take into account two different narrative worlds: the historical narrative of Jonah ben Amittai and the contemporary (to the author) spiritual narrative of the people of Israel for whom that narrative is "constructed" and to whom it is addressed.

In the latter, in *that* narratively constructed world, Jonah must be imaginatively seen as a representative of Israel who is playing out a role "on the vast stage of the world" (39) while Nineveh (and the frightened sailors) also represent the Gentile nations who are both threatened by God's judgment and the objects of his "pity." Furthermore—a point not developed by Stek—God's turning of Jonah's hard heart toward an understanding of divine mercy is accomplished *imaginatively* by having Jonah enter into yet another metaphorical/narrative world where vines grow wondrously, supply the benefits of needed shade, and then, as wondrously, wither and die. Finally, it must be noted that our Lord uses the Jonah narrative itself as a "sign" for his audience (Matthew 12:39-41, par.). The historicity of Jonah's prophetic mission is pregnant with multilayered signification that transcends its *mere* history.

Finally, the prophecy of Jonah cannot be preached to a contemporary audience without homiletic narrative imagination. My point here is not to insist that someone attempting to preach on Jonah use a specific narrative homiletic technique such as set forth by Eugene Lowry, for example, in *The Homiletic Plot*,[47] but that the preacher understand that the very task of proclamation itself is, as Walter Brueggemann has stated, one of helping a congregation reimagine. Thanks to the unhappy association of the term *reimagining* with the efforts of some radical feminists to reimagine the God and Father of our Lord Jesus Christ into the categories of pagan Baalism, it must be said clearly that the reimagining that must take place is not about God but about the narrative of our personal and communal lives. Our life stories must be rescripted by the narrative of God's kingdom.

Thus, where those narratives are twisted by idolatries, they must submit to the surgery of divine judgment; where they flounder in despair and hopelessness because of sin and brokenness, they need the infusion and reorientation of divine forgiveness, grace, and hope. Reading a congregation's narrative is one of the most demanding challenges to a preacher's empathetic imagination.

In short, we need to let the Holy Spirit direct us to and through the scripted, *scriptural* plot that begins with Creation and ends in Consummation. As living characters in the drama of redemption we remember what God has done ("the Lord's death and resurrection") in hopeful anticipation of his glorious coming again. It is the *sacramental world* that is the only real world, the only real narrative—the world where we are baptized into Christ's death and resurrection, and where we, in memory as well as in anticipation, eat and drink at the eschatological banquet.

Here we recall Erich Auerbach's famous comment about the key difference between the narratives of the Homeric myths and biblical narratives such as Abraham's call to sacrifice Isaac in Genesis 22: "The Bible's claim to truth is not only more urgent than Homer's, it is tyrannical—it excludes all other claims. The world of the Scripture stories is not satisfied with claiming to be a historically true reality—it insists that it is the only real world, is destined for autocracy."[48]

---

[47]Eugene Lowry, *The Homiletic Plot: The Sermon as Narrative Art Form* (Atlanta: John Knox, 1980); other advocates of some form of narrative-imaginative preaching include Frederick Buechner, *Telling the Truth: The Gospel as Tragedy, Comedy, and Fairy Tale* (San Francisco: Harper & Row, 1977); John R. Donahue, *The Gospel in Parable* (Philadelphia: Fortress, 1988); Calvin Miller, *Spirit, Word and Story: A Philosophy of Marketplace Preaching*, rev. ed. (Grand Rapids: Baker, 1996 [1989]); Richard A. Jensen, *Thinking in Story: Preaching in a Post-Literate Age* (Lima, Ohio: C.S.S. Publishing, 1993); William J. Bausch, *Storytelling: Imagination and Faith* (Mystic, Conn.: Twenty-Third, 1984).

[48]Erich Auerbach, *Mimesis: The Representation of Reality in Western Literature*, trans. Willard R. Trask (Princeton, N.J.: Princeton University Press, 1953), 14-15.

Perhaps what the church needs today is less preoccupation with so-called relevance (the strategy of accommodating to the world's narrative) and more attention to reimagining what it can be to participate as living characters and agents in the only true narrative plot scripted and directed by the Lord of history who came onto the world's stage to be the "leading man" in its definitive redemptive scene.

Seeking God Through Preaching

Cornelius Plantinga, Jr.

INTRODUCTION

In "The God with Whom We Can Be Confident,"[1] the final sermon of his ministry at Fourth Presbyterian Church of Chicago, the great Welsh preacher Elam Davies told of an incident that stuck in his mind. During their years in Chicago, Davies and his wife Grace used to return to Wales on holiday, and every so often they would visit a favorite spot called the Rock at Orme. Orme is at land's end, right at the seaside, and people gather there to watch sunsets. On clear nights, people watch the yellow sun drop steadily into the pewter sea, backlighting strands of clouds in such a way that the whole horizon turns into a kaleidoscope. Because the sunsets are so spectacular and because the people who watch them are so Welsh, the spectators at Orme sometimes weep.

On one particular night, the Davies were parked there, taking in the beauty, when a beat-up car drew alongside. In this car were an elderly couple and a man who seemed to be their son, likely the son of their middle age. Some accident or illness had come to this son along the way, with the result that he was clearly disabled. There he lay in the backseat behind his parents, limp, and maybe exasperated with the condition that held him captive.

Then, as the great ball of fire began its final descent toward the sea, the two old folks got out of their junker and came around to the backseat. They reached in, hoisted their son up to a sitting position, and maneuvered him forward to the edge of the seat. And, according to Davies' account, just as the sun in its full flame dropped below the rim of the world in a final burst of glory—just then the old parents reached under their boy's chin, raised his head, and "pointed him out there toward the horizon."

"And I knew at that moment," said Elam Davies in his sermon, "that God can dazzle us with all the magnificence of the universe, but that the *secret* of the universe lies in a love that comes to us in our weakness and in our need."

God's glory was in the sunset that night. Of course. That's what everybody at Orme came to see. But the greater glory of God was in the hearts of two old parents and in the fingers that lifted the chin of their son. And the simple name of this glory is love.

---

[1] Elam Davies, "The God with Whom We Can Be Confident," a sermon preached in Fourth Presbyterian Church, Chicago, May 6, 1984 (cassette tape).

WHAT DOES PREACHING DO?

Let's say that preaching is the presentation of God's Word at a particular time to particular people by someone authorized to do it. Like telling others of one's spiritual experiences (some Christians call it "sharing" or, in intellectually chaste moods, "just sharing"), good preaching is personal and concrete. A sermon is not a lecture. But even a highly personal and concrete preacher, such as Elam Davies, does not create his message from scratch. He works from the Bible, which is his community's book. How he personally feels about his message matters, but it matters less than how faithfully he brings it. After all, he himself is addressed by his message, just as his listeners are. In fact, the sermon's message ultimately comes only through, and not from, the preacher, and it centers on the same God who sends it. "For we do not proclaim ourselves," as St. Paul put it, "we proclaim Jesus Christ as Lord" (2 Cor. 4:5).

Then Paul adds these words (vv. 6-7): "For it is the God who said, 'Let light shine out of darkness,' who has shone in our hearts to give the light of the knowledge of the glory of God in the face of Christ. But we have this treasure in clay jars, so that it may be made clear that this extraordinary power belongs to God and does not come from us."

Imagine a preacher at work on this text. In a classic way of proceeding, he or she studies the text for a time—listening to it, questioning it, probing it, looking at it from several angles. The preacher compares it with kindred texts in Scripture and reads what biblical scholars have said about the text and its family. The preacher also attempts to fit this text into his or her biblical and theological network of understanding, so that the text can speak from its context there. All along, the preacher imagines strategies or "moves" for getting the text's message across to listeners—apt illustrations, dramatic contrasts, perhaps the use of a refrain that stitches the sermon together. Then one day the preacher stands before a congregation and preaches this text.

How so? Classically speaking, to preach a text is to do in other words what the text does. Depending on the text, the preacher might warn people one Sunday and comfort them the next. She might prophesy, counsel, teach, or rebuke. She might provoke people if her text is provocative enough. She might begin by challenging a popular opinion and end by reinforcing it, but only after moving this opinion inside a biblical view of the world. She might reproduce an interrogative text by turning a big part of her sermon into a repeated question.

If she is preaching 2 Corinthians 4:6, perhaps she will tell her listeners a story like the one of the people at Orme, not just because the story inspires, but especially because the story inspires listeners right along the same line as the text does. This is a line that runs from creation to redemption, showing us, at both ends of the line, a God who says, "Let there be light."

We should notice that redemption is the harder piece of work. The reason is that in redemption God cannot start fresh. Instead, God must salvage human beings who have already been damaged by years of sin and misery. The difficulty of this salvage project may be measured by the kind of pain it takes, namely, the self-giving passion and death of Jesus Christ, the Son of God, who had to cut the loop of retaliation by absorbing evil without passing it on.

As every faithful preacher knows, the death and resurrection of Jesus Christ occupy the center of human history and the center of Christian preaching. In the death of Christ, God adopts a "like-cures-like" strategy of defeating death by way of another death. Then God follows up with a similar strategy for passing along the death benefits of Christ to his followers. Remarkably, God elects to salvage human beings by deputizing other human beings to preach Christ to them—other human beings who are just as damaged and foolish as their audience. In 2 Corinthians 4:7 Paul compares the preacher (he has himself especially in mind) to a baked clay jar. To find the flame of love in such homely ware, to find the flame of God's glory in human hearts as Davies found it one night at Orme, is to find a kind of miracle.

What Davies found that night also provides a first-rate sermon illustration, which reminds us that the preacher's job is not just to repeat a text, but also to outfit it for the hearing of a congregation. The preacher not only does in other words what the text does. He also says in other words what the text says—dressing it up or down, shaping and coloring and amplifying it in such a way that when people hear the preached text they hear God's Word to them. For example, they might hear a warning that sin is not only an offense against God and neighbor, but a form of self-abuse. They might hear that we do not belong to ourselves, that we are not our own authors or centers, and that, surprisingly, this is a comfort. They might hear that idolaters want to carry their gods around with them, but that the God of Scripture carries us, and that a central question of religion is "Who is carrying whom?"

When preaching works well, the result is eventful. People feel pierced, or assured, or blessed. They sense that they are somehow joined to God by this religious event, just as they are by partaking of baptism or of the Lord's Supper. Indeed, Christians think of a preached and heard sermon as "an audible sacrament," to use a phrase attributed to Augustine.[2] Sacraments are ligaments of the covenant between God and believers— covenant "binders," we might say. So preaching naturally binds believers to God by making God audible to them. But a sermon may also take hold of others. A well-designed sermon may make God audible to unbelievers, or to seekers, or to people who

[2]Mary Catherine Hilkert, "Preaching, Theology of," in *The New Dictionary of Sacramental Worship*, ed. Peter E. Fink, S. J. (Collegeville, Minn.: Liturgical Press, 1990), 996-1003.

are so consciously ambivalent about God that they would hardly know what to call themselves.

BRINGING GOD HOME

In fact, one of the main functions of preaching is to make God real to listeners, including to the preacher who is always a sermon's "pioneer listener."[3] Of course God is real whether people in church think so or not. Presuming to "activate" God by preaching a sermon would be a prime piece of arrogance.

But in another way, sermons do render God actual to listeners. I mean that in healthy preaching God's grace and power come home to people; these qualities are brought to mind, raised up in consciousness, affirmed by the heart. A Godly life is at least a God-conscious life, and the preacher stimulates such a life by re-presenting God to listeners. When this is done effectively—that is, when the preacher's good efforts are energized and focused by the power of the Holy Spirit (the unpredictable variable, or "x-factor," in preaching)—then once more God seems large and luminous to people who are listening.

But because a sermon bears God's Word, it also calls for response on the part of those who hear it. A dynamic sermon goes to human hearts and stirs them. When people hear such a sermon they feel faith rising in them. They feel passion rising in them. They may feel very much like *doing* something. When Martin Luther King, Jr., preached one of the great prophetic texts of Scripture, such as Micah 6:8 ("What does the Lord require of you but to do justice, and to love kindness, and to walk humbly with your God?"), or when he made a political speech that arose from this text, the effect was the same. People were moved to believe that God was on the side of racial justice. They were moved with a passion for seeking this justice. But people listening to King were especially moved in their hearts to shout "Yes!" and then to start marching. Sometimes King would urge them: "Let us march on ballot boxes!" he would proclaim. "Let us march on ballot boxes till we send to . . . the United States Congress men who will not fear to do justice!"[4]

"True religion," said Jonathan Edwards, "consists in great measure in . . . the fervent exercises of the heart."[5] Edwards meant that, at its core, true religion has to do not only with kindling our passions, but also with aiming them in the right direction. The world is full of good. The Godly person must say "yes" to it with all his heart and then

[3]Roger E. Van Harn, *Pew Rights: For People Who Listen to Sermons* (Grand Rapids: Eerdmans, 1992), 18.

[4]Stephen L. Carter, *The Culture of Disbelief: How American Law and Politics Trivialize Religious Devotion* (New York: Basic Books, 1993), 48.

[5]Jonathan Edwards, *Religious Affections*, ed. John E. Smith. Vol. 2 of *The Works of Jonathan Edwards*, ed. Perry Miller (New Haven: Yale University Press, 1959), 99.

act accordingly. The world is also full of evil. The Godly person must say "no" to it with all his heart and then act accordingly. The world is full of the mixture of good and evil so that the Godly person sometimes needs the gift of discernment before he knows *what* to say or *how* to act.

In any event, true religion always begins from the central place in us where we "hate what is evil" and "hold fast to what is good" (Rom. 12:9). A sequence of hearty "yes's" and "no's" lies at the center of true religion, said Edwards, and this is why we sing our praise instead of merely saying it. This is why we preach the Word instead of simply reading it. This is why in the Lord's Supper we eat and drink our God.[6] The reason in each case is that we want to get our hearts going again, and we want the passions of our hearts to find their true target. For example, we want love and joy to start up, and we especially want these "affections," as Edwards called them, to be aimed at God. We want the reality of God to be big enough to see with the eyes of faith and good enough to taste with the mouth of faith. To "taste and see that the Lord is good" (Ps. 34:8) meant for Edwards, and for many writers on spirituality before him, that we need preaching and other spiritual exercises to give us a sense of God's "sweetness" and "glorious brightness."[7]

But here a caution is in order. To say that preaching helps to make God real to us does not mean that it helps to make him obvious. Nor, certainly, does the preached God somehow become our possession to be shaped and used as we see fit. Any attempt to possess God or the Word of God in this way would be raw idolatry. "Bringing God home" to believers gives nobody a license to domesticate God.

The truth is that God may be known, but he is also hard to know. God does approach us in sermons and sacraments, but only by his grace. The mystery of God's grace and the majesty of his nature combine to generate one of the most basic of biblical paradoxes: God is both present to us and absent from us, both immanent and transcendent, both available and also perfectly free in power and grace. Karl Barth, a theologian who never met a paradox he didn't like, wrote that God was both veiled and unveiled, and veiled in his unveiling.[8] Though Barth sharpened the point of the paradox more than most, he was working from a solid biblical base. On the one hand, "the Lord used to speak to Moses face to face, as one speaks to a friend"; on the other hand, "The Lord said to Moses . . . 'you shall see my back; but my face shall not be seen.'" So basic is this paradox to biblical thinking that in Exodus these two testimonies appear next door to each other (Ex. 33:11, 23).

---

[6]Edwards, *Religious Affections*, 115.

[7]Ibid., 95.

[8]Karl Barth, *Church Dogmatics*, ed. G. W. Bromiley and T. F. Torrance. Various translators. 4 vols. (Edinburgh: T. & T. Clark, 1936-1939; Second edition, trans. G. W. Bromiley, 1975), 165.

Human suffering seems to heighten the paradox instead of collapsing it. On the one hand, believers who suffer great pain sometimes lament what feels like the withdrawal of God: "My God, my God, why have you forsaken me?" (Ps. 22:1, Matt. 27:46). On the other hand, many believers testify that it is just when they are imperiled that they most fully experience the presence of God: "Even though I walk through the darkest valley, I fear no evil; for you are with me" (Ps. 23:4). In one of the eloquent passages of his *Confessions*, Augustine states the paradox with simple depth: "Who then are you, my God? . . . deeply hidden, yet most intimately present."[9]

A biblical word that is faithfully preached and believed will usually bring the reality of God home to people at both of these depths—at the depths of God's hiddenness and also at the depths of his intimate nearness.

While taking part in the drama of bringing these things home, a preacher inevitably clothes a text not only with stories and images, but also with many features of his own mind and personality. God is personal, and it is therefore fitting that the gospel of God should be preached by persons. Thus, when a preacher stands before a congregation, his posture, energy level, choice of language, tone of voice, degree of eye contact with his audience—even his manners—may all serve to make God real to us. Some of his "fruit of the Spirit," such as generosity and patience, will help as well. If the preacher has a history of self-giving strength, the God of whom he speaks may seem especially plausible to hearers.

Such plausibility is crucial, because it's the matrix of faith. To play his part in creating this matrix, the preacher must bend heart, mind, and voice to his calling. He must preach the Word of God quite deeply into our lives. He must give up the hope of thrilling people all the time, and of amusing them, and of confirming their favorite ideas. Because he must rebuke as well as comfort, he must give up the hope of regularly endearing himself to listeners. Moving to the pulse of God's Word and not to the breezes of fashion, he must give up the hope of mere popularity. In short, he must give up anything that threatens his integrity as a preacher.

By guarding his integrity, the preacher becomes available to God as a lamp. When he preaches—when he says in other words what the text says, and does in other words what the text does—a part of the glory of God may shine from him. And then his audience may spot "the light of the knowledge of the glory of God in the face of Jesus Christ."

God's light shines from acts of love and justice, as Elam Davies discovered at Orme and as the followers of Martin Luther King discovered when he shamed a whole nation

---

[9]St. Augustine, *Confessions*, trans. with an Introduction by Henry Chadwick (Oxford: Oxford University Press, 1992), I. iv (4).

into passing civil rights legislation. But God's light shines especially from his Word made flesh and from his Word made audible. To praise God, says Augustine, we must call upon him; to call upon God we must know him; to know God we must believe in him. And to believe in God we need a preacher.[10]

BRINGING GOD HOME TO PRACTICAL ATHEISTS

The preacher's job of bringing God home to human beings is necessary not because most of the people in earshot of the preacher are atheists, but rather because many of them are "practical" atheists. I do not deny that even devout believers sometimes doubt the sheer existence of God. So luminous a believer as C. S. Lewis testified that just as he had once doubted his atheism, so too, after he had become a Christian, he endured certain moods in which the whole Christian religion seemed "very improbable" to him.[11] So sturdy a Puritan as Increase Mather wrote in his diary for July 29, 1664, that he was "grieved, grieved, grieved with temptations to Atheisme."[12]

But such temptations are rare enough among believers as to be remarkable. What is more common among them is to forget about God. It happens all the time, and it happens right in the middle of a religious life. Religious people get distracted by the traffic of daily living—getting educated, making a living, juggling the responsibilities of various relationships. They get distracted by their joys, forgetting to thank God; they get distracted by their pain, forgetting to lament to God.

In one of his sermons, my teacher John Stek remarked that God is working on a big building project. God is building a kingdom of peace and justice, and, in so doing, has entrusted people like us with some of the jobs in this project. The problem is that we keep getting distracted by our own interests. We keep wanting to borrow God's tools to attempt side projects of our own, and then we complain that God doesn't bless these side projects as much as we would like.

As this last example suggests, some of our forgetfulness is owed to sin. We neglect God because we find ourselves more interesting. We avoid God because the knowledge of God makes us feel guilty or small by comparison. Above all, we ignore God because we prefer to lead our lives without divine interference. This forgetfulness is usual, but it is not normal and it is not trivial. As George MacDonald somewhere remarks, "the one principle of hell is 'I am my own.'"

According to Psalm 14, "the fool says in his heart, 'There is no God.'" Most believers who read these words think of classic theoretical atheists. They think of Marx,

[10]St. Augustine, *Confessions*, I. I (1).

[11]C. S. Lewis, *Mere Christianity* (New York: Macmillan, 1960), 109.

[12]Michael G. Hall, *The Last American Puritan: The Life of Increase Mather, 1639-1723* (Middletown, Conn.: Wesleyan University Press, 1988), 65.

Nietzsche, and Freud. Or nowadays they think of scientific naturalists who insist that the great engine of life is ungoverned randomness. *That's* atheism—complete with gross inhospitality to God and a stubborn insistence that plain, dumb luck must be the ultimate source of life. To believers, such naturalistic atheism sounds narrow-minded. It sounds absurd. In a world of staggering complexity inside a single cell, what could be more provincial than refusing to make room for God? Only a fool would say in his heart, "There is no God."

How awkward it is that when Christians speak of such folly they discover that their words are a boomerang. The psalmist isn't talking about scientific naturalists. He's not talking about those who scorn the very idea of purposeful design in the world. Of course the psalmist would have found such naturalists foolish too, but he's not talking about them. He's talking about religious people who say they believe in God, but who live as if heaven has closed its doors.

These are practical atheists, and every church has them. They are theists in their heads, but atheists in their hearts and therefore in their practice. Practical atheism of the sort that we find in Psalm 14 has almost nothing to do with sheer disbelief. It has almost everything to do with sheer disobedience. Practical atheists discount God because they presume that God is "shut up idle in heaven" and that we are free to do what we want.[13] To be a practical atheist is to say with our lips, "There is a God" and to say with our hearts, "but he's out to lunch."

It's important to emphasize that practical atheism is a disease of the religious. In fact, when we are most religious we may be most at risk of contracting this disease. It is true that the spiritual exercises of religion may make God real for us in some of the ways that I have described. Reading Scripture, preaching and listening to sermons, singing hymns of praise and thanksgiving, answering the call to fight for social justice—all such things tie us to the living God in such a way that by repeating them we may come to know God more keenly and to serve God more fruitfully. Honest religious practice builds spiritual momentum. "To those who have, more will be given" (Mark 4:25).

But not all religious practice is honest. Some of it gets diverted from the kingdom of God to side projects of our own, as John Stek said. For example, people use religion to get rich or to get happy or to feel good about themselves. They use it to build a power base and to bend other people to their will. Believers are entirely capable of using religion to *conceal* the character of God, as in those cases where they turn God into a racist or a sexist or a fascist or a New Democrat. It's not only secularists who "suppress the

---

[13]John Calvin, *Institutes of the Christian Religion*, ed. John T. McNeill and trans. Ford Lewis Battles. The Library of Christian Classics, vols. 20, 21 (Philadelphia: Westminster, 1960), I.4.ii.

truth" about God. This famous Pauline characterization of sinners in Romans 1:18 indicts believers as well. Believers, not only secularists, exchange "the glory of the immortal God for images resembling a mortal human being" (Rom. 1:23).

Why else do new revised versions of God keep appearing? Why else does God emerge in believing communities as a fashionably correct socialist, capitalist, or chauvinist? If we are intellectuals, God is our tenured professor in heaven; if we are anti-intellectuals, God is a small group leader who hates theology; if we are poor, God is a revolutionary; if we are propertied, God is night watchman over our goods. If we are theologians of a certain sort, God is the essential and existential dynamic of our ultimate horizon situation. The gods of the Persians always look like Persians. "Unbelief is not the only way of suppressing the truth about God," writes Merold Westphal, "it is only the most honest."[14] (1990, 214).

The preacher's job is to bring *God* home to us—not some blown-up portrait of ourselves.

STRATEGIES FOR BRINGING GOD HOME TO PRACTICAL ATHEISTS

What this means in the pulpit is that the preacher must be willing to practice not only faith, but also suspicion. He must suspect us all, including himself, of a tendency toward idolatry, and he must suspect us all, including himself, of a tendency to mix some hypocrisy with our idolatry.

These religious sins are triply dangerous. In the first place, they make God's actual character and will obscure to us. In the second place, these sins typically hide under a cloak of innocence, or even of holiness, with the result that they are hard for others to detect. (If you say Jesus' name often enough and piously enough, people might not notice that you are a fraud.) In the third place, particularly in the case of hypocrisy, these religious sins corrupt our own consciousness so that they are hard for *us* to detect too. There is no more fertile field for self-deception than the presumption that we are sincere in our faith, and there is no scarier figure than a sincere hypocrite—a person who is false to the core, but who really believes in his integrity. This is a person who does not hesitate to burden others with legalisms, which he typically attributes to God and from which he may partly exempt himself. One gathers from Matthew 23 that Jesus saved his sharpest words for such hypocrites not only because he wanted to penetrate the skin of their self-deception, but also because he wanted to challenge their religious tyranny.

In order to bring God home to us, the faithful preacher will try to counter our tendency toward idolatry and hypocrisy. He will adopt a healthy self-suspicion, and he will encourage the rest of us to follow suit.

[14] Merold Westphal, "Taking St. Paul Seriously: Sin as an Epistemological Category," in *Christian Philosophy*, ed. Thomas P. Flint (Notre Dame, IN: University of Notre Dame Press, 1990), 214.

One way in which preachers may express both faith and self-suspicion is by asking questions about God. Psalm 14 says that fools turn their backs on God but that the wise "seek after God" (v. 2). So, in the spirit of Psalm 14, wise preachers adopt the posture of a seeker. They know that God is not only intimately present, but also hidden. They know as well that seekers are not limited to the ecclesiastically homeless folk who happen to visit a mission-minded megachurch. A seeker is anybody in search of God. This means that many long-term believers qualify for seeker status. Many ministers qualify, as well as some theologians and theology students, for in its most famous definition, theology is "faith seeking understanding," and the main object of our understanding in theology is God.[15]

The wise seek after God in their preaching and in their listening to preaching. What makes them wise is that they have discovered something about God and the world, and they have discovered a knack for fitting themselves into God's world. At the same time, they have also discovered how little they know of God and of his purposes, and how clumsy are some of their attempts to fit themselves into God's project in the world.

How do the wise make such discoveries? By taking an alert and receptive attitude toward reality. By assuming that reality is a lot bigger than what happens within the confines of their own skull. By letting Scripture teach them and the Holy Spirit lead them. By apprenticing themselves to saints. And, all along, by spending time in the interrogative mood.

The wise seek after God by asking questions. How simple it sounds, and how seldom it happens. The wise ask questions and then they wait for a response. Fools, on the other hand, don't ask anything. They just make statements. As the saying goes, fools are often in error, but never in doubt. They don't *wonder* about anything.

But the wise, including wise preachers, ask a lot of questions. They know that we have not created our own natural riches—beauty, memory, will—and this thought leads them to wonder who did. They know that we human beings are finite and corruptible, and they wonder who might be infinite and incorruptible. They know that if we human beings try to put the weight of our longing and adoration on other human beings, those other human beings will break and so will we, as in the case of a celebrity who cracks under the pressure of our worship and leaves disillusioned fans to sift through the wreckage. The wise person wonders if anyone in the universe can actually satisfy our longing, forgive our folly, and bear the weight of our worship. In short, the wise and restless heart seeks a supreme good to bring it to rest.[16]

---

[15]St. Anselm, *An Address (Proslogion)*, in *A Scholastic Miscellany: Anselm to Ockham*, ed. and trans. Eugene R. Fairweather. The Library of Christian Classics, vol. 11 (Philadelphia: Westminster, 1961), Preface.

[16]St. Augustine, *Confessions*, I.I (1).

Wise persons keep seeking God. They wonder about things and they wonder about persons and so, like Augustine, they wonder about God. How does God speak? they wonder. Is God inside or outside? How can God be immense without a body? Is God more like a single complex person or more like a close society of three persons? Is Jesus the same as God or different? Can a person under the wings of God get brain cancer there? Where is God's home? How masculine is God? Can we cause God to suffer? If so, is God at our disposal? If not, can God have compassion? When human beings lobby God in group prayer, does this really make any difference to God's plans?

The wise seek God by wondering, and by asking questions that arise from their wondering, and often they do these things by preaching and listening to sermons.

"Most persons," wrote Rufus Jones, "would listen on their knees to anyone who would make God absolutely real to them."[17] Maybe so and maybe not, but nobody should underestimate the challenge of making absolutely real to us the God who is both hidden and intimately present. The challenge is big enough in those cerebral churches where God is unspeakable and remote—less a person than an idea. Here the portrait of God seems to have been drawn by an abstract impressionist; here the pious hesitancy of the faithful is hard to tell from agnosticism.

To rebalance Augustine's equation in such settings, the wise preacher will lean hard on the truth of God's intimate presence with us. She will speak of hearts that have been strangely warmed by God. She will testify of lives that have been renewed by the Spirit of God, and she will share the words "born again" when she testifies. She will tell of "a personal relationship with Jesus Christ," and she will have something thoughtful to say when people ask her the meaning of this phrase. Most important, to Christians whose God seems remote, the wise preacher will bring good news of great joy: God has come to us. A child, Immanuel, has been born to us, and even the wise men from the East—those from Harvard, Yale, and Princeton—belong on their knees before him.

The challenge of making God real to believers is big enough in cerebral churches where the knowledge of God "merely flits in the brain"[18] (Calvin, 1960, 1. 5. 9). Surprisingly, the challenge is just as big in those evangelical churches where a sermon about God has to get through layers of old bumper-sticker piety. Here the sermon must reach people whose God doesn't seem to them hidden at all. Aren't their lives filled with signs and wonders? Doesn't God speak to them in plain English? Didn't they just talk with God face to face this very morning—the way a man talks to his friend?

[17]Rufus Jones, *Social Law in the Spiritual World: Studies in Human and Divine Inter-Relationship* (Philadelphia: John C. Winston, 1904), 33.

[18]Calvin, *Institutes of the Christian Religion*, 1.5.9.

To rebalance Augustine's equation in such settings, the preacher must lean hard on the "hiddenness" side of the equation. Here the wise preacher will offer a tart and astringent God for people with too much spiritual fat in their diet. He will preach a strange and elusive God for people who have become too familiar with God. He will preach an austere God to straighten the spines of evangelical Christians whose lyrics have slumped into sentimentality already at ten o'clock on the first morning of the week ("I felt every teardrop when in darkness you cried; and I came to remind you that for those tears I died"). Most important, he will preach the advent of Jesus Christ, the Son of God, and he will sometimes choose Mark as his witness.

Why? Because Mark's gospel gives us no space to get sentimental with the God who comes home to us in Jesus Christ. Mark's gospel begins not with the little Lord Jesus asleep on the hay, but with a thoroughly grownup Jesus being baptized on a day when the heavens get torn apart, and the Spirit descends upon Jesus, and the Spirit drives Jesus out into the desert where the wild things are. In Mark 1:12-13, the Spirit drives Jesus into the desert as if to exorcise him from polite company, and this strange incident anticipates the rest of the gospel in which, frankly, most people don't really want the advent of God.

Why should they? Sentimental Christians sometimes suppose that a meeting with God would be like a walk in a garden or a coffee date with a friend. But the truth is that it might be more like getting electrocuted. Calvin comments that the saints in Scripture who feel the presence of God are "stricken and overcome." In fact, they are "so shaken" as to be "almost annihilated."[19]

CONCLUSION

In this fact lies a sobering truth, namely, that no matter what our religious style, we probably want God less than we think. We human beings do seek God in prayer and in sacraments and in the push toward justice. We do seek God in preaching sermons and in listening to them. We seek God, and we should. It's natural for creatures to want their creator, and it's wise for sinners to want their savior.

But the people who really want God—the ones who thirst for God the way a parched creature thirsts for water in a desert—are typically people who are in deep trouble. It's the lepers and the lame and the besieged who want God in their lives. It's people who have been sickened and deprived who cry out for God their savior. The rest of us have reason to keep the search going as long as we can. Comfortable people have reason to hear sermons about God with half a mind, and to launch prayers toward God with half a heart, and to sing hymns to God with words they cannot recount five minutes later.

[19]Calvin, *Institutes of the Christian Religion*, 1.1.3.

The reason is that God slays in order to save, and the search for God is therefore a death wish.[20] That is why our interest in God is often so mild. We do not relish the idea of being almost annihilated. And so we retreat from God. Or we approach God, but keep our distance. Like an ambivalent prodigal son, we leave the far country but settle somewhere short of home.

The gospel of grace says that this strategy will fail. The reason is that although our interest in God is mild, God's interest in us is fierce. That's why the heavens get ripped open in Mark 1. According to Donald Juel, it's not as if we keep "bumping our heads against the glass ceiling" as we try to get at God. Just the opposite. God rips open the heavens to get at *us*. Mark's gospel says that God is on the loose in Jesus Christ and that nobody is safe.[21] None of our favorite sins is safe. Everything in us that is smug or envious has to die. Everything grudging or greedy has to die. All our self-indulgence has to die. Because these sins have grown into our hearts (the place where we say there is no God), we cannot be rid of them unless we ourselves die and rise with Christ.

The upshot is that when we think of meeting God, we ought to do so with a sense not only of joy, but also of horror. We ought to count the cost. According to C. S. Lewis, who was an accomplished seeker, when we talk of searching for God, we "might as well talk about the mouse's search for the cat."[22]

The truth is that we are divided creatures who want God, but also flee from God. We are like Cain in Genesis 4. He wants neither to obey God ("Am I my brother's keeper?"), nor to lose God. And so when God banishes him, the desolate Cain first protests ("My punishment is greater than I can bear") and then grieves ("I shall be hidden from your face!").

That's who we are, and the preacher must say so. She must speak the truth not only about God but also about us—people who look so much like God, have wandered so far from God, and so urgently need to accept the grace of God.

[20]Stanley Sturing, "To See God," an unpublished course paper (Grand Rapids: Calvin Theological Seminary, November 20, 1997), 3.

[21]Donald Juel, "What Makes for 'Engagement?' Interpreting at the Beginning (Mark 1:1-15)," a lecture at the St. Olaf Conferences on Theology & Music, St. Olaf College, Northfield, Minn.: St. Olaf College, July 15, 1997.

[22]C. S. Lewis, *Surprised by Joy: The Shape of My Early Life* (New York: Harcourt, Brace & World, 1955), 227.

Application in Preaching
Old Testament Texts

Sidney Greidanus[1]

"Great preaching is relevant preaching." This is the conclusion of the editors of *Twenty Centuries of Great Preaching*. They explain, "After studying the lives of hundreds of preachers and reading countless sermons, we concluded that the preachers who made the greatest impact upon the world were men who spoke to the issues and needs of their day."[2]

Speaking to the issues and needs of the day is the heart of application. Although one can find a variety of definitions of the term, all have a common core. In his popular text of 1870, John Broadus offered a definition that has stood the test of time:

> Application, in the strict sense, is that part, or those parts, of the discourse in which we show how the subject applies to the persons addressed, what practical instructions it offers them, what practical demands it makes upon them.[3]

Application of the message of Old Testament texts is notoriously difficult because the message must be carried across the immense historical-cultural gap between Old Testament Israel and the contemporary church. Perhaps this is why many pastors concentrate on preaching the New Testament and have largely given up on preaching the Old Testament. On the basis of reports from several denominations, I estimate that the average church member hears at most two sermons on an Old Testament text for every ten sermons on a New Testament text.

The apostle Paul, however, declares that the Old Testament is "profitable" (RSV) for the Christian church: "All Scripture is God-breathed and is useful [profitable] for teaching, rebuking, correcting and training in righteousness, so that the man of God may be thoroughly equipped for every good work" (2 Tim. 3:16-17, NIV). Paul commands Timothy and all Christian preachers: "Preach the Word," that is, the Word of God as it is found in the Old Testament (2 Tim. 4:2).

---

[1] On this occasion of honoring John H. Stek, I wish to express publicly my appreciation for his valuable insights in his publications and my gratitude for his superb proofreading of my *The Modern Preacher and the Ancient Text* (Grand Rapids: Eerdmans, 1988), and for promising to do so again for my forthcoming *Preaching Christ from the Old Testament*.

[2] Clyde E. Fant, Jr., and William M. Pinson, Jr., *Twenty Centuries of Great Preaching*, Vol. 1 (Waco: Word Books, 1971).

[3] John Broadus, *On the Preparation and Delivery of Sermons*, rev. ed. (New York: Harper, 1944), 211.

Preaching from the Old Testament is still "profitable" today, for it proclaims truths not found in, but assumed by, the New Testament—think of the creation account, the fall into sin, the long covenant history between God and his people Israel, God's promises, the ten words of the covenant, the sacrifices God requires, God's concern for social justice, the Psalms, and so on. Congregations receive a balanced diet only when they hear sound preaching from both Testaments.

Here we shall focus on application in preaching from the Old Testament. We shall first explore the historical-cultural gap that makes application of the Old Testament so difficult. Next we shall test some bridges often used for crossing the gap, but which turn out to be too flimsy to bear the weight. Then we shall explore the foundations of the only solid bridge across the historical-cultural gap and suggest practical ways in which this bridge may be used for sound application.

THE HISTORICAL-CULTURAL GAP

In seeking to apply the message of the Old Testament to the contemporary church, preachers must cross the historical-cultural gap. Lessing voiced the frustration of many preachers when he graphically called this gap "the ugly ditch." More helpful is Fred Craddock's description, which uncovers the many different layers of the gap. He observes, "The geographical, linguistic, psychological, cosmological and chronological gulf between the ancient Near East and modern America yawns frighteningly wide."[4] Let us briefly look at the two major layers—the historical and the cultural.

The Cultural Gap

While the Old Testament authors originally addressed their messages to listeners in an Eastern, agricultural, patriarchal society, contemporary preachers address listeners in a Western, urban, postindustrial, democratic society. These cultural differences hinder direct application.

For example, in the Old Testament, polygamy and slavery were accepted and regulated. How do preachers today apply messages regarding polygamy and slavery in a culture where monogamy is the law of the land and slavery has been abolished? And what about regulations for holy war? Clean and unclean animals? Sabbatical years and years of jubilee? The many cultural differences seem like an "ugly ditch" that cannot be crossed for contemporary application.

The Historical Gap

Even more of a hindrance for direct application is the historical gap. Here we should think especially of the redemptive-historical gap; the Old Testament authors

---

[4]Fred Craddock, *As One Without Authority* (Nashville: Abingdon, 1971), 117.

addressed Israel before the coming of Christ while preachers today address the church *after* the coming of Christ—a church that claims the Old *and* New Testaments.

For example, how are Christian preachers to apply Old Testament regulations regarding temple worship, animal sacrifices, or being clean and unclean? The redemptive-historical gap makes the cultural gap even wider.

Instead of viewing the historical-cultural gap as an "ugly ditch" that prevents contemporary application, Christian preachers can see the ditch in a more positive light. The challenge is to preach the Old Testament message so that it is as relevant for the church today as it was for Israel in the past.

Before we discuss how we can properly cross the historical-cultural gap, we should identify several bridges that cannot carry the weight of the Old Testament message and therefore should be avoided.

INADEQUATE WAYS OF BRIDGING THE HISTORICAL-CULTURAL GAP

Direct Transference

Some preachers seek to apply the Old Testament message directly to the contemporary church by ignoring the gap. But, writes William Willimon, "transference, in its assumption that there are no differences between our time, our concepts, and our lives and those of the Bible, usually does injustice to Scripture."[5]

The bridge of direct transference fails for two reasons. First, transference tends to ignore the original historical-cultural context addressed by the text. And second, it ignores the historical-cultural context of the Christian church in modern society after the coming of Christ. Ian Pitt-Watson writes, "Every sermon is stretched like a bowstring between the text of the Bible on the one hand and the problems of contemporary human life on the other. If the string is insecurely tethered to either end, the bow is useless."[6] Direct transference usually fails to tether the bowstring securely at both ends and therefore tends to misunderstand the original word and to misapply it today.

Universalizing

Another popular bridge across the historical-cultural gap is universalizing. Ernest Best describes universalizing as follows: "The selected text . . . which was set originally in one situation is now interpreted so as to apply to a whole range of situations and circumstances."[7] For example, God gave Israel the promised land, therefore God will give his people today "the promised land" (the United States, South Africa). God com-

[5]William H. Willimon, *Preaching and Leading Worship* (Philadelphia: Westminster, 1984), 70.

[6]Ian Pitt-Watson, *Preaching: A Kind of Folly* (Edinburgh: St. Andrews, 1976), 57.

[7]Ernest Best, *From Text to Sermon: Responsible Use of the New Testament in Preaching* (Atlanta: John Knox, 1978), 86.

manded David to fight the enemy, therefore kings, presidents, prime ministers, and ordinary citizens must fight the enemy today.

The bridge of universalizing fails to do justice to the unique historical-cultural context addressed by the text. As Willimon puts it, universalizing ignores the fact that "Scripture arises out of concrete needs of the community of faith in specific situations."[8] Universalizing tends to overlook the uniqueness of the historical situation addressed by the Old Testament text and thus misjudges the depth of the historical-cultural gap.

Individualizing

Another inadequate bridge is individualizing, which is popular in individualistic cultures. Most of the Old Testament addressed Israel communally. Lloyd Bailey writes, "A text that initially was addressed to Israel as a whole should not be individualized. Seek its relevance for the community in the present, before inquiring about its meaning for the individual members."[9]

Spiritualizing

Spiritualizing is frequently used when preachers feel they cannot apply the earthly, physical, historical reality of the Old Testament. For example, how do we apply the story of Joseph being thrown into a pit? Not many of us today can relate to that. In seeking to bridge the gap, the *Interpreter's Bible* moves from Joseph being thrown into a pit to "the soul of man" being in a pit, "morally and spiritually." That is spiritualizing.

Unfortunately, the common bridge of spiritualizing cannot bear the weight of the Old Testament message. If the text speaks of physical, earthly realities, modern preachers have no right to twist the author's meaning and turn them into spiritual realities for the sake of application. Another unfortunate result of constant spiritualizing is that it undermines, in a gnostic way, the biblical message of the redemption of creation and the resurrection of the body. It is precisely the earthiness of the Old Testament that keeps the biblical concept of salvation tied to this earth and to our earthly existence. M. Reu rightly maintains,

> It is but a sorry fame when a preacher is ignorantly praised for his skill in twisting and turning his text and making it say things never dreamed of by the writer. . . . The main thought in the text must be the main thought also in the application; what is subordinate in the text must be subordinate in the application; what is not found in the

---

[8]Willimon, *Preaching and Leading Worship*, 71.

[9]Lloyd R. Bailey, *The Pentateuch* (Nashville: Abingdon, 1981), 92.

text has no place in the application; what gives the text its distinctive character dare not be absent from the application.[10]

Moralizing

Preachers also cross the historical-cultural gap by drawing little moral lessons from the text. Moralizing preachers attach these morals to mere elements in the text while they miss the text's message and its ethical implications. For example, preaching on God's command to Abraham to sacrifice his son, moralizing preachers quickly move to the application that we also must offer our dearest to God. Although this application is not unbiblical, it is not the point of Genesis 22.

Moralizing often takes the form of "imitation preaching," or holding up biblical characters as positive or negative "models" for the congregation. For example, Roy De Brand, among others, advocates biographical preaching where the application consists of imitating the biblical characters: "Biographical sermons . . . carry the automatic bonus of example. . . . We learn from others. Sometimes the lessons are positive and we emulate them. Other times we learn what not to do, think, or say from the example of others. Often both positive and negative lessons can be learned from the same Bible character."[11]

Biographical imitation preaching allows easy applications. When preaching on the book of Ruth, preachers can make the following applications: like Ruth, we must decide to join the family of God, confess, and belong (a three-point sermon with three imitation applications); or, like Naomi, we must discourage insincere Orpahs; or, unlike Orpah, we must not return to our old gods; or, like Boaz, we must love the poor and feed them. Again, these applications are not unbiblical, but they lack the authority of the text. They turn the biblical author's *description* into *prescription* for hearers today. Imitation preaching twists the message of the author into practical do's and don'ts, and in the process turns the God-centered character of Old Testament texts into human-centered sermons.[12]

Moralizing may seem practical, but a constant diet of moralizing applications is terribly harmful to the gospel and the church. Leander Keck minces no words:

> It is hard to conceive of any mode of preaching more deadly to the
> hearer or more inimical to the Bible itself than the prevailing pattern

---

[10]M. Reu, *Homiletics: A Manual of the Theory and Practice of Preaching* (Grand Rapids: Baker, 1967), 362.

[11]Roy E. De Brand, *Guide to Biographical Preaching* (Nashville: Broadman Press, 1988), 23.

[12]See further my *Sola Scriptura: Problems and Principles in Preaching Historical Texts* (Toronto: Wedge, 1970). Bailey, for one, advises, "We must learn to look beyond the morality of a story's characters to the overall reason the Community preserved the story, if we can discover it. It is not so much that *Abraham* is hero or villain, as that the story is about *God* as hero: It is the deity who preserves Abraham and provides for a future." *The Pentateuch*, 91-92.

of drawing lessons for today from a text that has been explained briefly. . . . Moralizing "application" of the text is a markedly unbiblical way of preaching the Bible.[13]

Direct transference, universalizing, individualizing, spiritualizing, and moralizing—all fall short of bridging the historical-cultural gap authentically. Biblical preachers require a better bridge.

FOUNDATIONS FOR BRIDGING THE HISTORICAL-CULTURAL GAP

Before exploring valid ways of bridging the historical-cultural gap, we need to lay a foundation, or the bridge to application will collapse. We shall briefly discuss four indispensable principles that lead to sound application.

View the Old Testament as a Relevant Proclamation to Israel

Preachers sometimes view the Old Testament as objective revelation or as objective history that they must *make* relevant by adding one or more applications. Because all of the Old Testament is *kerygma*, that is, relevant proclamation to Israel, contemporary preachers need not *make* their text relevant; they need only discover the text's past relevance and determine how that relevance applies today. It is important that preachers seek to discover the author's goal as well as the text's theme. The goal helps one discern the specific relevance, the result anticipated in response to the message.

Focus on God-Centered Interpretation of the Text

Preachers often are so enamored with biblical characters that they fail to see beyond the human characters. But the Bible is God's *self-revelation*. The Old Testament is the story of God and his creation, God and his coming kingdom, God and his covenant people. Consequently, if we fail to find God in our text, we have missed the very purpose for which the Old Testament was written. And, as will become clear below, we have also missed the key component for sound application. Preachers need to ask with every text, What does this passage reveal about God and his relationship with his people? What does it say about God's acts of redemption, his covenant of grace, his promises, his providence, his judgment, his will for his people Israel?

Understand the Text in Its Redemptive-Historical Context

Redemptive-historical understanding views the message of the text in the context of the whole of redemptive history. It views the text first as a message addressed to

---

[13]Leander Keck, *The Bible in the Pulpit: The Renewal of Biblical Preaching* (Nashville: Abingdon, 1978), 100. Cf. J. Daniel Baumann, *An Introduction to Contemporary Preaching* (Grand Rapids: Baker, 1972), 255, "They append little 'preachy' additions to sermons which are at once offensive and childish." Cf. Willimon, *Peculiar Speech*, 72, "Moralism unintentionally but blasphemously puts us in the place of God in Scripture, stresses people's misdeeds more than God's deeds, and talks about what we should do rather than what God is doing."

Israel at a certain stage of redemptive history (historical interpretation). Second, it seeks to relate this historical message to God's ongoing work of restoring his creation through the seed of the woman (Gen. 3:15) until his kingdom comes on earth in perfection (Rev. 22). This context of redemptive history from creation to new creation provides biblical depth and scope to the message. Moreover, viewing the text in the context of redemptive history provides a solid bridge across the historical-cultural gap, enabling preachers to discover the continuity in God's actions for Israel then and for the church today—continuity in God's promises to Israel then and to the church today, continuity in God's requirements of Israel then and of the church today. "Because God is in His nature the same now as He was in the past, His Word is still valid today. . . ."[14]

Along with continuity on God's side, redemptive-historical understanding acknowledges the continuity in humanity's condition and need. "Man's heart continues the same with its needs, its joys and sorrows, its follies and sins, but also with its inextinguishable longing after God."[15] In short, redemptive-historical understanding enables preachers to see that the word God addressed to Israel in the past is also addressed to the church today because of the continuity in God's kingdom history. As Israel was God's people and agent in the world in Old Testament times, so the church is God's people and agent in the same kingdom history in New Testament times.

Understand the Text in the Light of the New Testament

Understanding in the context of redemptive history leads one to discover not only continuity but discontinuity as well. Redemptive history is not static; it is like a mighty river that is constantly on the move, moving forward, sometimes switching back, but gradually reaching its destination in the perfect kingdom of God.[16] One of the major turning points in the river of redemptive history was the coming of Christ. It divided kingdom history into a "before Christ" and an "after Christ." Since the Old Testament was addressed to Israel before the coming of Christ, and preachers today address the church after the coming of Christ, application needs to reckon with discontinuity as well as with continuity.

Church history shows the complexity of sorting out what is continued or discontinued from the Old Testament era to the New. In making this difficult decision, however, preachers have a definitive guide. Since the New Testament was written after the coming of Christ, discontinuity in the message can best be established by understanding

---

[14]Reu, *Homiletics*, 361.

[15]Ibid.

[16]The graphic metaphor of a river was first suggested to me by Walther Zimmerli, "Promise and Fulfillment," in *Essays on Old Testament Hermeneutics*, ed. Claus Westermann (Richmond: John Knox, 1964), 112.

the Old Testament message in the light of the New Testament. For example, if the message of Genesis 17 for Israel was that they ought to circumcise their baby boys on the eighth day or break God's covenant, Acts 15 reveals that after the coming of Christ circumcision is no longer required, and baptism gradually replaces this sign of initiation into God's covenant. Or take Exodus 20:8-11. If God required Israel to rest on the seventh day of the week, the New Testament makes clear that the seventh day gradually shifts to the first day of the week, the Lord's day of resurrection.

In applying an Old Testament text, therefore, preachers need to be aware of discontinuity as well as continuity. The bridge across the historical-cultural gap that can do justice to both aspects is redemptive history. The oneness of redemptive history accounts for the continuity in God's dealings with Israel and the New Testament church, while the progression in redemptive history accounts for the discontinuity. A comprehensive view of redemptive history, I believe, is the only solid bridge across the historical-cultural gap. But this single bridge provides a number of tracks, often used in combination, across the gap. We shall next explore these different tracks or ways that can cross the gap with authority and integrity.

VALID WAYS OF BRIDGING THE HISTORICAL-CULTURAL GAP

Focus on the Goal of the Author

R. P. Richard rightly claims that "the first step in discovering the application of Scripture in general is determining what application was expected of the original audience."[17] This first step anchors present application in past application. What was the author's purpose for writing, his aim, the response he desired from Israel?[18]

Inquiring after the author's goal is important because it exposes the text's original relevance and directs the way to contemporary application. For example, it is clear that the goal of the author of Exodus 20 is to urge Israel to obey the ten covenant words, and that the goal of the author of Isaiah 40 is to comfort Israel in exile, and that the goal of Amos is to admonish Israel for injustice and idolatry. Preachers today may not be able to have exactly the same goal for their sermon as the original author had for his text, but their goal ought at least to be in harmony with it. In other words, if the author's purpose is to comfort Israel, we can use this text today to comfort the church or to encourage it, but we ought not to use this text to admonish or to warn, for then we would be working at cross-purposes with the inspired author.

---

[17]R. P. Richard, "Methodological Proposals for Scripture Relevance," *Bibliotheca Sacra* 143 (1986): 207.

[18]Walter Liefeld suggests with respect to the New Testament that preachers ask, "What purpose did the passage serve? . . . I am not only asking what the teaching *is* but *why* it is given here. . . . What immediate results did the author seek? . . . . Now we are thinking about intended outcome." *New Testament Exposition: From Text to Sermon* (Grand Rapids: Zondervan, 1984), 97.

Look for an Analogous Situation in Contemporary Life

Because of the continuity in redemptive history, there are analogous situations between Old Testament Israel and the church addressed by contemporary preachers. Finding such an analogy leads to relevant preaching. As Keck puts it, "The preacher must identify what today's hearers share with the author's original readers so that the text confronts them both. When this happens, the event of the text repeats itself." And again, "Preaching that emerges from the awareness of these continuities will not 'apply' the text to life today; rather, it will communicate the discovery of its pertinence because today's church is already addressed along with the original readers."[19]

Haddon Robinson similarly advises, "In order to apply a passage accurately, we must define the situation into which the revelation was originally given and then decide what a modern man or woman shares, or does not share, with the original hearers. The closer the relationship between the modern man and biblical man, the more direct the application."[20]

Preachers must be careful, of course, not to force an analogy between Israel and the present congregation. The analogy may not be posited at the cost of leveling the unique situation of Israel and of the church today.[21]

Uncover the Underlying Principle

Sometimes the author's goal is so culturally specific that we cannot find an analogous situation today; the discontinuity is so great that the message simply cannot cross the historical-cultural gap unchanged. In this case, preachers can seek to discern the principle behind the message, that is, the principle of which the message is a concrete expression. Perry Yoder writes, "In moving from the meaning of the passage to application, it is the principle involved that is our best guide to present application."[22] He explains, "Since principles are more general, less tied to specifics, they usually have a wider range or scope of application. This means that the same principles can take on a variety of forms in different cultures and thereby help us transcend cultural relativity."[23]

---

[19]Keck, *The Bible in the Pulpit*, 116.

[20]Haddon W. Robinson, *Biblical Preaching: The Development and Delivery of Expository Messages* (Grand Rapids: Baker, 1980), 90.

[21]Ernest Best cautions against what he calls "historicizing exegesis": "Stories from the history of ancient Israel are taken to have a message for what is happening to us. This takes place easily in time of war or conditions of national stress or jubilation." *From Text to Sermon*, 70.

[22]Perry A. Yoder, *From Word to Life: A Guide to the Art of Bible Study* (Scottdale, Penn.: Herald Press, 1982), 223.

[23]Ibid., 40. Cf. Jay E. Adams, *Truth Applied: Application in Preaching* (Grand Rapids: Zondervan, 1990), 47-55.

Determine Whether the Author Intended Israel
to Identify with a Biblical Character

Proponents of narrative preaching argue for identification as the way to cross the historical-cultural gap. If preachers can enable the congregation to identify with one of the biblical characters, the distance has been bridged. Craddock writes, "Without the factor of recognition of our common lot, the preacher cannot build enough bridges between text and listener; with the factor of recognition, those structures are unnecessary."[24]

Unfortunately, the way of identification with biblical characters is fraught with hazards. The obvious danger is that a God-centered biblical narrative will be turned into a human-centered sermon. Another danger is that the biblical story will be preached in isolation of its function in the canon and in redemptive history. Still another danger is that identification with a Bible character will turn into a sophisticated form of moralizing. When congregations have to learn the "lesson" learned by the Bible character, we are but one step removed from imitation preaching that uses the Bible character as a moral example.[25]

Many other questions could be raised. Since there is always more than one character in biblical scenes, with which character should hearers identify? Who decides this? And was it the author's intention that Israel identify with the characters they sketched? Best states flatly, "The stories of the Bible were not told to illustrate character but to awaken their hearers to the judgment and love of God. Concentration on 'identification' and the consequent production of moral lessons can lead us to missing what Scripture is really about."[26]

I suggest that we begin identification at a different level than is customary. Preachers usually seek to have the congregation identify with a certain Bible character. A better way is to help the congregation identify with the first hearers of the story, that is, with Israel. Hear the story the way Israel heard it. This is an attempt to hear the original relevance of the story. Then the question will arise, Did Israel identify with one of the characters? If Israel did, then the church can identify with that character through Israel. But if the author did not intend Israel to identify with a certain character, we have no right to impose such identification.

For example, there is little doubt that Israel identified with the patriarchs Abraham, Isaac, and Jacob (Israel). Gerhard von Rad writes regarding Abraham, "Now there is no doubt that in reading this ancient story ancient Israel recognized itself in Abraham

---

[24]Fred Craddock, *Preaching* (Nashville: Abingdon, 1985), 134-135.

[25]See further *The Modern Preacher and the Ancient Text: Interpreting and Preaching Biblical Literature*, 175-181.

[26]Best, *From Text to Sermon*, 92.

as believing community, as people of God (and not primarily as individuals)."[27] John Stek has done some astute detective work in bringing to light some of the less obvious characters with whom Israel was to identify. For example, he makes the case that the Samson story "confronted Israel with a mirror image of herself":

> As Samson was given birth by a special act of Yahweh (out of bar-renness), so Israel herself was the product of Yahweh's special inter-vention in history (remember Isaac, Jacob, and the exodus). As Samson was consecrated to Yahweh (as a Nazirite) from birth, so Israel was to be wholly consecrated to Yahweh (circumcision). As Samson was constantly drawn to the blandishments of Philistine women, so Israel was constantly drawn to the blandishments of the peoples around her (she "made love" to the gods of the neighboring peoples, as the prophets charged). As Samson called on Yahweh only when in a life crisis, so Israel called on Yahweh . . . only when she was in deep crisis.[28]

See the Old Testament Message in the Light of the New Testament

Some thirty years ago, John Stek first made me aware of the fact that progression in redemptive history requires a new hearing of earlier revelation. He writes,

> The fact of progression in salvation history demands an ever-new hearing of the word of the Lord spoken at an earlier moment in salvation history. The hearing must be new because it is a hearing in the context of the later events and circumstances in salvation history, and in the light of the word of the Lord spoken later in salvation history.[29]

For example, Stek suggests that the message of the book of Jonah was heard in one way by Israel in exile, somewhat differently when the remnant had returned, and still differently when living under the oppression of Antiochus. The reason for this new hearing was that Israel was living at a later stage of redemptive history and was read-ing Jonah in the context of later events and circumstances. Our place in redemptive history today cries out for a new hearing of the Old Testament, for we live after the com-ing of Christ. Therefore we need to read Jonah not only as Israel read this book, but also through the lenses of the gospel of Jesus Christ as revealed in the New Testament. As

[27]Gerhard von Rad, *Biblical Interpretations in Preaching* (Nashville: Abingdon, 1977), 27.

[28]John H. Stek, *The Former Prophets: A Syllabus* (Unpublished. Grand Rapids: Calvin Theological Seminary, 1985), 32.

[29]John H. Stek, "The Message of the Book of Jonah," *Calvin Theological Journal* 4/1 (1969): 47-48.

Stek puts it, "Although Israel because of her unfaithfulness failed to be a salvatory agent to all the world, God has in Jesus Christ, the true Israelite, and the anti-type of Jonah, brought salvation near to all the nations. If the 'elect' of the new age fail, Christ is still the Lord of history."[30] Jonah still speaks to the church today of the necessity of the church's involvement in the world as God's agent for the salvation of the nations—but with even greater urgency after Christ's resurrection and the outpouring of the Holy Spirit.

A new hearing is, admittedly, a risky way to arrive at an application because it leaves behind the safe harbor of the original meaning and application. Yet a new hearing need not mean being set adrift on the ocean of subjectivism and arbitrariness where every reader, as in reader-response criticism, brings his or her own meaning to the text, never mind the intention of the original author. For the new hearing envisioned here would not ignore the original hearing or the intention of the original author (our first step in application) but, in the light of the New Testament, it would *extend* this original meaning and application to our present situation in kingdom history. In other words, the New Testament is the compass that sets the direction for the application of Old Testament texts. This is as it should be. A text must be interpreted in its literary context; for the Christian church, the context of the Old Testament is the New Testament. Consequently, Christian preachers need to apply the message of Old Testament texts from the perspective of the gospel of Jesus Christ as revealed in the New Testament.

CONCLUSION

We have seen that the major obstacle to application in preaching from the Old Testament is the historical-cultural gap. Homiletical bridges such as universalizing, individualizing, spiritualizing, and moralizing do not bridge the gap; they twist the author's intended meaning for the sake of easy application. The only solid bridge across the gap is redemptive history with its twin characteristics of continuity and discontinuity. These two characteristics of redemptive history enable preachers to discern genuine analogous situations and identifications as well as valid ways of applying biblical principles to new situations. Redemptive-historical understanding offers a nuanced approach that can do justice in application both to the text as it spoke originally to Israel and to the changed circumstances in which the church hears this message today.

[30]Stek, "The Message of the Book of Jonah," 48-49.

Samson: The Riddle and the Reason

Roy M. A. Berkenbosch

There you have it—the beginning of one of the more sordid personal histories in the Bible—the tragedy of Samson, God's Rambo.

It's not a pretty story, and Samson is not a pretty character. An "over-sexed buffoon," one commentator calls him. He is ill-tempered, slaughters people when he doesn't get his way, takes his vengeance-seeking anger out on three hundred innocent foxes whose tails he amazingly ties together and sets ablaze. He's a womanizer, falling head over heels for every pretty face. He has no self-control, he is disrespectful of his parents, and he's contemptuous of the sacred calling for which he was born. I'm not sure I'd want my kids to play with him, and I am very sure I wouldn't want my daughter to marry him. Let's be honest. This story is embarrassing to read and hard to explain at family devotions or in church school.

QUESTIONS ABOUT SAMSON

That raises the obvious question, If it's as bad as all that, then why on earth is this story in the Bible at all, and why are we reading it?

At least two reasonable answers come to mind. First, because the history of God's mighty acts is both grand and gritty, full of grace and grime; it includes unpleasant episodes where God's grace gets dragged through the mud. The Bible includes the story of Samson because God is not embarrassed to use him, in spite of his folly and his contempt for his sacred calling. In fact, the measure of Samson's inadequacy and failure is also the measure of God's grace.

In the second place, Samson's tragic tale helps Israel and the church remember their past so they can learn from it. This story is both warning and encouragement, and we must listen for both.

Samson's life has a happy enough beginning. His birth is miraculous. To the barren wife of Menoah, an angel announces the best news she's ever heard. She will bear a son—no ordinary son, but a Nazirite with the special mission of delivering God's people from their enemies, the Philistines. That's good news for Israel and a good start in Samson's life. The story of his birth ends with the promising observation, "He grew and the Lord blessed him, and the Spirit of the Lord began to stir him . . . " (Judg. 13:24).

That would warm the heart of any Israelite. They liked stories that began that way because it reminded them of their own special beginning. They too were miraculously conceived in the barren womb of old Sarah and specially consecrated for God's mission in the world. Sounds like Samson will be a chip off the old block.

THE RIDDLE OF SAMSON: THE LION

More than the Spirit of God was stirring in Samson. Chapter 14 tells us that Samson really doesn't care all that much about his special consecration or the sacred purpose for which he was born. A chip off the old block all right!

Samson goes to Timnah, the heart of enemy territory, and falls in love with a pretty Philistine girl. Just one look was all it took. This is the one for him. He insists that his parents arrange a hasty wedding. But they protest, as they should, "Samson, you should find one of your own people. That's the will of God." Says Samson, "I know what I want, and I want it now. If that bothers God, too bad. I guess I'll learn to live with it."

Now, it is true that the Bible says this was all part of God's plan, for we read in verse 4, "His parents did not know that this was from the Lord. . . . " But that is confessional commentary supplied by the author. It was not apparent to Samson or to his parents that he was acting in accordance with God's purposes—far from it! He was only too willing to play fast and loose with his vows. So off to Timnah go Samson and his parents to make arrangements for the wedding. On the way, something very significant happens.

Near the vineyards at the outskirts of town, a young lion suddenly charges out of the forest and attacks Samson. Clearly not a smart lion! He doesn't know who he is dealing with, and he's no match for the young Samson. The Spirit of God comes upon Samson and he tears the lion apart as if it were a young goat. (Is this irony apparent?) Awesome strength!

But let's pause here for a moment. Why do you suppose this short episode is included in the story? Just to let us know that Samson was exceptionally strong? Perhaps, but there's more to it than that, especially when we see this story in the context of everything else that comes later.

This encounter with the lion is a pattern of Samson's entire career as God's judge. The lion that leaps out to destroy Samson is just like the bands of Philistine soldiers who leap out at him time and time again to destroy him. The lion is a symbol of the danger toward which Samson is headed, a warning that he's in dangerous territory. Since Samson easily defeats the lion, this is also a hopeful sign—a sign of the power and victory that will be his as long as he walks in the strength of the spirit of God. The dead lion is a hopeful, encouraging symbol.

But wait—a lengthening shadow falls over the story. Samson doesn't heed the warning of the lion, and he carries on his love affair with the Timnite girl. Some time later, when he's on his way to the wedding, he passes by the lion's carcass and sees it buzzing with life. Honeybees have made their home in it and the honeycomb is full. Samson dips in, pulls out a handful of honey, and eats it. He gives some to his parents, but doesn't tell them where he got it. And why not? Because he doesn't want them to know that he has broken his Nazirite vow. As a Nazirite he wasn't even supposed to come close to a dead body, much less touch it or eat from it. But touch and eat he does, and in that moment Samson defiles himself and spoils his consecration.

Do you see what's happening? The lion Samson defeated now returns to defeat him. The lion, once a hopeful symbol of Samson's victory, now becomes a symbol of his defeat.

There is a terrible division and contradiction in Samson's life. On the one hand, he can meet and defeat his enemy. On the other hand, the enemy easily overcomes him. He is awfully strong and terribly weak. Samson's life is a riddle.

THE RIDDLE OF SAMSON: THE HONEY

At this point, Samson doesn't recognize the division and contradiction in his life. But he does detect the contradiction in his experience with the lion. From that contradiction he fashions a riddle with which he taunts the Philistine guests at his wedding party:

> "Out of the eater, something to eat;
> Out of the strong, something sweet."

It's a good riddle, and he stumps his guests. But they are not good sports about it. The stakes are too high; they stand to lose a small fortune in tailoring bills if they don't guess the right answer. So they threaten Samson's new bride: "If you don't give us the answer we will burn you and your family." Their crude threat works. Samson's bride charms the answer out of him and passes it on to the Philistines. On the last day of the feast they answer Samson. But they also speak in riddles. Listen to the answer they give:

> "What is sweeter than honey?
> What is stronger than a lion?"

Samson knows he's been had, and in a fit of rage he murders thirty Philistines. (He didn't have much of a sense of humor either!) But Samson wasn't furious because he lost this contest. No, what really got to Samson was that the double irony of their answer exposed his real weakness and error. You see, the Philistines did more than solve a riddle—they also exposed Samson's deepest fault.

According to John Stek, the riddle "What is sweeter than honey? What is stronger than a lion?" was a common piece of folklore. Every Jew knew the answer: love, passion, desire. More to the point, lust; that's what is sweeter than honey and stronger than a lion. And it was lust that drew Samson to his Philistine honey in the first place.

Oh yes, he could kill a lion with his bare hands, but he could not resist the forbidden honey of beautiful Philistine women. Samson the lion-killer is defeated by the sweetness of his Timnite bride, who turned him over to his enemies. And he will not learn. He dips his hand into the Philistine "carcass" again and again, until he comes to tragic ruin through his passion for Delilah, the sweetest and deadliest honey of them all.

Because of her, God's chosen judge is rendered helpless and powerless. The riddle of the Philistines not only answers the riddle at Samson's wedding, but it also exposes the riddle of Samson's life. In chapter 16 we see the blind Samson shackled to a millstone, grinding food for the Philistines. "Out of the strong comes something to eat. . . . " And when he is called out to the Philistine party to entertain the guests, he is the eater who gives them something sweet. His life ironically fulfills the hidden prophecies of his own riddle, all because his passion was sweeter than honey and stronger than a lion.

THE REASON FOR THE SAMSON STORY

These word-plays are not immediately obvious to a twentieth-century North American congregation, but they would have been obvious to an attentive Hebrew ear. Any good Israelite with a conscience would feel the hot flush of shame on his cheeks when he heard this story. He would recognize that this is not just the story of Samson the man, but of Israel the nation.

Samson and Israel

Israel was the one who was specially born, specially nurtured, set aside to be God's invincible army against the powers that opposed God's kingdom. Israel was the crucible in which God was forming his movement of liberation for the whole world.

Israel was brought out of Egypt and given the law at Mount Sinai so she could defend herself against the stalking lion that sought to devour her and destroy God's cosmic plan of redemption through her. But when she was settled in the land of Canaan, this supposedly invincible host of the Lord became careless and, with hardly so much as a second thought, began to dip her hand into the carcass of Canaanite culture. She pulled out whatever sweets she craved, sometimes a golden calf, sometimes a Baal.

Israel had a wandering eye and a wavering heart. For the sake of the forbidden honey of Canaan she violated her consecration before God. You may ask, "How could God use such a blunt sword as Samson?" Surely the better question would be "How could God use such a blunt instrument as Israel the unfaithful?"

Samson and the Church

While we are on the subject of an unfaithful people, we may wonder how God can use faulty instruments such as ourselves, the twentieth-century church. Or, to bring it all the way home, how can God use me?

The truth is that you and I, Israel's spiritual heirs, are not much different from Israel or Samson. You and I sometimes bed down with the false gods of our age, dipping our fingers into the carcass of twentieth-century independence from God, hoping to find a little sweetening for our lives.

Like Israel, we are called to struggle against the powers of our age, and many of us do. But isn't it also true that we often find ourselves enchanted, lured by the sweets of our culture? Killing lions for God one day, but honey-dipping with abandon the next.

Perhaps we are very concerned about personal piety, minding our orthodox manners, and keeping all our liturgical ducks in a row. Perhaps in these things we are lion-killers. But what about when it comes to ordering personal relationships, or managing business affairs, or caring for the environment? Are we killing lions on Sunday but honey-dipping on Monday?

When it comes to political and economic life, we want to be supportive of policies that promote justice and equality. So we defend the rights of the poor. But do we not at the same time crave the economic advantages that will profit us and leave the weak impoverished? While we praise the God from whom all our blessings flow, others cry to him in frustration. Have our hands of justice and equality been killing the lion or dipping in the honey?

On the one hand, we establish Christian schools and colleges and organizations to confront human independence from God, to challenge the spirits of the age with the gospel of the kingdom of Jesus Christ. But when it comes to popular culture, TV, videos, and finding entertainment for ourselves and our kids, we become careless. We dip into popular culture as if it were a harmless carcass. But it isn't dead. Like the lion's carcass, popular culture bristles with sweet life, but it is a sweetness that masks the odor of corruption. The honey of popular culture can seriously weaken the character of the Christian community.

God's instruction to Israel at the beginning of her time in the promised land was clear. She was to occupy the whole land and displace the other nations and their seductive religions. In this way, Israel would declare that God's reign was total and that nothing was outside its purview. Whenever Israel failed by accommodating herself to the culture and worshiping other gods, that proved to be humiliating for God's reign among the nations.

So it is for the Christian community. All of life is to be claimed for God, lived for God's purpose, and reflecting God's values. When we fail to let that happen, when we accommodate ourselves to the culture, we become a thorn in the body of Christ and we contribute to the serpent's striking his heel.

That's one message the story of Samson has for Israel and for us. It exposes our own weakness; it forces us to own up to our own contradictions. It challenges us with the question, Are we slaying lions, or dipping for honey?

Samson and the Gospel

But we can't end there. We must end with the good news of the gospel, because that is the bottom line of Samson's tragic life story. The good news is that God used Samson, in spite of himself, with all his faults and honey-dipping ways. God used Samson as a judge in Israel to keep the fires of redemption burning through the most turbulent and unsettled times in Israel's history.

At the very end of his life, blind Samson is strung between two pillars at the temple of Dagon. He cries out, "Once more, Lord!" and the Spirit of God fills him. He literally brings down the house and in that single act kills more Philistines than during his entire career.

The bottom line is that Samson was a link in the chain of divinely guided events that led to the life of Jesus Christ, God's ultimate Judge, the lion-killer of Judah who denied himself even the sweet things of heaven to die on a lonely cross.

That's why Samson's name appears in Hebrews 11—it's an act of sheer grace. And if you have ever wondered about the riddle of Samson's life, or if you have ever wondered about the riddle of your own, better yet to wonder about the riddle of God's love, the miracle of grace, which sometimes gets dragged through the mud, but which nevertheless persists and makes saints out of the worst honey-dipping sinners.

If you need that grace in your life, I invite you to say, Amen!

Bibliography of John H. Stek

by Paul W. Fields

1952

"Inter-Church Principles." *Reformed Journal* 2 (August 1952):14-15.

1957

"The Centennial Synod of a Young Church." *The Banner* 92 (August 23, 1957): 6-7.

1958

"Daily Meditations." *Spires* No. 41 (January-February 1958):3-18.

"Woman Suffrage in the Church." *The Reformed Journal* 8 (January 1958):11-16.

Reviews of *Inspiration and Canonicity of the Bible: An Historical and Exegetical Study*, by Robert Laird Harris; *Biblical Criticism*, by Wick Broomall. *Torch and Trumpet* 7 (March 1958):22-23.

"The Rise of Fundamentalism." *The Banner* 93 (July 4, 1958):9, 21; (July 18, 1958):9, 25; (August 1, 1958):9, 21; (August 22, 1958):9, 25.

1959

"Amos: Herdsman from Tekoa." In *Lectures*, by Reformed Ministers Institute, 1-24. Grand Rapids: Christian Reformed Ministers Institute, 1959.

Review of *"Fundamentalism" and the Word of God: Some Evangelical Principles*, by James I. Packer. *The Banner* 94 (April 24, 1959):24.

Review of *The Theology of James Daane*, by Cornelius Van Til. *The Banner* 94 (October 16, 1959):28-29; (November 20, 1959):23; (December 18, 1959):22-23; 95 (January 22, 1960):18-19; (March 25, 1960):22-23.

"The Word" John 1:1, 14. In *Daily Manna* (December 3, 1959).

"The Son of Man" Luke 19, 10. In *Daily Manna* (December 4, 1959).

"The Good Shepherd" Ezekiel 34, 23-24. In *Daily Manna* (December 5, 1959).

"Immanuel" Isaiah 7, 14. In *Daily Manna* (December 6, 1959).

"The Lamb of God" John 1, 29. In *Daily Manna* (December 7, 1959).

"Jehovah Our Righteousness" Jeremiah 23, 6. In *Daily Manna* (December 8, 1959).

"Prince of Peace" Isaiah 9, 6. In *Daily Manna* (December 9, 1959).

1960

Review of *The Holy Spirit and Eschatology in the Gospel of John: A Critique of Rudolf Bultmann's Present Eschatology*, by David Earl Holwerda. *The Banner* 95 (September 2, 1960):28.

"Meeting the Christ." In *The Back to God Family Altar*. Chicago: The Back to God Hour (November 1960).

1961

Review of *Predestination and Other Papers*, by Pierre Maury. *Westminster Theological Journal* 23 (1960-61):200-04.

Review of *Facts and Faith in the Kerygma of Today*, by Paul Althaus. *The Banner* 96 (September 8, 1961):28-29.

"The Church's Certain Triumph" Numbers 23, 1-12. In *The Living Word* (September 28, 1961).

Reviews of *Calvin's Dying Bequest to the Church: A Critical Evaluation of the Commentary on Joshua*, by Marten Hendrik Woudstra. Calvin Theological Seminary, Monograph series 1; *Man Before God's Face in Calvin's Preaching*, by Carl Gerhard Kromminga. Calvin Theological Seminary, Monograph series 2; *Calvin's Doctrine of Predestination*, by Fred H. Klooster. Calvin Theological Seminary, Monograph series 3. *The Banner* 96 (October 13, 1961):28.

1962

"Interpreting 'The Infallibility Report.'" *The Torch and Trumpet* 11 (February 1962):10-13.

Review of *Job to Malachi: Part 2 of The Amplified Old Testament*, by Francis E. Siewert. *The Banner* 97 (August 17, 1962):28-29.

1963

Reviews of *Ezra, Nehemiah, Esther, Job*. Vol. 8 of *The Layman's Bible Commentary*, by Balmer H. Kelly; *Micah, Nahum, Habakkuk, Zephaniah, Haggai, Zechariah, Malachi*. Vol. 15 of *The Layman's Bible Commentary*, by James H. Gailey; *Mark*. Vol. 17 of *The Layman's Bible Commentary*, by Paul S. Minear; *Hebrews, James I and II, Peter*. Vol. 24 of *The Layman's Bible Commentary*, by John Wick Bowman. *Torch and Trumpet* 13 (September 1963):23.

Review of *Het Tweede Boek Samuel*, by Cornelis J. Goslinga. *Torch and Trumpet* 13 (November 1963):24.

Review of *The Bible and Archaeology*, by John A. Thompson. *Torch and Trumpet* 13 (November 1963):23.

"Was It? Wasn't It? What Was It?" *The Young Calvinist* 44 (November 1963):6-7.

1964

"Historiography and the History of Israel." *Torch and Trumpet* 14 (November 1964):16-19.

Review of *A Distinctive Translation of Genesis*, by J. Wash Watts. *Torch and Trumpet* 14 (April 1964):21.

Review of *Beschouwingen over Genesis I*, by Nicolaas Herman Ridderbos. *Torch and Trumpet* 14 (April 1964):22-23.

Review of *Treaty of the Great King. The Covenant Structure of Deuteronomy: Studies and Commentary*, by Meredith G. Kline. *Westminster Theological Journal* 26 (1963-64):180-182. Also in *The Banner* 99 (June 26, 1964):24-25.

Review of *Ras Shamra and the Bible*, by Charles Franklin Pfeiffer. *Torch and Trumpet* 14 (May-June 1964):32.

Review of *The Dead Sea Scrolls*, by Charles Franklin Pfeiffer. *The Banner* 99 (June 5, 1964):24.

Review of *Israel and the Nations*, by Frederick Fyvie Bruce. *Torch and Trumpet* 14 (November 1964):16-19.

1965

Review of *The Prophets and the Promise*, by Willis J. Beecher. *Torch and Trumpet* 15 (January 1965):23.

"Capital Punishment: Yes." *The Young Calvinist* 46 (January 1965):6-7.

"'Creation' Today." *The Banner* 100 (January 1, 1965):14-15.

"Providence." *The Banner* 100 (January 15, 1965):16-17.

"Studies in Jonah." *Young Calvinist* 49 (March 1968):30-31; (April 1968):28-29.

1966

Review of *He Gave Some Prophets: The Old Testament Prophets and Their Message*, by Sanford Calvin Yoder. *The Banner* 101 (January 7, 1966):24-25.

Review of *The Old Testament*, by Robert Davidson. *The Banner* 101 (February 4, 1966):25.

"KJV, ASV, RSV, NEB, NASB—or What?" *The Banner* 101 (March 18, 1966):4-5. Also in *The Presbyterian Journal* 25 (August 10, 1966):9-10.

"A New Theology of Baptism? Baptism: A Sign of Grace or of Judgment?" *Calvin Theological Journal* 1 (1966):69-73.

Review of *The Praise of God in the Psalms*, by Claus Westermann. *Calvin Theological Journal* 1 (April 1966):143-46.

Review of *Genesis*. Vol. 1 of The Anchor Bible, translated by Ephraim A. Speiser. *The Banner* 101 (July 22, 1966):24.

Review of *History and Theology in Second Isaiah: A Commentary on Isaiah 35: 40-66*, by James D. Smart. *Calvin Theological Journal* 1 (November 1966):217-23.

Reviews of *Our English Bible in the Making*, by Herbert G. May; *The Genesis Octapla: Eight English Versions of the Book of Genesis in the Tyndale-King James Tradition*, edited by Luther A. Wiegle; *Martin Luther: Creative Translator*, by Heinz Bluhm; *German Bibles Before Luther: The Story of Fourteen High German Bibles 1466-1588*, edited by Kenneth A. Strand. *Calvin Theological Journal* 1 (November 1966):229-34.

Reviews of *Creation Revealed: A Study of Genesis Chapter One in the Light of Modern Science*, by Frederick A. Filby; *Studies in the Bible and Science or Christ and Creation*, by Henry M. Morris. *Calvin Theological Journal* 1 (November 1966):253-57.

"The Message of Malachi." *Young Calvinist* 47 (December 1966):30-34.

"So Says Malachi." In *Information for Y. C. Leaders*. Folio 3 of *Faith, Fellowship & Service*, 27-31. Grand Rapids: The Young Calvinist Federation, 1966-67.

1967

"Jonah-Israel-Christ." In *Information for Y. C. Leaders*. Folio 4 of *Faith, Fellowship & Service*, 80-85. Grand Rapids: The Young Calvinist Federation, 1967-68.

"The Modern Problem of the Old Testament in the Light of Reformation Perspective." *Calvin Theological Journal* 2 (November 1967):202-25.

Reviews of *Psalms I: 1-50*. Vol. 16 of The Anchor Bible, translated by Mitchell Dahood; *Israel's Sacred Songs: A Study of Dominant Themes*, by Harvey H. Guthrie; *Introduction to the Psalms*, by Christoph F. Barth. *Calvin Theological Journal* 2 (November 1967):245-5l.

1968

"Roadblocks to Ecumenism." *The Banner* 103 (November 29, 1968):10-11.

"Israel-Christ: Forgiveness." *The Young Calvinist* 49 (April 1968):29.

"Israel-Nineveh: Repentance." *The Young Calvinist* 49 (April 1968):28.

"Jonah-Israel-Christ: Death." *The Young Calvinist* 49 (April 1968):30.

"Jonah-Israel-Christ: Resurrection." *The Young Calvinist* 49 (April 1968):31.

1969

"The message of the book of Jonah." *Calvin Theological Journal* 4 (April 1969): 23-50.

Review of *The Meaning of the Old Testament*, by Daniel Lys. *Calvin Theological Journal* 4 (November 1969):220-28.

Review of *The Basic Forms of Prophetic Speech*, by Claus Westermann. *Calvin Theological Journal* 4 (November 1969):247-49.

"Higher Criticism and the Bible." *The Banner* 104 (December 5, 1969):4-5.

1970

"Biblical Typology Yesterday and Today." *Calvin Theological Journal* 5 (November 1970):133-62.

"The Bible, the New Hermeneutic, and Calvin Seminary." *The Banner* 105 (October 30, 1970):10-11.

1971

Review of *The Glory of Christ, and Other Biblical Studies*, by Martin Jacob Wyngaarden. *Calvin Theological Journal* 6 (April 1971):60-63.

Review of *Sola Scriptura: Problems and Principles in Preaching Historical Texts*, by Sidney Greidanus. *Calvin Theological Journal* 6 (April 1971):109-16.

"My People Will Come Home." *Insight* 52 (May-June 1971):11-12.

"Symbols at the Seminary." *The Banner* 106 (August 20, 1971):6.

1972

"To the Jew First." *Calvin Theological Journal* 7 (1972):15-52. Also in *To the Jew First: An Exegetical Examination of a New Testament Theme*, 1-54. Grand Rapids: Committee for Home Missions of the Christian Reformed Church, 1973.

"The Fourth Commandment: A New Look." *Reformed Journal* 22 (July-August 1972):26-29; (November 1972):20-24; 23 (January 1973):18-22.

1973

"The Word Still Does It." *Insight* 54 (October 1973):6-9.

1974

"The Stylistics of Hebrew Poetry." *Calvin Theological Journal* 9 (April 1974): 15-30.

Review of *History of Israelite Religion*, by Georg Fohrer. *Calvin Theological Journal* 9 (April 1974):107-18.

"Address of Professor John Stek to the 1973 Synod of Haarlem Gereformeerde Kerken, The Netherlands." *The Banner* 109 (August 16, 1974):13-15. Shortened Dutch version in *De Wachter* 107 (1 Januari 1974):10-12.

1975

Review of *The Englishman's Hebrew-English Old Testament: Genesis-II Samuel*, by Joseph Magil. *The Messenger* 47 (October 1975):29.

Review of *A Manual for Problem Solving in Bible Translation*, by Mildred Larson. *The Messenger* 47 (November 1975):31.

1976

Review of *Torah and Canon*, by James A. Sanders. *Calvin Theological Journal* 11 (April 1976):136.

Review of *The Religion of Israel, from Its Beginnings to the Babylonian Exile*, by Yehezkel Kaufmann. *Calvin Theological Journal* 11 (April 1976):136-37.

Review of *The Psalms*, by Joseph Addison Alexander. *Calvin Theological Journal* 11 (April 1976):137.

Review of *Joshua and the Flow of Biblical History*, by Francis August Schaeffer. *Calvin Theological Journal* 11 (April 1976):137-38.

Review of *The Authority of the Old Testament*, by John Bright. *Calvin Theological Journal* 11 (April 1976):138.

Review of *Israel's Wisdom: Learn and Live*, by L. D. Johnson. *Calvin Theological Journal* 11 (April 1976):138.

Review of *The Typology of Scripture Viewed in Connection with the Whole Series of the Divine Dispensations*, by Patrick Fairbairn. *Calvin Theological Journal* 11 (November 1976):294.

1978

Review of *Solomon on Sex*, by Joseph C. Dillow. *Calvin Theological Journal* 13 (April 1978):115.

Review of *The Book of Psalms: A New Translation with Introductions and Notes, Explanatory and Critical*, by John James Stewart Perowne. *Calvin Theological Journal* 13 (April 1978):117.

Review of *Psalms: A Critical and Expository Commentary with Doctrinal and Practical Remarks*, by William Swan Plumer. *Calvin Theological Journal* 13 (April 1978):117-18.

Review of *Psalms*, by Charles Haddon Spurgeon. Condensed by David Otis Fuller. *Calvin Theological Journal* 13 (April 1978):119-20.

"Salvation, Justice and Liberation in the Old Testament." *Calvin Theological Journal* 13 (November 1978):133-65.

Review of *A Time to Mourn and a Time to Dance: Ecclesiastes and the Way of the World*, by Derek Kidner. *Calvin Theological Journal* 13 (November 1978):259.

Review of *The Bible in its World: The Bible and Archaeology Today*, by Kenneth Anderson. *Calvin Theological Journal* 13 (November 1978):259.

Review of *Knowing Scripture*, by Robert Charles Sproul. *Calvin Theological Journal* 13 (November 1978):261-62.

Review of *A Chronology of the Hebrew Kings*, by Edward Richard Thiele. *Calvin Theological Journal* 13 (November 1978):262-63.

Review of *Rocks, Relics and Biblical Reliability*, by Clifford A. Wilson. *Calvin Theological Journal* 13 (November 1978):263.

1979

"Dream." In Vol. 1 of *The International Standard Bible Encyclopedia*, edited by Geoffrey William Bromiley, 991-92. Grand Rapids: Eerdmans, 1979.

"Reactions to Lester Ronald De Koster's 'Method and You.'" *The Banner* 114 (September 21, 1979):8.

"Male/Female Created He Them." *The Banner* 114 (September 28, 1979):2, 24-25.

"What Is Man?" *Input* 9 (November-December 1979):8-9. Also in *Insight* 60 (November 1979):10-12.

"Response to Henry Vander Goot's 'Creation and Differentiation.'" *The Reformed Ecumenical Synod: Theological Forum* 7 (December 1979):17-21.

1980

"Children and the Lord's Supper." *The Banner* 115 (December 15, 1980):4.

1981

Review of *Balaam's Apocalyptic Prophecies: A Study in Reading Scripture*, by Calvin G. Seerveld. *Calvin Theological Journal* 16 (April 1981):114-16.

"De Klerk Deserves Better." *The Banner* 116 (May 25, 1981):6.

1982

"Elijah." In Vol. 2 of *The International Standard Bible Encyclopedia*, edited by Geoffrey W. Bromiley, 64-72. Grand Rapids: Eerdmans, 1982.

1984

Review of *I Kings* and *II Kings*, by Walter Brueggemann. *Calvin Theological Journal* 19 (April 1984):73-78.

Review of *Psalms 1-50*, by Peter C. Craigie. *Calvin Theological Journal* 19 (April 1984):378.

Review of *I Samuel–II Samuel*, by James D. Newsome. *Calvin Theological Journal* 19 (April 1984):73-78.

1985

The NIV Study Bible, edited by Kenneth Barker. Grand Rapids: Zondervan, 1985. Associate Editor and Contributor.

Review of *Angels, Apes, and Men*, by Stanley L. Jaki. *Calvin Theological Journal* 20 (April 1985):164.

1986

"What Happened to the Chariot Wheels of Exodus 14:25?" *Journal of Biblical Literature* 105 (1986):293-94.

"When the Spirit Was Poetic." In *The NIV: The Making of a Contemporary Translation*, edited by Kenneth L. Barker, 72-81, 158-61. Grand Rapids: Zondervan, 1986.

"The Bee and the Mountain Goat: A Literary Reading of Judges 4." In *A Tribute to Gleason Archer: Essays on the Old Testament*, edited by Walter C. Kaiser, Jr. and Ronald F. Youngblood, 53-86. Chicago: Moody, 1986.

Review of *Cross-Currents: Interactions between Science and Faith*, by Colin A. Russell. *Calvin Theological Journal* 21 (April 1986):124-25.

"Interrogating the Bible." *Christianity Today* 30, No. 14 (October 3, 1986):21-22.

"Spokesmen for God: Then and Now." *The Banner* 121 (October 6, 1986):8-10.

1987

Review of *In the Beginning: The Opening Chapters of Genesis,* by Henri Blocher. *Calvin Theological Journal* 22 (April 1987):240.

Review of *King Saul, the Tragic Hero: A Study in Individuation,* by John A. Sanford. *Calvin Theological Journal* 22 (April 1987):189-90.

1988

Review of *Harper's Bible Dictionary,* edited by Paul J. Achtemeier. *Calvin Theological Journal* 23 (April 1988):61-66.

Review of *Joshua, Judges, Ruth,* by John Gray. *Calvin Theological Journal* 23 (April 1988):121.

Review of *Creation or Evolution: A False Antithesis,* by M. W. Poole. *Calvin Theological Journal* 23 (April 1988):125-26.

1990

"God, Humanity, Earth: The Great Biblical Triad." *The Banner* 125 (March 12, 1990):10-11.

"The New Revised Standard Version: A Preliminary Assessment." *Reformed Review* 43 (Spring 1990):171-88.

"What Says the Scripture." In *Portraits of Creation,* edited by H. Van Till, 203-65. Grand Rapids: Eerdmans, 1990.

1991

"The New Revised Standard Version: A Preliminary Assessment." *Calvin Theological Journal* 26 (April 1991):80-99.

"The End Times? They're Already Here." *The Banner* 126 (April 8, 1991):8-11; (May 6, 1991):2.

"Forty Years of Seminarians." *The Banner* 126 (June 24, 1991):8-9.

"The Rapture: It May Be Near, Prophecy Watchers Say." *The Banner* 126 (April 1, 1991):8-10.

Review of *The Genesis Debate: Persistent Questions About Creation and the Flood,* by Ronald F. Youngblood. *The Banner* 126 (October 7, 1991):17.

1994

" 'Covenant' Overload in Reformed Theology." *Calvin Theological Journal* 29 (April 1995):12-41.

"Has the NIV 'De-Catholicized' Scripture?: A Response to James R. Payton, Jr." *Perspectives* 9 (April 1994):8-9.

1996

Review of *The Message of the Song of Songs,* by Tom Gledhill. *Calvin Theological Journal* 31 (April 1996):254.

Review of *The Psalms Through 3,000 Years: Prayerbook of a Cloud of Witnesses,* by William L. Holladay. *Reformed Worship* 40, No. 46 (June 1996):395.

1997

"Job: An Introduction." *Calvin Theological Journal* 32 (November 1995):443-58.